Jol

Gift from Ba

WARRIORS *and* WIZARDS

WARRIORS
and
WIZARDS

The Development and

Defeat of Radio-Controlled

Glide Bombs of the

Third Reich

Martin J. Bollinger

NAVAL INSTITUTE PRESS
Annapolis, Maryland

Naval Institute Press
291 Wood Road
Annapolis, MD 21402

Library of Congress Cataloging-in-Publication Data
Bollinger, Martin J., 1958-
  Warriors and wizards : the deployment and defeat of radio-
controlled glide bombs of the Third Reich / Martin J. Bollinger.
      p. cm.
  Includes bibliographical references and index.
  ISBN 978-1-59114-067-2 (alk. paper)
  1. Guided bombs—History—20th century. 2. World War,
1939-1945—Aerial operations, German. 3. Germany. Luftwaffe—
History. I. Title.
  UG1282.G8B65 2010
  940.54'4943—dc22
                              2010017194

Printed in the United States of America on acid-free paper

14 13 12 11 10   9 8 7 6 5 4 3 2
First printing

Contents

List of Tables and Illustrations   vii

Acknowledgments   ix

Introduction: "Wellsian Weapons from Mars"   xiii

ONE   *Egret* Explodes   1

TWO   Development of German Glide Bombs   9

THREE   Death of a Battleship and Crisis at Salerno   25

FOUR   Early Warnings from Agents and Analysts   41

FIVE   False Hope: Initial Countermeasures Development   52

SIX   II./KG 100's Struggles in the Mediterranean   60

SEVEN   Transition Time: KG 40 and the He 177   73

EIGHT   Intelligence Work Leads to Improved Electronic   89
        Defenses

NINE   Stalemate at Anzio and on the Convoy Routes   101

TEN   Lessons Learned, Moves, and Countermoves   122

ELEVEN Last Gasps: The Invasions of France   145

TWELVE How Effective Were the Glide Bombs   167
        and Electronic Countermeasures?

Epilogue   193

Appendix: Ships Sunk or Damaged with Glide Bombs   207

Notes   209

Selected Bibliography   247

Index   257

Tables and Illustrations

Tables

TABLE 11.1.   Commanders of Primary Luftwaffe Glide-Bomber   147
              Units

TABLE 12.1.   Luftwaffe Claims for KG 100 Glide-Bomb Hits and   168
              Near Misses Through 30 April 1944

TABLE 12.2.   Luftwaffe Claims for Ships Sunk or Severely Damaged 168
              by KG 100 Glide Bombs Through 30 April 1944

TABLE 12.3.   Ships Sunk or Damaged with Hs 293 or Fritz-X   171
              Glide Bombs

TABLE 12.4.   Defensibility of Ships Sunk or Damaged by Hs 293   176
              and Fritz-X Glide Bombs

TABLE 12.5.   Summary of Allied Jamming Technologies Deployed   185
              Against Kehl-Strassburg System

Graphs

GRAPH 12.1.   Success Rates for Glide-Bomb Attacks by Individual 173
              Luftwaffe Group

GRAPH 12.2.   Distribution of Glide-Bomb Launches by Time of   174
              Day

GRAPH 12.3.   Glide-Bomb Success Rates: Day vs. Dusk vs. Night   174
              Attacks

GRAPH 12.4.   Success Rates in Glide-Bomb Attacks by Luftwaffe   174
              Group Over Time

GRAPH 12.5.   Monthly Attrition of II./KG 100 Glide-Bombing   177
              Aircraft

GRAPH 12.6.   Monthly Attrition of III./KG 100 Glide-Bombing   178
              Aircraft

GRAPH 12.7.   Monthly Attrition of II./KG 40 Glide-Bombing   178
              Aircraft

GRAPH 12.8.   Doppler Shift of Reflected Kehl Control Signal vs.   183
              Aircraft Height and Distance

GRAPH 12.9.   Reflected-Path Kehl Signal Difference vs. Aircraft   183
              Height and Distance

GRAPH 12.10. Glide-Bomb Attack Effectiveness by Campaign and   187
              Jamming Technology

GRAPH 12.11. Glide-Bomb Hits and Near Misses Over Time by   188
              KG 100 Using Hs 293

GRAPH 12.12. Summary of Glide-Bomb Effectiveness vs. Jamming   190
              Technology

Map

Selected Locations of Glide-Bomb Bases and Attack Sites   xx

Acknowledgments

The author is very thankful for the professionalism and graciousness of many who labor quietly to maintain accurate historical records in national archives and other organizations. These individuals include Janet Delude (*Rohna* Association), Dori Glaser (Destroyer-Escort Sailors Association), Joel K. Harding (Association of Old Crows), Jonathan D. Jeffrey (Western Kentucky University), David Lincove (Ohio State University), Ed Marolda (recently retired from the U.S. Naval Historical Center), David W. McComb (Destroyer History Foundation), Nate Patch (U.S. National Archives and Records Association), Janice Schulz (Naval Research Laboratory), Katharina Schulz (Archiv Deutsches Museum), David R. Stevenson (American Society of Naval Engineers), and Ron Windebank (HMS *Newfoundland* Association). The staff at the UK National Archives were extremely skillful and helpful, as was Sebastian Remus, a professional researcher skilled in the ways of the Freiburg-based Bundesarchiv-Militärarchiv.

✦ ✦ ✦

This research was facilitated greatly by the support and cooperation of other more-accomplished authors in this field, including Ulf Balke, Nick Beale, David Bruhn, Henry L. de Zeng, Jan Drent, Chris Goss, Manfred Griehl, Greg Hunter, Carlton Jackson, Wolfgang-D. Schröer, and Theron P. Snell. Others who maintain an active interest also contributed greatly, including Franck Allegrini, Ed Hart, and Shamus Reddin. Al Penney of the

Canadian Navy was especially helpful in sorting out the development of British glide-bomb countermeasures.

The genre of naval and aviation history is well served by amateur and professional researchers who maintain, interpret, and make available data relevant to this story. Many of them are active participants in Internet-based forums that permit easy and effective transmittal of data, insight, and criticism. Two of these forums—*Warsailors.com* and *12oclockhigh.net*—were employed extensively here. Thanks in particular to Brian J. Bines, Hans Houterman, Doug Kasunic, Jerry Proc, and Derek James Sullivan

The author is also grateful to the veterans of this year of "warriors and wizards" who provided him with their time and insight. This includes several participants in the battles in air and sea: Roy W. Brown (convoy UGS-40), Kenneth C. Garrett (HMCS *Algonquin*), Russell Heathman (HMCS *Matane*), Jack Hickman (Operation Dragoon), Ian M. Malcolm (SS *Samite*), and Charles C. Wales (USS *Lansdale*). This group includes scientists who fought their own battle over the electromagnetic spectrum: J. T. Doyle (RCN *St. Hyacinthe*) and William E. W. Howe (Naval Research Laboratory).

Several family members of these warriors contributed to this effort, including K. C. Dochtermann (grandson of Luftwaffe pilot Hans Dochtermann), Chip Gardes (son of USS *Herbert C. Jones* captain Alfred W. Gardes Jr.), Rick Heathman (son of HMCS *Matane* crewman Russell Heathman), and Rainer Zantopp (son of Luftwaffe pilot Hans-Joachim Zantopp). Through their efforts I came to know more about the real people involved in this story. Thanks in particular to Chip for tracking down and sharing his father's personal files and his fascinating life story.

Two noted scholars in the field, Dr. Richard P. Hallion and Norman Polmar, acted as valued mentors to the author and graciously lent him their personal files on this subject that they had each accumulated over the years. Additional valuable assistance during the preparation of the manuscript was received from Anne Doremus, Declan Murphy, and Nic Volpicelli. Editors Adam Kane and Alison Hope were greatly helpful in turning tortured ideas and prose into clear and readable material.

The author is especially grateful to Dr. Allan Steinhardt, a former chief scientist with the U.S. Defense Advanced Research Projects Agency and an expert in radar, radios, and electronic warfare. Dr. Steinhardt, a former colleague of the author, contributed his valuable expertise in analyzing both the Kehl-Strassburg radio-guidance system and the Allied countermeasures. The author would also like to recognize an individual without whom this effort would never have been undertaken: author Rick Atkinson. It was Atkinson's account of German glide bombs in his book *The Day of Battle* that initiated the author's curiosity and led to this manuscript.

Finally, the author would like to acknowledge the critical role of his wife Maura, without whose friendship, patience, indulgence, encouragement, legal counsel, and constructive criticism he would accomplish little. Thanks!

The author retains responsibility for any mistakes, and that is as it should be.

Introduction

"WELLSIAN WEAPONS *from* MARS"

t was not easy in World War II for an aircraft to sink a warship. In our day of brilliant munitions, satellite-based navigation, and weapons calibrated in megatons, such difficulties may be hard to fathom. However, let us take ourselves back to 1943 for a moment and imagine the travails of a military tactician attempting to use an aircraft to destroy invading enemy warships or supply convoys.

◆ ◆ ◆

First, the weapon of any such aircraft has to be delivered to the target, at a time when that target is typically maneuvering at high speed. A bomb dropped from a great height, say above twenty thousand feet, might take forty seconds or more to fall to the water's surface; in that time, a warship moving twenty-five knots has advanced a half a kilometer (about a third of a mile) from where it was when the bomb was dropped. If nothing else is done to maneuver the bomb, it will miss. Clearly, the pilot can attempt to anticipate the ship's motion and adjust the aim, but the fact is that ships have rudders, and those rudders are prone to be employed urgently, heavily, and unpredictably when the ship is taking evasive action.

Air-launched torpedoes are not much better in that the target, assuming it knows it is under attack (hence the value of stealthy submarines over noisy aircraft), inevitably will adjust course in much the same way. Two of the

most notable raids in World War II by torpedo bombers against battleships—
by the British at Taranto and by the Japanese at Pearl Harbor—avoided this
difficulty by attacking moored ships or ships at anchor.

One logical response is to engage the target from low altitude and at
short distances in order to minimize the time between bomb release and
impact. The problem is that aircraft in close proximity to warships, including torpedo bombers, can easily be engaged by the full armament of those
warships, making the aircraft especially vulnerable. As pilots were fond of
saying, "If the ship is within range, so are we."

An alternative, used with impressive results in World War II, is to deploy
dive-bombers that approach the target at a high altitude and then drop vertically to the surface, releasing bombs at low altitude then pulling away—
assuming they have survived the journey thus far. In this way the pilot can
adjust aim until just before the bomb is released. One problem is that these
aircraft, and thus their weapons, are necessarily limited in size due to the
heavy g-forces encountered in the pull-up. As a result it takes large numbers
of them to successfully engage heavily armored targets such as battleships.
This fact is well demonstrated by the annihilation of battleships *Prince of
Wales*, *Repulse*, *Hiei*, *Yamato*, and *Musashi*. In each case, it took dozens of
aerial bombs and torpedoes to effect destruction, weapons that were often
delivered in orchestrated attacks in which dive-bombers and fighters sup-
pressed the antiaircraft defenses long enough for torpedo bombers to deliver
fatal blows. (Aircraft carriers, which in most cases did not have armored
decks in World War II, were especially vulnerable to dive-bombers, even
when attacked by relatively small numbers of aircraft.)

The reality, then, is that with conventional unguided bombs aircrews (1)
must approach the target closely to minimize time for evasion, or (2) successfully anticipate the movement of the ship and aim accordingly, or (3)
attack in such numbers as to simply overwhelm the ship and provide it with
no path of escape. The common element behind these complications is the
assumption that, once dropped, a bomb is a dumb ballistic object, subject
only to the command of Sir Isaac Newton.

The Japanese attempted to address this problem in the latter stages of
World War II by providing smart human guidance all the way to the target, in what Americans called *kamikaze* missions. Such missions caused
significant devastation, but complicated things for the attacker since an aircraft with a bomb is easier to target and shoot down than the much smaller
bomb itself. Relatively few *kamikaze* missions were successful, in part due
to aggressive ship defenses.[1] Moreover, in most cultures the supply of pilots
willing to perform these missions is typically scarce and the number of

successful missions per pilot—or for that matter, failed attempts per pilot—is necessarily limited to one. It is a questionable strategy in general, and a foolish one in particular for any prolonged war of attrition.

The Luftwaffe (German air force) in World War II came up with a different solution, one based on advanced technology. This approach involved radio-controlled guidance that allowed a distant bomb aimer to adjust course as he watched his bomb glide into its target, steering the weapon left or right and up or down until it hit dead on. Introduced in mid-1943, these "glide bombs" were the wonder weapons of the era, causing shock and awe among sailors of Allied navies. That they have largely been forgotten reflects the fact that they were eclipsed by the late arrival in the war of two other wonder weapons more properly associated not with World War II but with any future world war: ballistic missiles and nuclear bombs.

For a period of almost exactly one year, these German glide bombs, described by a contemporary witness on board a ship during an attack as "resembling some Wellsian weapon from Mars," terrorized naval and merchant sailors.[2] The weapons exploded suddenly onto the scene in August 1943 and drove frantic efforts by the unprepared Allies to devise an adequate defense. In the space of two months, a battleship was sunk with 1,254 sailors blown to bits or incinerated, while a few days later another battleship was crippled and nearly sunk. In that same period two light cruisers were virtually wrecked, and several other warships were sunk or severely damaged. One horribly successful mission led to the greatest loss of life of U.S. service members on board any single ship at sea across all the wars the United States has ever fought.[3] That specific incident remains generally unknown even to this day.

Yet the threat of these German innovations vanished almost as suddenly as it appeared, and the wonder weapons of autumn 1943 were largely discarded after summer 1944, just a year later. A small cadre of historians argues to this day about the cause for the eventual abandonment of the technology. Some, especially those in Germany, appropriately highlight the rise in Allied airpower over the European theater and the futility of German bombers attempting to close on high-value ships when surrounded by large numbers of Allied fighters. Others suggest sabotage played a role, believing that large numbers of the weapons were rendered ineffective by the intentional acts of forced labor or resistance workers. Still others blame the decline in training of Luftwaffe pilots: the veterans of early missions too often challenged the laws of chance with fatal consequences and were replaced by less-well-trained novices.

Many historians, somewhat likely to have been on the side of the Allies, point to another reason. In rapid response to the new German wonder weapons, the technical wizards in Allied laboratories came up with some of their own: electronic countermeasures that in early versions jammed the radio links between aircraft and glide bomb and that in later versions allowed an operator on board ship to take control of the bomb and steer it away from its target. These countermeasures arose from the brilliance of Allied science; also, they were informed through the efforts of the Allied intelligence services, including agents working for the American Office of Strategic Services (OSS) and analysts in the British Government Code and Cipher School (GCCS) in Bletchley Park. Thus the introduction of these revolutionary guided antiship weapons spurred another revolution, that of guided-missile electronic countermeasures. The electromagnetic interplay of these two technologies continues to this day, more than six decades later.

It is this interaction of Luftwaffe pilots, Allied sailors, scientists on both sides, and Allied intelligence that forms this story. It is a chronicle that has never been told in full. And while much has been written on this subject, the scholarship of that material is unfortunately mixed, often within the same tome. Other authors have endeavored to tell the tale from the vantage of pilots, sailors, scientists, or spies, but never from all four communities simultaneously. And it is in that interchange between the communities that the story can truly be found.

One should not be too hard on these earlier chroniclers, for several reasons. First, archives are incomplete. For example, the *Bundesarchiv-Militärarchiv* holdings of Luftwaffe operational records for the bomber units in question are particularly sparse.[4] Second, some critical documents in the United States, classified "Secret" in the years after World War II, were not declassified until so requested by this author and thus have not seen the full light of day until now. Third, even years after the fact, we remain victims of wartime news orchestration: ships very possibly struck with radio-controlled glide bombs were said in official reports to have been torpedoed or to have hit mines, in hopes of avoiding panic among anxious sailors.[5] As later reported by famed wartime correspondent "Beachhead Don" Whitehead, "Censorship prevented disclosure of the full effectiveness of this weapon until Winston Churchill announced its use at Salerno. Again, at Anzio, correspondents with the landing forces were forbidden to say the Germans were using rocket bombs against shipping. A directive said no mention was to be made of the glider projectiles."[6]

Paradoxically, as the years have passed, one senses it has become increasingly fashionable by survivors of these battles to link ship losses to these wonder weapons rather than to more prosaic torpedoes and bombs, even if the evidence is underwhelming. Other simple challenges confound the historian. For example, before the community had settled on a vernacular, the term "aerial torpedo" was used by some in Britain as shorthand for glide bombs, confusing the situation: conventional torpedoes launched by aircraft are quite accurately called the same thing.

Yet while records in any single domain are incomplete, there remains abundant information in discrete parcels, which, if packaged, can provide useful insight into exactly what happened between August 1943 and August 1944, and why. The available Luftwaffe reports can help inform occasionally unreliable naval records—and vice versa. An analysis of the effectiveness of glide bombs prepared by the Luftwaffe in mid-1944 is particularly helpful in supplying raw data, even if its findings are sorely lacking.[7] The history of wartime intelligence operations, especially the Allied success in cracking German and Japanese codes, turns out to shed important light on otherwise uncertain events and yields a few surprises of its own. Finally, the accounts of the technical wizards, toiling away in both missile research center and radio laboratory, fill in many of the missing pieces.

We are fortunate to have extensive firsthand information on this conflict from warriors and wizards, both in the form of personal accounts (published and unpublished) written by those who participated and in the form of direct contact with the survivors undertaken in preparation of this book. Their personal accounts help close many of the knowledge gaps in this obscure part of World War II.

The detailed technical information available on both missiles and (at least now) jammers, allows for useful analysis of their interplay according to the rules of the electromagnetic spectrum; this in itself informs and bounds what was reported in real time in the interplay of pilot and sailor at sea. In this book, for the first time, the actual workings and limitations of German guidance systems and Allied countermeasures are evaluated based on modern understanding of the theory and practice of electronic warfare. This analysis reveals that a phenomenon at the time underappreciated by both sides— multipath interference—may explain much of what occurred in the interplay of German and Allied scientists in this wizard war.

In the end, one must not be too intrigued by the scientific advances of the era and lose sight of their application. While this is a chronicle of technical achievement—on both sides—it is also the story of warriors drowning in darkened ships or burning in pools of flaming fuel oil. The number of sailors and passengers killed by these weapons approaches four thousand. Some of those lost have been hidden to history until now. Equally, this is the story of brave pilots struggling to escape their blazing and spiraling aircraft, or nurturing a crippled bomber over uninviting seas, hoping to reach distant land before the engines quit. The attrition rate for aircrews assigned to Luftwaffe bomber missions in World War II approached 90 percent.[8] In their honor and memory it is important that the story be told in full.

It becomes clear as one unravels the story that this interplay of "wizards and warriors" continues to this day. As we honor the memory of those who struggled and perished in World War II, we also recognize the sacrifice of modern soldiers on modern battlefields in Afghanistan and Iraq. A primary cause of these modern casualties is improvised explosive devices—roadside bombs—triggered remotely using radio links. As their grandfathers did in World War II, engineers and scientists in the United States and its coalition partners once again seek to develop sophisticated electronic countermeasures against these asymmetric weapons.

Plus ça change, plus c'est la même chose.

WARRIORS
and
WIZARDS

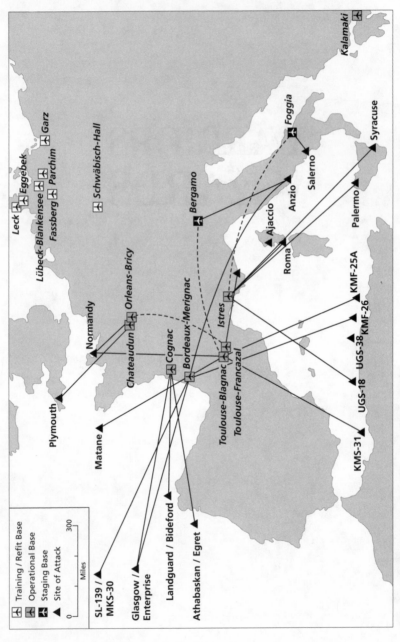

Selected Locations of Glide-Bomb Bases and Attack Sites

CHAPTER ONE

EGRET EXPLODES

B y the summer of 1943, the war in Europe was almost four years old and the Allies had finally taken the offensive across the Mediterranean. Allied ships were busy transporting men and materiel to sustain the recently victorious forces in North Africa, those engaged in combat on the island of Sicily, and those preparing for the impending invasion of mainland Italy. The German high command was equally determined to stop this flow of resources using the substantial air and naval resources at its disposal. In particular, ships transiting from England to the Mediterranean were subject to attack by Kriegsmarine (German navy) submarine forces, especially from German naval units operating from the southwestern coast of France. Following the dictum that the best defense is a good offense, the Royal Navy took the fight to the Bay of Biscay, deploying overwhelming numbers of escort ships to interdict U-boats as they traveled from havens in France to the Allied shipping lanes, where the U-boats' targets were fat, slow, and numerous. The Allies had achieved success in this effort, and the losses of U-boats to air and naval attack were slowly crippling the Kriegsmarine's offensive capabilities.

✦ ✦ ✦

In a naval war best remembered for its actions involving battleships and aircraft carriers, the campaign in the Bay of Biscay was one of those dominated by the light ships of the navies: corvettes, frigates, sloops, destroyers, and the occasional light cruiser.[1] Such was the case in the summer of 1943 with Operation Percussion, a British-led campaign to dominate the seas around Spain and France, thus depriving U-boats of safe transit to their undersea hunting lanes.

One particular area of focus was the northwest coast of Spain, at Cape Ortegal, where in 1805 a British fleet of sailing men-of-war under Rear Admiral Sir Richard Strachan caught up to and destroyed Rear Admiral Pierre Dumanoir le Pelley's French squadron, thus completing the final act in the Battle of Trafalgar. One hundred and thirty-eight years later, Commander John S. Dallison was performing a similar mission in the same location, leading the Royal Navy's 40th Escort Group on a sweep for enemy vessels—this time German submarines. Dallison had under his command British frigates *Exe*, *Moyola*, and *Waveney*, along with sloops *Landguard*, *Bideford*, and *Hastings*. *Bermuda*, a British light cruiser, was in support, should these slow and lightly armed frigates and sloops be challenged by heavily armed German destroyers.

On Wednesday 25 August 1943, the 40th Escort Group was to be relieved by the Canadian 5th Support Group, comprising Canadian corvettes *Calgary*, *Edmundston*, and *Snowberry*, accompanied by British frigates *Nene* and *Tweed*. As the two Allied naval squadrons approached each other they were shadowed by a Luftwaffe Fw 200 Condor, the familiar long-range German maritime-reconnaissance and attack aircraft. These lumbering four-engine transports were harbingers of air raids; suspicions of their hostile intent were confirmed when a group of Allied bombers in the vicinity reported a large group of German aircraft inbound to the ships' position.

Lookouts spotted the incoming aircraft at 1340 hours and identified some as Ju 88C fighter-bombers, familiar aircraft to these sailors, which often were deployed with torpedoes in an antiship role. Twelve of the aircraft divided into groups of three (called *kette*) and approached the small surface fleet while others circled nearby. As the attacking aircraft drew nearer, observers discerned that most were not Ju 88s, but instead were Do 217 bombers, a workhorse of the Luftwaffe bombing fleet. This was unexpected, because the Do 217 was not typically deployed in an antiship role and had not been seen previously even by many of these war-tested sailors. Moreover, the bombers did not continue on direct course for the armada, turning instead to parallel the fleet's course in the opposite direction, an action that must have confused those on board ship. Even more startling was the impression that, thousands of yards from their targets and while on this reciprocal course, the first wave of Do 217 bombers jettisoned the large bombs carried under their starboard wings directly over the empty sea.

Curiosity must have turned to shock when the first three of those items falling toward the sea stopped their descent and began, instead, to accelerate toward *Landguard*, a former U.S. Coast Guard cutter drafted into emergency wartime service in the Royal Navy. Shock transitioned to alarm as the three objects, resembling miniature airplanes trailing smoke and fire, maneuvered to track the British sloop despite whatever evasive course adjustments were commanded to the helmsman. One missile veered from its direct heading and crashed with a mammoth explosion into the sea four hundred yards away. Another just missed the ship, crashing only forty yards astern and showering the ship with shrapnel. The final weapon maneuvered sharply and spun into the sea barely forty yards away. *Landguard* escaped with serious damage from these last two near misses.

Five other weapons targeted *Bideford*. As reported in a British intelligence report filed a few days later, four were near misses and one hit the ship but failed to explode fully:

> The first hit the rigging, carried on and exploded on striking the water on the port side. . . . The second passed across the bows and headed for the second ship (HMS Landguard). The third one passed very close to the Bideford's stem and burst on the port bow holing all forward compartments and causing casualties. Portions of filling from this bomb were recovered indicating not only the type of filling—trialon, but that partial detonation only had taken place. If complete detonation had occurred much heavier damage would have resulted. The fourth struck the water thirty yards short abreast the bridge starboard side causing no damage.[2]

Though in the case of both *Bideford* and *Landguard* all of the missiles either missed or failed to fully detonate, the results of the attack were not trivial. On board *Bideford* one sailor—Able Seaman Charles W. Boardman—was killed, and another sixteen men were wounded; both ships had to return to England for repairs.[3] The crew was perplexed but relieved nonetheless, considering what might have happened had any of the twelve missiles actually struck and fully exploded. Clearly, this was something new.

Two days later the 1st Support Group under Captain Godfrey N. Brewer was on its way to relieve the Canadian 5th Support Group. Captain Brewer's antisubmarine force consisted of *Egret*, a sloop under the command of Acting Commander John Valentine Waterhouse, and less-powerful frigates *Jed* and *Rother*. Brewer also directed the covering destroyers, the Canadian Navy's *Athabaskan* and the Royal Navy's *Grenville*, intended to relieve light cruiser *Bermuda*. Sloop *Pelican* and frigates *Spey* and *Evenlode* also were under Brewer's command, though they had not caught up with the main force by 27 August.

History would be made on 27 August 1943. The events of that day are well documented. In addition to formal action reports filed later by Brewer and Waterhouse, we are fortunate to have an accurate depiction of what followed in the form of (then) Lieutenant Commander Roger P. Hill's detailed account. Hill, already a decorated officer for his heroic actions during a relief convoy to Malta, was commanding *Grenville* at the time and kept detailed records of his signals and orders, written up three decades afterwards in his biography *Destroyer Captain*.[4] Moreover, Hill's ship was outfitted with a special film crew that proved useful in documenting what followed.

On that morning of 27 August, Brewer and his colleagues proceeded on their mission to replace the Canadian 5th Support Group on the front line of the battle against Hitler's U-boats. The rising sun that morning revealed a fine day to come. The winds were light out of the northeast at about five knots. The sea was rippled with gentle waves rising to only a fraction of one foot. Observers on board ships recorded visibility of six to nine miles in a light haze. It was a gentle day in the Bay of Biscay, a body of water known for its occasional intemperate weather. Were it not for the war, it would have been a wonderful day to be at sea.[5]

But the war did encroach. Once again, the Allied maritime reinforcement process was observed by a distant Luftwaffe patrol plane, another Fw 200 sighted by the Allied ships at 0750 hours. The Luftwaffe aircraft, circling in the distance at eight thousand feet altitude, radioed back the position, course, and speed of the 1st Support Group. At 0800 hours another force of eighteen Do 217 bombers was readied for an assault. Just after 1230 hours *Athabaskan*'s radar operators intercepted air-to-air communications, indicating that an inbound raid was seventy miles to the north, and the ships prepared for attack. Perhaps to maintain formation with the slower ships, *Athabaskan* maneuvered at only twenty-three knots, well below maximum speed.[6]

The bombers were picked up on the destroyer's Type 291 air-search radar at 1255 hours and sighted visually shortly thereafter. The aircraft split into groups as the Allied forces opened fire on them at 1303 hours. Five Do 217 bombers engaged *Athabaskan*, pressing on despite intense antiaircraft fire put forward from that warship. The five aircraft each launched one missile. The first two projectiles appeared to fall into the sea in an uncontrolled descent. The last two fell short of the ship. But the third weapon, launched by the crew under the command of *Hauptmann* (Captain) Wolfgang Vorpahl, hit dead on, punching through one side of the hull and continuing on through the ship, punching through the other side on the way out before exploding about ten feet beyond the outside edge of the steel plates. *Athabaskan*, which had continued steaming at twenty-three knots, stopped dead in the water as smoke poured out of the crippled ship. Damage-control parties sprang into action to douse the fire and give aid to the wounded. Captain G. R. Miles and his crew managed a near miracle in saving the ship. When power was eventually restored some hours later, *Athabaskan* limped back to Plymouth, England, for repairs. The officers on board tallied up the losses: one man had been killed instantly, another blown overboard and lost, and fifteen had been wounded, of whom three later perished.

Grenville, with Hill in command, was targeted by six of the bombers but managed to evade all missiles via a combination of aggressive high-speed maneuvering (at thirty-two knots) and heavy antiaircraft fire. Hill quickly learned that by executing these sudden high-speed maneuvers at the very last moment he could circle inside the missiles' turn radius. When the missile operator in the distant Do 217 attempted to follow Hill's ship, the radio-controlled missile turned too sharply, stalled, and crashed into the sea.[7] This was useful information that soon would be relayed to other ships in the Royal Navy—useful at least to those capable of high-speed maneuvering. In the end, Hill and *Grenville* escaped shaken but unscathed.

While this was happening, just moments after *Athabaskan* was struck, sloop *Egret*, then trailing the rest of the formation, was busy fighting her own way out of seven attacking missiles. With less than half the speed of the destroyers, her ability to evade was substantially restricted. Five of the weapons missed, falling short of their target as they evidently exceeded their effective range, and a sixth was shot down by the antiaircraft fire. The seventh missile, launched by the aircraft commanded by *Oberleutnant* Paulus, tore into the ship right at the aft magazine, penetrating the hull and setting off the ordnance stored therein.[8] Within seconds *Egret* was ripped apart, its structure vanishing in an intense explosion that killed 197 of the 232 souls on board.[9] Forty seconds after the missile's impact, *Egret* was gone, and all that the other ships could do was to pick up the 35 survivors, who included Captain Brewer and Commander Waterhouse, both wounded.

Brewer survived the battle to write a firsthand account of what it was like to be on board the first ship in history to be sunk by a remotely guided weapon:

> At about 2 PM we sighted 21 aircraft coming over the horizon. They quickly sized up the situation and split up into three groups of seven, each one concentrating on an A.A. ship but keeping out of gun range. No normal bombing attack developed, but suddenly from *Egret*'s opponents a puff of smoke appeared underneath each aircraft, an object shot ahead

and above it for all of the world as if a tennis player was throwing up a ball to serve, and then turned and sped towards us at very high velocity. As they drew closer, five exploded in the water either short or over, and one coming straight for the bridge was hit and exploded by a 20-mm Oerlikon shell—a very fine piece of shooting. But the seventh, which had looked as if it was going to pass down our starboard side, turned in and hit us abreast the after magazine. There was an enormous explosion as the magazine blew up, the sky was filled with burning pieces of cordite which fell all around us and, with a strange sense of detachment, I looked at my clothing on fire and thought "How odd."[10]

The sudden loss of *Egret*, coupled with the crippling of *Athabaskan* and earlier damage to *Landguard* and *Bideford*, raised alarm in the Royal Navy and the Canadian Navy. The Germans appeared to be able to sink or cripple Allied warships at will with these radical new weapons. That very same day, the United Kingdom's Navy Department issued an "Ultra Most Secret" message warning to the Americans: "*Egret* was sunk today. *Bideford* and HCMS *Athabaskan* have also been damaged. New weapon employed apparently some type of rocket bomb with planes controlled by light impulses but expert appreciation awaited."[11]

The Allied interdiction force in the Bay of Biscay was pulled back another 400 kilometers (215 nautical miles) from the coast in order to take the vulnerable ships out of range of these new missiles.[12] This opened up a much larger safe travel lane for German U-boats, putting at greater risk the Allied supply convoys, just as the activity across the Atlantic was reaching fever pitch. With a couple dozen aircraft and a few guided weapons, the Luftwaffe had achieved a major tactical victory that threatened to undo the gains the Allies had made in protecting the vital Atlantic sea-lanes.

Anxiety was high. In mid-September British Prime Minister Winston S. Churchill addressed Parliament on the "aerial bomb which the enemy has begun to use at close quarters on our ships close to the coast."[13] The scientific community was kicked into high gear with the charge to understand and, it was hoped, defeat these new weapons. The world had indeed changed.

It often is said that the raids of 25 and 27 August 1943 came as a surprise to the Royal Navy, and that the story of the German glide bombs begins with these attacks. This is not the case: up to ten attacks with glide bombs had taken place before *Landguard* and *Bideford* felt their impact. In fact, not all those who perished on board *Egret* were sailors in the Royal Navy, which is our first clue that the attacks were expected. Several of the victims were personnel of the Royal Air Force (RAF) operating in a highly specialized and secret unit called the Y-Service, part of the extensive British signals intelligence and code-breaking apparatus.[14] Hunkered down inside the radio room, this contingent was described by Captain Hill of *Grenville* as "boffins, with pale faces, thick glasses and a special radio set."[15] The special radio set was part of the British signals intelligence network, and this Y-service detachment was on board *Egret* specifically to monitor the communications of attacking bombers and the radio links to the missiles.

Why this specific intelligence mission at this time and place? Hill reports that he and other ship captains had been warned prior to their sailing from Plymouth on August 25—*before* the attack on *Bideford* and *Landguard*—of special intelligence that the Germans were about to introduce rocket-propelled guided bombs, and that the Allied warships wreaking havoc in the Bay of Biscay were a logical target of Luftwaffe maritime attack squadrons armed with these new weapons, known to be based nearby in France. The Y-Service detachment on board *Egret* was there to monitor radio communications with German bombers as they used these new glide bombs. (Perhaps that is also why *Grenville* was equipped with film equipment to record the attack.) Hill suggests that if the Germans could be enticed to attack this group of ships, and if some of the fuel on board the rockets could be somehow collected in the aftermath of the attack, it might allow British intelligence to determine where the fuel was made, and thus allow the Allies to destroy the appropriate facility in a bombing raid.

Military historian Peter C. Smith goes even further, suggesting that *Egret* and its companion ships were purposefully put at risk as part of an intentional "decoy sweep," designed to bring on the German attacks and then allow the boffins on board *Egret* to monitor the radio frequencies used by the Germans to control their glide bombs. This would help the British scientists better understand these weapons, and perhaps develop countermeasures.[16] Hill himself questions why, if the British knew at 0800 hours from intelligence intercepts that bombers were taking off from France to intercept the 1st Support Group, the RAF did not respond by launching its own high-speed Mosquito or Beaufighter aircraft to disrupt this raid. He implies the Admiralty needed to have accurate records of the glide-bomb attack and thus did not want the RAF to interfere with the experiment by shooting down the attacking bombers.

If this were true, it suggests the British were well informed of the potential for this form of attack, and it further highlights the irony that the one ship sunk in the attack was the one in which the Y-Service detachment had been embarked. The names of these brave personnel have not surfaced in published works to date because they are excluded from the official rosters of victims of the loss of *Egret*. Therefore, it is worth noting that, in addition to the 194 Royal Navy personnel who perished on board *Egret* that day,

Squadron Leader Cuthbert William Prideaux Selby of the RAF Volunteer Reserve, serving as liaison between RAF Coastal Command and the Escort Group, also died in the attack. Also killed that day were two individuals—the boffins—sent by the Defence Signals Directorate to intercept radio transmissions: RAF Flying Officer Paul Geoffrey Scorer and a Telegraphist Signals Officer with the surname Keith.[17] Their presence on the ship indicates that there is clearly more to the story than is generally known.

CHAPTER TWO

DEVELOPMENT *of*
GERMAN GLIDE BOMBS

W here did these new weapons come from? How and why were they developed? The development and deployment of radio-controlled antiship weapons in Nazi Germany reflects foremost the failure of the German surface navy to effectively challenge Allied naval superiority after the first years of the war. Ultimately, even the vaunted U-boats would be driven from the Atlantic, leaving the Kriegsmarine unable to deny the Allies unfettered access to the seas off Europe. Second, these weapons reflect the great confidence that Nazi Germany placed in Hermann Göring's Luftwaffe, and the hopes that German airpower could succeed where the Kriegsmarine had failed.

◆ ◆ ◆

In the early years of the war, expectations had been high in Germany that the few but powerful battleships and cruisers of the German navy could engage and destroy vital convoys between the United States and Britain, crippling the latter and forcing the United Kingdom to the negotiating table. This faith had been shattered just months into the war when the Germans had to scuttle *Graf Spee* in Montevideo harbor—in full view of the world's media—lest the damaged "pocket battleship" be destroyed by British warships gathering off the Uruguayan coast. Any lingering hopes that the Kriegsmarine surface fleet could threaten British battleships ended in flames as the Royal Navy pounded *Bismarck*—the largest battleship and the pride of the German surface navy—until it sank beneath the cold waters of the Atlantic in May 1941.

From that point on it was up to the Luftwaffe and German submarines to deny use of the sea-lanes to Allied powers. If the Luftwaffe was to have a chance at crippling heavy British warships, it would need an appropriate bomb for the task, something sufficiently precise and destructive so it could penetrate the heavy deck armor of a battleship and put it out of action. Moreover, if convoys were to be attacked without heavy aircraft losses, some form of standoff weapon suitable for strikes against merchant ships and their escorts would be needed. Such a weapon would allow an attacking aircraft to remain out of range of the ships' guns—to stand off—while the aircraft's longer-range missiles bore in on targets.

As the needs emerged, the Luftwaffe was able to call on the fruits of German technical wizardry. Much of the groundwork had been laid. Development of precision, remotely controlled antiship weapons predates World War II, and, perhaps not surprisingly, originated in the German engineering and military community. In World War I the German navy developed remotely controlled surface craft designed to attack invading ships. Though controlled initially with cables, research into radio-controlled guidance mechanisms was under way when the 1918 Armistice brought the experiments to a close. A similar cable arrangement was employed on another weapon, a torpedo-laden glider designed to be deployed from airships against naval surface units. The glider was flown via the cable to a position near the ship, at which point the torpedo within it was released to hurl itself against the target. Neither weapon played a significant role in the combat of the era.[1]

In the postwar environment the advances in radio communication led, in many nations, to experimentation involving radio-controlled weapons and aircraft. In particular, the experience of the Luftwaffe in the Spanish Civil War led to renewed interest in weapons that might be more effective against maneuvering ships than were simple gravity bombs. Over time, these early innovations were to be enhanced into two radio-controlled weapons of considerably more sophistication. The programs were managed with strict secrecy—industrial participants knew only what their specific subsystems were designed to do and few people had a complete idea of the weapons under development. The development programs proceeded apace with good results, and both innovative weapons would be employed in summer 1943 with deadly consequences.

Ruhrstahl PC 1400FX ("Fritz-X")

In 1938 Dr. Max Otto Kramer initiated a research program into armor-penetrating guided bombs at the Deutsche Versuchsanstalt für Luftfahrt (DVL; German Institute for Aviation Research). In 1940, following the loss of *Graf Spee*, the Reichsluftfahrtministerium (RLM; German Air Ministry) formally established a priority program to develop radio-controlled weapons for use against heavily armored warships, building off Kramer's research. The result was the Ruhrstahl PC 1400FX ("Fritz-X") radio-controlled armor-piercing bomb. With this new weapon the Luftwaffe hoped to be able to defeat heavily armored British and Allied warships at sea.

✦ ✦ ✦

Dr. Kramer, by all accounts a brilliant and innovative engineer, was an ideal choice to lead this effort. Kramer was born on 8 September 1903 in Cologne, Germany, earned a degree in electronic engineering at Technische Universität München (the Technical College of Munich) in 1926, and received his doctorate in aeronautics from Aerodynamisches Institut, Technische Universität Aachen (the Technical College of Aachen) in 1931.[2] By the late 1930s he was already an authority on aerodynamics, working at Deutsche Versuchsanstalt für Luftfahrt (German Institute for Aeronautical Research) in Berlin, and holding patents for important innovations related to aircraft, such as landing flaps. His specialty was in the modeling of complex airflows, especially those related to laminar-flow dynamics. By 1938 he had written a definitive paper on the subject, based on his mathematical modeling of porpoises.

There is no consensus on the appropriate name for the battleship-sinker that emerged after 1940 from the genius of this scientist. The company that developed the weapon, Ruhrstahl AG, assigned the name X-1 to Kramer's project, thus it often has been referred to as the Kramer X-1. The bomb was a modified *Panzerbombe Cylindrisch* (PC), a 1,400-kilogram (3,090-pound) armor-piercing weapon known colloquially as the "Fritz." Modified with a new tail sporting cruciform (X-shaped) wings, the bomb was often called the "Fritz-X" or simply "FX" by both Allied forces and their German adversaries. While more formally it would be known as the PC 1400FX, by convention the bomb will be referred to in this book as Fritz-X.

What emerged from Dr. Kramer's laboratory was a massive bomb measuring 3.26 meters (10.7 feet) in length with short stubby fixed wings in the midsection measuring in total span 1.35 meters (4.5 feet). In the front was the PC warhead, and at the rear was a unique twelve-sided tail structure with vertical and horizontal fins and spoilers. Solenoids activated the spoilers to influence the path of the falling bomb by increasing or decreasing wind resistance on one side or the other. A tracking flare in the tail allowed the operator to keep the bomb in sight as it fell, and gyroscopic controls maintained stability during the descent.

Once dropped the Fritz-X no longer had any form of propulsion other than the force of gravity—it simply fell through the air. Its fins did not provide lift, just control. A typical descent required about forty seconds; the bomb could reach a terminal velocity of 260 meters (850 feet) per second—in other words faster than a bullet fired from a .38-special revolver. The four radio-activated spoilers allowed the operator in the launching aircraft to exercise limited control of range and azimuth as the bomb fell and the target maneuvered.

The Fritz-X was in effect a large guided bomb designed to be dropped close to its target from a high altitude and then steered into the deck of a heavy armored warship such as a battleship or heavy cruiser. With its high terminal velocity and armor-piercing warhead, the bomb would punch through the armored deck plates and explode deep in the bowels of the ship. The explosive charge of 320 kilograms (700 pounds) of Amatol would be sufficient to blow out the bottom hull plates, leading to massive flooding; if it by chance landed near a magazine, it would conflagrate the target in a matter of seconds. While effective against heavily armored targets, the weapon would be of little relevance to thinly armored ships such as merchantmen and their escorts. At this rate of descent, the bomb would punch a hole clear through the deck plates and not explode until well below the ship in the water.

In order for this bomb to be effective, the launching pilots had to head directly for the target and then drop the bomb from a high altitude, typically around 6,000 meters (20,000 feet). A minimum altitude of about 4,000 (14,000 feet) was required—anything lower and the bomb would not have sufficient fall time for the operator to provide effective guidance, especially since once dropped it took fifteen seconds for the radio-guidance system to provide effective control over the bomb.[3] Once the Fritz-X was dropped, the launching aircraft would reduce engine power or climb so as not to overtake the Fritz-X as the bomb's forward momentum was taken over by gravitational pull. In this way the operator in the aircraft could keep the bomb in sight as it fell far below. Once in its fast descent, the bomb was invulnerable to ship defenses of the era. The same could not be said of the launching aircraft, which—at this point flying slow, straight, and level—was extraordinarily vulnerable to large-caliber shipboard guns or protective fighters, if they were able to climb high enough to reach the bomber. If the launching aircraft were destroyed or forced to maneuver prior to bomb impact, the visual or radio link could be severed and the target could escape.

Initial ground and carry trials were conducted with an He 111 test aircraft at Peenemünde, an isolated village on the Baltic island of Usedom that became the center of German rocket testing in World War II. During spring 1942 the testing program was relocated to Foggia, outside Naples, Italy, in order to exploit better weather conditions. It did not take long for the outcome to impress observers. Test results suggested that the "circular-error-probable" for this new weapon was only five meters. This meant that there was a 50 percent probability that a weapon dropped from high altitude would land within five meters of the aim point—at least under test conditions. Of the one hundred bombs launched under test conditions, forty-nine achieved direct hits or misses sufficiently close as to have nearly the same effect as a direct hit.[4] The failures were written off to problems with manufacturing quality or operator error—sources of failure that might be expected to diminish over time.

Satisfied with these results, the weapon was taken out of developmental testing after only one month and was transitioned to operational testing with frontline aircraft and pilots. The RLM ordered an initial batch of one thousand Fritz-X bombs, ramping up to a full-scale production rate of three hundred per month. However, delays in development of the aircraft transmitter used for radio guidance delayed the program and production did not commence in earnest until April 1943.[5]

Henschel Hs 293 A-1

While the Fritz-X solved part of the Luftwaffe's problem—engaging heavily armored warships—it did not address the second challenge of standoff attacks against convoys. Fortunately for the Germans, the Fritz-X was not the only new antiship weapon emerging from German research facilities. In 1939 the industrial firm Henschel Flugzeug-Werke AG, housed in the Berlin suburb of Schöenfeld, was awarded a contract by the RLM to develop an unmanned bomber, based on the early design work performed by the Schwartz Propeller Werke on a remotely controlled glider. Led by Dr. Herbert A. Wagner, the engineers in Schöenfeld (including Otto Bohlmann, Wilfried Hell, Dr. Julius Henrici, Reinhard Lahde, and Josef Schwarzmann) modified the original Schwartz design into a rocket-powered miniature aircraft. This technology was ideal for the requirement of a standoff weapon able to destroy convoy merchantmen and their thinly armored escorts.

✦ ✦ ✦

Herbert Alois Wagner was a brilliant mathematician and designer of complex aircraft, gas-turbine engines, and missiles, operating well ahead of his time. Born in Graz, Austria, on 22 May 1900, he attended the Kaiserlich und Koniglich Marine-Akademie (the Austro-Hungarian Naval Academy) from 1914 to 1917 and served in the Austro-Hungarian navy as an ensign, surviving a torpedo attack on his ship. He returned to his studies after the war and received a doctorate in engineering from Technischen Universität Berlin (Technical University of Berlin) at the age of twenty-three. As remembered by a former colleague, Konrad Zuse,

> Wagner's work methods impressed us all. He was an extraordinarily confident and eclectic arithmetician. Lightning-fast approximations and cleverly chosen simplifications were his specialty. He could develop theories and calculations for hours on end, page upon page. The rest of us then sat around his desk and were hard pressed to follow his ideas, even in their most important points. Later, we often needed days to verify his calculations. But as far as I know, no one was ever able to catch a single mistake. The statements, as well as the calculations, were always correct.[6]

His aviation design career started in the mid-1920s working in Berlin for Rohrbach Betall Flugzeugbau on new flying boats, where he developed the Wagner-beam method of sheet-metal construction, a standard in the aircraft industry still employed today. After a short career as a full professor at the Technical University of Berlin, he returned to industry at Junkers Flugzeugwerke, working in the design of aircraft and aircraft engines. A disagreement with the president of Junkers around aircraft development priorities led to Wagner's resignation; he moved on to Henschel Flugzeugwerke in Berlin.[7]

In July 1940 work started on the adaptation of Wagner's initial design into a glide bomb for antiship purposes. Initially, the design called for an unpowered device, using small wings to slowly trade off altitude against forward speed, a concept evolved from that used in the Fritz-X. The difference here, though, was the desire for greater standoff range and the targeting of unarmored ships. Successful drop tests with these unpowered prototypes, labeled Henschel (Hs) 293 V-1, V-2, and V-3, demonstrated the viability of the basic aerodynamics and overall concept. However, two problems emerged. First, the descending bomb, relying only on gravity and slim wings, would be overtaken by the launching aircraft, making it difficult for the bomb operator to maintain control. Second, the operator often lost sight of the missile against surface clutter, making it hard for him to maneuver the weapon onto the target.

The first problem was solved by adding independent propulsion to the Hs 293. A Walter HWK 109-507 liquid-fuel rocket was mounted in a pod underneath the Hs 293 airframe and was ignited once the missile had safely cleared the aircraft. The second problem was solved by placing a flare in the tail section of the Hs 293. After the rocket was dropped, the flare would ignite, creating a visible tracking source for the operator for at least the first 100 to 110 seconds of flight.

Early testing used specially modified He 111 aircraft, with the first carry-and-drop tests performed in Karlshagen, a town on the Baltic Coast near Usedom.[8] The Hs 293 A-0 prototype proved the validity of the updated concept; after a string of early failures, the modified variant Hs 293 A-1 was ordered into production and operational testing on 1 November 1941, with three He 111 H-12 aircraft assigned to this mission. Initial pilot training began in February 1942; by May of that year fifty-three test firings had taken place, of which thirty-five worked as designed and eighteen did not, plagued by technical failures.[9] (This result, in which about one Hs 293 in three ran wild, would be witnessed throughout the operational life of this weapon.) Training missions with actual aircrews did not take place until spring 1943. As with the Fritz-X, deployment also was delayed by the lack of suitable production facilities; despite ambitious expectations, initial monthly production rates were barely adequate to meet testing and training needs.

What emerged from this development and testing process was a light-metal-alloy cylindrical structure with stubby wings measuring three meters overall in span, a conventional horizontal stabilizer, and a vertical stabilizer suspended below the aft body. The overall missile body extended 3.82 meters (12.5 feet), of which the forward part contained the warhead and the after part housed the control electronics and electric batteries. Protruding from the end of the missile was a flare and suspended beneath was the rocket pod. The rocket used a catalyst known in Germany as *Z-stoff* (a water-based solution of calcium or sodium permanganate) and a fuel oxidizer known as *S-stoff* (concentrated hydrogen peroxide). When mixed, the *Z-stoff* turned the *S-stoff* into steam, producing 5.9 kN (600 kilograms, or 1,320 pounds) of thrust, enough to propel the 1,045-kilogram (2,300-pound) missile well ahead of the attacking aircraft.

The addition of the rocket was an important innovation, distinguishing the Hs 293 from the Fritz-X. It provided for more-flexible combat engagements in that the missile could be launched from lower altitude and from a considerable distance. If the Fritz-X was a guided bomb, the Hs 293 A-1 was a genuine guided missile. In a typical deployment, the attacking aircraft would approach the target to within 12 kilometers (6 nautical miles), then fly a parallel course in the opposite direction. When the ship was about 45 degrees off the forward right side, the aircraft launched the Hs 293. The Walter liquid-fueled rocket, running for ten or twelve seconds, would accelerate the missile to about 600 kilometers per hour (325 knots), at which point the operator had turned the missile into the target. Once the rocket burned out, the missile continued with its forward momentum, maintaining a glide by virtue of short wings, until the operator steered it into the target. Depending on the final glide angle chosen, the terminal velocity could reach more than 900 kilometers (485 nautical miles) per hour. Dropped from low altitude, say 1,000 meters (3,300 feet), the missile could glide as far as 11 kilometers (5.9 nautical miles). At higher altitude, above 4,000 meters (13,100 feet), the range could be extended to 18 kilometers (9.7 nautical miles).

The business end of a glide bomb consisted of a 500-kilogram (1,100-pound) *Sprengstoffbombe Cylindrisch* SC 500 high-explosive bomb, without the heavy armor-piercing structure of the Fritz-X. The explosive charge itself was 300 kilograms (650 pounds) of a mix of RDX (15 percent), TNT (70 percent), and aluminum powder (15 percent). This made the Hs 293 suitable primarily for thinly armored warships and merchant ships, as distinct from the large battleships typically targeted with the armor-piercing Fritz-X.

Kehl-Strassburg Radio Guidance System

The genius of the Fritz-X and Hs 293 glide bombs lay not just in their aerodynamic qualities, but also in the sophistication of their guidance systems. Both weapons could be steered into the target by an operator in the launching aircraft via a radio link, known as the Kehl-Strassburg system. In the launching aircraft was a radio transmitter operating on one of eighteen frequencies between 48.2 and 49.9 megahertz (MHz), separated by 100 kilohertz (kHz). In the weapon was a receiver matched to the transmitter.[10] Before takeoff the Hs 293 or Fritz-X weapons were preset to one of the eighteen operational frequencies and a similar setting made in the launching aircraft. In this way up to eighteen different aircraft could launch weapons in the same mission concurrently, without interfering with each others' radio links.

◆ ◆ ◆

Since each aircraft was tuned to one frequency, this design meant that if an aircraft carried more than one Hs 293 or Fritz-X into action, it had to wait until the first had impacted before dropping the second. For the Hs 293 this was not a huge challenge because the aircraft could orbit miles from the target and proceed to launch one missile after another as the first ones impacted. In the case of the Fritz-X, it was far more complicated because it meant the aircraft had to fly over the target once again, putting it into harm's way without the chance of surprise. Thus, it was unheard of for an individual aircraft to carry more than one Fritz-X during any single mission.

The transmitter ("Kehl") was a FuG 203 unit manufactured by Telefunken, the German electronics conglomerate.[11] It generated about forty-five watts of power in normal use. About thirty watts of power would be passed to the receiver by its antenna, which would generate sufficient signal strength to maintain a command link within eighteen kilometers of the target, consistent with the operational range of the weapons. The Hs 293 and Fritz-X weapons shared a basic receiver unit known as the "Strassburg" subsystem, paired on the same VHF frequency range of 48.2 to 49.9 MHz as the Kehl transmitter.[12] The Strassburg receiver was naturally considered an item of the highest sensitivity, and it was intended that it should not fall intact into the hands of the Allies. A separate "explosive charge, fitted with a v.Z. (80) clockwork-arming all ways acting fuse [was] located under the radio control unit. The purpose of this charge is to destroy the radio control unit upon impact."[13] A similar device existed on the Fritz-X.[14]

The operator in the aircraft transmitted control signals via hand-activated devices known at the time as a *knüppel (club)*—it would be easily recognized today by any eight-year-old child as a joystick. As the operator moved the joystick left to right or up and down, it made contact with one of four different signal generators, each of which was allocated a specific frequency above the base signal frequency: +1 kHz (right), +1.5 kHz (left), +8 kHz (up), or +12 kHz (down) in the case of the Hs 293. The receiver on the guided weapon had four filters, one tuned for each of the control command frequencies. When a command signal was sent, it would be picked up by the appropriate filter and translated into an electrical power signal that would move a solenoid attached to a control surface.

For the Fritz-X the control surfaces operated in two dimensions—in essence left–right and up–down. A similar approach operated on the ailerons of the Hs 293, in what would later be known as a "bang-bang" control system. In this case, the operator could either deflect ailerons full left, neutral, or full right—with no gradations in between. Thus, the missile moved in a series of wide arcs left and right until it converged on the target. The vertical glide path of the Hs 293 was controllable as well, though with a dampening mechanism that helped avoid excessive oscillations. It took extensive training and experience to yield a competent operator under the best of circumstances, and in an aircraft attempting to dodge antiaircraft fire—not to mention Allied fighters—it was a complex task indeed. As will be discussed in more detail later, multipath interference also complicated the operator's task, especially as the weapon closed in on its target.

The Kehl-Strassburg system was prone to problems with moisture and condensation, especially during long-range high-altitude missions. To offset this limitation, an active heating device was installed in the aircraft that dispersed hot engine exhaust over the missile controls in an attempt to ward off condensation. This required the launching aircraft to be specially outfitted with both the Kehl-Strassburg system and the heating apparatus, and thus limited the number of aircraft able to deploy the weapons. The Allies would soon learn the value of targeting their own bombers against the airfields from which these special aircraft operated, in attempts (ultimately quite successful) to defeat the threat by destroying the aircraft on the ground.

Launching Aircraft

If there was a weak link in the overall glide-bomb scenario it was the ability of the aircraft carrying the weapons to reach the target and survive long enough to allow the operator to fly the weapon into the target. The deficiencies arose both from the combat limitations of the initial aircraft versions employed, especially in the face of advanced Allied fighter aircraft, and from the basic reliability of more-advanced bombers rushed into production in an attempt to redress that deficiency.

✦ ✦ ✦

The first aircraft to drop these weapons was the ubiquitous Heinkel (He) 111 medium bomber, employed as the primary test platform for each of the glide bombs. It often is written that the He 111 was a launching platform for these weapons on operational missions. However, while the He 111 H-12 variant was used in early tests of the Hs 293 and Fritz-X, it was apparently never deployed with these weapons in an operational role.[15]

The originally intended operational platform for the glide bombs was the He 177 *Greif* (Griffon) heavy bomber, a complex four-engine aircraft, with two engines in a single nacelle coupled to one propeller, and thus superficially resembling a twin-engine aircraft. The *Greif* is famous both for representing Germany's hope for a long-range bomber force and for the never-ending troubles it caused for flight crews and mechanics. Renowned for operational difficulties and in-flight engine fires, the troubled platform was delayed in production and did not enter operational use with the glide bombs until well after the initial missions had taken place. We will hear more about this aircraft in Chapter 7.

With the glide bombs nearing operational readiness, and with the He 177 suffering from extended teething pains, an interim solution was required. The Luftwaffe defaulted to a tried-and-true medium bomber in the form of the Dornier (Do) 217, then in the last stages of serial production and in the process of being replaced by advanced versions of the Junkers (Ju) 88. Essentially an enlarged version of the Do 17 bomber, the first flight of the Do 217 took place in August 1938. A versatile aircraft, variants of the Do 217 had been developed and deployed as a dive-bomber, level bomber, and night fighter. Its use as a carrier for glide bombs represented an expedient solution to the delays in development of the He 177. This new mission for the Do 217 also usefully extended the life of an aircraft design that was otherwise being overtaken by advanced models.

A unique variant of the Do 217, the Do 217 E-5, was produced in small numbers especially configured to handle the Hs 293. This aircraft was derived from the Do 217 E-4 dive-bomber.[16] The first modified Do 217 E-5 was delivered to the Luftwaffe in April 1942 and was deployed in support of the testing program at Peenemünde. The original Luftwaffe plan was for another 15 aircraft to be modified by 20 June 1942 and 23 more by the end of July. Another 80 aircraft were to be built to the E-5 standard by the end of 1942, leading to a total of 120 of the type. In the end, there were not enough trained crews or test missiles to support such a ramp-up, and in November 1942 RLM modified its plans, reducing the number of newly built aircraft on order to only 34, to complement the 40 already in hand, and switching the remaining aircraft to conventional bomber variants. According to some sources only 65 of these special aircraft were produced.[17] Others suggest the number was closer to 75; the records of the Luftwaffe group that operated these aircraft indicate that 74 aircraft were actually delivered, which is consistent with the numbers above.[18]

The Hs 293 would be carried by the Do 217 E-5 on special pylons located outboard the engines on the wings. Because of the weight of the weapons, and therefore the impact of that weight (and moment) on lateral stability, either two glide bombs were carried (one on each wing) or, more typically, one weapon was carried on one wing and a nine-hundred-liter drop tank with additional fuel was carried on the other. Of the 386 sorties of Do 217 aircraft armed with Hs 293 glide bombs from August 1943 to April 1944, 370 involved carriage of one weapon; only 16 sorties involved Do 217 E-5 aircraft equipped with two weapons.[19] Effective combat radius was about 800 kilometers (432 nautical miles) with two weapons carried.

Range could be increased to 1,000 to 1,100 kilometers (540 to 600 nautical miles) when only one missile was carried along with a wing-mounted fuel tank. If the aircraft departed and was unable to locate a target, it could still land without jettisoning the weapon(s).

Another variant of the basic Do 217 bomber, the Do 217 K-2, was developed specifically to carry the heavier Fritz-X at high altitude. Because of the need to climb above 6,000 meters (20,000 feet) for optimum deployment, the Do 217 K-2 had extended wings, lengthened in total 5.75 meters (19 feet). Superficially, the Do 217 K-2 also was distinguishable from earlier variants by its glazed and rounded forward fuselage, providing better downward visibility for the pilot and bomb aimer. Compared to the stocky and workmanlike appearance of the Do 217 E-5, the K-2, with its longer wings and rounded fuselage, projected a graceful and streamlined demeanor. As with the Do 217 E-5, ramp-up of the K-2 squadrons was hindered by the absence of trained crews and sufficient numbers of Fritz-X bombs. By May 1943, at the time the squadrons had been expected to go operational, only one hundred Fritz-X weapons were in inventory.[20]

Unlike the Hs 293, which was mounted on pylons outboard of the engines on the Do 217 E-5, the Fritz-X, with its smaller overall physical envelope, was carried on the wings between the fuselage and the engine nacelle on the Do 217 K-2. Operational radius was similar to the Do 217 E-5, from 800 kilometers (432 nautical miles) if two weapons were carried or 1,100 kilometers (600 nautical miles) if only one was carried. It was impractical to carry two of these heavy bombs because it meant the aircraft could not depart with full fuel tanks. Because of this, all the 102 sorties with Fritz-X weapons from July 1943 to April 1944 (at least) involved carriage of only one weapon.[21]

Over time, it became clear that a single version of the Do 217 able to carry either the Hs 293 or the Fritz-X would be desirable, so that the same group of aircraft on different missions could target either heavily armored naval targets or thin-skinned merchant ships. A new variant of the Do 217 K-2, the Do 217 K-3, was designed to launch either the Fritz-X or the Hs 293. A final variant, the Do 217 M-11, was produced in small numbers toward the end of the war; it could carry either weapon.

The deployment of either Do 217 variant for attack was a complex process, especially in comparison with traditional attack missions with ordinary bombs. Because of the weight of a fully loaded aircraft, both variants of the Do 217 required medium-length paved runways at least 1,500 meters (4,900 feet) in length, along with paved taxiways and parking aprons. Since the glide bombs had to be stored in weather-protected locations, they could not be loaded onto the aircraft until a few hours before takeoff. Once installed, tests had to be performed that required about twenty minutes per weapon. Overall, from the start of the process to takeoff, typically three hours was required for any individual aircraft; for a whole squadron (twelve aircraft), the preparation time could be double that.[22]

Once the aircraft were airborne and on the way to the target, another critical factor emerged: the weather at the intended point of attack. As a practical matter, since the operator had to track the weapon continuously from high altitude all the way to the surface, the Fritz-X could only be deployed in clear sky conditions with visibility above 20 kilometers (10.8 nautical miles). If the aircraft approached the target and discovered any cloud layers below the minimum effective drop altitude of about 4,500 meters (15,000 feet), the mission would have to be aborted. About one-third of all aircraft that departed on attack missions with Fritz-X weapons failed to launch them for one reason or another.[23]

Weather conditions also affected the operational use of the Hs 293, but since the launch altitude could vary from low to high altitude the primary consideration was one of forward visibility as opposed to ceiling height. The missions could proceed with cloud layers as low as 500 meters (1,640 feet). However, it should be noted that, in such conditions, it would be very difficult for the attacking aircraft to locate the targets: missions flown in poor weather conditions rarely led to success. From August 1943 to April 1944 about one-quarter of all departing aircraft carrying Hs 293 missiles aborted their missions, most typically for failure to find their targets.[24]

Enemy air defense became another critical planning element. The operational profile of glide-bomb missions made the aircraft especially vulnerable to Allied fighters and heavy antiaircraft guns. For this reason, the missions often were flown at dusk, at night during moonlit conditions, or at night with the use of flares to illuminate targets. Alternatively, glide bombs would be deployed during mass attacks in the hope that enemy air defenses would be overwhelmed. In particular, since attacks employing the Fritz-X were so dependent on clear skies—the same conditions that Allied fighter pilots and naval gunners also craved—missions with those weapons often were accompanied by Luftwaffe fighter units to distract enemy defenses.

One other aircraft besides the He 177 and Do 217 deployed with the Hs 293 in combat toward the end of its operational use. This was the Focke-Wolf (Fw) 200 Condor, which was a long-range maritime reconnaissance aircraft. All of these Hs 293–equipped Condors could be distinguished, first, by the more forward position of the ventral observers' station, and, second, by special fairings under the outboard engines on which the Hs 293 bomb racks were installed.[25] Relatively few glide-bomb missions were flown with these aircraft, and all of those missions were unsuccessful.

Operational Concept

There were debates within the German military commands about the best use of the new glide bombs, once they became operational after March 1943. By mid-1943, the war had turned against the Axis powers in Europe. On the Eastern Front, Soviet troops had launched a massive offensive in the Caucasus, which had forced the Germans to retreat and threatened their vital positions around the Black Sea. Farther north an offensive had pushed German troops back from Moscow and from positions outside Leningrad. In North Africa the Wehrmacht's Afrika Korps was reeling from combined blows by U.S. and British forces, and was only weeks away from collapsing altogether. In the Atlantic the vaunted U-boat offensive against Allied convoys had turned, and now German submarines were on the defensive against vastly improved antisubmarine units. By the end of May, Admiral Dönitz of the Kriegsmarine would withdraw his U-boats from the central Atlantic after fifty-six U-boats were sunk in April and May 1943 alone.

✦ ✦ ✦

In this context Hitler decided the best use of the new secret weapons would be against Allied convoys in the Atlantic, replacing the crippled U-boat fleet. However, the delays in deploying the delayed He 177 aircraft meant that the mid-Atlantic convoys were effectively unreachable by the Luftwaffe and its shorter-range Do 217. Colonel Werner Baumbach, late in the war the officer responsible for the Luftwaffe bomber fleet, argued that the glide bombs should be deployed in support of the war against the Soviet Union, targeting Soviet ships, which were bottled up at Kronstadt and Leningrad, and Soviet naval forces still active in the Black Sea.[26] Hitler overruled this decision on security grounds, afraid that the new weapons might fall into the hands of the Allies. With these constraints in hand, the deployment scenario shifted to targets at sea within range of the short-legged Do 217. This limited their use to convoys passing through choke points in the Mediterranean as well as naval units operating along the Atlantic coasts of France and Spain in the Bay of Biscay. Attacks against the Atlantic convoys would have to await deployment of the He 177.[27] Hitler also intended to deploy the weapons in large numbers to destroy any Allied attempt to invade continental Europe, and thus prepared weapons stockpiles in Italy, France, and Norway.[28]

Special Luftwaffe Units: KG 100 "Wiking"

The unique nature of the Hs 293 and Fritz-X meant that units deploying these weapons required special training and experience. It was not a weapon to be carried by just any of the many heavy-bomber, medium-bomber, and maritime-patrol units. To this end, in autumn 1942 two specialized units of the Luftwaffe were created. The Lehr und Erprobungs Kommando (LEK 21; Training and Test Command) was established in August 1942 to support service trials of the Fritz-X. A similar unit, LEK 15, was assembled for service trials and training for the Hs 293. On 20 February 1943 these LEK 15 aircraft ended service trials and were re-created into an operational unit with the Hs 293, based at Usedom. On 20 April 1943 LEK 21 was reorganized as an operational group based at Schwäbisch-Hall near Stuttgart.

✦ ✦ ✦

The Hs 293–equipped aircraft of LEK 15 were integrated into Luftwaffe *Gruppe* II of *Kampfgeschwader* 100 (II./KG 100), flying the Do 217 E-5 and under the command of *Major* Franz Hollweg.[29] The initial complement of aircraft was forty-five, five of which were destroyed in training accidents during the workup period from April to August. These losses were made good, and, when II./KG 100 embarked on its first operational missions in late August 1943, it had been provided additional aircraft and crews to bring its order of battle to forty-three bombers.[30]

In parallel, the Fritz-X–equipped aircraft from LEK 21 were incorporated into Luftwaffe *Gruppe* III./KG 100, operating forty-one Do 217 K-1 (for training purposes) and nine Do 217 K-2 aircraft, under the command of *Major* Ernst Hetzel. The K-1 aircraft were taken out of the *gruppe* by June and replaced with a somewhat lesser number of additional K-2 variants. Three aircraft were lost during the training period; by late July the equipment operated by III./KG 100 was down to only thirty-five Do 217 K-2 aircraft. Lack of suitable aircraft would remain a thorn in the side of III./KG 100 for its entire existence. Meanwhile, units of Luftwaffe *Gruppen* II./KG 40 (with the He 177) and III./KG 40 (with the Fw 200) also prepared for operational deployment, which would not occur until later in 1943. By late 1943, then, four groups of the Luftwaffe flying four types of aircraft would be deployed with glide bombs.

The crews of these units received special training in the tactics and operational use of glide bombs. Part of the training involved special simulators created by the Luftwaffe for this purpose. As described by a Luftwaffe pilot during an interrogation with his British captors,

An upright post with a horizontal area on top was mounted on a four-wheeled trolley. A white ball representing the bomb was suspended on an endless wire which ran round two pulleys, one of which was attached to the horizontal arm and one to the trolley. The trolley, which was fitted with an electric motor, travelled at a constant speed and by means of remote control could be turned to left or right as desired. . . . The movements of the bomb, which normally travelled on the endless wire in a downward direction at a constant speed, could also be regulated by means of this remote control. . . . The trolley was steered in the direction of a model ship on wheels, which was about six metres away. . . . The combined result of the motions of the bomb and the trolley is similar to that of a Fritz X bomb when controlled in flight. Informant found that this apparatus was surprisingly easy to control and he obtained a direct hit on the ship with his first attempt.[31]

By August both groups of KG 100 were ready for action, under the overall command of *Major* Fritz Auffhammer. Their presence was to be felt shortly.[32] It was II./KG 100 that carried out the successful mission in the Bay of Biscay, sinking *Egret* and damaging *Athabaskan, Bideford,* and *Landguard.* (Auffhammer claimed a near-miss during the first attack.)[33] And while III./KG 100 with its battleship-busting Fritz-X had yet to sink any ships, that was about to change.

CHAPTER THREE

DEATH *of a* BATTLESHIP *and* CRISIS AT SALERNO

I t is often written that the attacks by II./KG 100 in late August in the Bay of Biscay, in which *Egret* was sunk and *Bideford, Landguard,* and *Athabaskan* damaged, represent the first operational deployment of the German glide bombs.[1] That is not the case, though it does represent the first deployment of the Hs 293 and the first successful engagement with either the Hs 293 or Fritz-X. The first deployment of German glide bombs was not with Hs 293 missiles in the Atlantic but with Fritz-X bombs in the Mediterranean.

◆ ◆ ◆

Early Raids on Sicily

It was off Sicily in the Mediterranean that radio-controlled glide bombs had their debut. The Allied invasion of Europe began on 9 July 1943 when the first waves of British, American, and Canadian armies—eventually numbering 160,000 troops—stormed ashore on the beaches in southeastern Sicily. Operation Husky was under way. On 22 July units of General George S. Patton's Seventh Army moved from their landing zones in the south and took control of Palermo in northwestern Sicily. British units had moved north from their landing zones in the southeast, occupying the towns of Syracuse and Augusta along the eastern coastline. All three harbors—Palermo, Syracuse, and Augusta—provided refuge for Allied warships as they supported troops with naval gunfire. These harbors also served as unloading zones for Allied transports bringing reinforcements and material for units ashore.

✦ ✦ ✦

Such concentrations of ships proved all too tempting to the officers of III./KG 100, under the command of *Major* Ernst Hetzel, then based about 920 kilometers (500 nautical miles) away from Palermo at Istres, northwest of Marseilles, France. Arriving from Schwäbisch-Hall to Istres on 12 July, just days after the start of Operation Husky, the unit prepared for the initial operations of their radical new weapon, the Fritz-X. These were not to be full-fledged attacks of all three squadrons: 7./KG 100, 8./KG 100, and 9./KG 100. Instead, these operational trials under combat conditions were designed both to test the weapons in actual combat and to further the training of the aircrews.

The first combat mission using German glide bombs was flown on 21 July 1943.[2] A single *kette* (three aircraft; literally, a chain) of III./KG 100 loaded the Fritz-X on board and proceeded at dusk to attack Allied shipping concentrations in Augusta's harbor, without success. A similar attack two days later against Syracuse also ended without any demonstrable impact.

A similar small-scale raid took place a week later. Four Do 217 K-2 aircraft of III./KG 100 departed Istres after midnight on 1 August, destined for Palermo. These aircraft were part of a major air raid involving several dozen bombers from various units, including KG 26 (Ju 88s) and KG 100, the latter now under the command of *Major* Bernard Jope. The timing of the raid was ideal for the Luftwaffe. The afternoon before, Rear Admiral Lyal A. Davidson's invasion Support Force had sailed into Palermo harbor with cruisers *Philadelphia* and *Savannah*, escorted by destroyers *Gherardi*, *Nelson*, *Jeffers*, *Murphy*, *Trippe*, and *Knight*. Offshore, waiting in five passenger ships and seven Liberty ships, were the soldiers of the 9th Infantry Division.[3] It was a target-rich setting, made more inviting to attacking aircraft by clear skies and calm weather.

Arriving in the predawn hours over their target, some of the attacking aircraft released flares to illuminate the ships in the harbor below. Other aircraft of multiple squadrons dropped bombs. The aircraft of III./KG 100 released their Fritz-X bombs and attempted to guide the weapons onto the ships below, illuminated by the flickering flares and the periodic flashes of exploding ordnance.

It remains unclear exactly what damage, if any, was caused by the Fritz-X weapons on this raid. U.S. minesweepers *Skill* and *Strive* were damaged by bombers flying at high altitude—as opposed to dive-bombers—with a near miss ripping a four-by-eight-foot hole in the latter's hull. Tank landing ship *LST-373* was damaged.[4] It also has been reported that a British coastal freighter, *Uskide*, was sunk, though there are questions surrounding this account.[5] In the end, none of these losses can be definitely attributed to III./KG 100. Meanwhile, two of the attacking Do 217 aircraft were lost on the raid.[6]

It was the turn of Syracuse on 10 August. Another group of four Do 217 K-2 aircraft from III./KG 100 departed Istres during the night to travel some 1,130 kilometers (610 nautical miles), along with another two dozen bombers from other units and bases, arriving over their target in the early morning. Once again, no confirmed damage was caused by the Fritz-X. On the way back, one of the four attacking aircraft was attacked by an Allied night fighter and shot down.[7] A final raid on Sicily took place on 21 August with the target this time the port of Augusta, just north of Syracuse. Again, there was no damage from the air raid and all aircraft returned safely, so the novelty of the Fritz-X remained unknown to those on the receiving end of the attacks.

Another ten minor missions were flown in the month of August or first week of September 1943. The exact dates have been lost to history, though evidence exists that Calabria was targeted on 3 September and the Strait of Messina two days later.[8] The only Luftwaffe loss on these raids was one German aircraft, blown to bits by an accidental explosion of its own weapon on the Messina attack.[9] As before, these were limited trials of the Fritz-X, usually as part of a broad attack by Luftwaffe aircraft against naval targets. The high-flying Do 217 K-2 aircraft of III./KG 100 would arrive in advance of the main attack force in an attempt to disrupt the escorting warships and to distract enemy fire from the follow-on waves of dive-bombers and torpedo bombers.

It was unclear to the Allied sailors watching from below that some of the weapons dropped during these early raids around Sicily were innovative radio-controlled bombs. Not suspecting any such thing, and in the absence of any actual hits, the raids were dismissed as nothing special, one of the many Luftwaffe attacks during this part of Operation Husky. The most important part of the raid for historical purposes is not the damage caused by the new German weapon, but rather the fact that not all of the aircraft employed on these raids returned to base. Nor had all of the Luftwaffe airmen perished in the downed aircraft: some were taken prisoner. As will be seen later, the interrogation of these prisoners provided the Allies with critical early warning regarding the forthcoming storm of new German weapons.

Death of a Battleship

If the Allied navies did not know of the glide bomb's existence, that was to change on 25 and 27 August in the Bay of Biscay when II./KG 100 revealed the existence of the Hs 293 to devastating effect, as described earlier. The failure in August 1943 and early September of III./KG 100 with the Fritz-X contrasted with the striking success of II./KG 100 with the Hs 293 in the Bay of Biscay on 27 August. However, less than two weeks after *Egret* was obliterated by Dr. Wagner's rocket-powered missile, Max Kramer's radio-controlled armor-piercing bomb would realize the most significant success of all for these new weapons.

✦ ✦ ✦

It was Patton's seizure of Palermo that initiated this chain of events, because it led to the overthrow of Italian dictator Benito Mussolini and the initiation of discussions about an armistice that, in effect, would take Italy out of the war. Negotiations led to an agreement signed in secrecy on 3 September, one day after the first Allied landing on the Italian mainland, in the form of a small Canadian assault against Calabria. That agreement was released publicly on 8 September, just one day before the massive invasion by the U.S. Fifth Army against Salerno in Operation Avalanche and a similar landing of British forces at Taranto in Operation Slapstick.

It was greatly desired that the Italian navy, the Regia Marina (RM), not fall into the hands of Germany as a result of this armistice. The RM, ranked at the start of the war as the fourth-most-powerful navy in the world, had always been a major force in the Mediterranean. Even after the British had whittled away at its strength with a successful torpedo attack at Taranto, crippling three battleships, and after the decisive battle of Cape Matapan, sinking two heavy cruisers and damaging another battleship, the Italians still represented a potential threat. This was especially true of the RM's three modern battleships—*Roma*, *Littorio* (repaired after damage at Taranto), and *Vittorio Veneto* (damaged at Cape Matapan). Each ship mounted nine 15-inch (381-mm) main guns and was roughly equivalent in striking power to Germany's battleship *Bismarck*. If made available to the Kriegsmarine, these ships would have vastly complicated the Allies' efforts in the Mediterranean.

It was not surprising, then, that the Allies insisted that the Italian fleet, especially the three modern battleships, be handed over as part of the armistice. Fleet Admiral Carlo Bergamini decided to take his flotilla from La Spezia, the naval base on the northwestern coast of Italy near Genoa, on a course for Sardinia, at which point he would hand over the fleet to Allied authorities.

Unfortunately for the Italians, the German intelligence apparatus became aware of plans for the Italians to hand over the modern ships to the Allies, and had full knowledge of the likely timing and route of sailing. On 7 September *Major* Bernhard Jope, commanding III./KG 100, had been summoned in secrecy to the headquarters of the Luftflotte 2 (Air Fleet 2) in Rome and there ordered to prepare for a raid on the Italian fleet, once it had sailed from La Spezia. Preparations were made with absolute secrecy: only a small cadre of III./KG 100 officers knew of the mission.

At 0300 hours on 9 September, just as the Allies were preparing to go ashore at Salerno, Admiral Bergamini gave the order to weigh anchor from La Spezia, and the Italian fleet set course for La Maddalena in northern Sardinia. The fleet included battleships *Roma, Vittorio Veneto,* and *Italia,* the latter the new name for *Littorio,* rechristened after 25 July.[10] Accompanying these battleships were three cruisers and eight destroyers. At first all went smoothly as the fleet sailed in the early morning hours south along the western coast of Corsica. Around noon the fleet executed a turn to port toward the Bocche di Bonifacio, the strait that divides Corsica to the north and Sardinia to the south.

Not all was in order, however. At 0800 hours the German authorities in La Spezia informed Berlin that the fleet had sailed. At 1000 hours the alarm was issued at III./KG 100's airbase and the ground crews armed the Do 217 bombers with the Fritz-X and prepared the aerial machines for flight. The *gruppe* would launch two attacks: the first main wave was to depart as soon as the aircraft could be loaded and the second wave was to be refueled and rearmed upon return of the first.[11]

At 1340 hours Bergamini was informed that his intended destination, La Maddalena, was still in German hands so he reversed course to the west. Meanwhile, six Do 217 K-2 aircraft from III./KG 100 departed Istres at 1400 hours, each loaded with one Fritz-X, bound for the Italian fleet.

Shortly after 1500 hours the German aircraft were spotted. At first, the Italian officers did not know what to make of the Luftwaffe aerial armada. It was not known whether the Germans would actually attack the Italian ships, so no preemptive antiaircraft fire was offered. Believing the raid was designed to intimidate rather than destroy, the Italian officers on board ships were surprised to see the German aircraft release large bombs at 1530 hours. Those who still denied the Luftwaffe's hostile intent were relieved that these bombs had been dropped while the aircraft were still far away, on a 60-degree rather than 80-degree angle, which was more typical of aerial assaults on warships. The first few aircraft each dropped one bomb, all of which fell short of the fleet, thus appearing to the Italian commanders as the aeronautical equivalent to a shot across the bow. Since the Italians were under orders to fire only if first attacked, this unusual tactic led to an absence of evasive action or retaliatory fire.

It was no doubt with great surprise, then, when the first bomb dropped by the second group of Do 217s maneuvered away from its ballistic path onto a direct course for *Roma*. At 1545 hours a Fritz-X guided by *Unteroffizier* (Corporal) Klapproth of *Major* Jope's own aircraft hit *Roma*, passing through the hull and exploding in the water alongside, destroying an engine room and two boiler rooms. The badly damaged battleship staggered out of formation and attempted to recover. Five minutes later another Fritz-X guided by *Unteroffizier* Eugen Degan of *Oberfeldwebel* (Platoon Leader) Steinborn's aircraft hit the deck plating above the forward magazine, penetrated the armor plate, and exploded directly amid the large-caliber ammunition for *Roma*'s big guns. The resulting fire and explosion blew turret "B" completely off the ship, tossing the 1,500-ton structure high into the air as if it were made of paper. The resulting inferno threw flames three thousand feet upward, incinerating most of the crew in the process. Admiral Bergamini, along with 1,253 or more of his countrymen, burned to cinders in the conflagration on board his flagship.[12]

With the hostile intent of the attacking force now apparent, *Italia*'s anti-aircraft guns opened fire. However, because the Luftwaffe bombers had already approached a position dead overhead of the ship, beyond the maximum elevation of the guns, the Germans were safe from attack while they maneuvered their bombs for the kill. A Fritz-X penetrated *Italia*'s armored deck and then passed completely through the armored hull back outside of the ship before exploding with a massive plume just outboard. The hull was damaged across an area of twenty-one meters by nine meters, and the resulting leaks allowed 1,066 tons of water to penetrate the ship. The shock wave also disabled temporarily the ship's rudder, though the auxiliary rudder remained functional. Despite this damage, *Italia* was able to continue on course under its own power, suffering only one wounded sailor from what turned out to have been a massive bullet well dodged.[13]

As the victorious aircraft of III./KG 100 returned to base, the few survivors of the fire on board *Roma* evacuated the ship, leaving behind their many dead and incapacitated sailors. As *Major* Jope's Do 217 fleet was being rearmed and refueled, *Roma* turned over, broke into two, and sank, leaving only oil, debris, and bodies on the water's surface. Another wave of *Major* Jope's Do 217 aircraft took off for an evening attack on the battleship, which they believed would still be afloat, and searched in vain for *Roma*, not realizing until later that the ship had vanished below the waves.

The Italians, and the Allies, were stunned. A small flotilla of aircraft had managed in the space of a few minutes to sink Italy's most modern battleship and damage her sister ship. This was not a repeat of 10 December 1941 when hordes of Japanese aircraft sank His Majesty's battlecruiser *Repulse* and battleship *Prince of Wales* during an attack lasting several hours and involving a hundred or more torpedoes and bombs. Nor was this a repeat of the previous month's attacks in the Bay of Biscay, when thinly armored frigates and destroyers were incapacitated. Initially, the Italians concluded that the Germans had just been lucky with conventional bombs. As we shall see, the Allies knew better. Their Ultra intercepts of German Enigma-coded communications revealed the details of the attack and the instrumental role the new Fritz-X glide bomb had played.

The Allies had a better understanding of the success of these new weapons than did Adolf Hitler or Hermann Göring, who initially were told by their staffs that conventional weapons were responsible for this impressive victory over the Italians. The deception was promoted by *Generalmajor* Adolf Galland, head of fighter aircraft operations for the Luftwaffe. Galland was fearful that Hitler and Göring would be so enamored of the success of the new weapons that they would order production of fighter aircraft reduced in favor of more bombers able to carry the Fritz-X. Therefore Galland sought to underplay the impact of this new technology, at least for a while.[14]

Destruction at Salerno

Just as the smoke was clearing above the watery grave of Admiral Bergamini, a fleet of warships and transports stood offshore the Italian seaside town of Salerno, depositing General Mark Clark's Fifth Army on the Italian mainland for the first time. Salerno was within range (1,070 kilometers, or 580 nautical miles) of III./KG 100's base at Istres, but beyond the range of II./KG 100's base at Cognac. So it should not be surprising that on 9 September, the very day of the Salerno invasion, II./KG 100 relocated from Cognac to Istres, joining its sister *gruppe* there. For the first time both *gruppen* of aircraft equipped with glide bombs would be within range of the same Allied targets.

✦ ✦ ✦

The Luftwaffe also chose this time to make significant changes in personnel and leadership. *Major* Bernhard Jope, hero of the raid on *Roma*, was advanced to the overall command of KG 100, replacing *Major* Fritz Auffhammer, who was reassigned as the new commander of KG 3, a unit then engaged in heavy combat operations on the Eastern Front.[15] *Hauptmann*

Heinz Molinnus became the new commander of II./KG 100, replacing *Major* Franz Hollweg.[16] *Hauptmann* Gerhard Döhler replaced Jope as the officer leading III./KG 100.[17]

It may seem inevitable today, given the known outcome, that the Allies should persevere at Salerno. At the time, however, the invasion's success was very much in doubt and the hold of the amphibious forces, for a considerable period, was quite tenuous. Naval gunfire support from cruisers and destroyers off Salerno was instrumental in ensuring Allied success on the ground. The Allies knew this, and so did the Germans. Consequently, the Luftwaffe was ordered to throw everything it had at the armada of warships and transports off Salerno to relieve the pressure on the Wehrmacht and to allow the German counterattacks to smash the Allies back into the sea. Over the next few weeks III./KG 100 would launch six daytime missions with Fritz-X bombs at Salerno. Its sister unit, II./KG 100 using the Hs 293, executed three daytime raids involving a total of twenty-eight aircraft, as well as six nighttime missions.[18] KG 100 was just one of many Luftwaffe wings employed in this role. Unfortunately for the historian, the combined role of II./KG 100 armed with the Hs 293, and III./KG 100 armed with the Fritz-X, along with other Luftwaffe units armed with conventional bombs and torpedoes, has made it difficult to sort out exactly what happened at Salerno. There remains uncertainty to this day as to which weapons hit which ships, and which units were involved.

The first two attacks of the newly reorganized KG 100 took place on 11 September, two days after the landings at Salerno and the destruction of *Roma*. At dawn the Do 217 K-2 bombers of III./KG 100 unleashed their Fritz-X glide bombs on warships some three or four miles below them. This time the targets were cruisers providing critical fire support to besieged American soldiers and the diminutive escort ships protecting these cruisers. First to feel the effect of the glide bombs was *Flores*, an old Dutch sloop commanded by Lieutenant Commander Johannes Stephanus Bax, who described what happened in a postwar biography: "About half past five in the morning, while still dark, we are suddenly put into sunshine by the enemy. . . . [A]pproximately 16 bombers drop their charges directly above us. The sea becomes an ebullient mass. One bomb lands just off our port stern and the same time another lands off the opposite starboard side. The ship is lifted approximately one meter from the water and is twisted lengthwise. On the bridge, we stand as if in bathtub filled with water."[19] Contrary to what has been written, *Flores* did not sink from the attack, though it was severely damaged and its warfighting capacity was reduced by the shock of the explosions, with guns tossed from their mounts, the radar mast knocked down, and the sonar system put out of action.[20] *Flores* had to be towed by the tug *Moresco* to Palermo for repairs.

It may have been that the attack at dawn that damaged *Flores* was really directed at the *Philadelphia*, a light cruiser operating off Salerno in the vicinity of *Flores*. In any case, a few hours later at 0935 hours the second attack of III./KG 100 emerged and another bomb hit just fifteen meters off *Philadelphia*. The ship itself was not damaged, though several crewmembers were wounded in the explosion.[21] This would be the first of several strikes against this light cruiser, which emerged from Anzio with a well-deserved reputation as both an effective combatant and a lucky ship.

Ten minutes later during that same attack a far more devastating event unfolded as the Luftwaffe targeted *Savannah,* sister ship to *Philadelphia*. At that time, *Savannah* was lying to, preparing to execute the day's fire support mission. The crew was at General Quarters Condition I Easy, which meant that all battle stations were manned, though sailors could rest or sleep at those stations. This changed at 0930 hours when *Ancon*, the fleet's fighter director ship, raised the air-raid alarm after spotting twelve Fw 190 fighter-bombers on an attack run. The engines responded to commands from the bridge, and by 0941 hours *Savannah* was making fifteen knots and accelerating.

At 0944 hours, just as the ship's speed was reaching twenty knots, a Fritz-X glide bomb, launched from high above by a Do 217 K-2 of III./KG 100, hit squarely on the #3 turret of *Savannah* just ahead of the bridge. (*Savannah* had three turrets forward and two aft.) The impact of the Fritz-X validated all of the hopes and design objectives of Max Kramer's team.[22] The bomb penetrated through the 2-inch armored surface of the turret, tore through three more decks, and exploded in the ammunition handling room deep in the bowels of the ship. The explosion blew the whole structure of the turret up four inches and killed the entire turret crew instantly. The detonation also blew a twenty-four-by-thirty-foot hole in the hull of the ship, bending down the bottom plates so the torn edges of the steel dragged fifteen feet below the keel. The rapid flooding caused by this massive hole is what saved the ship: it inundated the magazines before flames could reach them.

Multiple fires erupted on board ship. Smoke and poisonous fumes broke through a too-thin bulkhead separating the turrets and incapacitated crewmembers in #1 and #2 turrets, killing many. The ship took an immediate list to port that reached 8 degrees after just three minutes. Forward momentum ceased briefly as the boilers went offline. Weighted down by tons of water, the bow of *Savannah* dropped until it was almost submerged.

Drastic efforts by the officers and crew saved the ship from greater destruction, a situation complicated by the fact that the Fritz-X had destroyed Damage Control Central. It was now that the countless hours of drilling in damage control procedures bore fruit. Slowly, power was restored and the fires put out. Flooding was controlled and the list corrected. By evening *Savannah* was sufficiently stabilized to make for Malta under her own power at eighteen knots. The ship was saved. However, 197 of *Savannah's* men had perished in this attack.[23]

It is worth noting that *Savannah's* antiaircraft crews had the German aircraft in their sights at 18,700 feet altitude but were not authorized to fire because a U.S. P-38 fighter had wandered into that airspace to attack the bombers, and *Savannah's* guns could not be fired without endangering that friendly aircraft. So, as with *Roma*, *Savannah* stood relatively defenseless as the Germans attacked.

The next day II./KG 100 entered the fray with its first daytime attack on the ships outside Salerno. This daytime mission failed to damage any ships, but two of the precious Do 217 E-5 aircraft never returned to base.[24]

The following day, 13 September, was a long one for the Allied ships off Salerno, this time with II./KG 100 and III./KG 100 taking turns raking the fleet. The Germans started early. About 0455 hours on 13 September Captain John Eric Wilson, master of hospital ship *Newfoundland*, noticed the sound of aircraft and proceeded to the bridge. At the time *Newfoundland* was steaming slowly (six knots) about 55 kilometers (30 nautical miles) off the coast of Salerno. It was this far from the invasion scene in order to reduce the possibility of aerial attacks, several of which the ship had survived the previous day. With three other British hospital ships (*Leinster*, *St. Andrew*, and *Amarapoora*), *Newfoundland* was brightly illuminated, with the red cross on its hull clearly visible. At 0510 hours Wilson "had the impression" that an aircraft flying at low altitude released a bomb that, according to Wilson, "travelled more or less horizontally" and that made "an intermittent swishing sound which was like the throb of a high-pitched aircraft engine."[25] Perhaps without knowing what he was describing, Wilson accurately depicted the attack characteristics of II./KG 100 and their Hs 293 rocket-powered glide bombs.[26] Wilson watched the bomb tear through the hull amidships and transform the interior of *Newfoundland* into a darkened and smoke-filled maze. In his own words,

> All the fire fighting appliances on the saloon and boat decks were completely destroyed, there was not a 6ft length of whole water piping left. The damage was devastating, extending over an area of about 100ft long by 50ft wide and 8ft deep, whilst underneath and two decks down there was more extensive damage. Everything within the midship area was destroyed, bulkheads had collapsed, accommodation wrecked with

splinter holes all over the place. As the missing people were accommo-
dated in this section I consider they must have all been killed instantly. The
bomb appeared to penetrate one deck before exploding. The boatdeck,
the stbd [starboard] side of which was completely destroyed, was shifted
bodily stbd and torn from the lower structure and turned completely over,
a portion of it hung down in the water. The ship was opened amidships
for a depth of 4 decks.[27]

Twenty of those on board *Newfoundland*, including six nurses, were
never found. One of the nine others injured in the attack later died of his
wounds. As for the ship itself, Wilson believed he could save it, and later that
morning volunteers went on board to start to repair the damage. However,
an escorting destroyer, *Plunkett*, came alongside that evening and reported
that orders had been issued to scuttle the ship, over the strenuous objections of Wilson. After removing Wilson and his crew, *Plunkett* fired about
seventy rounds of 5-inch shells into the hull of *Newfoundland*, all of which
seemed to have minimal effect. It was not until late the next evening on 14
September that the battered hull of *Newfoundland* succumbed to the sea.[28]

In the early afternoon on 13 September it was III./KG 100's turn with
their high-altitude armor-piercing weapons. The first target that afternoon
was *Uganda*, a British light cruiser. This attack had evidently not been
expected and a lone aircraft managed to elude detection, arriving unchal-
lenged and undetected in the sky high above *Uganda*. Sitting unmoving
at the time, the warship was an easy target for a radio-controlled Fritz-X,
which at 1440 hours plunged through seven steel decks and the bottom
hull, exploding in the water beneath the keel. The explosion ripped a hole
the size of a two-car garage in the hull of the ship. The structural damage
led to 1,400 tons of seawater flooding into the vessel, putting three of the
four engine spaces out of action.[29] Sixteen sailors were killed, but the ship
survived. A tug, *Narragansett*, towed *Uganda* out of danger, escorted by
three destroyers. *Uganda* would be out of service for well over a year, traveling to America and undergoing extensive repairs in Charleston Navy Yard
before being refitted in the United Kingdom. It was not able to return to
active duty (in the Canadian navy) until early 1945, and thus was effectively
out of commission for the duration of the war.

A more substantial group of airborne attackers arrived about 1530
hours that same afternoon, an hour after *Uganda* had been struck. Again,
the most likely protagonist seems to be III./KG 100 with their Fritz-X
bombs. Two British destroyers, *Nubian* and *Loyal*, were targeted and narrowly avoided destruction, escaping with light damage. *Philadelphia*, survivor of an attack on 11 September, also was a primary target of the afternoon

raid on 13 September. As the Luftwaffe bombers approached overhead on III./KG 100's second mission of the afternoon, Captain Paul S. Hendren maneuvered his ship at high speed to escape the threat. The closest bomb to fall missed by one hundred meters, once again demonstrating either via luck or skill that *Philadelphia* was not to be an easy target. Moreover, the afternoon attack was a damaging one for III./KG 100, with two of the special bombers lost.[30]

The next two days saw the Luftwaffe switch targets from the cruisers providing naval fire support to the vulnerable and equally vital merchant ships unloading supplies. It remains unclear which Luftwaffe group was involved and which weapons were deployed, though the nature of the damage and the types of ships targeted favor II./KG 100's Hs 293 rather than III./KG 100's Fritz-X, as argued by some.[31] Part of the confusion may arise from the fact that these cargo ships were hit in daytime, and it has been written that only III./KG 100 launched daytime raids over Salerno.[32] However, Luftwaffe records make it clear that both III./KG 100 and II./KG 100 were involved in daytime raids over Salerno so one cannot automatically assume that any ship hit during the daytime was hit by a Fritz-X dropped by an aircraft of III./KG 100.[33]

On 14 September at 1422 hours Liberty Ship *Bushrod Washington*'s cargo of gasoline caught fire when hit by a bomb from a Luftwaffe aircraft. On the nearby freighter *William Dean Howells*, Radioman Third Class Joseph A. Yannacci recorded what he witnessed:

> Holy Christ, they've cut their motors and are coming at us out of the sun. We can't see them. All ships open up right into the sun. One bomb meant for us drops off our port beam. One meant for the *John Payne* drops off her starboard quarter. But the one meant for the *Bushrod Washington* falls right on the *Bushrod W[ashington]*. It went right down #4 hold. Honest to God, you could see the refrigerator fly through the air. The port side is blown right off from the bridge up to #5 hold and is she burning.[34]

The weapon tore a hole in the side of the ship, killing six of the crew and one member of the Armed Guard. Despite heroic efforts of the ship's master, Jonathan M. Wainwright V, *Bushrod Washington* exploded the following day after the fires had raged out of control and reached 500-pound bombs stored in the forward compartments.[35] The explosion also destroyed the tank landing craft *LCT-209*, which had come alongside to render assistance.

It remains uncertain today what the exact cause was of the loss of *Bushrod Washington*. Most accounts credit the attack to an Hs 293 launched from II./KG 100. The nature of the destruction is consistent with a hit by an Hs 293, though it is also consistent with a conventional bomb. Certainly it is known that II./KG 100 was active above Salerno around that time, flying nine missions from 9 September to 30 September, three of them during the day. Original reports, possibly contrived to avoid mention of the glide bombs in accordance with U.S. policy at the time, suggest two conventional 250-kilogram bombs dropped from dive-bombers were responsible.[36]

The same morning that *Bushrod Washington* finally exploded, 15 September, another Liberty ship, *James W. Marshall*, became a victim of a Luftwaffe attack. *James W. Marshall* was anchored and in the process of unloading its cargo—gasoline, ammunition, and 250 tanks, trucks, and heavy artillery—into two tank landing craft (LCT) located alongside. During an air raid at 0745 hours it was struck by a bomb that penetrated through the boat deck on the port side.

It is uncertain exactly which bomb hit *James W. Marshall*; it has at times been written that the culprit was a Fritz-X from III./KG 100.[37] This latter scenario cannot be ruled out, though there is at least an equal case to suggest that if a glide bomb was involved the culprit was an Hs 293 from II./KG 100, as has been reported.[38] First, we do know that II./KG 100 with the Hs 293 glide bombs was active over Salerno that day. Second, it would be unusual for the heavy armor-piercing weapons of III./KG 100 to be employed against a simple cargo ship. That weapon was reserved for heavy cruisers and battleships. Third, the armored Fritz-X dropped from high altitude would probably have passed all the way through the ship before exploding, in contrast to the damage reported for *James W. Marshall*. Finally, not all of the Luftwaffe aircraft survived their missions that day, and the one glide-bomb carrier that failed to return to Istres on 15 September was an Hs 293–carrying Do 217 E-5 from II./KG 100.[39]

However, Radioman Joseph A. Yannacci, who watched the attack from the vantage point of the transport *William Dean Howells*, suggests German dive-bombers—not glide bombs—were responsible and that the bomb that actually struck *James W. Marshall* was a dud. He scribbled this account into his diary:

> 7:30. Wheat cakes, sausages, and a cup of coffee. Christ, I don't even get a chance to taste them and I'm starving. 10 Stukas cut loose and a stick drops right on the *"James Marshall."* One bomb went right through the bridge but it was a dud. One dropped right dead center in a barge tied alongside the *Marshall*. She went up in a puff of smoke. A destroyer pulled it away from the *Marshall* and sank it with depth charges. The crew has abandoned the *Marshall*. There was little damage done to it, but the dud might go off any time.[40]

Yannacci's account suggests that the fire was caused not by a glide bomb striking *James W. Marshall* but by a conventional bomb that hit the accompanying LCT, which was filled with gasoline. Whatever the source, the resulting explosion killed about fifty ammunition handlers from the Army, thirteen of the Liberty ship's crew, and seventeen of the Armed Guard. It is said the survivors, including Master Ragnar William Roggenbihl, were so terrified that they were unable to execute damage control procedures, and that they evacuated the ship in a panic even though the fire had been put out.[41] Certainly the presence of an unexploded bomb on board, if that was the case, might explain their reaction.

Captain Wainwright, whose own *Bushrod Washington* had just exploded, and nine volunteers from his crew came on board *James W. Marshall* to take control and complete unloading. The ship did not sink that day—it was eventually towed to Bizerte and then to England and saw invasion service off Normandy, being sunk to help form an artificial breakwater or "gooseberry" off Omaha Beach.[42] For his heroism Wainwright was awarded the Merchant Marine Distinguished Service Medal by President Franklin D. Roosevelt.

Warspite Narrowly Escapes

If uncertainty surrounds the weapons used to destroy *Bushrod Washington* and *James W. Marshall*, there is no such confusion regarding the last successful attack by KG 100 at Salerno. On 16 September at about 1425 hours six Do 217 K-2 aircraft from III./KG 100 unleashed their Fritz-X bombs on two veteran British battleships, *Warspite* and *Valiant*. These dreadnoughts, having arrived the day before, were providing critical gunfire support to troops ashore, massive salvos from their 15-inch guns systematically disassembling German hopes of a successful counterattack against the Allied invaders. At the time of the Luftwaffe attack they were cruising at about ten knots in congested waters, and therefore were unable to maneuver aggressively. They made ideal targets: big and slow, unable to evade.

✦ ✦ ✦

Most of the attention by the Luftwaffe pilots was paid to *Warspite*. The battleship was not a thinly hulled merchant ship like those sunk in the previous few days, but instead is remembered as one of the most honored warships of the twentieth century. A veteran of the Battle of Jutland in World War I, *Warspite* had achieved equal fame by steaming up a narrow Norwegian fjord toward Narvik and pummeling into wreckage a flotilla of German destroyers that had been harassing less-weighty British warships.

On this day *Warspite* was the prey, not the predator. In the characteristic pattern of III./KG 100 missions at Salerno, the attack started with a group of Fw 190 fighters diving out of the sun and attacking the ship from low altitude. This molestation was soon beaten off, but almost immediately afterwards the purpose of the diversionary maneuver became evident. *Warspite* captain (later admiral) Herbert ("Bertie") Annesley Packer described what followed in his formal report: "At 2.30pm only a few minutes after the fighter bombers had disappeared, the ship's lookouts sighted what were first thought to be three high level bombers at about 6000 feet. There were actually wireless controlled bombs, whose controlling aircraft were far away overhead at 20,000 feet. The three bombs when directly overhead looked like three very white mushrooms as they turned vertically down and dived for the ship at great speed."[43]

The first Fritz-X appeared to be headed for a point four hundred yards safely away from *Warspite* but then was guided back to the battleship by the crew under the command of *Oberleutnant* (First Lieutenant) Heinrich Schmetz. It just missed amidships on the starboard side and tore apart the hull plates, causing widespread flooding. The second bomb, guided by *Feldwebel* (squad leader, a senior noncommissioned officer) Meyer, tore through the armored deck and five other steel decks, exploding deep in the No. 4 boiler room and blowing out the double bottom of the ship. The third bomb, guided by *Obergefreiter* (Airman First Class) Mrowitzki, just missed on the starboard side, farther aft.

The ship was wracked by these explosions. In the words of R. A. Scott, an officer on board *Warspite* at the time, "It seemed as if an express train travelling at high speed had hit the ship; one tremendous explosion which seemed to jar every nerve in one's body. . . . The ship seemed as if it had been picked up by some devilish hand, then dropped. . . . A second explosion occurred, followed by more intense shuddering, which must have been the bomb exploding in the region of the boiler rooms. 12 members of the engine and boiler room staff were killed and about 30–40 people injured."[44]

Captain Packer, writing in his personal diary that same day, explained how he thought the ship might be lost after the second bomb crashed in the bowels of the ship, just behind the bridge:

> I was not thrown off my feet but for a fraction of a second had a kind of black-out like when you take a hard toss at football or fall off a horse. But I could see and think perfectly clearly all of the time. Black smoke and dirt from the funnels and a hell of a noise. Thought the whole mast was coming down as it rocked, bent and whipped. For a moment I thought

we were probably sunk and was quite prepared for the ship to break in two.[45]

The damage was intense and nearly fatal, but the tough old battleship did not break in two, despite Captain Packer's fears. Power was lost in five of the six boiler rooms, including the one utterly vaporized by the Fritz-X warhead, with the consequent loss of its entire complement. Five thousand tons of seawater rushed into the ruptured compartments, threatening to swamp the ship. Fortunately, there were no follow-on attacks; attentive damage control by Packer's crew saved the ship. After extensive repairs in Malta and Gibraltar she returned to service in time to return the favor by bombarding German defenses at Normandy.[46]

Gruppe II./KG 100 was in the air as well that day, without striking any targets and losing one of its aircraft.[47] Each *gruppe* would launch a final raid on 17 September, with III./KG 100 losing one aircraft on yet another unsuccessful attack on the lucky *Philadelphia* and II./KG 100 losing three bombers that same day.[48]

Ultimately, the aggressive actions by KG 100 were insufficient to deny to Allied navies the waters off Salerno. Increasing Allied air cover, now based at local airfields as opposed to distant Sicily, made daytime raids by either group of KG 100 an experience approximating suicide. Nighttime raids by II./KG 100 became problematic as the waning moon reduced the available light for targeting. Meanwhile, in part with naval gunfire support from the Allied ships off the coast, the Allied soldiers made progress inland, eventually reaching and liberating Naples and the naval support missions off Salerno decreased in importance.

The targets for the Luftwaffe had dispersed. The fears of the sailors were less easily lifted. The month of September had been troubling for the crews of warships and merchant ships alike. They had been surprised by these new weapons and no doubt anxiously awaited the next round of attacks.

CHAPTER FOUR

EARLY WARNINGS FROM
AGENTS *and* ANALYSTS

The twenty-two days from August 25 to September 16 were tumultuous for the British, American, Canadian, Italian, and Dutch navies, all of which had suffered losses due to the new German glide bombs. The destruction was severe: a battleship, a sloop, and two merchant ships sunk or written off; a battleship, two cruisers, and a destroyer crippled; a battleship and several frigates, sloops, and destroyers damaged. Roughly two thousand seamen had been killed as a result of these new weapons, all in barely more than three weeks. One can imagine the shock in London and Washington over this latest twist in the war. It may have looked to some as if the war at sea had begun to turn, and that the Germans might pick off Allied warships and merchantmen one at a time with near impunity.

✦ ✦ ✦

Scientists in the United Kingdom, United States, and elsewhere were engaged to develop ways to defeat these new technological marvels. But, first, the Allies needed to learn more about the Hs 293 missile, Fritz-X guided bomb, and the Kehl-Strassburg guidance system. By compiling what was known from all sources, it was hoped that analysts at the Admiralty in the United Kingdom and the Office of Naval Intelligence in the United States might assemble sufficient information to empower the Allied scientists in their search for an antidote. Thus the search went out for any kind of intelligence: witness accounts, POW interrogation results, reports from intelligence agents, or even fragments of exploded weapons. As the potential sources of information—naval officers, intelligence agents, and signals analysis—were pinged, it gradually became apparent that the Allies had already assembled considerable intelligence on these new weapons, albeit often in fragmented and underappreciated forms. It is appropriate to review what the Allies were able to piece together immediately after the events of August and September 1943.

Early Indications from Oslo

The first intelligence on German glide bombs was made available to the British in late 1939, almost four years before the first successful attacks. However, this information, contained in the so-called Oslo Report, is a classic example of useful information undervalued by military and intelligence authorities simply because much of it seemed too good to be true. In hindsight, there were very important clues regarding the development of German antiship weapons in this report.

✦ ✦ ✦

Dr. Hans Ferdinand Mayer was the author of the Oslo Report, although his identity would not be revealed until well after the war's end. Mayer was the director of the central research organization of Siemens & Halske AG, a leading German technology company in the 1930s and forerunner of today's industrial giant Siemens AG. Born in 1895 in Munich, he studied mathematics, physics, and astronomy and received his doctorate in the field of electronics under a Nobel Prize–winning physicist (and ardent Nazi supporter), Philipp Leonard. During his working career Mayer would receive more than eighty patents and would publish widely in technical journals. His work with Siemens & Halske involved extensive interactions with technical experts outside Germany; he traveled extensively on an international basis. His work also gave him access to a broad array of technologies across various German industries.

Mayer was also a spy, motivated by his anti-Fascist convictions. Just after war broke out in 1939 Mayer was visiting Norway, which at that time was a neutral country not yet occupied by Germany. Mayer, who opposed the Nazis, mailed an anonymous letter to Hector Boyes, the British Naval Attaché in Oslo, asking if Britain would be interested in technical research information from Germany. The letter asked that an affirmative response be communicated by changing the introduction to the German news broadcast of BBC World Service, a request to which the British complied.

On 5 November 1939 the British Embassy in Oslo received a package containing a vacuum tube and a seven-page document describing German research advances ranging across the spectrum from aircraft carriers to electric fuses. The first two items, a description of the Ju 88 bomber that contained nothing of substance beyond what was publicly available and a dismissed account of a nonexistent German aircraft carrier named *Franken*, led many observers to dismiss the report as a plant designed to mislead British intelligence.[1]

Unfortunately that dismissive characterization was applied to the third item described in the Oslo Report, a description of "remote-controlled gliders" being developed for use against ships. Dr. Mayer reported that these gliders were unpowered and "dropped by an aircraft from great height" and then a bit later that they "fly horizontally with rocket propulsion." This could easily be a description of the Bv 143 rocket-powered glider, or it could be a commingled description of the Hs 293 and Fritz-X. He correctly reported that the gliders were controlled "by Enigma-short waves in the form of telegraphy signals by which the glider can be steered to the right, to the left or straight ahead" and further that the test site was in Peenemünde. The weapon itself is described as three meters in length with a three-meter wingspan—a realistic depiction of the Hs 293 or Bv 143.[2]

British response to the Oslo Report was generally dismissive at first. It was considered improbable that any one person could know so much about such a range of devices as described in the packet. Moreover, the mere fact that some of the information could be verified was used, in an approach that years after the war would be characterized as Orwellian, as proof that it must be a plant, because good plants always contained at least some useful intelligence. As the war progressed, and as much of what Dr. Mayer described was revealed to be true, a greater appreciation was placed on the value of the Oslo Report.[3]

Hints from Ultra Intelligence

Human intelligence was not the only means of extracting technical information from German sources. Another valuable source of early warning was in the form of decoded German messages. In recent decades it has become well known that the Allies relied heavily on messages decoded from German communications, including those encoded by the Germans using their advanced Enigma machines. (Allied intelligence forces had managed to obtain Enigma code machines and subsequently broke the Engima codes.) Over time, Allied forces were able to penetrate many German military codes, including but not limited to Enigma, and thereby decrypt coded messages almost as fast as the Germans did themselves. This huge intelligence bonanza was code-named Ultra; it proved critical in accelerating Allied victory.

✦ ✦ ✦

Ultra began to pick up messages about unusual German antiship weapons as early as May 1943, months before the first attacks. A decrypted message revealed that "'objects Hs 293 and FX' were to be taken out of store and given, as new weapons, very special protection against espionage and sabotage."[4] However, the intelligence apparatus did not connect the dots with earlier indications that the Germans were developing radio-controlled bombs, and thus the advance notice disappeared into the intelligence ether. Information that was more concrete was made available by decrypts in late July 1943 that II./KG 100, equipped with the Hs 293–carrying Do 217 E-5 aircraft and III./KG 100 flying Do 217 K-2 aircraft armed with the Fritz-X, had just been declared operational, with missions approved for both day-time and nighttime. No alert was broadcast to the fleet generally, though the Mediterranean commands were informed of the new intelligence.[5] This warning, of course, was received days before the first operational missions against Palermo. However, it was not sent to the Atlantic commands operating in the Bay of Biscay, the location of the first losses to glide bombs.

The Allies had reasonably precise intelligence regarding the deployment of III./KG 100 and II./KG 100 against the forces of Operation Avalanche, the invasion of Salerno.[6] On 7 September the Allies decrypted instructions for II./KG 100 to redeploy to Istres from its Atlantic base. The Allies had learned that III./KG 100 was preparing to attack the defecting Italian fleet with radio-controlled bombs several hours before the attack took place, and that such bombs were responsible for the destruction of *Roma* early in the morning on 10 September, barely twelve hours after the attack had taken place. Intelligence decrypts also confirmed that the pace of attacks declined somewhat after 12 September and dropped off almost completely after 16 September.[7]

Intelligence revealed through Ultra also provided warning for many of the attacks that devastated the support ships off Salerno in the week starting 9 September 1943. At 0034 hours on 9 September, Ultra warned that III./KG 100 had been ordered to attack the ships in Operation Avalanche as quickly as possible, with cruisers and battleships explicitly identified as primary targets by messages intercepted at 0608 hours that day. *Luftflotte* 2 ordered the attacks to coincide with a German ground counteroffensive on 11 September, the day when *Savannah* was almost destroyed by a Fritz-X.[8] The Allies also knew that at 1015 hours on 13 September III./KG 100 had been ordered to make another attack at Salerno—this was the raid that crippled *Uganda*. The same message indicated another attack was ordered by the same unit against battleships that had been crushing German resistance, and that the unit should operate independently at its discretion. It may have been this attack, delayed for some reason, that resulted in the near-loss of *Warspite*. Overall, the British code breakers at GCCS were providing near real-time intelligence to the Mediterranean commands on orders being cut for German antiship bomber units.[9]

POW Interrogation Reports

There is another known source of early warning, one that comes originally from Germany. The first operational mission of III./KG 100, the attack on Palermo on 1 August, yielded mixed success for the combined fleet of twenty-five Ju 88 bombers from KG 26 and the four Do 217 aircraft of KG 100. However, it did produce a major intelligence coup for the Allies. The reader may recall that this raid was not without loss: as the aircraft approached Sicily they were jumped by Malta-based Spitfire fighters flown by U.S. pilots. Fighter pilots Captain Normal L. McDonald and Lieutenant Norman E. English each downed one Do 217 bomber from III./KG 100.[10] German records confirm that two Do 217s were lost in the raid—one commanded by Luftwaffe *Leutnant* Werner Bürckle and another by *Unteroffizer* Silvio Schenk.[11] Of the eight crewmembers on board the two aircraft, only one survived and was taken prisoner: *Leutnant* (Lieutenant) Christian Köbke, of Bürckle's crew.

✦ ✦ ✦

Another Do 217, this one piloted by *Leutnant* Hans-Joachim Zantopp, had been lost on the 10 August raid on Augusta. Pilot Zantopp and observer Walter Arnold were taken prisoner, one crewmember went missing, and a fourth managed to return to friendly units.[12] So by mid-August 1943 British intelligence officers had access to three III./KG 100 airmen as POWs.

It is certain that Zantopp and Arnold were interrogated by British intelligence and RAF authorities; Bürckle might have been interrogated as well. This questioning, conducted in the ancient Tower of London, yielded insights that the Germans had developed not one but two new antiship weapons, that both were radio controlled, that one of them was rocket powered, and that the weapons had been declared ready for operational use shortly before the interrogations. So within weeks of the initial attacks by III./KG 100 the British knew (almost) the name of the inventor of the

Fritz-X ("a certain Anton Kramer") and that Fw 200 aircraft from KG 40 were being equipped with Hs 293 glide bombs. Interrogation of Zantopp and Arnold also revealed the operational details of both the Hs 293 and Fritz-X weapons and their carrier aircraft, the Do 217.[13]

Critically, however, the information given during the interrogations to the Air Ministry on the Kehl-Strassburg radio-control frequencies was incorrect. This is not surprising, because it appears that this information was not available to the pilots and observers. Crewmembers were simply provided with a box of radio crystals marked "1" to "18" and told which they were to use for any specific mission. At the time, the British suspected either a 19.2 MHz or 40.2 MHz signal was being used, based on radio intercepts in the Mediterranean. Zantopp informed his interrogators that the 40.2 MHz frequency would be implausible, given that it would interfere with the communications radio carried in the KG 100 aircraft. Another prisoner, unidentified, informed the British that the wavelength in use was about sixteen meters, which translates to a frequency of about 19 MHz. Evidently this inaccurate information initially led the British and their Allies down a path of countermeasures operating in the 20 MHz region, instead of in the actual 48–50 MHz bands.[14]

This intelligence from POWs was provided by the Air Ministry to the Admiralty in the form of warnings about new weapons about to be deployed against warships.[15] This is quite possibly the source of intelligence that led to the decision to deploy Y-Service technicians on board *Egret*, as well as the source of warnings to Captain Hill and his colleagues about new German weapons. It may even be, as suggested by some, that the mission of *Egret* and other ships was to act as decoys to precipitate a German attack so the interrogation reports could be confirmed and augmented. This is also one possible explanation for why British fighters were not dispatched to intercept and prevent the incoming raid, despite more than four hours' warning.

Though an alert to the fleet was provided right away, the full text of the initial POW interrogation reports, which were remarkably comprehensive, did not make it to the Admiralty until 27 August. By that point the Royal Navy was aware that two different radio-controlled weapons had been declared ready for operational use, one ("FX") that had been deployed in the Mediterranean and the other, only identified as a glide bomb with wings, that had been assigned to II./KG 100 operations in the Atlantic. Thus, when reports arrived from the 40th Escort Group and the 1st Support Group of strange new guided missiles, it should have been quite straightforward for naval intelligence in Britain to assemble the pieces of the story.

Reports from Intelligence Agents

Intense desires to learn more about the Hs 293 and Fritz-X led U.S. intelligence agencies such as the Office of Strategic Services (OSS), as well as their British counterparts, to hunt down whatever clues they could on these new weapons. After the losses off Salerno, the intelligence organizations redirected their efforts against this emergency. Some of these intelligence efforts were successful but most were not.

✦ ✦ ✦

The first tantalizing clue emerged from a Danish officer who came across an unpiloted miniature airplane at Bornholm, not far from the new German rocket test center at Peenemünde. The strange vehicle—which fit the general description of the Hs 293—had crash-landed on 22 August, and the Danish officer's detailed photographs were in the hands of British intelligence on 27 August, the very day the *Egret* was lost. Alas, this was a false lead as far as the Hs 293 was concerned: it turned out the Danish officer had actually captured an early test version of a more significant German development, the V-1 "buzz" bomb that would soon be falling across London. However, at the time it was assumed that this rare find provided useful insight into the Hs 293.

Winston Churchill himself made this error in a congratulatory note to his Minister of Economic Warfare—and head of the Special Operations Executive—Roundell Cecil Palmer, dated 16 October 1943: "Thank you for your letter of September 29. The photographs which you send with it are certainly an excellent example of the work which S.O.E. is doing, and that of the control gear will I imagine be especially interesting to the experts. The weapon which the Danish agent saw, however, was not any long-range rocket but the Glider Bomb (HS 293) which has been used against our Escort Groups in the Bay of Biscay."[16]

The advancing forces in Italy provided additional opportunities for intelligence forces, and many of these turned their attention to the problem of German glide bombs. As recalled by Max Corvo, an OSS officer in Italy at the time, "[A] new dimension was added [to Operation MacGregor] on September 19 when the Luftwaffe first started to use its radio-guided bombs against the Allied fleet in Salerno Bay with telling accuracy, inflicting losses on the British and American naval units supporting the invasion. British and U.S. naval brass immediately put a top priority on intelligence regarding the threatening new weapons."[17]

It was hoped that Italian navy personnel might have insight into these new weapons. As an example of how the OSS pursued any possible source, the chief of naval ordnance production was quickly spirited out of the country and placed before Allied scientists. Nothing emerged from this source that addressed the glide-bomb threat, however.

Another intelligence mission in September 1943 involved the Simmons Project, a high-priority effort by the OSS to obtain intelligence on the Hs 293. A German informant advised the OSS that an aircraft carrying the bomb might be found at Kalamaki, an airbase outside Athens. It was hoped an agent would be able to penetrate the airfield and obtain parts or photographs of these weapons. This was not an unreasonable scenario. Preceding units with the designation II./KG 100 and III./KG 100 had operated He 111 aircraft out of Kalamaki, though only prior to April 1943, before these units had been reconstituted with the glide bomb–carrying Do 217 aircraft.

Military action in Greece reinforced the arguments of those who surmised the Allies would find a Do 217 at Kalamaki. In mid-September 1943, over the protests of the Americans, the British began seizing the Italian-occupied Greek Dodecanese islands off the coast of Turkey, before they could be reoccupied by the Germans. The Germans retaliated with fierce air assaults, and on September 26 British destroyer *Intrepid* and Greek destroyer RHS *Vasillisa Olga* were both sunk. The suddenness of the assault led naval analysts to conclude that KG 100 units might again be operating from Kalamaki, 280 kilometers (150 nautical miles) west-southwest of Leros, this time with their advanced glide bombs.

With this in mind, the OSS dispatched agent Nikolaos Sotiriou, a former lieutenant in the Greek army, to Aretsou, near Salonia. In a dangerous trek lasting several days, almost all of it accomplished in canoes and other small boats, Sotiriou made it to the airfield at Mikra where he observed activity for several days. In the end, he came away empty-handed.[18] There were no Do 217 bombers to be found.

Sotiriou was not the only one to look to Greece for evidence of glide bombs. Over the decades several writers have claimed *Intrepid* and *Vasillisa Olga* were victims of Hs 293 glide bombs, despite clear evidence that the losses were caused by aircraft from II./KG 51, II./.KG 6, and II. and III./StG 3.[19] The actual attack on these two ships by Stukas and Ju 88 aircraft (neither of which carried the Hs 293) was observed from a nearby seaplane base by Adrian Seligman, an officer in the Royal Navy Reserve, who described it in his memoir:

> Two fleet destroyers—Queen Olga and Intrepid—had entered harbour and anchored half a mile away in the upper arm of the bay. An enemy agent (there were many among the local people) must have informed the German Command by radio, because within a short while formations of

Stukas and Ju 88s came over. No Italian anti-aircraft batteries opened up on them, fearing no doubt that they would become targets themselves. The Italian naval barracks were flattened and Queen Olga was sunk straight away by a direct hit amidships. Intrepid was also hit, but was successfully towed into shallower water, and so did not sink immediately. Three more attacks soon followed, resulting in further direct hits and in the end Intrepid capsized and was a total loss. . . . From the seaplane base we watched, fascinated but helpless.[20]

Further evidence that glide bombs were not involved arises from a consideration of where the suitably equipped aircraft were stationed on 26 September. That day, all three squadrons of II./KG 100 and two of the three squadrons of III./KG 100 were based at Istres, which, at 2,000 kilometers (1,080 nautical miles) from Leros, was well beyond the operational range of the Do 217. The third squadron of III./KG 100, 8./KG 100, had just been relocated to Fassberg, south of Hamburg, to begin transition training with the He 177.

In the end, the decoy sweep of the Bay of Biscay provided some of the best intelligence, in this case from eyewitness reports. Captain Hill of *Grenville* had learned that high-speed and highly maneuverable ships could turn inside the Hs 293's own turning radius, and that if the missile operator attempted to follow, the weapon could stall and fall into the sea. (We will see in Chapter 12, in technical analysis of the Hs 293, that Hill's analysis was valid.) This defensive approach required the ship to initiate an aggressive turn as soon as the missile was launched. Hill had filmed the attack and brought back quite clear images of the weapon in flight. Finally, *Athabaskan* returned to Plymouth not just with survivors from *Egret,* but also with fragments of the Hs 293 missile and traces of its fuel from the direct hit she had received.[21] Scientific analysis of the fuel traces was undertaken immediately, and by mid-September reports were issued describing the fuel as novel and otherwise unknown.[22]

The Beginnings of a Defense

By the end of September, it was clear to the Allies that three squadrons of Do 217 aircraft armed with the Hs 293 and another three squadrons armed with the Fritz-X represented a clear threat to Allied naval and merchant shipping. The threat was most pronounced in cases where ships were stationary or moving slowly, and especially when Allied air cover was inadequate to threaten the attacking aircraft.

✦ ✦ ✦

From a defensive standpoint, there were five responses identified initially.[23] The primary imperative was to provide Allied air cover over friendly ships. The Allied fighters would deter approaching bombers, shoot down those that continued their approach, and disrupt those that did launch weapons such that the radio control would be lost. Likewise, ship-based airdefenses could be used to target both the missiles (with light weapons) and the more distant attacking aircraft (with the heavier guns).

These aerial and ship-based defensive measures had already exacted heavy losses from KG 100, to such an extent that on 19 November 1943, III./KG 100 (except for 8./KG 100 training at Fassberg) was repositioned away from the front line to Eggebek, near the Danish border, for a six-week period of rest and recovery. *Gruppe* II./KG 100 (except for 5./KG 100 in Greece) was moved to Leck, just north of Eggebek and out of the war zone, on the same day.

Should the German bombers make it through the air and shipboard defenses, the second defense was to attempt to shield the vulnerable ships, especially those at anchor, in a cloud of smoke. Given that the radio-controlled weapons were visually aimed and guided, a thick layer of smoke would make it difficult for the bomb aimers to track the target, the weapon, or both. However, smoke also frustrated the ability of shipboard gunners to target aircraft and weapons.

The third layer of defense was the ability of some ships in some circumstances to maneuver at high speed, turning inside the missile's turn radius, or to open the distance between attacker and target to reduce the effectiveness of the radio links or to move beyond the effective glide range of the bombs. This had saved *Grenville;* these lessons were spread throughout the fleet. Of course, as was demonstrated at Salerno, ships that were stationary or moving slowly were especially vulnerable.

A fourth measure, more preemptive than defensive in nature, was to attack the enemy airbases at Istres and Cognac and, after November 1943, at Toulouse-Blagnac and Toulouse-Francazal. Courtesy of POW interrogations and Ultra, the Allies had good intelligence on the location of these special bomber units. Waves of Allied bombers would soon be on their way to these targets in an attempt to destroy as many of the specially equipped Do 217 aircraft as possible. The first such attack took place on 17 August 1943 when 180 American heavy B-17 bombers pulverized Istres le Tube and Salon-de-Provence airfields, the former then the home of III./KG 100.[24] This was very possibly in response to Ultra intelligence intercepts in July warning Allied authorities that III./KG 100 had been declared operational with its Fritz-X bombs. This raid did not destroy significant numbers of aircraft but killed and wounded several III./KG 100 airmen.[25] Istres would be hit again on 16 November, at which time both 7./KG 100 and 9./KG 100 were in residence. It would be attacked again by American 15th Air Force B-17s on 21 January and 27 January 1944, though by that time the bombers of KG 100 would have returned to Germany.

The fifth defensive measure was to exploit the figurative and literal weak link in the bombing system: the tenuous radio connection that allowed the operator in the launching aircraft to steer the bomb. If this command signal could be overwhelmed it might degrade the advanced glide weapons into nothing more than traditional bombs. With the limited information available, the Allied wizards went to work.

CHAPTER FIVE

FALSE HOPE:
INITIAL COUNTERMEASURES DEVELOPMENT

The new German weapons were christened "Chase-me-Charlies" by the crews and officers of British ships under attack. Novel means of defense were soon proposed from a variety of sources. As author Terrence Robertson reported (perhaps apocryphally) in his biography of legendary Royal Navy captain Frederic John Walker,

> Against the "Chase-me-Charlies" there was no defence until, one day in the Bay [of Biscay], an escort was attacked by an aircraft which launched its "glider bomb" just as a scientist aboard switched on his electric razor to test out a theory. To the amazement of the ship and the enemy aircraft, the new weapon gyrated about the sky in a fantastic exhibition of aerobatics finally giving chase to its own "parent." In some inexplicable way, the "Chase-me-Charlie" control system has been affected by electric waves given off by the razor. This method was never officially admitted by the Admiralty as a defence measure, but the ships who sailed into the "Chase-me-Charlie" area found it foolproof. In Liverpool there was a sudden run on shops selling all makes of electric razors.[1]

✦ ✦ ✦

It has never been demonstrated that the use of electric razors somehow defeated the guidance mechanism of the Hs 293 or the Fritz-X, though, as will be described in Chapter 12, a very large number of electric razors operating together might just jam the baseband frequency of the Strassburg receiver. Fortunately for the Allies, while Captain Walker's crew was buying razors in Liverpool, a certain Howard Lorenzen was working on the same problem.

Howard Lorenzen

Howard Otto Lorenzen, sometimes described as the "Father of Electronic Warfare," was born in 1912 in Atlantic, a small town almost dead center in the state of Iowa, now the self-proclaimed "Coca-Cola Capital of Iowa." Lorenzen received a bachelor's degree from Iowa State College in Electrical Engineering in 1935 and began his professional career by designing commercial radios for Colonial Radio, and then Zenith Radio. This work nicely complemented his lifetime personal interest in amateur radio communications, which was perhaps a natural outcome of growing up in rural Iowa and being curious about electronics.[2]

✦ ✦ ✦

In 1940 Lorenzen left the commercial world to work for the Naval Research Laboratory (NRL), which at the time was a small research organization in Washington, D.C., with fewer than four hundred employees. It was founded in 1923 under the sponsorship of the U.S. Navy. Once there Lorenzen helped design air-search radars, high-gain receivers, and other electronics for Navy ships. Perhaps by virtue of having been raised in a farming community, he was adept with machinery and established his own machine shop for rapid prototyping of new electronic systems. He also collaborated with British scientists on challenges related to the air war in Europe. This combination of electronics design expertise, familiarity with shipboard systems, collaboration experience with the British, and an ability to turn out rapid prototypes made Lorenzen an ideal choice to oversee an NRL effort to build countermeasures for the Hs 293 and Fritz-X when frantic requests for such a system emerged in late August 1943. In response, NRL established a "crash" program to develop a jamming system to counter these missiles.[3]

Basics of Electronic Jamming

How does electronic jamming work? Perhaps an analogy will help here, at least for those who recall a stirring scene in the film *Casablanca*. Midway through the film the German interlopers in Rick's Café commandeer a piano and begin to sing *Die Wacht am Rhein*, an emotional German patriotic song that celebrates German victory over France in the Franco-Prussian War. The sounds of the Wehrmacht soldiers fill the café, to the frustration and disappointment of the other patrons, most of whom are sympathetic to Free France. In response, the café's orchestra is instructed to play *La Marseillaise*, an equally patriotic French song. As more and more singers join the orchestra, the French words fill the room, the lyrics of *Die Wacht am Rhein* are overwhelmed in the ears of the audience, and eventually the German soldiers abandon the effort. This, in a nutshell, is electronic jamming, the use of a powerful signal to overwhelm another, either to cause the receiver to lose its original connection or to allow an external entity to command the attention of the receiver for its own purposes.

✦ ✦ ✦

In our case the challenge was to overcome the reception of the signals of the aircraft's Kehl transmitter by the glide bomb's Strassburg receiver. The Kehl represents the German soldiers singing *Die Wacht am Rhein*. The jammer represents the orchestra playing *La Marseillaise*, and the audience represents the Strassburg receiver. If all we can hear is *La Marseillaise*, we will no longer be able to understand the German words of *Die Wacht am Rhein* and the original signal will be overwhelmed with a new one. More specifically, the scenario above is analogous to "spoofing" or deception jamming, in which a new signal displaces the old one. If the French patrons in Rick's Café had replied to the Germans by pounding on the floor with pneumatic jackhammers, it would have been analogous to noise jamming, overwhelming a signal with meaningless noise. Allied jammers against the Kehl-Strassburg system would ultimately include both technologies.

Initial Jammer Development: NRL's XCJ

When Lorenzen went to work on this challenge in late August, the Allies knew only a small bit about these weapons, mostly from POW interrogation reports and Enigma intercepts. Small traces of fuel had been recovered by *Athabaskan* and analyzed by the British, and fragments of the physical structure of the Hs 293 had been recovered from various ships damaged in the attacks.[4] However, the critical information related to the radio-control links was absent. Allies did not yet know for certain the precise radio frequencies or the power output of the Kehl-Strassburg system, nor did they know the way in which control inputs from the aircraft cockpit were translated into radio waves, or, in turn, how the radio waves were translated into control surface movements on the weapons. Finally, they did not yet know whether the launching aircraft had the ability to detect the presence of Allied electronic countermeasures and to implement procedures to undermine their effectiveness. Since jamming works best when the adversary is unaware of its use, such information would be critical to development of jamming procedures and technologies. Otherwise, the Allied gambit would be revealed to the Germans who just might then move the whole system to a different frequency band.

✦ ✦ ✦

The team at the NRL proceeded, therefore, on two parallel paths. The first effort, directed by Lorenzen himself, was designed to gather more-precise information on the Kehl transmitter frequencies and power output, and, perhaps, on the specific characteristics of the radio signal being employed. This involved the development of a wire-based magnetic recording system to allow the transmitter signals to be retrieved and stored for later analysis. In addition, it is probable that the Allies deployed special observers to the fleet to scrutinize the apparent movement of incoming glide bombs and to correlate those movements with the radio signals being recorded. If every time the frequency jumps 8 Hz an observer notes the missile climbing, and every time it jumps 12 Hz the observer sees the missile descending, something very useful has been learned about the radio control system. In this way, a first-order approximation could be developed regarding the relationship between radio signals and missile control inputs. It is worth noting that *Grenville* had on board a movie camera that was used to record the attack on the 1st Support Group back on 27 August, perhaps with this objective in mind.

The second crash program involved the development of a countermeasures system—one able to be tuned across a wide range of frequencies—in the hope that high-power radio signals across this range of frequencies just might overlap with and overwhelm the Strassburg receiver in the Hs 293 or Fritz-X, thereby breaking the radio connection with the guiding aircraft. The first step in this process was to prepare radio receivers to indicate when a Kehl transmitter was operating so that ships would know to take evasive action and so those ships equipped with jammers would know to start radiating their disruptive signals. To this end the NRL team adapted twenty sets of Hallicrafters S-27 radio receivers operating across the frequency range of 27.8 MHz to 143 MHz into threat warning receivers with the U.S. naval designation RBK. The S-27 was teamed with the Hallicrafters S-36 (given product code RCK) operating across the range from 130 MHz to 220 MHz, which brought the combined frequency coverage from 27.8 MHz to 220 MHz. The effort to build these receivers was supported by William E. W. Howe, then a twenty-three-year-old with a bachelor's degree from Yale who was recruited in June 1942 by the NRL while he was undertaking postgraduate studies at the University of Alabama.[5]

The specific frequencies chosen for the receivers were largely an educated guess, based on the underlying physics, perhaps informed by British

Admiralty reports. The engineers and scientists at NRL knew they were developing a system to combat German radio-controlled weapons but knew little more than that. In fact, Howe himself was not even aware at the time that the weapons had already been deployed successfully against British ships.[6] As Howe relayed to author Alfred Price,

> At the time, we had no idea in which part of the frequency spectrum the missile guidance signals were being transmitted. So, to cover the probable bands, we modified Navy versions of the Hallicrafters S-27 and S-36 receivers (respectively the RBK and RCX) for our purposes, which together covered the spectrum from 27 to 220 MHz. . . . During a period of six weeks we hastily modified some 20 pairs of receivers this way. They were installed on warships and went to sea, and that was the last I heard of them.[7]

The operator of the RBK and RCK receivers would manually troll through the frequency range and observe movements of the needle on the signal strength meter. When the needle jumped one might infer that a radio control link could be operating on that frequency. Clearly, this appears to have been a slow, imprecise, and hit-or-miss approach.

The next step was to prepare transmitters to jam the radio links, a more complex task since the early jammers required the operator to tune the jammer to a specific frequency. This effort was headed by Carl Miller, a twenty-three-year-old engineer who had just graduated from the Oklahoma Agricultural and Mechanical College.[8] The theory was that once the RBK or RCK receivers indicated a potential threat and identified a likely frequency, the operator would assign that same frequency to a jamming transmitter and begin to radiate transmitter power. The project to develop such a transmitter was assigned an AAA1 priority, which meant that work could not be interrupted, and that it continued around the clock, including weekends.[9] Carl Miller described the process to author Alfred Price:

> Building a transmitter to cover the required band was a bear. That is one of the most difficult frequency spreads to cover. In the end, we managed it by dividing the coverage into a couple of bands. We [ultimately] built a series of experimental jammers, the XCJ, XCK and XCL, which solved the problems in different ways. We never had any time to test the jammers, however, because as each hand-built set was completed, somebody from the fleet would come and grab it from the laboratory. It would be hastily installed into one of the warships, and off it would go to sea.[10]

The critical decision to make was what frequency range to employ in the jammer. Guess correctly, and the device might have a chance of working.

Guess incorrectly, and all the broadcast noise in the world would be as use-less as the cries of seagulls. In the end, the frequency range chosen for the first generation of jamming transmitters, the XCJ, was for the most part in the High Frequency (HF) band, from 10 MHz to 35 MHz.[11] However, the German Kehl transmitter actually worked in the lower end of the Very High Frequency (VHF) band, between 48 MHz to 50 MHz. This meant that, while the Kehl transmitter signal would be received by the RBK receiv-ers, the initial two custom-built first-generation jammers developed by NRL could not have been effective in overriding that signal. At the time, this was obviously not known to the Allies.

How was the 10 MHz to 35 MHz band chosen? It is not clear, though the evidence from early attacks off Sicily and in the Bay of Biscay indicates that a frequency in the 20 MHz range was that most likely to yield success. For example, British light cruiser *Orion* had picked up and reported a spu-rious transmission in the 20 MHz range during an earlier air raid, perhaps while operating off Sicily in August 1943. Interrogations with pilots involved in that raid, who had been captured and interrogated by the British, had sup-ported the view that a frequency around 19 MHz to 20 MHz was involved.

A countervailing argument had been advanced that the actual frequency might be nearer to 40 MHz, based on interference seen by *Orion* in its Type 279 radar during that same attack. However, this band had been ruled less likely because, according to reports from captured Luftwaffe pilots, it was also the frequency used for Luftwaffe plane-to-plane communications.[12] In the end the British Admiralty concluded that the best course of action was to jam the frequency range of 17 MHz to 20 MHz; this information was almost certainly shared with the NRL, given the high degree of Anglo-American scientific cooperation at the time.

Herbert C. Jones and Frederick C. Davis

The first two countermeasures systems were installed on *Herbert C. Jones* and *Frederick C. Davis*, two American destroyer-escorts recently completed by the Consolidated Steel Corporation of Orange, Texas. Both were *Edsell*-class ships, two of the eighty-five of that class that had been constructed for use in World War II. Generally equivalent to contemporary British frigates, these were relatively slow ships (twenty-one knots maximum speed) pow-ered by diesel engines as opposed to steam turbines, lightly armed with three 3-inch guns, two 40-mm guns, and eight 20-mm guns. Their primary role was convoy escort duty and antisubmarine warfare, and for this they were well equipped. However, in the special case of these two ships, the primary role was neither surface attack nor antisubmarine warfare, but instead the new world of electronic combat.

✦ ✦ ✦

Herbert C. Jones and *Frederick C. Davis* were both commissioned in July 1943, the former skippered by Lieutenant Commander Alfred W. ("Skeeta") Gardes Jr., and the latter skippered by Lieutenant Commander O. William Goepner. Each commanding officer had already earned fame in the early days of World War II. Gardes was serving as executive officer of the U.S. Navy gunboat *Tutuila* on the Yangtze River when, on 31 July 1941, it was crippled and stranded during a Japanese aerial attack. The *Tutuila*'s commanding officer ordered that the damaged ship be abandoned after the outbreak of formal hostilities with Japan on 8 December, and stayed with the vessel to hand it over to the Nationalist Chinese. Meanwhile, Gardes took the ship's full complement along the just-completed and almost-impassable Burma Road all the way to India, and from there to South Africa and thence to a reunion with the U.S. Navy in Trinidad. It was with pride that the month he turned thirty years of age he took command of *Herbert C. Jones,* named in honor of an ensign killed at Pearl Harbor who had been awarded the Medal of Honor. (After the war, the Gardes family moved to Coronado and lived right around the corner from the parents of Ensign Jones. The two families become very close.)[13]

Meanwhile, Goepner had already earned eternal fame as the American who arguably fired the first shot in anger in the new war against Japan. (This contribution was deemed sufficiently important to earn him an obituary in *The New York Times*.) As officer-of-the-deck and gunnery officer of the destroyer *Ward*, he commanded the gun that fired two shells into a Japanese Type A "midget" submarine attempting to enter Pearl Harbor early on the morning of 7 December 1941.[14] This assault happened in the early morning hours *before* the armada of Japanese bombing and torpedo aircraft arrived over the American naval base at Pearl Harbor.

Initial shakedown operations of the two new destroyer-escorts took place in the Caribbean, after which both ships departed for the Washington area, arriving on 27 September.[15] There the ships were put in the hand of Dr. Ernest H. Krause, a thirty-year-old scientist with a doctorate in nuclear physics from the University of Wisconsin. Krause's team, in a crash effort, prepared the ships for combat. Each was outfitted with the Hallicrafters RBK and RCK receivers developed by Bill Howe, the NRL's custom-made XCJ jammer designed by Carl Miller, and perhaps most important, ultimately,

Howard Lorenzen's special magnetic recording system. Once prepared, both *Herbert C. Jones* and *Frederick C. Davis* departed Washington to conduct exercises in the Chesapeake Bay, and from there to Norfolk, Virginia, to prepare for convoy escort duties. On 7 October the two sister ships departed Norfolk for the Mediterranean, stopping in Gibraltar before arriving in Algiers on 16 October.

The departure was recalled by Motor Machinist Mate William F. Placzek, on board *Herbert C. Jones*: "With land falling away astern, the captain called the crew topside to discuss our mission. He told us about the enemy radio-controlled bomb that was raising havoc with Allied shipping and that our new equipment was a jamming device to counter it. The radiomen were to intercept the frequencies of radio-controlled bombs and jam them so they would fly off on erratic courses and miss their targets. The operation was code-named *Shingle*."[16]

Operation Shingle was, of course, the code name for the upcoming operation to break out of the Salerno beachhead, involving a major amphibious operation at Anzio in January 1944. The Allies were preparing for this next offensive push by moving additional men and materials into the battle zone. These convoys represented the next sphere of battle between III./KG 100 and the Allied navies and merchant marines.

Expectations for the success of the jamming ability of these two ships were not very high. One of the fathers of the NRL's efforts in electronics, A. Hoyt Taylor, described how *Herbert C. Jones* and *Frederick C. Davis* were to be employed: "Navy engineers took the NRL devices to the Mediterranean aboard two 'guinea pig' destroyers. Acting as bait for a large number of German bombs was a nerve-racking experience, but the operation paid off by the acquisition of the necessary technical intelligence needed for development of a practical counter-device."[17]

CHAPTER SIX

II./KG 100's STRUGGLES
in the MEDITERRANEAN

The campaign against Allied shipping did not pause while *Herbert C. Jones* and *Frederick C. Davis* sailed for the war zone. But as the Germans reflected on the success of the initial glide-bomb campaign, several hard-won lessons emerged. Primary was the vulnerability of the Do 217 in circumstances where Allied ships had fighter cover, such as over major amphibious landing sites. In such circumstances not only did the Luftwaffe find it challenging to approach the target area within effective range of the Hs 293 or Fritz-X, but also it found the losses in aircraft shot down to be at unacceptable levels.

✦ ✦ ✦

As the Allies consolidated their beachhead in Salerno in September 1943 and the war in Italy ground to a bloody stalemate, the Luftwaffe looked elsewhere for targets of opportunity. The slow and thin-skinned merchant ships plying the Mediterranean seemed attractive prospects, especially because they served as the lifeline for the Allies' Italian campaign. More suitable for Hs 293 weapons than the armor-busting Fritz-X, the primary responsibility for the antiship campaign shifted from III./KG 100—still recovering from losses over Salerno in any case and with only five serviceable aircraft—to II./KG 100, continuing to operate from Istres.[1]

Ajaccio: A Pyrrhic Victory for the Luftwaffe

After Salerno, the first round of II./KG 100 attacks was felt in Corsica, where Free French troops were retaking the island, displacing the Italian soldiers who had occupied Corsica after France's surrender to the Axis powers in 1940. The harbor of Ajaccio was a staging ground for merchant ships operating across the region, providing a nice target of opportunity for II./KG 100's Do 217s. Known to history primarily as the birthplace of Napoleon Bonaparte, Ajaccio is only 400 kilometers (215 nautical miles) south of Marseilles, and thus an easy distance to cover for the German bomber squadrons. However, the raid on Corsica also was to yield an important intelligence coup for the Allies; in the end the attack on Ajaccio ill served the interests of the Luftwaffe.

✦ ✦ ✦

On 30 September 1943 a small force of Do 217 E-5 aircraft from II./KG 100 was sent to attack Allied ships in Ajaccio.[2] Not all the aircraft were able to attack—a group of defending Spitfires dove into the formation and drove off parts of the attack, destroying three of the attacking aircraft.[3] Those bombers that managed to escape the Spitfires launched their Hs 293 glide bombs onto the vessels confined in the small port, which were unable to maneuver to escape. French air force mechanic Sergeant Pierre Perruquet witnessed the attack and described what happened:

> I found myself at the harbor [of Ajaccio] when my attention was attracted by the DCA [anti-aircraft artillery] opening fire on some enemy aircraft. I could see the German bombers out over the water when a flash of light and then smoke emerged from the wing of one aircraft. I immediately thought that the aircraft had been hit . . . except that a glide bomb then fell free from the aircraft and I was able to watch its sinusoidal trajectory until it fell close to the semaphore station. Soon after two more of these glide bombs, or missiles, fell next to a docked destroyer, causing huge eruptions of water. After the explosion a *tôle* [metal roofing sheet] passed over my head and I was knocked down by the shockwave.[4]

One glide bomb ripped into *LST-79*, built in the United States but at the time in the operation of the Royal Navy.[5] *LST-79* was a large amphibious assault ship designed to carry tanks into a battle zone and then land them using small on-board LCTs (tank landing crafts). Despite their stout construction LSTs were known with irreverence by crews as Large Slow Targets. In this case, *LST-79* had not been carrying tanks, but instead was couriering a special cargo, an air-surveillance radar designed for management of air battles over the region, and which was therefore critical to the defense of the newly liberated island. S. Peter Karlow of the OSS, having just arrived on board *LST-79*, described what happened:

> The morning was clear and sunny when we sailed into the beautiful bay of Ajaccio and tied up at the main dock. I got off and was waiting for our OSS people in Corsica to meet us when suddenly an armada of German planes flew overhead. This was accompanied by sporadic anti-aircraft fire. I ducked under a balcony of a nearby building and peered out cautiously. Five or six of the planes had been shot down and were tumbling out of the sky in flames. It turned out they were new German guided glider bombs with their own motors that flared fiery exhaust. They were not shot down at all but [were] on their final guided run for the target. They headed for and hit the LST and sank it, with the much needed anti-aircraft radar still on board.[6]

Of more interest, however, were reports reaching Allied intelligence shortly after the attack. Witnesses at Ajaccio claimed two of the five glide bombs seen to reach the harbor area hit the water—without exploding—near a destroyer moored at the jetty, most likely the French *Le Fortune*. Motivated by the prospect of finding a relatively intact Hs 293, British search parties previously engaged in similar and unproductive hunts at Salerno were instead redirected to Ajaccio. Here, unlike at Salerno, their efforts would be rewarded. Vital components of five missiles were recovered from the shallow harbor and immediately flown to the United Kingdom for detailed analysis.[7]

Moreover, it turns out that one of the three Do 217 aircraft lost was no ordinary bomber: it was a specially outfitted aircraft designed to detect the presence of Allied transmissions, such as those designed to jam the Kehl transmissions.[8] This would have alerted the Luftwaffe to the potential vulnerability of the Kehl-Strassburg system. At the time of this attack, there was nothing to detect. However, the absence of such a capability would prove critical in future months.

Convoy Attacks by II./KG 100

Perhaps with the recent losses from heavily defended Ajaccio fresh in the crew's memory, II./KG 100's next wave of attacks were against convoys operating in the Mediterranean that were more thinly defended. First to feel the weight of II./KG 100's attack was convoy UGS-18, a large collection of ships and escorts bound from Hampton Roads in the United States ("U") to Gibraltar ("G") at slow speed ("S"). From Gibraltar they would sail on to Port Said, Egypt, making stops at Algiers, Oran, and Bizerte. *Gruppe*

II./KG 100 paired up for this mission with torpedo bombers from KG 26, attacking the convoy at dawn on 4 October.

+ + +

The specifics of the attack remain somewhat confused, with German claims of successes with glide bombs not matching reports from those on the other end of the missile's flight path. Pilots from II./KG 100 claimed one ship sunk and three others damaged with their Hs 293 missiles.[9] Indeed, one ship was destroyed as a result of the combined raid, British-flag merchant ship *Fort Fitzgerald,* which was set afire and eventually had to be scuttled by gunfire from an escorting destroyer. However, the clearest accounts of the attack, including those from eyewitnesses, indicate the ship was sunk by a torpedo from KG 26 as opposed to a glide bomb from II./KG 100. John Slader, who was on board at the time, is certain regarding the mechanism of his ship's destruction: "From out of the northern sky at over 200 mph came a formation of twenty Do 217s, equipped with the new glider bombs, and twenty-five [He] 111H-6s, carrying two 1,686-pound torpedoes. The explosion was deafening when the torpedo struck. Clambering from the cabin through the porthole, my only means of escape, I found myself on the outside alleyway. Bleeding from head wounds, I was safely brought aboard the corvette *Lotus* thirty-five minutes later. This was my fourth escape from the enemy."[10]

Conversely, it is believed that both British-flagged *Samite* and U.S. Liberty ship *Hiram S. Maxim* were damaged by Hs 293 missiles. *Samite* was lucky—the ship was filled with explosives in every hold except No. 3. The Hs 293 struck the ship right in the middle of hold No. 3, thereby saving those on board from almost certain obliteration.[11] *Hiram S. Maxim* was seriously damaged by a near miss, again most likely of an Hs 293.[12] The crew abandoned ship after thirty minutes under the belief that the bulkheads would give way. Both freighters lost power and had to be towed into Algiers for repair, but survived to carry cargo another day. The Norwegian freighter *Selvik* also was damaged in the raid and fell behind the convoy, possibly from another near miss of an Hs 293. The damage proved relatively light, and soon after *Selvik* was able to rejoin the other ships headed to Gibraltar.

In contrast, the raid on UGS-18 proved damaging to the rapidly depleting squadrons of II./KG 100. One aircraft was shot down, with three killed and one survivor rescued by a British escort ship after four hours in the water.[13] Perhaps more critically on the return to base *Major* Molinnus, commander of II./KG 100, was killed when his aircraft crashed on landing.[14]

Hauptmann Heinz-Emil Middermann took over command from Molinnus, who had served in that position for less than a month. Three additional aircraft from II./KG 100 crash-landed at Istres, though with damage sufficiently contained as to allow effective repair.

Five days later another mission was launched, this time involving an attack at dusk against a convoy thought to be moving along the North African coast. In the end, the aircraft of II./KG 100 returned to Istres without finding the convoy or launching their weapons.

The next convoy to be found and attacked by II./KG 100 was MKS-28, which ran from the Mediterranean ("M") to the United Kingdom ("K") and consisted of ships capable only of slow speed ("S"). This convoy of more than forty merchant ships and five escorts was subject to repeated air assaults with torpedoes by KG 26, with attacks almost like clockwork every morning and evening. On 21 October, between 1845 hours and 1905 hours, thirteen Do 217s from II./KG 100, once again paired with the torpedo-carrying aircraft of KG 26, launched twelve Hs 293 missiles at the convoy. Luftwaffe pilots claimed two targets damaged with Hs 293 missiles and another fifteen damaged by torpedoes. Only two freighters were lost, in the end: American *Tivives* and British *Saltwick*. *Tivives* is confirmed as a victim of an aerial torpedo. However, some have suggested *Saltwick* may have been hit by an Hs 293 launched by *Feldwebel* Bruno Obst of 6./KG 100.[15] In reality, the ship was sunk by a conventional aerial torpedo, as is made clear in the Survivors' Report by Captain William Wilson: "The 3rd Mate was the first to see the torpedo approaching the ship, and as he shouted, I saw the torpedo travelling along the surface of the water towards the port quarter, at a speed of approximately 30 knots. The gunners opened fire on it with the Oerlikons, but this had no effect. The torpedo struck under the mainmast on the port side, on the watertight bulkhead between the two after holds."[16]

The next mission, on 4 November, involved another aborted raid: the pilots were unable to locate any convoys. Thus far, in four convoy missions, II./KG 100 had only located its target twice and had not yet managed to sink a ship, though it had hit and damaged several.

The slump continued in the next convoy attack on KMF-25A, a convoy from the United Kingdom ("K") to the Mediterranean ("M") operating at fast ("F") speed. This procession of transports departed Liverpool on 27 October, stopping by Algiers and then sailing for Alexandria, Egypt, with twenty-six merchant ships and nineteen escorts. Noteworthy among the warships joining the escort group at Algiers were *Frederick C. Davis* and *Herbert C. Jones*, the destroyer-escorts especially equipped with NRL's newly developed system for recording and possibly jamming the glide-bomb radio links. The two destroyer-escorts operated as Task Group 80.2 under the command of Lieutenant Commander Gardes on board *Herbert C. Jones*. The plan was for the two specially equipped destroyer-escorts to meet convoys off Gibraltar, outside bomber range, and then assume positions on either side as the convoy proceeded through the Mediterranean.[17]

In the now-familiar pattern, at 1600 hours on 6 November II./KG 100 linked up with KG 26 in a combined attack, with sixteen torpedo bombers of KG 26 targeting the merchant ships and with nine Do 217 aircraft of II./KG 100 targeting the escort ships with Hs 293 missiles. The troop transport ships of KMF-25A were organized into three columns, surrounded by the screen of destroyers and destroyer-escorts. The destroyer *Tillman* guarded the rear starboard side of the convoy while another destroyer, *Beatty*, guarded the rear port "coffin corner." As the Luftwaffe aircraft flew in from the east, exploiting the darkening twilight skies to help disguise their presence, the escort ships made smoke in an effort to hide the convoy. The first wave of Luftwaffe aircraft targeted *Tillman* and *Beatty* in an attempt to break up the protective ring of warships and open up a safe access path for follow-on waves of aircraft to the troop transports in the rear of the convoy. Under the command of Lieutenant Commander Francis D. McCorkle, *Tillman*, a modern destroyer rated at thirty-seven knots, evaded all three glide bombs launched in its direction, two of which landed only 160 yards away, with the third destroyed by the ship's guns. (McCorkle would go on to command battleship *New Jersey*.) *Beatty* was not so fortunate: targeted by the He 111s of KG 26, it took a torpedo that broke the back of the ship. *Beatty* sank later that evening.

Tillman's success and the loss of *Beatty* reinforced the fact that high-speed destroyers continued to be elusive targets for the Hs 293, although they still were vulnerable to conventional torpedo attacks. However, this is a narrow view of the situation. At the same time that *Tillman* was engaged in self-defense, and after *Beatty* was torpedoed, the rear escort screen ceased to be effective, and the Luftwaffe torpedo bombers penetrated the weakened defenses and pounced on the vulnerable merchant ships. Here they were successful, sinking two of the troop transports (*Santa Elena* and *Marnix van St. Aldegonde*) using conventional torpedoes, though fortunately for the thousands of soldiers on board the ships succumbed with minimal casualties. Once again, II./KG 100 came up empty with no sinkings, but at the same time played an instrumental role in the overall success of the convoy on the attack by distracting the escorts.

Frederick C. Davis and *Hebert C. Jones* were not targeted during the attack on KMF-25A, though *Herbert C. Jones* took credit for one aircraft destroyed. As the internal newspaper of *Herbert C. Jones* reported in its edition for 7 November, "The USS HERBERT C. JONES got its baptism of fire last night during an air raid on our present convoy. Our ship succeeded in downing a H.E. 111 which fell in flames off our starboard bow. . . . Three ships in the convoy were damaged. . . . The Commanding Officer announces, that, as soon as the appropriate insignia is determined, we'll 'chalk up' our win."[18]

The success against enemy bombers was not matched by any success in the jamming of the enemy missiles. Because of their defensive position abeam the merchant ships and the fact that II./KG 100 targeted its glide bombs against the escorts at the rear of the convoy, the two modified destroyer-escorts may not have been in the best position to test their new jamming systems. *Herbert C. Jones* reported that three radio signals were detected, and an effort was made to jam them, though the results were uncertain.[19]

Part of the problem clearly was that the jamming devices were set to the wrong frequency band: 10 MHz to 35 MHz instead of the required 48 MHz to 50 MHz. The destroyer-escorts could have broadcast all day long and the only result would have been some overheated vacuum tubes. Complicating the problem was that, while the Kehl transmitter antenna was omnidirectional—it radiated in all directions, thus making the signal easy to detect—the Strassburg receiver antenna on the Hs 293 and the Fritz-X was partially shielded by the glide bomb's airframe and thus jamming signals radiated from in front of the weapon might see only limited reception.[20] Such a design was logical in that while the missile's direction from the aircraft might vary as it moved parallel to the target, the missile itself would always be between the aircraft and the target. This meant that the jamming ship would need either to radiate at very high power or position itself between the controlling aircraft and the weapon. If *Herbert C. Jones* and *Frederick C. Davis* were guarding the flanks of the convoy while the attack happened from astern, they might not be in a position to effectively jam the radio link, even if they had the right frequency. Finally, while both destroyer-escorts were clearly interested in jamming the weapons fired at their convoy, their primary mission was to record the signals in the hopes that jammers that were more effective could be developed. Thus they often would wait until such recordings had been made before initiating their jamming systems, even if that meant the jamming might be less effective.

It is apparent that at least one of the two officers commanding the destroyer-escorts was frustrated by the apparent lack of success and communicated this frustration back to Washington. Evidently, the commanding officer of *Herbert C. Jones*, Lieutenant Commander Gardes, wrote an account critical of his radio detection and jamming equipment, especially the converted S-27 receiver. While his original letter of 22 November 1943 has not surfaced, a reply to the Chief of the Bureau of Ships from Commander John L. Reinartz, on behalf of the Director of Naval Research, suggests that NRL bristled at these criticisms from the field:

> This receiver was the preliminary laboratory model of the RDC and its development had not been complete when placed aboard the JONES. However, it had been used successfully for jamming tests and was considered the best equipment available for its purpose at the time. This receiver failed abruptly during the jamming practice held between the JONES and the Chesapeake Bay Annex and could not be repaired before the JONES sailed. It is evident that "despite the many improvements made by countermeasures technicians" [on board *Herbert C. Jones*] this receiver was never thoroughly repaired. Such inaccurate comments as "Too rapid scanning does not allow the highly selective IF stages to build up to a sufficient potential to give a visual pattern on the oscilloscope screen" indicate that the personnel were not sufficiently familiar with the technical aspects of this receiver. . . . The comments and recommendations made indicate a lack of technical understanding of this equipment.[21]

A subsequent attack with glide bombs was made on KMS-31, a convoy of fifty-two merchant ships that departed Liverpool on 27 October and arrived at Gibraltar on 10 November. A subset of the ships continued on through the Mediterranean for points farther east. That convoy, code-named *Untrue*, was shadowed by Luftwaffe Ju 88 aircraft as soon as it had departed Gibraltar, with reports early on the morning of 11 November confirming the convoy's course and speed, information that made its way back to Luftwaffe headquarters. By 1320 hours the shadowing aircraft had been instructed to transmit further contact reports on the same frequency as used by incoming bombers, a sign that an attack was in progress. All of these Luftwaffe aerial communications were picked up and deciphered by RAF signals-intelligence units, providing ample warning of the attack. A group of Allied P-39 fighters was providing air support to the convoy in anticipation of this raid, and, at 1755 hours, with the attacking force seen on radar, the ships began to make smoke to further complicate the mission of the Luftwaffe pilots.

The attack began at 1820 hours as the first wave of ten or twelve Do 217 E-5 bombers launched their Hs 293 missiles, targeting the escort ships in an effort to clear a path for the follow-on torpedo bombers. Some explosions were seen within five hundred yards of the convoy but no ships were hit. Torpedo and conventional bombers from KG 26 then entered the fray, directly targeting the merchant ships with conventional bombs and torpedoes. Meanwhile, another group of four to six Do 217 bombers maneuvered around the convoy, attacking the starboard side from a westerly direction. Ships exploded and aircraft were shot down in a confusing mêlée. In the end, the combined Luftwaffe attack of II./KG 100 and KG 26 on convoy KMS-31 cost the Allies four merchant ships: British-flagged ships *Birchbank* and *Indian Prince*, Belgian cargo ship *Carlier*, and French tanker *Nivose*. Several other ships were damaged but continued on.

Exactly which units and weapons were responsible for these losses remains uncertain. Luftwaffe pilots from II./KG 100 claimed to have sunk three of these ships: British-registered *Birchbank* and *Indian Prince* and Belgium-flagged ship *Carlier*.[22] (*Nivose* was torpedoed and then sank after a collision with another ship.) However, most postwar published accounts dispute these claims from II./KG 100, suggesting the ships were victims only of conventional torpedoes and bombs rather than glide bombs.[23]

Upon closer examination, it is by no means certain that torpedoes were solely responsible for these losses; the claims of II./KG 100, dismissed by some, may be correct. For example, the Survivors' Report of the sinking of *Birchbank* makes clear that the most likely cause of the ship's loss was a glide bomb. That account, by Captain A. Ellis of Birchbank, follows:

> At 1815 on 11th November, when in position 36° 10' N. 00° 06' W. steering a course of 063° at a speed of 7 knots, an explosion occurred amidships on the starboard side. . . . I did not know whether it was a torpedo or a bomb which struck the ship, but my 2nd Officer and Chief Engineer both definitely stated that they saw a glider bomb strike on the starboard side, describing it as a "miniature fighter." The Master of the ANGLO FARMER, the vessel next astern of me, told me subsequently that he definitely saw a torpedo dropped between columns eight and nine, which circled, near-missed his ship, and in view of the explosion which followed a few seconds later from my vessel, he was of the opinion that we had been struck by a torpedo which he had seen. A later examination showed, however, that the hole in the ship's side was well above the water-line when the ship was on an even keel; it therefore seems hardly likely that it was made by a torpedo. . . . The explosion was not as violent as I would have expected, but I was amazed to see, on entering the wheelhouse, the large amount of internal damage, especially as I was standing only three or four feet away at the time of the explosion.[24]

The eyewitness accounts, the fact that the bulk of the damage was internal with a moderate explosion as seen from the outside, and evidence that the impact point was above the water line all help to confirm that an Hs 293 was the most likely cause of the sinking of *Birchbank*, which is also what the official Admiralty report concluded.

The Survivors' Report for *Indian Prince* reached a different conclusion. Certainly a torpedo was reported as the official cause of the loss of *Indian Prince,* though the account of Captain R. C. Proctor does not indicate that anyone actually saw the torpedo, in part because observers were distracted by the sight of a German bomber on fire and crashing nearby, brought down by the gunners on board *Indian Prince*. The report also provides important facts that raise interesting questions about which type of weapon struck *Indian Prince*: "[A]t 1845 on November 11th, when in position 35' N.E. from Oran, steering a course of 062° at a speed of 7 knots, we were struck by one torpedo from an aircraft. The weather was fine and visibility good, with a full moon just rising. The explosion was heavy, there was a violent rending and tearing noise, but no flash was seen and no column of water was thrown up."[25]

A torpedo, exploding against the hull of the ship and underwater often creates a massive column of water that can extend far above the tallest part of the ship. The flash of the explosion, which takes place outside the hull of the ship, is also often seen. In contrast, an Hs 293 glide bomb was designed to penetrate the ship's skin before exploding. Since the explosion would occur inside the ship as well as above the water line, it would be less likely to generate the massive column of water typical of a torpedo attack and might generate less of a large flash visible to observers on deck. It must be considered at least plausible that, in contrast to what was concluded by Captain Proctor, *Indian Prince* was another victim of a glide-bomb attack.

The fate of *Carlier*, steaming in the center column of the convoy directly behind the lead ship, remains unclear. The most detailed account, by maritime historian Thierry Bressol, indicates the ship was hit in rapid sequence in a full interval lasting only three minutes by three bombs (of a nature otherwise unspecified) and two torpedoes, the last of which hit a hold filled with ammunition, causing the entire ship to erupt in a massive explosion.[26] Casualties were heavy, with twenty-four survivors out of the total complement of ninety-one. It is unclear whether *Carlier* was hit by any of the glide bombs.

One more convoy had been ravaged by the Luftwaffe and it is reasonable to conclude that one or two of the ships lost were victims of glide bombs. We will not know if the losses would have been lower had Allied countermeasures been deployed since escorts *Frederick C. Davis* and *Herbert C. Jones* were not involved in this attack and no other ships in the convoy were equipped with countermeasures.

Dodecanese Campaign

If II./KG 100's attacks in the Mediterranean and Atlantic against convoy escorts yielded minimal success, its mission against similar targets in the Dodecanese campaign were more successful, with three ships hit on eight dusk or nighttime missions, involving a total of twenty-two sorties.[27] The three successes took place despite serious restrictions on operational deployment, because British ships would hug the nearby Turkish coast, perhaps with the knowledge that the Luftwaffe was under strict orders not to do anything that might involve an intrusion into Turkish airspace.[28]

✦ ✦ ✦

As described earlier, the British embarked on an effort to occupy the Greek island of Leros off the coast of Turkey, albeit with disastrous consequences. A Greek and British destroyer had already been sunk by conventional bombs in late September in an attack often erroneously attributed to KG 100 and the impetus behind unsuccessful campaigns in Greece to gather intelligence on the Hs 293. While KG 100 could not be held accountable by the Allies for the attacks in late September, that situation changed on October 24 when *Staffel* 5./KG 100 (about a dozen aircraft) relocated from Istres to Kalamaki airfield outside Athens. A *kette* (three aircraft) of III./KG 100 also deployed to Kalamaki, though it never launched a mission with its Fritz-X battleship-buster glide bombs, most likely because the British destroyers and landing craft found in that theater were more suitable for the Hs 293. Dropping a Fritz-X on a destroyer would be like trying to kill a fly with a sledgehammer.

The first successful attack by the Do 217 of 5./KG 100 took place early in the morning on 11 November, the same day other aircraft of II./KG 100 were targeting convoy KMS-31 in the eastern Mediterranean. Two groups, each of three Allied destroyers, had been on patrol around Leros in a vain attempt to stop an incoming German assault force embarked in landing craft. On the night of November 10–11, one of those two groups had bombarded the islands of Cos and Calino, locations where the Germans had been assembling their assault force. It was while these destroyers were retiring that 5./KG 100 claimed its first victim in that theater, the British destroyer *Rockwood*.

The attack on *Rockwood* yielded important results for each side, and both the British and Germans could claim victory. The destroyer was under the command of Lieutenant (later Captain) Samuel Richard le Hunte

Lombard-Hobson and in company of British destroyer *Petard* and Polish destroyer *Krakowiak*. Lombard-Hobson himself explained what happened:

> At twenty minutes past midnight, at a moment when the nearest enemy aircraft was three miles distant, I felt a thud onboard, as though the ship had hit a baulk of timber in the water, or someone had dropped a heavy weight on deck. I then noticed that we were dropping back from our position, third in the line. I telephoned the engineroom but could get no reply. Within five minutes *Rockwood* was stopped in the water. . . . The First Lieutenant then came on the bridge and said that we had been hit by some large object, like a meteorite, which had penetrated the deck, causing extensive damage and plunging the ship into darkness below. . . . There was a hole in the deck, large enough to take two jeeps.[29]

It was not a meteorite that had struck *Rockwood* but an Hs 293 glide bomb. The missile did not explode—which explains why Lieutenant Lombad-Hodson remained alive and in a position to ponder the unusual circumstances of this encounter. Instead, perhaps because of the oblique angle, the missile "pancaked" (Lombard-Hobson's word) off the deck. Moreover, the missile broke up on impact and large portions could be collected for analysis while others continued through the ship and out the side, carving a path directly through a bulkhead.

Lombard-Hobson explained what happened after the situation was clarified and the remains of the missile collected: "The parts, recovered intact, were carefully packed into two sacks, and transferred to Petard for passage to Alexandria. Later we learned that they were immediately flown to England, where the mechanism was re-assembled and an effective-countermeasure to this new weapon quickly designed. Later still, we were thanked by the Admiralty for the part we had played."[30]

Rockwood was never repaired. Returning to Plymouth, England, she was surveyed by keen-eyed shipyard assessors and determined to be beyond the point of economical restoration. Instead, the ship was laid up for the war and then scrapped in West Hartlepool once peace had returned.[31]

Another British formation came under attack from glide bombs later that same day. This was British minesweeper *BYMS-2072*, escorting some landing craft about three miles off Leros early in the evening of 11 November. Perhaps as a result of a long white wake, the ship was spotted by the Luftwaffe and put under attack. According to survivors, the ship dodged three or four bombs before a glide bomb struck the ship on the port side forward.[32] Several crewmembers were killed, but *BYMS-2072* survived only to be captured the next day by German units. The Royal Navy's Adrian Seligman observed the attack from the safety of his nearby seaplane base:

From Navy House we had a clear view down the bay and out to sea. One night, early in November, we saw a glider bomb, easily recognizable by its red tail-light, pounce on a Brooklyn Yard Mine Sweeper (BYMS) passing the entrance to the bay. "Pounce" is an exact description of the way the bomb came cruising along then suddenly tipped up and fell upon its wretched victim. The funnel and deck clutter after took the full force of the explosion, thus saving the lives of the people in the great palace of a wheelhouse further forward.[33]

Two days after *Rockwood* and *BYMS-2072* were struck the aircraft of 5./KG 100 returned to the area, this time catching British destroyer *Dulverton* and two other destroyers off the island of Kos on a reinforcement mission to Leros, yet still twenty-five miles short of the island. An Hs 293 glide bomb rammed through *Dulverton's* hull directly under the bridge where Commander Stuart Austen Buss spent the last seconds of his life directing the defenses of his ship. The resulting explosion and fire killed Buss and another seventy-five of the ship's complement. Other ships came to the rescue, saving the remaining six officers and 114 sailors. *Dulverton* was beyond repair, and destroyer *Belvoir* sank the wreck with gunfire two hours later.

The following day the hunters of II./KG 100 went looking for other targets. Instead of finding new victims, they stumbled into two Beaufighters of the RAF: *Unteroffizier* Walter Pink and his Do 217 crew were shot down.[34] It was the last mission of the campaign. Two days afterwards, the British rout at Leros was completed as Wehrmacht units took control of the island, and the Grecian adventures of 5./KG had come to an end.

Not all of the losses involving 5./KG 100 took place during aerial combat. As was the case in France, the Luftwaffe operations from Kalamaki airport attracted the attention of Allied authorities, who assigned bombing missions against this airfield. On 15 November B-25 medium bombers from the American 12th Air Force attacked the field, destroying two of II./KG 100's Do 217 E-5 bombers while damaging five more and another from the *kette* of III./KG 100 also present at the field.[35] This one raid effectively depleted about half the fighting strength of 5./KG 100; it was followed up with another raid two days later. After that, the remnants of 5./KG 100 returned to France to meet up with its sister squadrons. The Allies continued to pummel Kalamaki just in case, with 56 American B-17 heavy bombers from the 15th Air Force striking the field on 6 December and 150 heavy bombers hitting the airport and nearby targets on 14 December.[36]

CHAPTER SEVEN

TRANSITION TIME:
KG 40 *and the* HE 177

Despite the losses, Allied navies had proven capable of mounting at least some defenses against the Hs 293, especially when it was deployed from the Do 217 bombers against high-speed targets such as destroyers. Merchant ships were more vulnerable; before reaching those ships, though, the attacking aircraft had to pass through the protective screen of warships and airborne fighters, which proved quite difficult in the relatively slow Do 217. After the initial successes at Salerno, albeit primarily against stationary or undefended targets, losses of warships to these glide bombs had diminished considerably. Fritz-X operations effectively vanished after Salerno altogether, not to reemerge for seven months.

✦ ✦ ✦

The threat from KG 100 diminished for a while after both II./KG 100 and III./KG 100 were pulled off the line in late November, abandoning their Istres base. The three squadrons of II./KG 100, including the parts of 5./KG 100 temporarily based in Greece, were relocated to Toulouse-Blagnac. Similarly, on 19 November *Staffeln* 7./KG 100 and .9/KG 100 of III./KG 100 were redeployed to Eggebek in northern Germany to prepare for Operation Carmen, a planned surprise attack on the British Home Fleet at its base in Scapa Flow, located in the Orkney Islands in the far north of Scotland. (The attack never took place, however.) In late October 1943 8./KG 100 had already been redeployed to Fassberg to begin conversion to the new He 177 aircraft. After just 104 days the glide-bomb offensive of KG 100 had been, in effect, put on hold.

In that short period glide bombs actually hit about fifteen ships (including two possible hits). Two things are noteworthy across these incidents. First, in most cases the ships successfully hit with glide bombs were either moving at slow speed or were not in a position to provide significant defense, for one reason or another. Only *Athabaskan* was capable of maneuvering at high speed while simultaneously engaging distant aircraft with long-ranging guns. It is noteworthy that both *Athabaskan* and *Egret* were hit by glide bombs before the operational limitations of the weapons had been observed by Captain Hill on board *Grenville*, which was present in the same attack. Second, there are only three cases where ships were sunk immediately by these weapons. In two cases (*Egret* and *Roma*) it was because a glide bomb detonated in the ship's magazine, leading to a tumultuous explosion. A third, *Bushrod Washington*, was not sunk immediately but succumbed the following day when the fire caused by the glide bomb reached ordnance stored in the ship's hold. All of the other ships remained afloat after taking the hit or hits from glide bombs, though in three cases the damage was such that the ship was scuttled, sometimes over the objections of the ships' masters. In aggregate, the new wonder weapons proved less of a threat to Allied ships than the traditional threats of bombs and torpedoes.

Moreover, the attacks undertaken by II./KG 100 and III./KG 100 had exacted a massive toll on the Luftwaffe. *Gruppe* II./KG 100 had been in action from late August through mid-November 1943, starting with a fleet of 43 Do 217 E-5 aircraft. By late November the Group had lost six aircraft to enemy action, fifteen more to accidents, another eleven that had been taken out of service for extensive overhauls, and one that was transferred out of the Group. Before the end of the year the squadrons of II./KG 100 would be rebuilt around eighteen newly built aircraft, with another sixteen aircraft transferred in from other units, bringing II./KG 100 back up to a roster of fifty-six aircraft by year-end.[1]

III./KG 100 had suffered even more. Starting with only thirty-five of its unique aircraft at the beginning of August, the Fritz-X squadrons had lost seventeen aircraft to enemy action, another twelve to accidents, and ten others to overhauls or other units by the end of November. Another five aircraft were lost in accidents in December alone. Losses in equipment were made up with forty-seven newly built aircraft, two repaired aircraft, and thirteen transferred in; by year-end III./KG 100 had expanded its fleet to a record fifty-three aircraft.

The equipment losses of KG 100 could be made up with new aircraft, but the dead, missing, and wounded crewmembers were not so easily replaced. By the end of November, fifty aircraft in KG 100 had been destroyed by enemy action or accidents. While some of those crewmembers may have survived to fly again, the overall shortage of trained and experienced crewmembers had become a critical issue.

Göring's Long-Range Bomber: The He 177

During this operational lull, some units of KG 100 began to transition to the long-awaited He 177 *Greif* now entering operational service, albeit in limited numbers. Powered by two Daimler Benz DB 606 power plants, each of which consisted of two side-by-side DB 601 twelve-cylinder engines in a single nacelle, the four-engine bomber was Germany's answer to such aircraft as the U.S. B-17 Flying Fortress and the British Lancaster bombers.

✦ ✦ ✦

An innovative engine design allowed this large four-engine bomber (superficially resembling a twin-engine aircraft) to carry a heavy weapons load and still operate with an effective combat radius (A-5 variant) of 2,000 kilometers (1,080 nautical miles), twice that of the Do 217 it replaced. Speeds of 490 kilometers an hour (265 knots) were possible at altitude. A crew of six staffed the aircraft and its considerable defenses against enemy fighters.

The He 177 A-3 and A-5 variants were those equipped to carry Hs 293 glide bombs. The former could carry two bombs, one under each wing; the latter, with upgraded DB 610 power plants (each consisting of two DB 605 engines), could carry a third under the fuselage, though it is not evident that this was ever done operationally. The aircraft also was equipped to launch Fritz-X glide bombs, though this seems to have been of secondary importance.

If the He 177 looked great on paper, its operational performance suffered by comparison. The major problem involved the unusual engine configuration, which led to problems with both overheating and fuel leaks—never a good combination when flying more than twenty thousand feet above the ocean. Nicknamed the "flaming coffin" by crewmembers, the He 177 was difficult to fly and suffered an atrocious accident rate, especially with inexperienced crews.

A final limitation of the He 177 is that its four DB 601 or DB 605 engines drank copious quantities of high-octane aviation gasoline on these long missions: each bomber could consume six tons of fuel on a single raid. This became a challenge because Germany's ability to produce petroleum products declined during the war, especially after its oil production capacity was crippled by concentrated Allied air attacks after March 1944.

Development of the long-range bomber had begun in the late 1930s; the first prototype had taken to the air on 20 November 1939.[2] Problems in development, including the eventual crash of the first prototype, led to delays in preparing the bomber for operational use. Finally, in February 1942 the experimental squadron *Erprobungsstaffel* 177 was created under the leadership of famed Luftwaffe pilot (then-) *Hauptmann* Rudolf Mons, who had earned admiration for daring maritime attacks while flying the Fw 200 Condor. By summer 1942, based from Orléans-Bricy, *Hauptmann* Mons counted only eight new (and nonstandard) He 177 available for training and only four complete crews.[3]

Gruppe II./KG 40

The first unit to employ the He 177 A-5 in an operational role was not KG 100 but instead a newcomer to the glide-bomb role, although it was by no means a newcomer to antiship missions. *Kampfgeschwader* 40, as a whole, had a storied history in the antishipping role, having engaged numerous targets in the Atlantic with its Fw 200 aircraft. *Gruppe* II./KG 40 was formed initially around the Do 217 and He 111, to be engaged alongside Fw 200 in an antishipping role, but it was not equipped to handle the Hs 293 or Fritz-X. In September 1943 II./KG 40 began to transition to the new He 177 A-3 bomber along with the Hs 293 glide bomb.[4] At the end of October, as the group was preparing to migrate to operational roles, it had acquired forty-nine of the new bombers, two of which were lost in fight accidents. In late October the group redeployed to Bordeaux-Mérignac airfield, on the Atlantic coast of France, and prepared to transition from operational training to real attack missions.[5] With the range of the He 177, this base provided ready access to convoys between the United Kingdom and the Mediterranean, both on their transits down the Atlantic and while in the western Mediterranean. This long reach would be demonstrated as the group successfully attacked a convoy in the Atlantic and another in the Mediterranean—more than 1,800 kilometers (970 nautical miles) apart—in the space of just five days.

✦ ✦ ✦

On 25 August 1943 Royal Navy sloop *Egret* became the first ship in history to be destroyed by a remotely guided missile. *Imperial War Museum, FL22644*

Athabaskan was hit by an Hs 293 glide bomb on 25 August 1943, as seen from an attacking aircraft. *Personal Collection of Ulf Balke*

Egret exploded after an Hs 293 struck the ship's magazine, as witnessed from nearby *Grenville*. *Imperial War Museum, A19448*

The wrecked bow of *Egret* is all that remained after *Grenville* arrived at the scene. Almost two hundred officers and crew were killed. *Imperial War Museum, A19449*

Herbert A. Wagner's Hs 293 glide bomb allowed bombers to pick off merchantmen and escort ships while attacking from a safe distance. *Personal Collection of Ulf Balke*

An Hs 293 presented an intimidating image to crewmembers of ships under attack. *UK National Archives, HO 199-365*

This Do 217 E-5 from II./KG 100, shot down over Salerno, carried an Hs 293 glide bomb under its right wing. *Personal Collection of Ulf Balke*

The Do 217 K-2, with its longer wings and glazed nose, was designed to carry the Fritz-X. *Bundesarchiv, Bild 101 III-Pachriike-041-24A*

Max Kramer's PC 1400FX "Fritz-X" glide bomb was designed to penetrate the thick armored decks of battleships. *Collection Manfred Griehl*

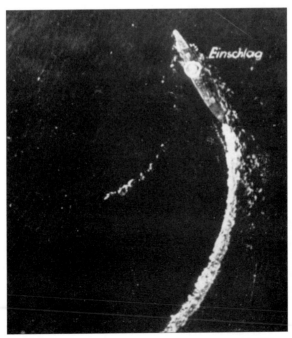

The modern Italian battleship *Roma* took a direct hit by a Fritz-X, in a strike photo taken from an attacking aircraft. *Personal Collection of Ulf Balke*

An estimated 1,254 officers and sailors were blown to bits or burned to death when *Roma* exploded after a direct hit from a Fritz-X. *Ufficio Storico Marina Militare Italiana*

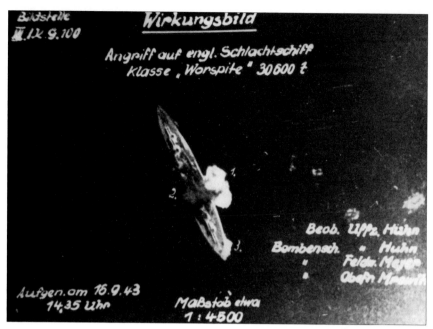

Warspite suffered a direct hit by a Fritz-X at Salerno, as seen from the attacking aircraft overhead. *Personal Collection of Ulf Balke*

Advanced He 177 A-5 bombers of II./KG 40 initiated attacks with Hs 293 glide bombs in November 1943. *Personal Collection of Ulf Balke*

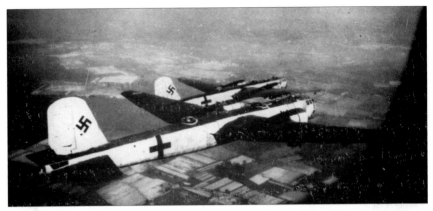

He 177 bombers of II./KG 40 flew in formation to their Aalborg airbase. *Dochtermann Family Archives*

Some versions of the Fw 200 patrol aircraft were equipped with glide bombs in late 1943. *Bundesarchiv, Bild 1011-619-2663-06*

The Ju 290 A-7 was the largest Luftwaffe aircraft equipped to launch glide bombs. *Bundesarchiv, Bild 141-2472*

Convoy SL-139/MKS-30

II./KG 40 enjoyed its baptism of fire while flying the He 177 on 21 November 1943. *Gruppe* II./KG 40's victims were the ships of convoys SL-139 and MKS-30. SL-139 had departed Freetown in Sierra Leone on 2 November and was making its way north to Liverpool with about two dozen merchant vessels. MKS-30 left Gibraltar on 13 November and also was headed toward Liverpool, with another two dozen or more ships. The convoys had joined up off Gibraltar and were proceeding north under the escort of seven warships of the 40th Escort Group, including Canadian corvettes *Calgary* and *Snowberry* accompanied by British frigates *Foley* and *Exe* and British sloops *Crane* and *Chanticleer*.

✦ ✦ ✦

On 16 November the familiar Fw 200 reconnaissance aircraft spotted the convoy and the seafarers braced themselves for the inevitable attacks. First to arrive were *Grossadmiral* Karl Dönitz's U-boats. However, the Allies had been forewarned of the U-boat positions by Enigma intelligence intercepts and the submarines emerged as the loser in this sea battle with four submarines destroyed against only two escorts in the convoy damaged, specifically *Exe* and *Chanticleer*. Reinforcements were sent by the Admiralty from bases in England to help bring the convoy home. Included in the convoy were Canadian armed merchant cruiser *Prince Robert*, configured especially as an antiaircraft ship; British destroyers *Watchman* and *Winchelsea*; and frigates *Calder* and *Drury*.

On the morning of 21 November, while the convoy was only five days from its destination, twenty-five He 177 aircraft of II./KG 40 were assigned to an attack. They dispatched at 1215 hours from Bordeaux-Mérignac, with two Hs 293 missiles under the wings of each aircraft. Some aircraft on this maiden run had to turn back and only twenty approached the convoy, reaching attack positions about 1527 hours. Weather was not ideal, with 6/10 coverage of low clouds obscuring the targets, making it difficult for the missile operators to maintain visual contact with their intended victims.[6] A few aircraft launched missiles at *Calder* and *Drury*, but each ship was able to evade the glide bombs. Similarly, an attack by a single He 177 on *Watchman* and *Winchelsea* also failed.[7]

Many of the bombers never even made contact with the main convoy and instead targeted two merchantmen that had fallen behind the convoy and therefore suffered from lack of effective support from the convoy's escorts.[8] Under the command of Rudolf Mons, now a major, this group of

Luftwaffe pilots took their time, launching a missile at the two stragglers with a deliberate pace every four or five minutes. Most were targeted at *Marsa*, a 1928-built cargo ship of 4,405 tons that had been struggling to keep up with the convoy and therefore made easy pickings. The captain of the doomed freighter, Thomas H. Buckle, after surviving the attacks of four aircraft and eight missiles, explained what happened as the fifth He 177 launched an Hs 293:

> I brought my stern round, but as it travelled round the stern I lost track of [the missile], consequently I was unable to take any further avoiding action, and it struck the water between the davits of the port lifeboat, exploding in the engine room near the main discharge. The detonation did not appear to be particularly loud. The blast, however, was terrific. I was walking from the starboard to the port side of the bridge at the time, endeavoring to trace the bomb's path, when a gunner and the Second and Third Officers were blown in through the door for which I was heading. . . . The ship was hit near the water line. I could not see the extent of the damage to the shell plating because it was underwater, but the deck was indented for the full length between the two boat davits, and the engine-room flooded so rapidly that I think there must have been a hole in the ship's side.[9]

Marsa was too badly damaged to save and was abandoned, despite the heroic efforts of its skipper. (Buckle would later receive OBE honors for his performance that day.)

Delius, the other straggler proceeding at only seven and a half knots, was the next target of II./KG 40. Its chief officer, Gordon Marshall, reported the events later to British intelligence authorities:

> At 1615 hours the bomb struck the ship. The starboard wing of the glider-bomb hit the foremast; this turned it inboard and downwards, then it hit No. 3 derrick and exploded on the port side of the hatch. The explosion was extremely violent, and debris was thrown to a tremendous height. I was knocked over by the blast and was dazed for a few minutes. The master on the bridge, the lookout on the monkey island and the assistant steward in the saloon were all killed instantly. . . . The explosion shattered the bridge, chartroom, wireless-room, etc. leaving them a complete shambles. . . . Fortunately the engine room was undamaged.[10]

Marshall was able to restore control and eventually rejoined the convoy, delivering his cargo to its intended destination.

By 1705 hours, after an hour and a half of semicontinuous attacks, the aircraft of II./KG 40 withdrew. On balance, II./KG 40 could not view the mission as a great success. Except for one aircraft, flown by *Hauptmann*

Nuss, who was responsible for both hits on *Delius* and *Marsa*, all the other aircraft missed their targets.[11] Bad weather played a role, but also, no doubt, did inexperience and perhaps the aggressive defense put up by the convoy's escorts, a defense sufficient to allow the main convoy to escape without loss.

Moreover, three He 177 aircraft were shot down, and several others were badly damaged.[12] Two of the losses occurred in a highly unusual confrontation with a patrolling Liberator bomber, under the command of Pilot Officer A. Wilson of No. 224 Squadron from RAF Coastal Command. While performing an antisubmarine watch over the convoy, Wilson sighted the formation of enemy bombers and decided to transform his lumbering four-engine patrol aircraft into an interceptor, engaging in air-to-air combat against the flock of He 177s. The German bombers, at that moment committed to a straight and level course as they guided their Hs 293s, were relatively easy targets, and several He 177s were hit by the gunners on board Wilson's Liberator. His intervention helped break up the main attack.[13]

Two other aspects of the raid are worth noting. First, at least one engine of the He 177s was seen to burst into flames spontaneously, reinforcing the views that the aircraft suffered from chronic engine overheating problems. Second, a number of the missiles appeared not to work, either refusing to launch or falling out of control after launching. There were no ships equipped with jamming gear in the convoy, so such aberrant behavior cannot be attributed to electronic countermeasures. While later we will offer a potential technical explanation for such a high rate of failure (multipath interference), at the time it was suggested within the Luftwaffe that sabotage was to blame. *Feldwebel* Fritz Trenkle, who was based with II./KG 40 at Bordeaux-Mérignac, reported after the war to author Alfred Price on the discovery of apparent sabotage in one of the Kehl transmitters:

> The command guidance signals from the aircraft transmitter were carried to the antenna via a co-axial cable, and somebody had cut the central conducting wire half-way along its length and then reassembled the cable. It was very clever, and obviously done by an expert. When we tested the transmitters on the ground with the aircraft engines stopped, the central conducting wire made a good enough contract and the signals were radiated properly. But, when the engines were running, the vibration caused the gap in the wire to open and close, so that for long periods, the guidance signals never reached the antenna. Once we had discovered the reason for the failure, we checked all of the Henschel 293-carrying aircraft—Do 217s and He 177s—and found that about half had been "doctored" in this way. The security service carried out exhaustive inquiries at Mérignac in an effort to find the culprit but without success.[14]

Convoy KMF-26 and Loss of *Rohna*

The somewhat depleted II./KG 40 was back at it again five days later, on 26 November 1943, as part of a combined aerial assault on KMF-26, a big troop convoy carrying soldiers to destinations in the Middle East and Asia. Two dozen large transports had departed the Clyde eleven days earlier bound via Gibraltar for Alexandria, the convoy's last port in the Mediterranean before heading through the Suez Canal. A large number of the passengers were U.S. Army Air Corps personnel on their way to India to serve with the 10th Air Force, which then was engaged in offensive operations in the China–Burma–India theater. Some 1,981 of these soldiers and airmen sailed on board HMT (His Majesty's Transport) *Rohna*, bound from Oran through the Suez Canal to Bombay (now Mumbai), India.

✦ ✦ ✦

Rohna—the name comes from the name of a village in Punjab, India—was an aging transport ship built in 1926 and operated before the war by the British India Steam Navigation Company, a unit of the Peninsular and Oriental Steam Navigation Company. In the prewar years it operated between India and other parts of the global British empire, carrying cargo in the hold, wealthy voyagers in comfortable cabins, and native Indian passengers in less-commodious spaces belowdecks and on the exposed surfaces. Designed in part to accommodate as many low-fare Indian travelers as possible, the ship was originally certified for 5,065 passengers, an astoundingly high number given the ship's gross tonnage at 8,602.[15] (The passenger certification was later reduced to 3,851.)

As the sun set behind the east-bound convoy, and as the families back home of the Suez-bound American troops were preparing for a Thanksgiving dinner, the darkened transports made their way along the North African coast between Algiers and Philippeville (now Skikda). The columns of cargo ships were surrounded by an impressive array of escorts from the U.S. Navy and Royal Navy. Once again, these escorts included *Frederick C. Davis* and *Herbert C. Jones*, equipped with NRL's first-generation jamming system, the same that had failed to protect other troop transports some twenty days earlier.

A few hours before sunset twenty-two He 177 bombers from II./KG 40 had departed Bordeaux-Mérignac for the long flight to the North African coast. One aircraft crashed on takeoff, leaving twenty-one under the command of *Major* Mons for the attack on KMS-26.[16] The first wave of bombers, arriving at 1645 hours, targeted the escort ships, especially *Colombo*, an antiaircraft cruiser. *Colombo* evaded all the missiles fired at it, and destroyer *Atherstone* did likewise with the five glider bombs sent in its direction. Troopship *Banfora* was almost hit by an Hs 293. *Herbert C. Jones* dodged a pair of missiles, as the shipboard newspaper reported the following day:

> Last night, commencing about 1700, the officers and crew of this ship were galvanized into action by two sounds—the General Alarm and the firing of the 40 mm guns. . . . In this attack, which lasted an even two hours, the new Nazi invention, the control glider bomb, was used extensively. It is definitely known that this ship was the target of at least 2 of these bombs. The first of the bombs aimed at us described a circular pattern and then came straight in at the [ship] at about 005° relative. It is estimated that this bomb crashed within not more than 200 yards of the ship. The second bomb that originally had our name on it but wound up in Davy Jones's locker, was entirely unobserved until it struck the water within not more than 50 yards from the ship, almost directly amidships on the port side. The reason this bomb was not observed was due to a change of wind which blew our smoke screen back into our faces. That was more than close.[17]

Fortunately for the Allies, in the midst of this attack friendly fighter aircraft arrived on the scene including French Spitfires of GC 1/7 Squadron, American P-39 Airacrobras of the 350th Fighter Group and British Beaufighters of No. 143 Squadron.[18] The combination of German bombers and British, American, and French fighters resulted in a confused mêlée in which six of the attacking He 177s were shot down. Two of the Luftwaffe officers lost in those flaming aircraft were none other than *Major* Mons, commander of the mission, and *Hauptmann* Nuss, hero of the attack five days earlier that had claimed *Marsa* and *Delius*.[19] The aerial combat was described by a pilot engaged in the combat:

> We passed a convoy near Bourgie at 16:15 hours when R/T [radio] told of enemy formations approaching from the north. We turned north on an intercepting vector, climbing from 7,000 to 12,000 feet. . . . We spotted a big one about 10 miles away going full speed for the deck and gave chase. After ten minutes we caught him just in the base of a broken cloud layer around 2,500 feet. Some miles back from a quarter view Allemand and I had identified the long nose, two nacelles etc. as an HE-177. Now we could also see two glide bombs along outside the engines. He went into a slow starboard turn, so at 300 yards with 10 degrees deflection, I gave him a long burst with cannons and machine guns, raking him from outside the left nacelles, through the fuselage to the right nacelle. Oil and pieces of the ship, one of which could have been an engine cowl or escape hatch, flew past and both engines were on fire as we ducked into the clouds for a second. Dropping down on a parallel, we saw him jettisoning fuel and one of

the radio controlled bombs shaped like a plane. One man bailed out. We closed to 250 yards, firing him again in both engines; this time he started losing altitude, and I think the fuselage was on fire. Then for good measure, we went in a third time to 100–150 yards, leaving the whole ship a mass of flames as it dove into the sea. . . . This was the first HE-177 to be shot down in the area.[20]

As the Allied fighters were engaged in destroying the first wave of bombers, another group of He 177s entered the fray; at 1725 hours one of these broke through the barrier of escorting warships and launched a missile directly at troopship *Rohna*. Those watching the battle on deck saw the Hs 293 drop from the wing of the bomber and accelerate toward the port side of the merchantman, crashing through the hull plates just above the waterline and exploding in the engine room. Survivor and 2nd Officer J. E. Wills reported the details of the battle:

Shortly after 1700 several other enemy aircraft appeared, and at one time I saw four in formation off the port quarter. The escorts gun-fire, however, appeared to be keeping the planes from attacking. At 1725 [hours] on the 26th November I observed two bombers approaching the ship from the port quarter, flying at a height of approximately 3,000 ft. One of them attacked the ship ahead, the other, when he was just abeam of us, swerved towards us and launched a bomb from about two points before the beam. At this time we were 15 miles N. from Jijelli, North Africa, steering 100 degrees (approx) at 12 knots. The weather was fine and cloudy, the sun was setting and visibility good; there was a moderate sea with a long swell, and North Westerly wind, force 3. When first released the bomb appeared to be a little below and to the starboard of the plane, it then closed the plane, shot downwards, swerving to the right of the plane and a red glow appeared in its nose. When it was half way I realised that it was a glider bomb; I gave orders for the port Oerlikon to open fire, which order was carried out, but I do not think any hits were scored. The bomb struck the ship in the engine room, on the port side, just above the water line. There was not a loud explosion; in fact the near miss explosions were far more violent.[21]

The perspective from the Luftwaffe's side has also been captured. The pilot responsible for the hit on *Rohna*, *Major* Hans Dochtermann, survived the war and years afterwards wrote an unpublished paper providing details of the mission. He describes the situation from his aircraft commander's seat:

Upon reaching the target distance, Uffz. [*Unteroffizier*] Zuther launched the Hs 293 and I pressed the seconds pointer of the stop clock in my control column. As the massive bomb fell through about 100m, the red flare in the rear lit up and the rocket engine gave the bomb additional thrust for about 10 seconds. Uffz. Zuther came up a bit on his control raising the Hs 293 to eye level. His eyes and the red flare had to be brought together over the ship. I could not see the flight of the bomb myself from my seat on the left side of the cockpit. I concentrated solely on my [flight] instruments and counted off in 10 seconds increments the duration of the flight. . . . At 92 seconds a loud eager scream about the BzB [intercom] sounded at the same time from all 5 occupants: "Direct hit amidships!" The rear gunner, Uffz. Warnecke, announced: "Just as the captain has a ship's whistle, we have our harmonica." From his flight bag he dragged out his harmonica and played *Denn wir fahren, denn wir fahren, denn wir fahren gegen Engelland*. Every soldier in WWII knew this song.[22]

On *Rohna* a different cacophony ensued, one of a ship tearing itself to pieces amid screams of panic. The engines and electrical power failed, bulkheads started to collapse, and black smoke—and bodies—poured out of the hole created by the missile. The evacuation order was a shambles and ill-prepared troops and sailors attempted to abandon ship. Some survivors later alleged that the Indian crew and English officers were negligent in organizing the evacuation, a charge rejected by many of the ship's volunteer complement of merchant sailors.[23] In the chaos large numbers of troops were left behind on board to drown or burn to death as *Rohna* sank.

Casualties on board *Rohna* far exceeded one thousand, though precise numbers are hard to pin down. By most accounts, a total of 1,149 persons perished on board the transport as it sank or afterwards in the water. The death of the 1,015 U.S. troops, by far the largest contingent within this total of 1,149, remains the greatest loss of U.S. service members at sea in a single ship in the history of the United States. In addition, 120 of the ship's crew were killed, along with three Red Cross personnel and eleven naval gunners. To the total of 1,015 U.S. service members lost in the actual sinking should be added the 30 other U.S. personnel who were rescued but died later of their injuries, contributing to total losses of U.S. personnel in this incident of 1,045 and those of all nations to 1,179.[24]

The loss of *Rohna*, and specifically the fact that an Hs 293 glide bomb caused the destruction, remained generally unknown for a long time, though contrary to what some have written the loss itself was not kept an official secret for decades after the war. It is true that many survivors were told not to mention the incident in letters home.[25] However, the loss was acknowledged only three months after the sinking in February 1944, though the ship was unnamed, the cause of the sinking was attributed to a submarine, and the location identified only as "European waters."[26] In June 1945 the name of the ship as well as the precise number of deaths were made public, though the role of glide bombs in the sinking was still not revealed, noting only that it occurred during a German "aerial attack."[27]

Escorts *Frederick C. Davis* and *Herbert C. Jones* again distinguished themselves in the battle in their conventional escort role, with their guns adding to the defense of the convoy. Their special abilities with respect to electronic countermeasures proved far less substantial, though at least one author suggests some glide-bomb signals were jammed.[28] No doubt the operators of the "newfangled" radio-jamming equipment tried their best to deflect some of the glide bombs, but it proved difficult in such mass attacks. First, the number of different signals being used—one for each glide bomb in the air at the same time—made it difficult for the electronic warfare technicians to pinpoint the specific control frequencies for any single missile in time to initiate effective jamming. Second, it would have proven useless in any case because this first generation of jamming equipment, as we have seen, was set up to jam the wrong set of frequencies.

Of far more long-term consequence were the results achieved by Howard Lorenzen's magnetic wire recording system. As the attack took place, and as more than a thousand sailors and soldiers on board *Rohna* went down with the ship, the special naval officers dispatched from NRL took careful note of the multiple radio signals picked up and recorded for analysis. Their primary mission completed, *Frederick C. Davis* and *Herbert C. Jones* returned immediately to Oran. As reported by crewmember Placzek on board *Herbert C. Jones*, "After the November 26 raid, we went to Oran. Two officers on board, who had been supervising the jamming operation, flew back to the states to report. The mission was very successful. We also had two army radiomen aboard who translated conversations between German pilots and gave that information to the skipper."[29]

One of these individuals carrying the precious recordings back to the scientists and intelligence agents was none other than Bill Leonard, who in later life would become the head of CBS News. As he reported in his biography,

Meanwhile I spent . . . four years in the U.S. Navy, where my radio background landed me in the middle of a push-button electronic war within a war that was many dreadful years ahead of its day. . . . The Germans . . . developed several types of radio-guided bombs, the most deadly of which was the HS293, a tiny pilot-less aircraft containing a single 500-kilogram bomb. . . . A way had to be found to discover what frequencies were being used, and then, if possible, to throw the bombs off target with special jamming equipment. . . . I found myself in charge of a special unit aboard two ships, the *Herbert C. Jones* and the *Frederick Davis*. Our orders were to get into the middle of a few attacks and see what we could find out. . . . The Germans arrived on the minute, and the air was presently alive with guided missiles. By a lucky accident, a radio in our communications room had been inadvertently left tuned to a particular channel. That just happened to be one of the frequencies the Germans used to control the missiles. In the next attack, a few hours later, we were able to make a recording of their missile control. I was flown to Washington with the precious record, and on the basis of its information, we began to develop jamming equipment.[30]

As for II./KG 40 the losses suffered in the battle over KMF-26 were massive. Of the twenty-one aircraft dispatched, one crashed before getting airborne, six were shot down over the convoys, and another two crashed on landing.[31] Another nine had to be sent to overhaul centers for major repairs. *Gruppe* II./KG 40 started the month of November with forty-seven He 177 A-3 aircraft. By the end of the month, and losses from attacks on both SL-193/MKS-80 and KMF-26, the three squadrons of II./KG 40 were down to only twenty-six serviceable aircraft. The group commander, *Major* Mons, also had been lost and was replaced by *Major* Walter Rieder, former commander of a squadron within III./KG 40.

Defending the Blockade Runners

The remaining operations of KG 40 in 1943 were of a defensive rather than offensive nature, designed to support the struggling German war economy. As the military conflict with Hitler progressed past its fourth year, the Allied naval blockade of Germany took an increasing toll. There were materials critical to the German war effort that simply could not be sourced within the territories occupied by the Wehrmacht or its contiguous allies. Examples include rubber, tin, tungsten (wolfram), molybdenum, zinc, opium, and quinine. However, much of this material was available via the territories occupied by Germany's Axis partner, Japan. Prior to the breakout of hostilities with the Soviet Union in June 1941, Germany obtained such items from Japan via the Trans-Siberian Railway. Once that avenue was shut off by the Red Army, a result of Hitler's invasion of the Soviet Union in June 1941, Germany was forced to transport these supplies in merchant ships or submarines across the open ocean. These blockade runners made the dangerous journey from Japanese territory to German-controlled ports, typically in occupied France.

✦ ✦ ✦

These were strategic missions, and they precipitated an escalating series of battles in December 1943. First, the Allies launched Operation Stonewall, a concerted attempt by naval and air forces to locate, identify, and sink the freighters making the run from Japan. In response, the Germans sent a group of destroyers to meet the incoming blockade-runners and to escort the ships and their essential cargoes the remaining distances to France. In counter-response the Allies brought three cruisers and other ships into the battle in an attempt to intercept and destroy the German naval escorts. The German reaction was to deploy aircraft from II./KG 40 and III./KG 40, armed with Hs 293 glide bombs, as a protective umbrella.

Action started on 22 December when the approaching German block-ade-runner *Orsono* was sighted by a German patrol aircraft. On both 23 December and 24 December two *kette* (two chains of three aircraft each) of II./KG 40 were dispatched to provide protective air cover. Due to failure in communications compounded by poor nighttime weather, the He 177 bombers never met up with *Orsono* and one was lost to enemy action.[32] A similar mission flown the next day also failed to engage the enemy, and another aircraft was lost to a fighter attack.[33] *Orsono* survived a gauntlet of air attacks from Allied aircraft and, abandoning hope of actually making port, beached itself on the French coast where its vital cargo of tin, tungsten, and rubber was unloaded to feed the voracious Nazi war machine.

Meanwhile, the blockade-runner *Alsterufer* approached the coast, and once again German destroyers sortied to escort it in. Before they could reach it, on 27 December *Alsterufer* was attacked and sunk by an Allied bomber. With the mission over, the German destroyers turned about to head back to port. However, British light cruisers *Glasgow* and *Enterprise* had maneuvered in position to cut off the escape of the retreating Kriegsmarine destroyers, hoping to trap the German destroyers and to sink them in a sur-face naval action.

Once again the Luftwaffe launched antiship missions in support, this time targeting the British cruisers in an effort to unspring the British trap. The tactics this time changed slightly. Luftwaffe officers observed that the He 177s of II./KG 40 had struggled to find *Osorno* a few days earlier, ham-pered by the poor weather and the relatively limited maritime electronic nav-igation and surveillance equipment on board those aircraft. They realized that in missions launched before daybreak the He 177s had trouble form-ing up in the dark and therefore had to struggle on their own to reach the target. With this in mind, the Luftwaffe first dispatched four of the Fw 200 aircraft of III./KG 40, well equipped for maritime surveillance and recently upgraded to accommodate the Hs 293. They departed on 28 December in the predawn darkness, with the expectation that another attack from II./KG 40 would be launched later during daylight.

Only four such Hs 293–equipped Fw 200s existed in the entire air fleet, and all four departed Bordeaux-Mérignac on the first operational mission combining this aircraft and weapon.[34] Each carried two Hs 293 glide bombs, positioned on special fairings underneath the outboard engines. Again, weather frustrated the attempt and only one of the four large patrol aircraft could reach the scene of the impending ambush. The crew of this Fw 200 attempted to intervene in the battle, and at 1346 hours sent the first of its two weapons in the direction of *Glasgow*, with a similar effort following forty-five minutes later.[35] Neither launch succeeded because the low ceiling made effective operation of the visually guided missiles too difficult; the mission was a complete failure.[36] Compounding the failure was the loss of *Hauptmann* Wilhelm Dette's aircraft, forced to ditch due to engine failure or fuel exhaustion, after what may well have been the only time Fw 200 aircraft engaged targets with a glide bomb.[37] The general disappointment in these missions led to a de-emphasis on Hs 293 strikes for the Fw 200, and the aircraft were gradually reassigned to other roles.[38]

A more ambitious effort followed that same afternoon, after sixteen He 177s from II./KG 40 lifted off from Bordeaux-Mérignac to intercept the British ships. Each Luftwaffe bomber was armed with two Hs 293 weapons. Again, poor weather intervened and only nine of the He 177 aircraft were able to reach the battle; none of their eighteen missiles reached any targets. (The British cruisers, unimpeded by glide bombs, also destroyed three of the German destroyers.) One or two of the attacking aircraft did not survive the mission.[39] In an episode reminiscent of that from 21 November, it is possible that one of the He 177 was lost due to the intervention of an American Liberator patrol aircraft. At 1745 hours that same afternoon Lieutenant Commander James R. Reedy, commanding a PB4Y-1 in that vicinity, reported attacking and crippling an He 177 bomber.[40]

Meanwhile, the Allies went on the offensive in this confrontation with glide bombers. As was the case at Istres and Kalamaki, the use of Bordeaux-Mérignac as a base for glide-bombing aircraft did not escape the notice of Allied intelligence analysts, and once again the heavy bombers of the U.S. Army Air Force were called into action. Bordeaux-Mérignac had already been visited by 58 B-17s of the 8th Air Force on 24 August 1943, even before glide-bomber units were operational at that field. A more substantive attack occurred on 5 December when a larger force of 236 B-17s of the 8th Air Force was dispatched against the field. On 5 January the B-17s returned, with 112 hitting the airfield. The Allied pilots claimed more than fifty aircraft destroyed, including three He 177 A-3 bombers from II./KG 40.[41]

Thus ended the year in which the Hs 293 and Fritz-X made their combat debuts. II./KG 40 went off the line at the end of December in an effort to rebuild the group and recover from the recent losses. *Gruppe* II./KG 100 likewise had already stood down, and both of these groups would not see action again until late January, when they attempted to destroy the Allied invasion force at Anzio. *Gruppe* III./KG 100, redeployed to northern Germany in preparation for raids against the British Isles, was out of action even longer, not to appear in the skies above Allied ships until an ambitious mission to Plymouth in late April 1944.

CHAPTER EIGHT

INTELLIGENCE WORK
LEADS *to* IMPROVED
ELECTRONIC DEFENSES

The first wave of electronic defenses had been developed in the period immediately following the strikes of August and early September 1943. At that point Allied scientists could rely on nothing more than fragments of exploded bombs, traces of rocket fuel, reports from interrogated Luftwaffe POWs, and—when it came to the critical radio-control frequencies—only educated guesses. These early guesses had proved inaccurate, as the losses on the Mediterranean convoys in November had demonstrated. In particular, misled by early intelligence reports from British sources, the NRL's engineers had targeted the wrong frequency band to jam. As the Allied scientists regrouped, they were able to exploit an increasing wealth of information on the Hs 293 and Fritz-X, including a growing set of fragments and pieces from exploded weapons.

✦ ✦ ✦

Evaluating the Threat: The Allied Engineers' First Look

Each attack on Allied ships created the possibility that more fragments of the Hs 293 and Fritz-X would be recovered. Some bits of an Hs 293 had arrived at the Royal Aircraft Establishment (RAE) in Farnborough as early as 1 September 1943, almost certainly from the attacks on *Athabaskan*, *Bideford*, and *Landguard*.[1] Unfortunately, this did not include any meaningful components of the Strassburg receiver and thus provided no additional insight into the potential mechanisms to jam the Kehl-Strassburg radio links.

◆ ◆ ◆

Components of the Hs 293 that were more substantial began arriving in UK and U.S. laboratories in October and November 1943. The RAE conducted an assessment of all the available physical information on the Hs 293 and Fritz-X through 24 November 1943, and issued its reports a few weeks later in December.[2] That report centered on a reconstruction of the Hs 293 from pieces obtained during seven previous attacks, with the most substantial segments coming from Ajaccio and the attack on *Rockwood*. Based on these fragments, the engineers at the RAE were able to reconstruct large portions of the wing, propulsion system, center fuselage, and tail section, all which were seen to be of "striking robustness." There were only limited bomb fragments recovered, but photographic evidence taken by *Grenville* during the attack on August 27 indicated the bomb was "a 500 K.G. SC type, probably fitted with Kopfring. A certain amount of Trialen filling has also been recovered."[3]

The examination of the wreckage did reveal some important aerodynamic characteristics of the Hs 293. Specifically, the scientists were able to duplicate from an examination of the control and lifting surfaces the nature of the weapon's ability to bank and turn. It is worth noting that an attempt to turn the Hs 293 too sharply in the final stages of flight would create a flight characteristic quite similar to that envisioned by a successful jamming operation: "The minimum radius of turn (1,500 ft.) in a horizontal plane implies banking to about 80°. In the absence of any rudder control this turn would clearly fail and hence the minimum radius for horizontal manoeuvre will be much greater. Attempts at extreme control in the later stages of attack have been described by observers; the weapon has banked very steeply and slipped into the sea."[4]

Unfortunately for the Allies, as relayed above, relatively little information about the radio-control system could be deciphered from the available wreckage of the radio unit. As reported by the RAE engineers, "The initial material which has been recovered is, up to now, very incomplete and while a general picture of the system of control may be given, no details of the mechanism are possible. . . . Only a part of the servo has been recovered. . . . No significant part of the master control unit has been recovered. A single gyro rotor is of normal pattern, but the number of gyros and their function is not known."[5]

Most frustrating for the Allies was that the one Strassburg receiver unit captured so far, again most probably from *Rockwood*, was damaged beyond the point of detailed evaluation. It was only possible to develop a general circuit diagram and description of surviving components, which did not include any of the radio tubes.[6]

Two Critical Intelligence Finds

As operations off Salerno wound down and the Allies (and Luftwaffe) recovered from the bombing campaign, the intelligence units went to work. Two major intelligence finds occurred in the period from late September to early November 1943, and these were to transform the jamming technology employed by the Allies.

✦ ✦ ✦

The first critical intelligence find occurred at the airfields around Foggia, Italy, a staging area for the bombers of KG 100 from 17 September to 23 September 1943. Since early 1943, Foggia had also served, along with locations in France and Norway, as one of a handful of armament stockpiles for the Hs 293 and Fritz-X weapons. As the Allies approached Foggia in September 1943, the German aircraft deployed there were ordered back to the relative safety of Istres. Evidently, though, not all of what was taken into Foggia by III./KG 100 was taken out when the Germans departed, and on 27 September Allied intelligence units exploring Foggia made an important discovery.

What was found at Foggia in September 1943 has been a cause of confusion for many years, at least in the published literature. Some sources have suggested that the Allies discovered a bevy of FuG 203 transmitters, perhaps stockpiled as spares and inadvertently left behind.[7] Other writers have suggested the British Eighth Army recovered "fully intact and crated" examples of the Hs 293 or Fritz-X glide bombs.[8] This seems highly unlikely, given the timing and sequencing of Allied intelligence operations, since there was still frenetic activity directed toward obtaining an intact Hs 293 or Fritz-X well into 1944.[9] Moreover, the intelligence assessment by the RAE of all available Hs 293 components on 9 December 1943, ten weeks after the seizure of Foggia and reflecting all sources of information through late November, made it clear that "reconstruction of the German Weapon Hs 293 has been carried out at R.A.E. with the help of fragments obtained from seven attacks, and of photographs taken in flight from an attacked ship. The material available allows a confident reconstruction of the main features of the airframe and a detailed picture of the propulsive unit. Virtually none of the radio control gear which is subjected to a secondary destructive charge, or the bomb section has been recovered."[10]

We know what was found at Foggia from contemporary Allied intelligence reports.[11] What the Capture Intelligence Team of the Headquarters Section of the Northwest African Air Force discovered at Foggia were the remains of nine KG 100 aircraft, left behind as the Germans evacuated, as well as "fragments" of exploded glide bombs.[12] These aircraft were almost certainly victims of concentrated air attacks by heavy bombers at Foggia on 19 August, 25 August, and, most critically, 19 September. This last raid was particularly devastating and is yet another indication of how Allied intelligence thwarted glide-bomb threats through offensive operations. Aileen Clayton was an officer with the RAF Y-Service and later explained what had happened:

> Four days later [on 18 September], Y was to be incidental in a highly successful operation. The Wing had intercepted messages during the late afternoon which indicated that, owing to bad weather, a great many aircraft were grounded on the Foggias. . . . Immediately *Ancon* [a ship housing a Y-Service unit] command sent a signal to the North Africa strategic Air Force in Tunisia giving them details of the number of Ju.52s, Do.217s, Ju.88s and fighter bombers on Foggia and satellite airfields. A request was made for their immediate destruction. As a result of this a force of ninety-one [P-38] Lightnings [fighter-bombers] was dispatched to reach Foggia by first light, and this was backed up by eight heavy bombers of the R.A.F. The resultant destruction of forty-five enemy aircraft with a further seventeen seriously damaged curtailed considerably the Luftwaffe's efforts over the battle area during what was one of the most critical periods of the Salerno operations.[13]

Some of the aircraft damaged in this or earlier raids belonged to KG 100. Their fractured and burned remains were left behind as the Luftwaffe evacuated Foggia just before the airfield was seized by Allied forces. The RAE intelligence report goes on to describe how the Germans attempted to sabotage the wreckage before leaving: "All of the aircraft examined had been partially destroyed by the enemy before they were abandoned, and in most cases particular attention had been paid to the destruction of this 'Secret Weapon.' The following details are therefore based on an aggregation of evidence from all Do 217 K aircraft examined."

Despite the efforts at sabotage, the find was an intelligence bonanza for the Allies. Pieces of the aircraft and transmitters were dispatched by aircraft to Farnborough for detailed examination. Fragments of multiple demolished Fritz-X bombs, including components of the receiver, also were recovered at

Foggia and Palermo. Within weeks it proved possible to run the recovered components through extensive testing in order "to establish the frequency" at which they operated, confirmed at 47.5 MHz to 50 MHz.[14] Sufficient fragments of Fritz-X bombs were recovered that it was "possible to reconstruct the control mechanism directing the bomb's flight." Analysis of the Do 217 aircraft left behind also revealed that while power output of the Kehl transmitter was forty-five watts, the radiated power after antenna loss was only about thirty watts.[15]

The second major intelligence find involved the special recording systems on board U.S. Navy's destroyer-escorts *Herbert C. Jones* and *Frederick C. Davis* commanded by Lieutenant Commander "Skeeta" Gardes and Lieutenant Commander O. William Goepner. The attacks on 6 November and 26 November (the latter being the raid where *Rohna* was sunk) provided accurate recordings of Kehl transmitter signals, using the innovative recording apparatus developed by Howard Lorenzen at NRL. On 7 November 1943 the Allied Commander in Chief Mediterranean broadcast the news to the relevant Allied commands that the mystery of the glide-bomb frequencies had finally been solved, adding that the initial jamming efforts had (not surprisingly) failed: "Following received from C.T.G. 80.2 begins. 3 Gliders Control Frequency established 49–50 mc/s. during attack. Spacing 200 kc/s 49.1, 49.3 49.5 mc/s. Amplitude modulated about 800 CPS [cycles per second] tone continuously keyed about 5 CPS. Amplified report upon arrival at port. Result jamming not definitely established."[16]

The data obtained from captured bomb fragments and radio intercepts were supplemented by information gleaned from interviews with captured Luftwaffe pilots. By late September a substantial number had been captured following raids on various convoys at Salerno; slowly, these interrogations revealed secrets regarding both the Fritz-X and the Hs 293 beyond those discernable from physical examination of wreckage. An Allied intelligence report prepared on 14 November by Major Gordon Davis of the RAF laid out many of the critical elements of the glide bombs themselves as well as of their operational deployment.[17] The range of the weapons was understood, the method of control was known, and the limitations of the system were well understood. The report also suggested eight potential means to counteract the weapons, number seven of which was jamming:

> This is a likely field of study and experiment. The latest information is that a frequency of 50 megacycles [MHz] is used for radio control of the glider. A careful listening watch should therefore be kept on this band when there is any indication of an attack developing. It is not known what value of modulation is used for the control. It may be supersonic in which case

only the carrier will be heard. It is probable that more than one frequency will be used to enable several gliders to be controlled simultaneously. If any suspicious transmission is heard, the frequency should be measured, and all available transmitters in all ships in the vicinity should be used for jamming MOW, IOW or R/T if suitable apparatus is available. On R/T as much noise as possible should be transmitted, either by violent agitation of the microphone or by attaching an electric razor to the microphone. If receivers are available, searching should be made around 50 megacycles, while the 20 meg. Band is a possibility. The frequency and a description of any suspicious transmissions should be reported by signal to the Admiralty. If controlling aircraft is shot down, every endeavour should be made to recover the transmitter.[18]

Via the intelligence finds at Foggia, combined with operations at sea by *Frederick C. Davis* and *Herbert C. Jones*, an important unknown—the precise frequencies to target for jamming—had finally become known.

Development of Second-Generation NRL Jammers: XCJ-1 and XCJ-2

Early in December a second generation of U.S. jamming equipment was developed exploiting this new intelligence. The NRL in Washington executed another crash program to prepare six such jamming systems, with improved broadband receivers now able to pick out the precise frequencies in use and then pass that information on to the operator of the jamming transmitter.[19] Several such units were rushed to Africa to be put on board *Herbert C. Jones, Frederick C. Davis,* and *Woolsey* (DD-437), the first wave of ships to operate this equipment off Anzio.[20] Meanwhile, two other destroyers—*Madison* (DD-425) and *Hilary P. Jones* (DD-427)—were outfitted in Norfolk with the new gear and then sailed to meet the rest of the invasion force preparing for the Anzio mission, arriving after the initial assault. *Lansdale* (DD-426), accompanying *Madison* and *Hilary P. Jones* in the second wave of jamming ships at Anzio, appears to have been the final ship so equipped, though it is uncertain whether this happened in Norfolk or on arrival in theater.[21]

✦ ✦ ✦

Each of these updated installations consisted of six major modules.[22] A receiver, designated the RAO, was a modified National NC-120 unit, specially upgraded to be very quiet, with minimal electromagnetic emissions. The Allies were evidently concerned that the radio-frequency amplifiers in the NC-120 might betray the presence of the ship to Luftwaffe direction finders, so the RAO was shielded carefully.[23] The responsibility of the

RAO unit was to alert operators to the potential presence of enemy aircraft—a sort of tripwire—as well as to gather intelligence on enemy tactics and capabilities. A second receiver unit called an RBK, most likely a modified Hallicrafters S-36, scanned the airwaves from 27.8 MHz to 143 MHz, looking for signals that indicated the actual use of the Kehl transmitter and identifying to the operator the approximate frequencies in use. These receivers were supported by two panoramic adapters—devices that when tuned to the approximate frequency indicated the precise frequencies to be jammed—denoted as RBW and RXX. The business end of the suite was an upgraded XCJ-1 transmitter (also known in its production variant as TX) that, once tuned properly, could emit a powerful five-hundred–watt signal on the same frequency used by the Kehl transmitter, hopefully overloading the Strassburg receiver embedded within an Hs 293 or Fritz-X. The final system components were the antennae, a pair of which was mounted on either side of the ship to provide equal coverage to port or starboard.

Installation was rushed in order to have at least some units available for Anzio. Destroyers such as *Lansdale* had not been designed to accommodate this new equipment and had no designated spaces available for it. Consequently, the executive officer was moved out of his quarters and that space taken over by the electronic equipment. In the case of *Lansdale*, that executive officer was none other than Robert M. Morgenthau, the future district attorney for New York County, who would serve for thirty years in that role.

While considerably advanced over the first-generation systems, this second-generation system shared a common weakness with its predecessor: each jammer could only be tuned manually via several steps to one of the eighteen specific frequencies in use by the Kehl-Strassburg system. With three ships defending the invasion force at any given time, only three missiles could be jammed simultaneously. Therefore, in the case of a massed attack the operators of the jamming systems could be overwhelmed. It is conceivable, also, that multiple ships with jamming gear could select the same frequency, allowing other guidance signals to move unimpeded from aircraft to weapon. The XCJ-1 system was appropriately considered as only part of a layered defense, starting with friendly air cover, continuing with ship self-defense weapons, and culminating in the point-defense capability represented by the upgraded jammers.

British Type 650 Jammer

While the United States was upgrading its jammers to allow an operator to target a precise frequency between 48 MHz and 50 MHz, the British were working on their own designs. This effort was overseen by Norman E. Davis, senior engineer in the field of radio countermeasures with the Admiralty Signal Establishment (ASE). Davis, a pioneer in the development of television while with the Marconi Company, was seconded as a civilian employee to the ASE in November 1940 to work on techniques to jam German radar systems being used to aim coastal gun batteries. When the threat of the glide bombs emerged in 1943 his organization was directed to develop an electronic countermeasure for the new German weapons.

✦ ✦ ✦

The British scientists and engineers, in a project led by Laboratory Assistant David Denys Silvester, took an entirely different approach from that employed by the Americans in Washington. Engineers at the ASE, under the direction of the twenty-one-year-old Silvester, concluded that the operational approach embedded in the U.S. solution was prone to failure. They were afraid it would take too long for an inexperienced operator to manually tune the receiver across the range of frequencies in the hope of identifying which precise position of the tuning dial caused the signal indicator to jump, read from the analog display the relevant frequency, and then turn the dial of the transmitting to the same frequency—all while under attack. Given that the jamming would work best once the missile had passed the escort ship and was inbound to its target (given the directional nature of the Hs 293 antenna), there might only be ten or twenty seconds for this entire process to take place. A Most Secret memo from late 1943 explained the problem: "[The first possible method of jamming is] by using a monitoring receiver to bring the transmitter on to the frequency in use. This is the most efficient means of jamming when the power of the jamming transmitter is small, but not only is the Army 36 [wireless unit] unsuitable for use in a monitored system, but the high degree of skill required to achieve effective jamming on a number of controlled frequencies separated by a very small amount, rules out this method."[24]

Moreover, there was no guarantee that in a mass attack, when perhaps as many as eighteen missiles could be in the air, a single operator could keep up. If there were multiple operators in multiple ships jamming at the same time there was no guarantee that the operators would appropriately share the load across the entire threat, as opposed to all jamming one frequency while leaving others uncontested.

As a result, the British focused on systems and procedures that would jam across the entire frequency range and that could be employed during an attack by Hs 293 missiles or Fritz-X glide bombs. Several such barrage-jamming options were considered. One scenario was to equip various ships with equipment operating at different frequencies and have them combine forces to cover the full spectrum. As the director of Signals Department reported in a (formerly) Secret memo on 9 October 1943,

> It is considered that insufficient time will be available to enable individual ships to receive the transmitted signal, measure its frequency, and set their transmitters accordingly to jam. It is therefore recommended that the W/T organisation should be arranged so that the transmitters on all ships in company are adjusted to varying frequencies within the band according to their particular capabilities of frequency coverage, and that immediately an attack develops, all ships should transmit on full power regardless of whether they, themselves, are attacked or not.[25]

Another approach would be to employ a motor-driven tuning mechanism to allow a single jammer to sweep across the frequency range, covering the entire relevant portion of the spectrum. However, this approach was impractical in late 1943 or the first part of 1944 due to the absence of such tuning mechanisms: "It would of course be most advantageous if transmitters could be made to sweep automatically over a frequency band, by means of a motor driven condenser, or other device. No set in its present form is responsive to such treatment, and the introduction of such a measure would involve considerable development work and no early production of suitable equipment in quantity can be envisaged."[26]

In the absence of such advanced equipment, the British scientists were forced to apply off-the-shelf systems in an effort to achieve effective barrage jamming. Analysis of fragments of recovered Hs 293 weapons led British scientists, under the direction of Silvester, to a far more elegant solution. It turns out that a system broadcasting just two signals, one at 47 MHz and another at 50 MHz, would create a third signal that jammed not the primary receiver, tuned to one of the specific eighteen control frequencies, but rather that jammed the intermediate frequency mixer that operated at 3 MHz downstream of the primary receiver.[27] (The Americans had also considered this approach but had ruled it out due to lack of confidence in the intelligence data that indicated the Strassburg 3 kHz intermediate frequency was in fact at 3 MHz.)

> The third method of jamming, on which the present policy of fitting Type 650 sets is proceeding, is based upon the knowledge that the intermediate

frequency mixer circuit of the bomb receiver is tuned to 3 Mc/s. [MHz] and accepts signals over a band of 80 Kc/s [kHz]. Two transmitters are employed, each working into a separate aerial. One transmitter is tuned to 47 Mc/s. and the other to 50 Mc/s. These two frequencies are separately radiated and will be accepted without loss by the aerial and first amplifier stage of the bomb receiver and pass[ed] on to the grid circuit of the mixer stage. By cross modulation the two carriers will give a resultant signal of 3 Mc/s. in the anode circuit of the mixer valve [vacuum tube] and so pass this to the intermediate frequency amplifier. By this method of operation, a jamming signal is made to enter the receiver irrespective of what radio frequency is used for the control in the 47 to 50 Mc/s. band and by this means maximum protection, with the minimum number of transmitters, is achieved, coupled with the simplicity of operation.[28]

The RAE had been busy at work developing this system, referred to as the Type 650, since November 1943.[29] The program was built around two hundred ex-Army No. 36 wireless sets and R208 receivers, originally developed in 1941 as a portable system used to connect various air-defense sites and released by the British Army for this vital mission. Trials were undertaken on board *Woodpecker* in December 1943 and were seen as successful.[30] The other ninety-nine pairs of transmitters were installed on board an array of ships in the Royal Navy, in a program led by Lieutenant John C. G. Field, a twenty-three-year-old lieutenant of the Royal Navy Volunteer Reserve, and the ASE lead officer for radar countermeasures at Anzio.[31] First to be equipped were the command ships used in the invasion fleet—the air-defense fighter-director ships and the escort carriers. Within months, fifty ships in the Mediterranean and another fifty in the Home Fleet were scheduled to be equipped.[32]

It is not clear how many Type 650 systems were actually deployed in time for the Anzio invasion. On 3 January 1944 it was reported that three complete systems were to be dispatched the following day by air from England to Gibraltar.[33] A later message on 20 January 1944—just two days before the Anzio invasion—reported, "a number of equipments Type 650 are being sent to the Mediterranean for allocation by C. in C. Mediterranean," and further suggested that the only ship equipped to date was *Woodpecker*, then operating in the Atlantic.[34] It does not appear from available records that the Type 650 made it to the fleet in time to make a difference at Anzio.

Interim British Countermeasures:
"Jostle" and Lieutenant Field's System

It took awhile for the Type 650 jammers developed by the Royal Navy to make their way to the fleet, leaving British ships at Anzio relatively undefended, at least by electronic means. To fill the gap, two interim jamming approaches were employed by the British, though neither appears to have been particularly successful.

✦ ✦ ✦

There is little known about the first interim jammer, though it appears this was an early variant of a barrage jammer, one that would attack all frequencies within a narrow frequency band at the same time. In this way the operator did not have to intercept, decipher, and then manually tune the correct frequency. For this purpose in early 1944 six "Jostle" airborne jammers, designed to disrupt Wehrmacht and Luftwaffe communications, were adapted for shipboard use. The Jostle system, developed in great secrecy, transmitted five hundred watts of energy simultaneously across multiple frequency bands ranging from 20 MHz to 80 MHz. By the standards of the day, it was an electronic warfare "beast," filling the entire bomb bay of a large aircraft such as the B-17. It remains uncertain how many were developed and whether they were actually deployed in the fleet. Available records point only to six such systems prepared in mid-January for delivery to the Royal Navy.[35]

A second early effort by the British was undertaken by Lieutenant Field himself. While waiting for Type 650 units to arrive in theater he attempted to improvise an interim solution using the hardware at hand. As Field's colleague, Frederick A. Kingsley, explained years after the war,

> Lt. Field was able to intercept about a dozen radio-control signals in the 6-metre waveband during the attacks [at Anzio]. Field deduced that the Hs 293 guidance system was based on a variable mark-space ratio, two-tone modulation system, for asimuth and elevation steering respectively. Armed with the information, he set up a workshop in Naples to design and manufacture a simple 150-watt tunable spot-frequency jammer. The transmitter used parts obtained mainly from R.A.F. V.H.F. transmitter spares. He fitted some 12 of these systems in Ships of the Mediterranean Fleet, but the difficulty of rapid turning of the transmitters after detection of the missile control signal remained.[36]

However, as before, the challenge was in allowing for sufficiently rapid transfer of information from the radio receivers—which identified the specific frequency in use for any particular missile—to the jamming system, which had to be tuned for that specific frequency to be useful. In the end, Field's interim solution was seen as inadequate to the challenge.

Summary

In all probability, then, the initial jamming burden at Anzio fell to only three U.S. ships: destroyer *Woolsey*, and destroyer-escorts *Frederick C. Davis* and *Herbert C. Jones*. As time went on, and these ships were rotated off the line, they would be replaced by destroyers *Madison*, *Hilary P. Jones*, and *Lansdale*. The three ships on station at any one time would have to stand against the full power of the Luftwaffe, which for the first time would combine the forces of KG 100 and KG 40.

CHAPTER NINE

STALEMATE *at* ANZIO *and* ON THE CONVOY ROUTES

While the Luftwaffe was repairing its battle-damaged aircraft and aircrews, the Allies were hard at work preparing for the next confrontation in the Mediterranean with the persistent Wehrmacht. Ironically, it was Allied weakness and Wehrmacht strength that drove this decision: the next action was born from frustration over the stalemate that had emerged following the landings at Salerno in September. German resistance, abetted by terrain more suited to defense than attack, had caused the U.S. and British armies in southern Italy to bog down. Rome, an important original target of the Salerno landings, seemed ever more out of reach behind the German Gustav defensive line.

✦ ✦ ✦

Winston Churchill, always a fan of attacking soft underbellies, advocated an amphibious end run around the Gustav Line. By landing Allied divisions around the beaches of Anzio and Nettuno and proceeding inland to the dominant terrain of the Alban Hills, the German line at Salerno would be outflanked and the Wehrmacht forced to withdraw. Yet another effort to break through the Gustav Line would be launched simultaneously in an effort to draw German resources south from Rome, making the Allied trap even more effective. At least that was the theory.

In contrast with the abundance of naval power that accompanied other Allied operations, the invasion force at Anzio was done on the cheap, compromised by the need to divert most of the landing ships and escort vessels to the upcoming invasion of western France at Normandy and the follow-on assault in southern France. The Allies would have to accomplish the landing at Anzio with only minimal naval support, comprising just five light cruisers and twenty-four destroyers.

The air-defense capability over the landing site was also going to be modest. As reported by General Henry Maitland "Jumbo" Wilson, Supreme Allied Commander of the Mediterranean Theater (and architect of the ill-fated Dodecanese campaign described in Chapter 6), "The enemy air menace was not considered to be great; the long range bomber force of Luftflotte II had been withdrawn from Italy and plans to blast enemy airfields prior to D-day should reduce his available force considerably. To economise in shipping space, it was planned to put only one Spitfire squadron ashore on the beachhead. The greater part of the air support was to be provided by aircraft based in the Naples area."[1]

Preparations for Battle at Anzio

In mid-January, a flotilla of transports and escorts weighed anchor and departed from harbors in southern Italy and across the western Mediterranean. The slow transports, heavily laden with soldiers and equipment, moved in a steady close formation surrounded by prancing destroyers, sloops, and frigates, one of which was Lieutenant Commander Roger Hill's *Grenville*, both of them recently recalled from the Adriatic. Nearby the heaviest warships of the naval contingent, the American and British light cruisers, prepared to stand offshore and bombard enemy positions with their 6-inch guns. (Such cruisers would fire shells weighing between 51 and 68 kilograms. By contrast, the 15-inch guns used in support of ground forces at Salerno could fire shells weighing 871 kilograms.)

✦ ✦ ✦

The Allied invasion force began to arrive off Anzio and Nettuno at about 0200 hours on 22 January 1944; within hours five cruisers, two dozen destroyers, four hospital ships, nine transports, and about 226 landing craft were off the beaches. The day emerged clear and sunny, with warm temperatures for that time of year. The friendly environment provided by Mother Nature was matched by the almost complete absence of German resistance that first day. Within the first twenty-four hours, 36,000 troops had been landed, with only thirteen Allied troops killed. However, in a decision that remains hotly debated to this day, rather than move inland quickly the Allied commander, American Major General John P. Lucas, decided to reinforce his beachhead, believing it to be insecure from the expected German counteroffensive. No doubt he was heavily influenced by the recent experience at Salerno, when German counterattacks nearly threw Allied forces back into the sea.

Exploiting this delay, the Germans began pouring troops into the area. By 24 January Lucas's invasion force was more than matched by a greater number of German defenders, dug into strong defensive positions. As Allied forces continued to land, reaching 70,000 by month's end, German forces also expanded, more than matching the Allied expansion. Instead of the rapid outflanking maneuver anticipated by Churchill, Anzio evolved into another slow slugging match between Allied invasion troops and well-dug-in German defenders.

Luftwaffe Order of Battle for Anzio Glide-Bomb Missions

At the time of the Anzio landing, the special bomber units trained to attack ships with the Hs 293 and Fritz-X were widely dispersed across France and Germany. Two of the three squadrons of II./KG 100—5./KG 100 and 6./KG 100—were recovering at Toulouse-Blagnac, where they had relocated after abandoning Istres in early November 1943. The depleted aircrews of these two squadrons were supplemented by transfers from IV./KG 100 who were already familiar with the Do 217 aircraft and who therefore only needed to be trained on the Hs 293. *Gruppe* II./KG 100 as a whole remained under the command of *Hauptmann* Heinz-Emil Middermann. Squadron 5./KG 100 was led by *Hauptmann* Wolfgang Vorpahl, whose aircraft launched the Hs 293 that struck *Athabaskan;* his colleague *Hauptmann* Willi Scholl commanded 6./KG 100.

✦ ✦ ✦

The third squadron in II./KG 100, 4./KG 100, did not participate in the upcoming attacks at Anzio. It had relocated its eleven surviving Do 217 E-5 aircraft to Leck in northern Germany to begin transition training to the new He 177 aircraft.[2] Therefore the force available to II./KG 100 at Anzio was only two-thirds the size of that deployed at Salerno.

Toulouse-Blagnac was about 950 kilometers (515 nautical miles) from the invasion site and was thus at the outer limits of the range of II./KG 100's Do 217 E-5 bombers, now numbering forty-five. A safety margin was built in by having the aircraft stage out of Bergamo airfield in northern Italy, shuffling between Toulouse-Blagnac and Bergamo by day and between Bergamo and the Allied fleet after sunset. On these missions the aircraft would carry one Hs 293 under one wing and an additional discardable fuel tank under the other.

Gruppe III./KG 100 missed out entirely on the opening salvos of the Luftwaffe counteroffensive against Anzio and only became available for deployment there in February 1944. Two of III./KG 100's squadrons, 7./KG 100 and 8./KG 100, had been based in the north of Germany of Eggebek, just south of the Danish border, in preparation for the never-executed raid on the British Home Fleet's base at Scapa Flow, and subsequent missions against targets in Russia. The time in Eggebek had not come cheap: eleven of the unique aircraft, along with vital aircrews, had been lost in training missions or accidents. Three weeks after the Anzio landing these two squadrons of III./KG 100 were relocated to an airbase at Toulouse-Francazal, landing their thirty-five remaining Do 217 K-2 and Do 217 K-3 bombers there on 13 February. Without enough of these Fritz-X carriers to go around the remaining aircrew of III./KG 100, those of 8./KG 100, remained at Fassberg near Hamburg, to begin transition training for the He 177. However, because it turned out that the Allies deployed light warships not suitable for attack by the battleship-busting Fritz-X, the aircraft of III./KG 100 never participated in missions at Anzio. In aggregate, then, only two of the six squadrons of KG 100 were available to repulse the Allies at Anzio.

Conversely, though, the He 177 long-range bombers of II./KG 40, still based at Bordeaux-Mérignac, were also within range of the Anzio battlefield, some 1,150 kilometers (620 nautical miles) distant. Each of these four-engine aircraft would be able to carry two Hs 293 missiles on these attacks, offsetting (at least on paper) the shortfalls of KG 100. However, after the disastrous missions of November and December 1943, in which twenty-five He 177 aircraft had been lost, II./KG 40 could muster only twenty-four aircraft, enough for only two effective squadrons.

For the first time the depleted squadrons of II./KG 100 and II./KG 40 would be employed against the same Allied invasion force—but they would not operate alone. These two glide-bomb units would be accompanied by four others dropping conventional ordnance.[3] Fighters would be mustered to provide some level of protection, also. As before, the Luftwaffe would engage in mass raids of aircraft, with torpedo bombers flying in low above the water, dive-bombers screaming down from above, and, in the distance, the Do 217 and He 177 aircraft standing off with crews attempting to steer Hs 293 missiles onto their targets.

If the Anzio battle itself was born of the frustration of Allied commanders over the slow progress in Italy, any historian attempting to reconstruct what happened in the seas off the Anzio beach will share that frustration.

Challenges include the presence of both II./KG 100 and II./KG 40; the simultaneous use of glide bombs, conventional bombs, and air-launched torpedoes; and the general mistakes that creep into accounts made at a time of confusion, danger, and distraction. Some accounts track events in local time; others are in Greenwich Mean Time. All these make it next to impossible to precisely and confidently articulate known facts of this aerial-naval battle. Witness accounts made long after the war often conflict with official reports produced immediately after the actions. Attacks made at dusk and at night, as was the case for many attacks at Anzio, are inevitably more difficult to illuminate than those made in bright sunshine. The contemporary casual use of the term "aerial torpedo" as shorthand for an Hs 293 glide bomb helps produce confusion, because that term is properly associated with an air-launched conventional torpedo. Luftwaffe records of the battle, especially those of II./KG 40, are very limited and the participation of that *gruppe* needs to be reconstructed from bits of evidence here and there. Finally, it still is argued that the Allies intentionally understated the damage from glide bombs, attributing their success to torpedoes or mines, in an effort to buttress lagging morale. In short, we might never know precisely what happened in the first week after troops landed at Anzio and Nettuno in January 1944.

The First Terrible Week

The Allies had one day largely immune from air attacks as they executed their surprise invasion at Anzio because it took a while for Göring's forces to organize against this new threat. By the next day II./KG 100 and II./KG 40, along with other units of the Luftwaffe, were able to mount a serious challenge to the swarm of ships discharging troops and cargo onto the Italian coast and the warships providing fire support to those already engaged in combat. The Allies were certainly prepared for the attack. The destroyers and light cruisers readied their 6-inch and 5-inch guns to take on any distant circling aircraft. Closer in, masses of 20-mm and 40-mm rapid-fire guns would attempt to shoot down approaching glide bombs, torpedo bombers, or dive-bombers. Around the convoy, the specialized ships equipped with NRL's RAO and RBK receiving sets monitored the airwaves for the telltale signals that indicated an impending glide-bomb attack. These ships also prepared to apply the new XCJ-1 jammers, for the first time tuned to the right frequencies, albeit only one at a time. On D-day at Anzio this flotilla of jamming ships consisted of *Woolsey* along with our old friends *Frederick C. Davis* and *Herbert C. Jones*.

✦ ✦ ✦

It would turn out that the most effective defense of shipping at Anzio was employed in the air as opposed to at sea. Marauding bands of British and American night fighters, in many cases guided by sophisticated aerial radar sets, pounced on Luftwaffe squadrons as they made their way to and from the battlefield. In many cases they shot down approaching bombers before they reached the Allied invasion fleet, depleting the attacking Luftwaffe units of up to half their strength before they could even engage. The night fighters, mainly Beaufighters and Spitfires, pounced again on the bombers as they returned from battle against the fleets off Anzio, decimating the forces available for any subsequent attacks. Meanwhile, once the points of departure of the German raiders could be pinpointed, legions of Allied bombers launched to drop tons of ordnance on the airfields, hoping to destroy the specialized aircraft on the ground, kill the highly trained personnel, and disrupt airfield operations.

The Luftwaffe, fully appreciative of the aerial threat, chose dusk for most of its operations over Anzio. In this way the vulnerable bombers could escape some of the Allied fighter cover while the ships at sea would still be silhouetted against the setting sun. All three missions at Anzio flown by II/KG 40 were at dusk. Of the twelve missions executed by II./KG 100, eight were at dusk, three at night, and one during late afternoon.[4] The night missions were supported by aircraft dropping powerful flares, designed to illuminate targets while hiding the aggressors. The other Luftwaffe squadrons—torpedo planes and dive-bombers—employed a similar strategy.

Glide bombs initially appeared over the battlefield about 1645 hours on 23 January as the Do 217 E-5 bombers of II./KG 100 arrived at the scene for the first time. Seven aircraft had taken off from Bergamo in Northern Italy, the convenient staging point between the Anzio beaches and the home base at Toulouse-Blagnac. Each carried one Hs 293. One aircraft crashed near Anzio, and it is not known whether this bomber was able to launch its missiles.[5] Those bombers that reached Anzio fired their Hs 293 into the silhouetted ships. A number of missiles targeted two British destroyers of the 14th Flotilla, *Jervis* and *Janus*, then engaged in a duel with Luftwaffe torpedo bombers.[6]

In the case of *Janus*, it remains unclear what happened next. The official action report from *Janus* describes an attack in which both *Janus* and *Jervis* were dodging torpedoes launched from He 111 aircraft when an explosion ripped open *Janus* between the bow and foc'sle, leading to a huge fire and secondary explosions. Historian Barbara Tomblin, who has written a detailed account of the battles off Anzio, concludes the culprit was a torpedo.[7] Other accounts disagree, suggesting a glide bomb was to blame. A near-contemporary report of the Anzio campaign, written in 1946 by General Henry Maitland Wilson, the Supreme Allied Commander in the Mediterranean, states quite clearly, "[D]uring an air raid at dusk, glider bombs sank *Janus*."[8] Author G. G. Connell, who served with the 14th Flotilla in the Mediterranean, wrote a book about *Jervis* in 1987 and compiled an account of the various actions, many of which included *Janus*, from primary sources and interviews with participants. He also concludes, based on accounts from participants in the battle, *Janus* "had been struck by radio controlled glider bombs, launched and guided by parent Do 217 aircraft."[9]

Recollections by participants in the battle, recorded decades after the event and therefore best handled with caution, also suggest a glide bomb was to blame. Ron Douglas, a sailor on board *Spartan* at the time, recalls what he saw during the battle, confusingly using the term "aerial torpedo" to describe a glide bomb:

> The *Janus* and the *Jervis* had been giving fire support for two days, but in the meantime approximately 30 or 40 Luftwaffe aircraft came over the area. They would circle the area at a very high altitude and let go their bombs. These bombs were made with maneuverable flight surfaces so that a crewmember in one of the bombers could control the bomb and direct it to its target. Hence the reason for the two [*sic*; there were actually three] American jamming ships to try to jam the radio signals that were used to guide the bombs. Unfortunately, some got through and the *Janus* was hit on the bridge and foc'sle by an arial [*sic*] torpedo. She broke in two and capsized with the loss of 100 or more officers and men.[10]

On balance, given the circumstances of the loss, contemporary accounts, and the fact that we know Do 217 aircraft were attacking with glide bombs at the very moment *Janus* was hit, a strike with an Hs 293 is a very reasonable scenario, perhaps even likely.

In contrast to the uncertainty surrounding *Janus*, the accounts of the attack on *Jervis*, one of the most celebrated ships of the Royal Navy in World War II, are quite clear. At 1750 hours, just after the crew witnessed the destruction of the *Janus*, a loud swishing sound was heard and observers watched an Hs 293 plow into *Jervis*'s forward hull. The resulting explosion tore off the entire bow of the ship all of the way back to the ninth bulkhead. It was a somewhat lucky hit for the British, in that the ship maintained its watertight integrity and suffered no casualties.[11]

After losing only one aircraft, III./KG 100 withdrew from the raid.[12] Seven longer-range He 177 A-3 bombers of II./KG 40 also participated in the battle that evening, though without achieving any hits.[13] Moreover, two of the precious heavy bombers were shot down by Beaufighters even before they could reach Anzio in an attack that scattered the rest of the squadrons, making a coordinated strike more difficult.[14]

Meanwhile, *Jervis* was made seaworthy and then prepared to sail back to Gibraltar for an extensive repair. The skipper of *Jervis*, Captain Harold Pitcairn Henderson, also served as flotilla leader and therefore required an appropriately intact and equipped ship for that purpose. He summoned Lieutenant Commander Roger Hill of *Grenville*, who had witnessed the destruction of *Egret* in the Bay of Biscay in August 1943, and informed him that a switch of ships was to be made. In this way Hill, who had managed to dodge glide bombs in both the Atlantic and Mediterranean and who had returned critical intelligence from the first glide-bomb attacks, was reduced to skipper of a destroyer whose bow had been blown off by a glide bomb.[15]

The sudden loss of *Jervis* and *Janus* created near panic across elements of the naval force off Anzio, bringing to memory the similar losses at Salerno. The commander of the 15th Cruiser Squadron, Rear Admiral J. M. Mansfield, ordered a withdrawal of cruisers *Orion, Penelope,* and *Spartan* to Naples, concluding that the aerial threat was too overwhelming. The order was partially countermanded by Rear Admiral Frank J. Lowry, overall commander of the naval assault force at Anzio-Nettuno.[16]

Those hoping that the losses of 23 January were an aberration would be sorely disappointed on the following evening, as both II./KG 100 and II./KG 40 returned to do battle as the sun set. U.S. destroyer *Plunkett* was a primary target of the Luftwaffe that night in a coordinated attack that combined glide bombs with conventional ordnance. At 1738 hours the air-raid alert was sounded, and shortly thereafter two glide bombs were sighted coming toward the ship off the port beam, just as two Ju 88 bombers were seen directly ahead. *Plunkett* was thrown about by its skipper, Commander E. J. Burke, in radical high-speed maneuvers; the ship managed to avoid the two glide bombs, which exploded in a roar about two hundred yards away. However, by then aircraft armed with conventional bombs had joined the battle; at 1757 hours horrified crewmembers watched as a 250-kilogram conventional bomb hit directly on the 1.1-inch gun mount, between the aft funnel and the aft 5-inch guns, creating a massive fire that almost destroyed the ship. *Plunkett* survived the attack, limped to Palermo on one engine for emergency repairs, and eventually made it back to New York for further repair and upgrading.

Shortly after *Plunkett* was hit, at about 1804 hours, an alarm rang in the form of an SOS from a group of hospital ships moored some twenty-five miles off the beach. *St. Andrew*, *St. David*, and *Leinster*, plainly marked and illuminated as hospital ships, were under attack by a combined formation of dive-bombers and II./KG 100's Do 217s equipped with glide bombs. One Hs 293 ripped into *St. David*, turning the converted passenger ferry into an inferno. By the time help arrived within an hour, the ship had sunk, taking about 100 of the crew and patients down with it, though an aggressive rescue operation saved about 130 others.

As with most of these events, it remains difficult even sixty years afterwards to reconstruct what happened next to *Mayo* (DD-422). What is known is that just after 2000 hours a large explosion tore open the hull of this destroyer, killing seven crewmembers and wounding two dozen others. Some, including the captain, Commander Albert D. Kaplan, in the official report, have reported that the culprit was a mine or "circling torpedo."[17] A contemporary shipboard account, however, provides important clues:

> In the gathering dusk the air attacks increased; there were several near misses, and we knew we were coming in for another night. We needed something to keep us awake it was not long in coming, for at one minute past eight PM, *as we were stopped*, quietly waiting for *the last air raid to subside*, there was a large explosion in the midship section of the ship and we knew that our luck had run out. . . . For thirty seconds no one breathed; the ship took a deep lurch to port and straightened up again; shortly thereafter it became apparent she would not sink immediately, as was the case with so many destroyers. . . . It soon became apparent that the after engine room and fireroom were completely out of commission, and that neither shaft would turn the propellers; this was extremely unfortunate as *we were drifting out of the swept area into mined waters*. (emphasis added)[18]

This account suggests that the attack took place during an air raid. It is known that the attack coincided with a strike by II./KG 100 with Hs 293 glide bombs, in which the Luftwaffe pilots claimed hits on several destroyers. Moreover, *Mayo* was stationary at the time, and, in addition, was in an area that had been swept for mines, which is not consistent with a mine strike. Conversely, the crew did not report inbound glide bombs in the ship attack report, and the damage to the hull is consistent with an inward explosion at the waterline (as from a mine) as opposed to an outward explosion above the waterline (as from an Hs 293 penetrating the hull). Therefore, the evidence remains ambiguous.

One other ship was damaged that night by a near miss: minesweeper *Prevail* (AM-107). As with *Mayo* and *Janus*, the exact cause of the damage remains uncertain. Some sources indicate that it was hit in the same glide-bomb attack that almost caught *Plunkett* and possibly damaged *Mayo*. The official chronology of the U.S. Navy in World War II only indicates the cause of damage was a "horizontal bomber," which could well apply to a Do 217, or for that matter to an He 111 or Ju 88.

The damage to Allied ships that night was matched by losses on the German side. II./KG 100, which had escaped with only one loss on the first night's raid, lost three of the eight aircraft launched on 24 January, with some indications a fourth may also have been lost.[19] II./KG 40, which departed with eleven aircraft and did not strike any targets on this raid, lost another two aircraft on the mission.[20] Across the two nights of 23 and 24 January the two groups lost seven (possibly eight) aircraft of twenty-five deployed, for an unsustainable loss rate of at least 28 percent. In turn, the Allies had one ship lost (HMHS *St. David*) with one other damaged in a confirmed glide-bomb attack (*Jervis*). In addition, glide bombs might have been responsible for one other ship sunk (*Janus*), one other damaged by direct hit (*Mayo*), and one damaged by a near miss (*Prevail*).

The next day, 25 January, turned into a day off as each side licked its wounds. The glide-bomb squadrons of both II./KG 40 and II./KG 100 were back on 26 January, this time shifting targets to the assemblage of merchant ships bringing supplies to the beachfront. II./KG 100 struck at dusk, launching its first Hs 293 glide bombs about 1645 hours. Allied air defense remained intense and the bombers once again had difficulty reaching targets. One glide bomb—or, in many accounts, a German dive bomber—narrowly missed Liberty ship *Hilary A. Herbert*, striking the water on the starboard side only five yards away from the anchored vessel.[21] Seconds later a glide bomb struck near the port side, some ten yards away. The force of explosions lifted the ship from the water and caused a 15-degree list. Hull seams were separated and the engine room began to flood. About 1900 hours Captain Percy Harold Hauffman put his ship on the beach and allowed nonessential personnel to depart.[22] He then calmly continued his unloading operations, an indication of the courage that would earn him the Silver Star, one of the few merchant mariners to be given that honor during World War II. There were no crew lost in the attack and *Hilary A. Herbert* was repaired and returned to service.

While Hauffman was struggling to save his ship, Liberty ship *John Banvard*, then anchored off Anzio and in the process of unloading, came under attack by six Do 217 bombers about 1815 hours. One Hs 293 missile—and possibly two—landed only fifteen yards off the stern with the resulting explosion cracking frames, wrecking cargo gear, and rupturing steam lines. *John Banvard,* under the command of Captain John Lind, survived this hit and managed to limp to Naples under her own power.[23] However, upon returning to the United States the ship was declared a total loss and scrapped.

If the twelve aircraft of II./KG 100 all survived the attacks on the cargo ships off Anzio that day, the 26 January mission later that night proved to be a disaster for II./KG 40, mimicking the heavy losses of the attack on *Rohna* two months before. A small number of these He 177s, probably numbering ten to twelve, departed Toulouse-Blagnac for Anzio. On the way, they were jumped by U.S. Army Air Force fighters based in Corsica. In the mêlée that followed, the U.S. fighters claimed six He 177 aircraft shot down and one other damaged. German accounts of the battle are incomplete, though the losses of three of these aircraft can be confirmed.[24] In any case, the cumulative losses were so severe that II./KG 40 was pulled out of action at heavily defended Anzio and reallocated toward softer targets in the Atlantic and Mediterranean.

II./KG 100 stood down for a few days to recover from this hectic pace, including three missions in four days, and did not reach the skies above Anzio again until 29 January, in what turned out to be the most significant raid of the campaign. On that evening twelve Do 217 E-5 aircraft departed Bergamo field for another dusk mission over the Allied fleet, the fourth of the campaign for II./KG 100. Weather conditions were generally favorable, and the bombers arrived over the warships and transports off Anzio just as the area entered nautical twilight. An eyewitness describes the scene:

> On the eighth night the Nazis made a desperate effort in force. The sky was slightly overcast, with here and there a break in the clouds. It was just that period between dusk and darkness when the alert sounded and the guns all over the harbor opened up. The enemy was using radio controlled glider bombs. They looked like comets, like devilish red fire balls gliding through the sky. They didn't seem to move as fast as everyone knew they actually did; instead they seemed to soar leisurely and deadly seeking their targets.[25]

First to feel the effects was Liberty ship *Samuel Huntington,* loaded with gasoline. An initial attack at 1705 hours caused no damage. Then at 1800 hours, during a second attack, one Hs 293 penetrated the port side of the transport and exploded deep in the engine room, killing four men instantly.[26] Had it struck just about anywhere else on the ship the resulting fireball would have been instantly catastrophic. In any case, the ship began to burn furiously from the explosion of the Hs 293. It would be hit again by a conventional bomb later that night at 2130 hours, capsize, and then explode the following morning when the flames finally reached the gasoline storage area.

Two other transports were almost struck that evening: *Alexander Martin* was targeted but undamaged in a raid at about 1930 hours. *Lawton B. Evans* narrowly survived a glide-bomb attack, with the weapon landing only fifty yards away. Captain Harry Ryan and his crew claimed they shot down both the missile and the aircraft that launched it. While the claim cannot be proven absolutely, 4./KG 100 did lose one aircraft that night.[27]

However, the most crippling attack that night involved *Spartan*, a new light cruiser barely a year in service and widely described as a beautiful ship. *Spartan* was lying at anchor off Anzio, ready to provide fire support and anti–air defense as needed. As the air raid progressed, local commanders ordered that smoke be deployed to hide the fleet. However, as late as 1730 hours smoke still had not fully covered the ships. *Spartan*, in particular, was highly visible due to the intense antiaircraft fire put out by the ship's crew. That visibility proved a beacon for the Luftwaffe—five Hs 293 glide bombs were sent toward her. At 1756 hours one of these was sighted on a direct course for the ship and within seconds exploded through the starboard hull of *Spartan*, destroying parts of the engine room and starting a serious fire. The official report into the loss of *Spartan* describes what happened next:

> As a result of the explosion, "B" Boiler Room and compartments abreast it on the port side (including the main switchboard room) flooded rapidly. The main bulkhead stop valve between "A" Boiler Room and "A" Engine Room was closed (probably by shock) and accordingly all steam and electric power was lost. SPARTAN was thereby immobilized and all lighting, pumping and ventilation failed throughout the ship. The port lower deck space over "B" Boiler Room became filled with smoke and steam, and was inaccessible; the lower deck spaces 83 to 99 and 117 to 135 were also troubled with acrid smoke and steam.[28]

Spartan was in serious trouble. Without power, it was impossible for it to combat the fire or order counterflooding to counteract the list that emerged as the ship took on water. By 1840 hours the list had reached 18 degrees, and by 1900 hours the list had increased to a dangerous 30 degrees and the ship was ordered abandoned. By 1915 hours the ship had settled on its side in six fathoms of water. Some forty-five officers and crew perished in the attack.

The loss of *Spartan* was a serious blow to the Allied forces off Anzio and engendered a strong reaction from them, including attacks on the airfields from which the bombers of II./KG 100 had flown. An air raid by American B-24 heavy bombers at Istres airfield on 27 January would have disrupted II./KG 100 operations had the Group not been moved to Toulouse-Blagnac a few months before. The Allied response to the events of 29 January, which took place on the following day, involved a new twist. As the heavy bombers approached and were detected by German observers, the Luftwaffe knew its best course of action was to flush its aircraft and fly them out of the region. What they did not know is that large formations of U.S. fighter aircraft had moved in at low altitude ahead of the bomber raid, hoping to catch the Germans just as they were departing the airfield for presumed safety. The American fighter pilots claimed they shot down thirty aircraft with a total of sixty-eight Luftwaffe lost in that day's operations, including those destroyed on the ground.[29] While none of these was from II./KG 100, the devastation inflicted at Bergamo ruled out its use as a staging point for several days, and it would be a week before the glide bombs returned to Anzio.

Ongoing Attrition at Anzio

By the first week of February 1944, II./KG 100 was ready to resume missions over Anzio. The first two attempts were nighttime raids on 5 February and then again two days later. It does not appear the aircraft actually engaged any targets on those missions, though two Do 217 E-5 aircraft were shot down on the first of those two attempts.[30] A dusk mission on 12 February also disappointed the Luftwaffe, with hazy weather complicating the approaches and Spitfires disrupting the formation as it passed Florence.[31] Though the Germans claimed hits on a Liberty ship and landing craft, Allied records do not indicate any ships hit or lost that evening.[32]

✦ ✦ ✦

On 13 February the aircraft of III./KG 100, up to that point held back in Eggebek for never-executed raids against Soviet economic targets, relocated in a secret maneuver to the airport of Toulouse-Francazal. Each Do 217 dispatched with two ground crewmembers on board; these crew lacked oxygen masks, which forced the whole flight to operate at a lower altitude than normal. Radio silence was maintained in the hope of avoiding roving patrols of Allied fighters. The aircraft passed over Cologne and Paris and reached Toulouse late in the afternoon. A special train bringing technical crews and vital equipment had already been dispatched, arriving that same day in Toulouse to mate up with the aircraft.[33] *Gruppe* III./KG 100 was now ready to take on the Allies at Anzio with its Fritz-X glide bombs. In the end it was to no avail: the battleships and heavy cruisers most suitable for the Fritz-X never made an appearance off Anzio and III./KG 100 was unengaged in the Anzio combat.[34]

Meanwhile, II./KG 100 continued its dusk mission over Anzio with a successful operation on 15 February, after more than two weeks without scoring any hits. That night about a dozen Do 217 E-5 bombers approached the fleet still in residence off Anzio, making their first strike at about 1808 hours. One Hs 293 plunged through the deck of freighter *Elihu Yale* and exploded in the empty #4 hold, just as the crew was unloading artillery shells into a tank landing craft (*LCT-35*) moored alongside. The resulting explosion on board *Elihu Yale* blew out both sides of the ship down to the waterline—you could see completely through the sides of the ship to the open sea beyond—and wreaked havoc above deck, lighting numerous fires. As the freighter settled by the stern, the fires spread to the landing craft; despite heroic firefighting efforts by fleet tug *Hopi* (ATF-71), both *Elihu Yale* and *LCT-35* had to be written off as total losses. Those killed in this incident included three of the ship's crew, two of the Armed Guard on board ship, and seven stevedores in the process of unloading cargo.

Unfortunately for the Luftwaffe the raid also cost them one aircraft when it crashed the next morning as it was returning from Bergamo to Toulouse-Blagnac. Even more important was that the aircraft was commanded by *Hauptmann* Heinz-Emil Middermann, leader of II./KG 100.[35]

One other ship may have been damaged that evening, according to Luftwaffe sources, though if a near miss did cause damage it was sufficiently light as to not affect immediate operations.[36] The ship in question was none other than destroyer-escort *Herbert C. Jones*, one of the ships equipped with the Kehl-Strassburg jamming system operating off Anzio. Since the beginning of Operation Shingle, *Herbert C. Jones* had alternated with its sister ship *Frederick C. Davis* in providing jamming services against the German glide bombs, using the updated XCJ-1 systems installed in Oran. Each had a special detachment of three Army radio technicians who operated the sophisticated equipment. As reported earlier, some destroyers at Anzio also had just been equipped with this jamming system, though, perhaps because the crews were less experienced than those on board the destroyer-escorts, it is believed they had less success than did *Herbert C. Jones* or *Frederick C. Davis*.[37]

It is unclear whether this ship was targeted by the Luftwaffe, though some have speculated to that effect, noting the ship was nicknamed "Frau Maier" by the Luftwaffe pilots, at least as determined by the radio intercept operators on board *Frederick C. Davis*. These operators interpreted that phrase to mean "Old Gossip" and suggested it indicated Luftwaffe knowledge of the role these two destroyer-escorts were playing in the defense of the Anzio beachhead. Immediately after this signal was intercepted, *Herbert C. Jones* was surrounded by exploding plumes of water, just barely escaping a concerted attack by four Luftwaffe aircraft.[38]

It certainly would have been logical for the Luftwaffe to target the ships jamming the Kehl-Strassburg system. At a minimum, they provided excellent advance warning of raids, with the result that local commanders were rarely if ever surprised by an air attack. (Ultra intelligence was also supplying advance notice of raids.) The extent to which these two ships along with the other equipped with the NRL's countermeasures system actually jammed missiles remains unclear. Certainly the ships were able to identify when the glide-bomb frequencies were in use. The challenge was to tune the transmitter quickly enough to counteract the signal and to ensure that all of the jamming ships did not target the same missile while allowing others to pass through unimpeded. The apparent success of these efforts was enough to lead to Navy Unit Commendations for both destroyer-escorts for their valuable service at Anzio. Captain Harry Sanders, Commander of Destroyer Squadron (DesRon) 13—the unit of destroyers patrolling Anzio—wrote this in his battle report:

> During the period 22 January–2 February, 1944, there were some 26 bombing attacks by the German Air Force. Radio-controlled bombs were dropped during four of these attacks. . . . The efficiency with which *F. C. Davis* and *H. C. Jones* jammed radio-controlled bombs is an outstanding achievement on the part of these vessels. . . . A feature of the glide-bomb attacks was the effective deflection of the bombs by jammers in *F. C. Davis* and *H. C. Jones* and to a lesser extent by *Woolsey*. On the last attack two glider bombs were seen to suddenly break off from their flight path and plunge into the sea.[39]

Another glide-bomb attack was planned for 17 February, though it was cancelled due to poor weather, the risk of which was clearly demonstrated when two aircraft crashed upon landing at the transfer airport at Bergamo. One aircraft suffered severe damage, with one crewmember killed and another suffering serious fractures in both legs.[40] The glide bombs next returned on 19 February, during a dusk attack by II./KG 100. The Luftwaffe pilots claimed one hit on the stern of a large transport, while acknowledging one loss of its own.[41] No such hit occurred. The ship in question, *Edward Rutledge*, survived a near miss only fifteen yards astern. Another ship, *Samuel Ashe*, was also targeted in this raid and had a similar experience, with an Hs 293 exploding only fifteen to twenty yards away.[42] A follow-up raid was launched two days later on 19 February, though there is no record of any successes. Yet another aircraft was lost on that mission as it crash-landed while transiting to Bergamo in preparation for the raid.[43]

The penultimate attack by II./KG 100 was also the last to achieve success. On 25 February Royal Navy destroyer *Inglefield* was stationed off Anzio to provide fire support and antiaircraft defense. It was targeted in a dusk raid by *Major* Jope's force, which achieved a direct hit on this nearly two thousand–ton warship with an Hs 293.[44] Eric Alley, a seaman on board ship at the time, reports his experience:

> The attackes [sic] came every night just on dusk and on 25 February *Inglefield* was hit just three miles off Anzio lighthouse. There was an extremely strong sirocco wind blowing at the time with a very heavy sea. We abandoned ship into these extreme conditions and of the ship's company of 192, 35 shipmates were lost that night. Minesweepers and other destroyers rescued many of our survivors, and in particular the American *LCI-12*, equipped as a salvage vessel managed to pull 23 of us from the water.[45]

Inglefield was to be the last ship lost at Anzio to glide bombs. Only one more raid followed, an unsuccessful night attack of about thirteen aircraft once again staging out of Bergamo. No targets were hit in that raid—indeed no such raid has even been reported on the Allies' side. In the end, the Luftwaffe concluded that the process of staging the Do 217 out of Bergamo played a large part in the minimal success of the campaign because it exposed the aircraft to the dangers of air attack by enemy fighters as well as to the inevitable hazards of flying in winter conditions in mountainous northern Italy. The Do 217 just did not have the legs for these missions, and only the He 177 offered the opportunity for effective offensive operations. After the final raids at Anzio, most of 5./KG 100 was taken off the line and transferred to Aalborg to join up with its sister unit, 4./KG 100, for He 177 conversion training.

Attacks Against Anzio Supply Convoys

As the battle at Anzio moved inland and control of the skies over the landing zone migrated to the Allies, the Luftwaffe shifted resources from that precarious battle zone toward attacks on more-vulnerable convoys at sea. First to be diverted was II./KG 40, which had engaged in three night missions over Anzio without any success while losing seven of the precious He 177 bombers in the process. On 1 February, while the battles over Anzio were in a mid-campaign pause, the Luftwaffe's attention shifted back to Allied merchant ships in the Atlantic, with occasional forays into the Mediterranean.

◆ ◆ ◆

First to undergo an assault was UGS-30, a set of fifty-five freighters, tankers, and transports transiting from the United States to Casablanca with a stop in Gibraltar. Once again II./KG 40 came up empty with no confirmed kills against one reported loss, though accompanying Luftwaffe torpedo bombers did achieve a hit on freighter *Edward Bates*. It is possible that UGS-30 was also attacked by II./KG 100, in a temporary deviation from their missions over Anzio.[46]

The next mission was against convoy SL-147, homebound from Gibraltar with eighty-one ships, many of which were repositioning to support the planned Normandy invasion. Four He 177s took off for the attack but contact was never made and the mission was aborted.[47]

The next objective was the eastbound convoy OS-67/KMS-41, which was targeted by both II and III *Gruppen* of KG 40 on 12 February. However, things had changed from the days of autumn 1943 when convoys were relatively easy pickings for KG 40 and KG 100. In this case, the convoy was protected not just by destroyers, sloops, frigates, and corvettes, but also by its own airpower. This came in the form of *Pursuer*, an escort aircraft carrier equipped with a squadron of Wildcat fighter aircraft.

The first attack on OS-67/KMS-41 was made by four Fw 200 of III./KG 40 equipped to launch Hs 293 glide bombs. One was shot down en route; the three surviving aircraft were never able to make contact with the convoy. A follow-on raid was launched with nine He 177 of II./KG 40 while the convoy was about 500 kilometers (270 nautical miles) west of Cape Finisterre. At 1844 hours, eight minutes after sunset, there arrived an alert from the Admiralty, most likely from Ultra, warning of an impending attack. Radar picked up the bandits shortly afterwards and four Wildcats took off from *Pursuer* to intercept. The Wildcats sighted the incoming bombers and shot one down, which, unfortunately for the Luftwaffe, was the aircraft of *Major* Walter Rieder, commander of II./KG 40.[48] Only three of the remaining aircraft ever fired missiles at the convoy (one other jettisoned its missiles while under attack) and there were no hits. Four more He 177s attempted to strike the convoy in a third attack that day and were sighted on radar at 1930 hours. Again, fighters were dispatched, but the incoming attack force of bombers never engaged the convoy and instead was seen to be retiring at 1950 hours.[49]

After this disappointing experience II./KG 40 stood down for several months, not to appear again in force until its last campaign against the invasion force at Normandy. The campaigns at Anzio and against the convoys had cost it dearly, with seventeen aircraft—one in three—lost to enemy action, and another three destroyed in accidents. Spring 1944 was a time of renewal, and of preparation for the invasion of France that was all too evident from Allied actions. The tired He 177 A-3 aircraft were replaced by newer and more powerful He 177 A-5 variants able to carry three Hs 293 missiles, with one under the forward fuselage and two under the wings. The first four of the newer models arrived in February, with seventeen in March, sixteen in April, and seven in May. The twenty-two then-surviving A-3 models were taken out of service, with only one left by the end of April.[50] Finally, the renewal during that time extended as well to personnel. Replacing the former II./KG 100 group commander, *Major* Rieder, who had been killed in the attack on OS-67/KMS-41, was *Major* Hans Dochtermann, up to that point in command of 5./KG 40 and the commander of the aircraft that had sunk *Rohna* four months previously.

Introduction of the Ju 290

There is a possible epilogue to the convoy attacks of February 1944. It has been written that on 16 February convoy ONS-29 was the recipient of a glide-bomb attack by a unit new to this story, *Fernaufklärungs Gruppe* (FAGr) 5 based in Mont-de-Marsan, France, and equipped with the massive Ju 290 long-range patrol aircraft.[51] The account suggests that the two Ju 290 aircraft, which to that point had been used for surveillance operations only, attempted to engage the convoy with Hs 293 glide bombs but were defeated when defending fighters shot them down.

✦ ✦ ✦

It is known that the Ju 290 was adapted as a potential launch platform for the Hs 293 but unclear if it was ever used operationally for this purpose. This four-engine aircraft was developed by Junkers as a derivative of the Ju 90 commercial airliner, and then adapted for military use as a very-long-range transport and patrol aircraft. First flown on 16 July 1942, the aircraft was intended to replace the slower Fw 200, which had grown increasingly vulnerable to Allied defenses. Relatively few Ju 290s were completed, perhaps fifty in all.

Only one production variant, the Ju 290 A-7, was equipped to carry the Kehl transmitter and could be armed with either Hs 293 or Fritz-X glide bombs. Very few were built and delivered, perhaps about a dozen.[52] This differed significantly in appearance from the other Ju 290 variants in that the solid nose was replaced with an extended glazed nose to permit the bomb operator to see the glide bomb and control its flight. In addition, three ETC 2000 bomb-release mechanisms were installed—one under each wing and the third under the fuselage.

FAGr(5) was a new Luftwaffe unit stood up for purposes of operating the Ju 290 in its maritime patrol and attack role. This unit did deploy its limited numbers of Ju 290 A-3 and A-5 patrol aircraft to shadow Allied convoys, including ONS-29. However, since FAGr(5) did not receive its first Ju 290 A-7 until late in March 1944, it is not possible for ONS-29 to have been engaged by Hs 293 missiles launched from a Ju 290 in February 1944.[53] As a final indication of the implausibility of this scenario, the two Ju 290 aircraft shot down in that attack on ONS-29 were A-5 variants, not the glide bomb–carrying A-7s.[54] Karl Kössler and Günther Ott, authors of the definitive study of the Ju 290, have assessed this claim and report the following regarding the loss of the first aircraft on the morning of 16 February: "Reports from British sources suggest this aircraft might have dropped a glide bomb on one of the ships, though it missed its target. This statement cannot be correct, because the A-5 had still no Kehl [radio-transmitting] equipment, though it was equipped with an ejection mechanism for Schwan buoys."[55]

The reference to Schwan buoys may provide an explanation for the report from British sources. The Schwan, more correctly identified as the FuG 203 Schwan-See, was a floating radio beacon dropped by Luftwaffe maritime patrol aircraft and used to record the position of convoys for follow-on attacks. This buoy looked like a conventional bomb and was dropped in a similar manner. It could very well be that the Ju 290, thought by observers to have launched a glide bomb, had instead dropped one of these buoys.

An Intelligence Holy Grail

In the end, the decisive element of the Anzio campaign may have been achieved in scientific laboratories and not the battlefield. By observing the missiles in operation, and via the use of improved receivers, the Allies were able to decipher more details about the Kehl-Strassburg control system. A particular contribution was made by Lieutenant J. C. G. Field, who intercepted German guidance signals and was able to deduce from their patterns that they were azimuth- and elevation-steering signals.

✦ ✦ ✦

Another intelligence find at Anzio, also involving the ever-present Lieutenant Field, was more critical still. Sometime during the attacks in late January, most likely on 22 January, an intact Hs 293 was found on the beach at Anzio, possibly jettisoned by a Luftwaffe bomber attempting to evade attack; it might also have been a missile targeted against the invasion force that failed to explode.[56] Moreover, the explosive charge designed to destroy the Hs 293's radio control unit also failed, thereby providing for the first time an intact Strassburg receiver for the Allied scientists to explore. Lieutenant Field salvaged the weapon; by 15 February the captured German missile had been taken on board *Inglefield*—not yet destroyed by another Hs 293—to Field's lab at Naples. From there it was sent on to the scientists at the RAE at Farnborough in the United Kingdom.[57] Now the Allied scientists had a complete glide bomb to disassemble and examine. Not only would it confirm the specific frequencies used, but it would also close any gaps in the knowledge of how the missile control actuators reacted to specific signal inputs.

Moreover, one of the aircraft shot down on 23 January helped provide important clues for the ultimate defeat of the Kehl-Strassburg system. This aircraft (F8+AM from 4./KG 40) was destroyed at 1750 hours by a Beaufighter of the American 414th Night Fighter Squadron, based out of Ghisonaccia, Corsica.[58] The Beaufighter, crewed by 2nd Lieutenant Clyde William George and Flight Officer Herbert C. Penn, encountered the Hs 293–laden He 177 over Corsica and crippled it with cannon fire. Luftwaffe *Oberleutnant* Georg Dietrich and four members of his crew parachuted to safety and were captured. The fifth member of his crew was never found. The abandoned aircraft itself plowed into the ground near Urtaca, Corsica.[59] As a subsequent Most Secret British intelligence report confirmed, "The aircraft disintegrated after hitting the ground so that only the battered remains of the aircraft transmitter were recognizable, but the glider bombs buried themselves upon impact and were subsequently recovered. The photographs of the radio equipment will indicate the extent to which the bombs were damaged, much additional information has been obtained although there is still insufficient evidence to give the complete system of control."[60]

British engineers and scientists at the Radio Department of the RAE were able to reconstruct two of the major modules of the Strassburg receiver, as well as develop detailed circuit diagrams for two others, and a partial diagram for the fifth. They were also able to validate the specific frequencies (1 kHz, 1.5 kHz, 8 kHz, and 12 kHz) that provided the basic mechanism for transmitting guidance commands to the missiles' control surfaces. By March 1944 the analytical teams had garnered much of the information required by countermeasures experts to develop devices not only to jam the Strassburg receiver with noise, but also to "spoof" it with false commands. A U.S. intelligence report prepared in March later illustrates just how far advanced the Allies' knowledge of this previously secret weapon had become. Within a few months the Allies were able to put forward a complete and accurate description of the Hs 293.[61]

CHAPTER TEN

LESSONS LEARNED, MOVES, *and* COUNTERMOVES

The discovery of an intact glide bomb at Anzio, the recovery of two others on Corsica, and the lessons learned during operations at Anzio precipitated yet another flurry of crash-development programs designed to yield better countermeasures. Scientists at the NRL in Washington, the ASE in the United Kingdom, and the Royal Canadian Naval communications center at Sainte-Hyacinthe, Quebec, exploited the intelligence finds to improve the mediocre performance of first-generation systems at Anzio. Once the Allies had tinkered with the recovered Hs 293 missiles they understood almost as much about it as the German designers did.

✦ ✦ ✦

The immediate challenge was to address the operational shortcomings of the early NRL and British jammers and to quickly get such improved systems into the field. The upgrades took several forms. One stream of effort was designed to automate the process of identifying and jamming specific frequencies in use. The United States also began work on a spoofing jammer that would allow operators to take over the control of the missile and drive it into the sea in spite of whatever counteractions were taken by the Luftwaffe missile operator in the distant Do 217, He 177, or Fw 200. Other efforts were designed to yield very powerful jammers that would flood the airwaves with noise across multiple frequencies. There was a flurry of activity; by the time the threat was removed about a dozen different countermeasures systems had been developed.

U.S. Plans for Advanced Countermeasures

The American XCJ series of jammers deployed in the Mediterranean had met with mixed success (at best) because a well-organized attack could overwhelm the operators of these early manually tuned and relatively imprecise systems. Evidence had accumulated in late 1943 and early 1944 that the Germans had learned of this vulnerability in Allied capabilities. The Luftwaffe aircrews began switching on large number of transmitters on different frequencies in unison in order to flood the airways and disguise the few signals actually being used to guide missiles.[1]

✦ ✦ ✦

In contrast to the British, who favored technologies that would jam the intermediate frequency thus disabling the Kehl-Strassburg system regardless of the radio frequency in use, the Americans still pursued "spot-jamming" approaches that involved identification and then jamming of specific radio frequencies. (The Americans remained concerned that the British approach was too dependent on sketchy intelligence regarding the intermediate frequency actually in use.)[2] The follow-on systems to the XCJ series were designed to improve the ability of an operator to quickly identify a glide-bomb radio signal and to seamlessly pass information about that signal to the jamming transmitter. As Howard Lorenzen himself described in a private memoir written in 1983 but classified until 2008, "It soon became apparent that the 'crash' system built for the two ships [*Herbert C. Jones* and *Frederick C. Davis*] to protect them from the glide bombs was hardly the system the Navy needed for the countering of future threats. What was needed were receivers that would search wide portions of the frequency spectrum rapidly; the intercepted signal frequencies could then be passed to narrow-band, manually tuned receivers which would set the jammers on frequency."[3]

To this end the countermeasures system was upgraded substantially to include a new low-frequency (LF) receiver suite, a new high-frequency (HF) receiver suite, and upgraded jammers. For the LF suite the original manually tuned RBK receiver was replaced with a modified Hallicrafters S-27 unit with a special variable condenser that was rotated at high speed. The unit, designated RDG, would automatically identify the rough frequencies of any radio signals in use between 0.5 MHz and 30 MHz, which would then be displayed on an oscilloscope—either a commercial DuMont 241 device or a special military XCA unit. Complementing this was a manually tuned receiver, which was a modified National NC-100 designated as RAO whose output could be seen by the operator on a panoramic display derived from a Panoramic Radio Corporation SA-3 and designated RCX. The operator could detect all radio signals captured by the RDG on the oscilloscope, then use the RAO to tune in precisely any signal of interest and read that frequency information on the display of the RCX panoramic adaptor.

The HF suite operated in a similar way. A modified S-27 Hallicrafters unit designated RDC would automatically scan the airways for radio signals between 30 MHz and 170 MHz and indicate any signals received on the oscilloscope. Having detected a signal of interest, the operator would tune it in with a manually tuned RBK receiver (another S-27) and use another panoramic adaptor (designated RBW) to pinpoint the frequency. With these two advanced suites the electronic warfare operators on board ship could continuously scan the frequencies from 0.5 MHz to 170 MHz, instantly read out any reported signals on the appropriate LF or HF panoramic display, and feed that information to the jamming transmitter. With training the whole process could be done in seconds.

The receivers were also equipped with an innovative optional "look through" capability. This allowed the operator to see both the jamming signal and the original Strassburg guidance signal at the same time and to adjust the former until it exactly overlapped with the latter. This was accomplished by turning off the jammer and enabling the receivers for one cycle in four during the sixty-cycles-per-second sweep rate of the system. Once the frequencies had been matched precisely, the look-through capability could be disabled by the operator, allowing the jammer to operate full time against the Strassburg signal.[4]

The next challenge was to select a jammer to go along with these advanced receivers. Initially, NRL endeavored to advance its original line of jammers, the XCJ series. The XCJ-1 transmitters installed on board six ships in the Mediterranean were upgraded to a new XCJ-2 model with improved tuning ability. Simultaneously, the NRL wizards were developing a highly advanced follow-on model of the XCJ series designated the XCJ-3. (All three of these transmitters are referred to as TX in their production variant.) The NRL engineers intended to pair the XCJ-3 (TX) with the new XCK transmitter (to be designated TY when in production), operating across frequencies from 40 MHz to 130 MHz. This was an interim step toward an even more advanced jammer under development, labeled the XCL (and to be designated TEA when in production).

However, because of the urgency of the situation—ships were still sinking at Anzio—an off-the shelf transmitter was required as an interim solution. For this the U.S. Navy looked not only within its own research laboratories, but also to its sister service, the U.S. Army, and to the private sector.

The First Interim Jammer: ARQ-8

First to come to the assistance of the U.S. Navy was the U.S. Army Air Force, which was itself developing a jammer to protect its bombers. The U.S. Army recently had ordered fifty advanced airborne transmitters known as the ARQ-8. These systems put out up to fifty watts of power across a frequency range of 25 to 105 MHz; they were intended to jam German fighter communications. In addition to the designation ARQ-8, the system was known under the name DINA or DINA-MATE.[5] These advanced devices were developed by the then-secret Radio Research Laboratory at Harvard University, which was the less-familiar sibling of the more-illustrious Radiation Laboratory at the Massachusetts Institute of Technology.

✦ ✦ ✦

The ARQ-8, made by Hallicrafters, just happened to encompass the critical frequencies of the Kehl-Strassburg system. The Navy requested an allocation of these precious devices; twenty units of the fifty ordered were dispatched for Navy use, with the first two shipped from Harvard to the NRL the first week of January 1944.[6] The intention was to install these units on board destroyers, destroyer-escorts, and cruisers, perhaps in emulation of British efforts to adapt the airborne Jostle jammer for the same purposes.

It is not clear the ARQ-8 solution was seen as effective—or that it was even widely adopted—by the U.S. Navy. The wizards at the NRL were highly critical of this system, which had been designed originally for aircraft installations rather than for shipboard use. The NRL engineers cited the excessive "complexity of this equipment, together with its limited usefulness [and] the difficulty of its installation because of the 400 cycle power supply required."[7] (U.S. Navy ships used 60 Hz power systems.) Also, they complained it was "too complicated to produce on a crash basis in the necessary quantities because it involves multiple modulation and RF [Radio Frequency] power amplification, with inductive tuners and other precision parts crowded into ATR [Air Transport Rack] racks to conserve space and weight." The tuning mechanism came in for particular criticism: "The particular method of tracking the transmitter frequency by tuning the receiver as exemplified by the present Dinamate equipment is not considered to be applicable to a properly designed system for general guided missiles countermeasures application. The Dina-Dinamate device, as designed, is fundamentally limited to single-control tuning over a limited frequency range such as 5 mc. [MHz], for example. In order to change this 5 mc. range to other bands requires a rather extensive, and hence slow tuning procedure involving several controls."[8]

Most important, many of the ARQ-8 installations made in response to the urgent need had evidently been completed without the additional B3200 power amplifier—which had been intended to boost output to three hundred watts—due to production shortfalls of the latter. This meant that the output of the installed system would be only thirty to fifty watts, far below the two hundred watts thought to be needed to jam the Hs 293's directional antenna.[9] It was as if the ships equipped with this jammer but not with the B3200 amplifier would only be firing electromagnetic blanks.

It remains unclear how many ARQ-8 systems were actually deployed in combat. It is likely that no more than twenty were actually installed.[10] Other sources suggest up to thirty-five were fitted because over "several weeks, five to ten destroyers and destroyer escorts at a time were ordered into the Boston Navy Yard for installation of the jamming units and training of navy electronic ratings in their use."[11] In any case, the ARQ-8 was soon supplanted by another interim solution that proved much more aligned with Navy needs.

The Second Interim Jammer: CXGE

The NRL recommended that the Navy look elsewhere besides the ARQ-8 for both an interim and a more permanent solution. The permanent solutions were the XCK and XCL jammers then under development. For the interim solution the NRL put forward its own XCJ-3 prototype, the most advanced version of the XCJ jammers. A search of available hardware indicated that the General Electric Company's models No.4AF-1A1-1 and -2 commercial radio transmitters could be adapted as an interim production variant of the XCJ-3 design. This powerful transmitter, designated as the CXGE, emitted three hundred to one thousand watts over a frequency range of 15 MHz to 55 MHz. The Hammarlund Manufacturing Company of New York was engaged to modify the GE units to match the performance attributes of NRL's prototype XCJ-3. This turned out to be more complicated than envisioned, and the Hammarlund final product bore little resemblance to the GE original.

✦ ✦ ✦

The General Electric Company amplifier was so modified as to become the approximate equivalent of XCJ-3 equipment previously designed and developed at NRL, see Ref. (b). The principle [sic] modifications involved the installation of the necessary special coils, condensers, and mechanical controls to provide operation over the range 15–55 mc, tunable by means of a single control; also the necessary modifications of the existing power supply. A modulator look-through unit similar in electrical characteristics to that in the XCJ-3 equipment had to be installed. It may be briefly stated that the modifications necessary were of such magnitude as to leave little resemblance between the original and modified units. Except for some minor components, the only parts of the original equipment utilized in the modified unit were the power supply and frame assembly.[12]

Fourteen units were ordered, with the first delivered to NRL on 1 March. At least five units, and probably all fourteen, were shipped to the Exeter naval depot in the United Kingdom for use in ships preparing for the invasion of Normandy.[13] All fourteen installations were matched with RBW-1 Panoramic Adaptors from the Panoramic Radio Corporation, upgraded specifically for operation with the CXGE jammer.

Some of the units sent to Exeter were used in laboratory tests with recovered (and rebuilt) Kehl transmitters and Strassburg receivers, generating results that encouraged the scientists. To overcome skepticism of the operators, those whose lives were on the line, it also was deemed important to test the equipment under conditions that were as realistic as possible. To do so the scientists relocated to the Navy's electronic test range at Rosneath in Scotland for operational trials. There a ship equipped with the CXGE system attempted to jam captured enemy Hs 293 Strassburg receivers mounted on a motor launch while those same receivers attempted to receive signals from a captured enemy FuG 203e (Kehl) transmitter on another motor launch, an appropriate distance away from each other and from the jammer. As a British analysis revealed,

> With the FuGe 203 [transmitter installed in a motor) launch at 2250 yards from the CXGE jammer it was found that with the Hs293 receiver [motor] launch 750 yards from the FuGe 203 [transmitter unit], control was erratic and the rhythm of the relay contact was somewhat irregular. This irregularity was severe 1000 yards from the FuGe 203 launch and at 1250 yards distance [between Kehl transmitter and Strassburg receiver] the relay contact was hard over, and the FuGe 203 [Kehl transmitter] could do nothing to change this condition. The CXGE was then changed from a modulation frequency of 1000 c/s [steer left] to 1,500 c/s [steer right] and the relay was observed to fall in the opposite direction. It should be noted that the CXGE transmitter was not tuned until the FuGe 203 signal was received on a panoramic receiver. Monitoring showed that the delay in bringing the jammer on to frequency occupied only a few seconds.[14]

In realistic operational tests, it was clear that the CXGE jammer, when combined with the upgraded receivers, could quickly identify and jam the

Strassburg receiver, overcoming the Kehl signal. This took place even when the distance between Kehl transmitter and Strassburg receiver was half the distance between the CXGE transmitter and that same receiver. The results not only encouraged the scientists, but also reassured the operators that they finally had an effective electronic defense against German glide bombs.

Hector Skifter's Type MAS System

As prototypes of these interim solutions were being developed, a group of engineers at Columbia University was engaged by the NRL to assist in large-scale production of the interim (and apparently unloved) ARQ-8 system. This group was led by Dr. Hector R. Skifter, a specialist in the design and production of sophisticated electronic systems and founder of a company specializing in electronic countermeasures that continues to operate to this day on similar missions, albeit under different corporate ownership. What resulted from this dialogue was possibly the most effective glide-bomb jammer to emerge from U.S. industry during the war.

✦ ✦ ✦

Skifter was born to Scandinavian immigrants in Minnesota in 1901. He got his early start with radios as a manager of WCAL, the broadcast station at St. Olaf College in Northfield, Minnesota. In the 1930s he became a highly respected consulting engineer in the field of directive antennae and field-intensity meters. Skifter, however, was also a skilled organizer of production operations and consulted frequently to companies in this area. He assumed these skills would be of interest to the U.S. government after the attack on Pearl Harbor, so he traveled from his home in Minnesota to Washington, D.C., to offer his services. Initially rejected, he returned home in frustration. A short while later he was summoned to New York's Columbia University to participate in a secret program to develop advanced electronic devices for the U.S. military. Skifter was asked in mid-1942 to head up product engineering and production operations at this new Airborne Instrument Laboratory (AIL).[15]

Working out of offices in Mineola, New York, about twenty miles east of Manhattan on Long Island, Skifter and his team at AIL specialized in the rapid prototyping and production of innovative electronic systems. His team initially was engaged by the U.S. Navy to develop an advanced device for finding submerged submarines—the magnetic-anomaly detector (MAD)—that sensed the magnetic signature of a large steel submarine even if it was hidden by sight. Developed and placed on board patrol aircraft, it radically improved U.S. antisubmarine warfare capability.

While looking for a follow-on project, Skifter was approached by the U.S. Office of Scientific Research and Development (OSRD), established by President Franklin D. Roosevelt and led by Dr. Vannevar Bush. OSRD was the body that coordinated all scientific research in the United States during World War II; by late 1943 it had established as its number-one priority the development of countermeasures for German radio-controlled bombs. Accordingly, on 1 January 1944 AIL was transferred from Columbia University to Division 15 (Radio Coordination) of the National Defense Research Committee, the same division in which the Harvard Radio Research Laboratory was housed, to help work on this challenge.

While the NRL pursued its interim jamming system around the ARQ-8 it also was developing, under the leadership of Howard Lorenzen, a more sophisticated recording system to better track the Kehl transmitter signals. This would allow the NRL to understand precisely how those signals were translated into movements of the Hs 293 control surfaces. However, J. C. G. Field's discovery of an intact Hs 293 at Anzio and the recovery of two intact missiles on Corsica changed all that, and the focus of activity shifted from the improved recording apparatus to a sophisticated jammer that could mimic the exact modulation of the Kehl transmitter. This transmitter would thereby issue false control signals that the Strassburg receiver would interpret as valid. In this way, the jamming system would take over control of the missile.

Skifter and his AIL team went to Washington in order to plan for the production of the ARQ-8. However, his team took one look at the proposed design for this system and, consistent with the findings of the NRL, concluded that a much more effective approach was possible:

A.I.L. representatives pointed out the needless complexity and the difficulty of producing this [ARQ-8] equipment and proposed the development of simplified equipment better suited for this application and which could be produced more rapidly. A conference to discuss these proposals was held in Capt. Detzer's office on 18 April 1944. [A. J. Detzer was a senior countermeasures officer in the U.S. Navy.] In the meantime the Communication Security Section of this Laboratory had built and tested the receiver and were building and testing the transmitter and modulator for the simplified jammer proposed at the April 6 conference. At the April 18 conference in Capt. Detzer's office A.I.L. representatives proposed a jamming system almost identical to the previous N.R.L. proposal. The N.R.L. representative outlined the status of its development and the results being obtained in preliminary tests. It was agreed that A.I.L. would take over the N.R.L. development and build 50 equipments on a crash basis with N.R.L. serving in a consulting and testing capacity. The designation, Model MAS, was assigned to this equipment. The A.I.L. representatives visited this Laboratory on April 18 and April 19, witnessed tests of the equipment and, on the authorization of Lt. Riddle, were supplied preliminary specifications (reference (c)) and circuit diagrams. The first model of this equipment was delivered by A.I.L. on May 1 and tests of this equipment have been completed at this Laboratory. A second unit, for installation aboard a CVE, is scheduled for delivery on May 10. It is believed that this will set a speed record for the conception, development, production and installation of countermeasure equipment.[16]

The NRL handed over to AIL all of the information it possessed on the Hs 293 radio-guidance system, including the control frequencies and the form of the signals as they related to movements of the missiles' control surfaces. Skifter biographer Gregory S. Hunter explains what happened next:

> Using commercial parts from various electronics stores in New York City, AIL built a working prototype in fifteen days, which they brought to Washington, along with an instruction book, a spare parts list, and a spare parts kit. The NRL tested the unit and found it satisfactory, whereupon the AIL staff returned to Mineola and started building several more units. Each was a fraternal twin because part sizes and shapes changed as they were purchased from stores in the metropolitan area. These hand-made units were developed around the clock. Many nights the staff caught a few hours sleep at their desk.[17]

This ultimate jammer, which AIL referred to as the "Type MAS Shipboard Jamming System," operated across the 41–51 MHz frequency band putting out a substantial 250 watts of energy, more than enough to overcome the thirty-watt Kehl signal at the relevant distances. Moreover, the MAS duplicated the exact square-wave pattern used by the Germans to communicate control instructions to the Hs 293 and Fritz-X. As described in a contemporary NRL memo,

> The Model MAS G.M.C.M. [guided missile countermeasures] jamming equipment consists of a simple dial tuned self excited oscillator which can be square wave modulated at 1.0, 1.5, 8 and 12 kc/s repetition rates, and a companion receiver consisting of a broad-band R.F. amplifier, mixer, and local oscillator followed by a high gain audio amplifier driving headphones. The local oscillator in the receiver is used only for preliminary search. "Listen-Through" operation is obtained by using the unmodulated transmitter to replace the receiver's local oscillator and tuning it to beat with the desired victim signal, and then applying the desired modulation. This type of adjustment enables the transmitter to be tuned to within a few kilocycles of the missile frequency rapidly and with ease. Separate

antennas are required for the transmitter and receiver. These antennas should be reasonably well isolated from each other to avoid coupling an excessive amount of the transmitted carrier into the receiver and thus reducing the sensitivity.[18]

It also was relatively simple to operate. A wide-band RBK monitoring receiver would seek out Luftwaffe air-to-air communications, the first clue that a raid might be in progress. (Ultra intercepts also would have provided advance warning.) Once on alert the operator would engage the MAS receiver unit to automatically scan the airwaves for an appropriate signal characteristic of the Kehl transmitter. When detected, the MAS transmitter unit would be switched to the "Search" setting and begin to beat with the MAS receiver's oscillator, automatically tuning the device to the appropriate frequency. Then, when switched to "Operate," the MAS transmitter would unleash a jamming signal on that same frequency. In this way, the system avoided the operational difficulties experienced with the early NRL XCJ jammers.

Detailed trials were conducted from 26 May to 30 May on board destroyer-escort *Otter* (DE-210), newly commissioned on 21 February 1944 and under command of Lieutenant Commander D. M. Kerr. These proved successful and systems were installed on other escort ships. Under the direction of engineer Robert Schulz, manufacture of the new system continued apace; as soon as each unit was completed, it was shipped down Long Island to the Brooklyn Navy Yard. The full production run of fifty was undertaken, with five of the first units flown to Scotland for installation on ships preparing for the Normandy invasion. However, some of the production variants experienced quality issues, and the week after D-day the NRL noted that substantial errors could creep into the system, often throwing the signal off by 40 to 60 kHz.[19] Work continued on the system throughout the summer of 1944.

It is possible that relatively few MAS systems were deployed against the German glide-bomb threat at Normandy. The number available for operations in June 1944 could have been as few as five—the quantity known to have been shipped by air to the United Kingdom to be installed on board ships preparing for D-day. At most it was thirty-one units, the total number not otherwise accounted for in installations that took place after Normandy.[20]

Other Advanced Systems: Type 651 and Canadian Naval Jammer

After the secrets of the Hs 293 were revealed, and as a possible replacement for the interim Jostle jammer, the British finalized plans for an improved jammer designated Type 651, with a very high power output of one kilowatt. Employing the same concept as the medium-power Type 650, the Type 651 would employ two transmitters at 48 MHz and 50 MHz with the combined signal jamming the Strassburg intermediate receiver at 3 MHz. A crash program lasting three months was undertaken under the leadership of David Silvester; after three months of development the Marconi Company began production.[21] First operational during the Normandy invasion, these systems were fitted only to large Royal Navy ships such as battleships and carriers. Their massive size and power requirements made them ill suited for anything smaller than a cruiser. For the *King George V*–class and the *Revenge*-class battleships the two antennae for the Type 650 (and follow-on Type 651) countermeasures were affixed to extensions from the mainmast. For *Rodney* and *Nelson*, the installation was off outriggers attached to the bridge.[22]

✦ ✦ ✦

The United States and the United Kingdom were not the only countries that exploited the intelligence finds of February 1944 for purposes of building advanced jammers. The Radar Branch of the National Research Council of Canada was engaged by the Royal Canadian Navy in February 1944 to develop improved jammers. Author William Edgar Knowles Middleton provides details on what became known as the Canadian Naval Jammer, a powerful unit that could jam all of the frequencies from 48 MHz to 50 MHz simultaneously:

> Five transmitters were requested, and also parts for twenty more to be assembled by the R.C.N. at St. Hyacinthe, Quebec. It is difficult to believe that the first equipment, complete with spares, was shipped to Halifax on March 28 and the other four in April. . . . The transmitter gave an output of 1 kW frequency-modulated at 150 Hz over 4 MHz in the region between 42 and 75 MHz. The output was also amplitude-modulated at 60 Hz; this may or may not have made it more effective but it certainly made the apparatus simpler by doing without a rectifier in the high-voltage supply. The frequency modulation was performed by a variable condenser rotating at high speed.[23]

By the time the Allied invasion fleets prepared for the invasion of France in both Normandy and the Riviera, perhaps 90 to 110 Allied ships in theater were equipped with countermeasures. This included the five remaining upgraded XCJ-2 systems on board destroyers and destroyer-escorts in the

Mediterranean (one had been lost on board *Lansdale*). Between twenty and fifty ARQ-8 systems (some of which were underpowered and thus not effective) also were installed, most likely on board destroyers and light cruisers preparing for the Normandy invasion. Between eleven and fourteen CXGE (XCJ-3) systems also were installed on the Normandy fleet, most probably in this case on bombardment ships such as battleships and heavy cruisers. Up to thirty-one (though more likely a lower number) of the new Type MAS systems were available. Thus, between 50 and 70 U.S. ships in theater were equipped to jam glide bombs, and half of those had exceptionally capable systems (CXGE and MAS).[24]

In addition, there were up to five ships equipped with the Canadian Naval Jammer, most likely including the two RNC infantry transport ships and their escorting destroyers.[25] Finally, thirty-four ships participating in the invasion had been equipped with the British Type 650 and one ship (most likely battleship *Anson*) had received the especially capable Type 651 in time for Operation Neptune, the sea-based component of the Normandy invasion.[26]

In short, in contrast to the situation at Anzio, when at most only three ships equipped to jam glide bombs had been on station at any one time, at Normandy a hundred or so ships were equipped with jammers. The correlation of forces in the electronic war was shifting toward the Allies.

Moreover, these jammers were very different from the early systems deployed in the convoy battles in November 1943 and then again at Anzio. The XCJ-2 was a major upgrade to the original XCJ system on board *Frederick C. Davis* and *Herbert C. Jones* and the modified XCJ-1 equipment installed for the defense of Anzio on those same two destroyer-escorts as well as on destroyers *Lansdale*, *Hilary P. Jones*, *Woolsey*, and *Madison*. The ARQ-8 may have suffered limitations in many installations, but those equipped with the appropriate power amplifier should have been able to generate three hundred watts of energy on the right frequencies. The CXGE was capable of generating between three hundred and one thousand watts (depending on the specific frequency), more than enough to disrupt the Kehl-Strassburg system, as tests in England with recovered Luftwaffe hardware had demonstrated. The British Type 650 and 651 systems and the Canadian Naval Jammer would effectively disrupt all potential control frequencies simultaneously. Most interestingly, the Type MAS system would not just override the Kehl signal: it also would spoof the Strassburg receiver into thinking it was receiving valid input for steep right turns, thus driving an Hs 293 right into the ocean no matter how determinedly the Luftwaffe weapons operator attempted to regain control.

Development of Advanced German Glide Bombs

As the Allied wizards worked feverishly to upgrade their countermeasures against the Hs 293 and Fritz-X, their German counterparts were no less engaged in improving the effectiveness of their weapons. Many of these improvements constituted relatively modest efforts to upgrade performance. A few were explicitly designed to reduce the vulnerability of the system to Allied countermeasures and, at least in the case of the Fritz-X, to deal with the next generation of Allied battleships.

✦ ✦ ✦

Max Kramer continued his research on the Ruhrstahl X-1, the basic design behind the Fritz-X. While the Fritz-X had achieved excellent results against prewar battleships (*Roma* and *Warspite*) there were concerns it might not have the penetrating power to destroy the more-heavily armored ships of the British *King George V* class or the American *North Carolina* and *Iowa* classes. One way to address this would be to increase the terminal velocity to give the weapon even greater penetrating power. By replacing the straight fins of the X-1 with swept fins, Kramer's X-2 was stable through much higher terminal speeds and thus could be dropped from as high as 10 kilometers (33,000 feet). A more refined X-3 would be able to maintain controlled descent even at the speed of sound. Of course, this presupposed that the Germans could develop a turbocharged aircraft engine and airframe capable of reaching sufficient altitude to allow those speeds to be achieved.[27]

A second approach to enhancing the penetrating power of the Fritz-X was to increase the explosive charge itself. Toward this end the Germans investigated a larger 1,500-kilogram (3,300-pound) weapon, one specifically designed for use against the American *North Carolina* class of battleships.[28] A Kramer X-5 variant was larger still at 2,250 kilograms (almost 5,000 pounds), with a dense armor-piercing warhead that would have overcome the deck armor of any ship. A final variant, the X-6, replaced the heavy steel armor-piercing warhead with an enhanced explosive charge that would have been crippling against lightly armored ships.[29] (The missing weapon here, the X-4, was a highly innovative wire-guided air-to-air missile that did not have antiship applications.)

In the end, none of these upgraded Fritz-X derivatives ever entered large-scale production and none was moved from concept development and design into operational use. Moreover, Kramer's focus in increasing the lethality of the weapon by improving its penetrating power or expanding its warhead suggests a fundamental misunderstanding of the actual limitations of the system. When the Fritz-X hit a target, whether a light cruiser (*Savannah*, *Uganda*) or a battleship (*Roma*, *Italia*, *Warspite*), the result was typically devastating and the ship was either sunk or put out of action for a very long time. The challenge with the Fritz-X was less its lethality than the low probability that an aircraft that departed with such weapons under its wing or fuselage would ever be in a position to successfully launch and guide it.

A small research effort was undertaken to adapt a wire-guided capability to the basic Fritz-X, thus frustrating any attempts by the Allies to jam the more vulnerable radio link. Assigned the code name "Düren-Detmold," this new FuG 208/238 system mounted two bobbins, each with wires that could stretch 8 kilometers (just over 4 nautical miles). As the Fritz-X was dropped from its launching aircraft the bobbins would unwind and the wire would connect the bomb to the operator's control station. Simple up–down and left–right signals would be transmitted via these wires. In the end, though a few systems were developed, the new technology was never deployed.[30]

Likewise, about a dozen variants of the basic Hs 293 A-1 were developed by Herbert Wagner's team as the war progressed, and they addressed all aspects of the weapon's performance. One avenue of investigation led to the Hs 293 C and Hs 294, designed to strike ships below the waterline, thus intensifying the effects of the explosive charge. Some minor upgrades to the basic Hs 293 design were embedded in various experimental versions, including the Hs 293 E (replacing ailerons with spoilers), the Hs 293 F (a tailless design), and the Hs 293 G (for high-altitude drops and attacks using a near-vertical profile). Another approach, embodied in the Hs 293 I and Hs 295, contained a much larger warhead; in the latter case the approach employed two rocket motors to provide for faster and more-sustained acceleration toward the target.[31]

Unlike Kramer, Wagner also directed his developments to ensure a higher probability that a weapon deployed in combat would actually strike its target. Three such challenges were evident. First, the radio-guidance link represented an area of vulnerability, though it remains unclear whether the Germans felt that vulnerability had already been exploited or might merely be so in the future. Second, the launching aircraft often was in a position of poor visibility with respect to the weapon and therefore was unable to optimally time its detonation. And third, it was difficult for the operator in the launching aircraft to maintain visual contact with the target and missile and thus to guide it seamlessly to its target. The innovative responses to these challenges created a foundation for many of today's guided-missile systems.

The Hs 293 B was designed to avoid the possibility that the radio-control link might be jammed. Rather than use electromagnetic waves to transmit signals to the missile from the operator, the command signal would instead be sent over thin wires that would trail behind the missile, maintaining a continuous connection with the launching aircraft. Assigned the code name "Dortmund-Detmold," the FuG 207/237 system involved wires thirty kilometers long that were wound on bobbins in both the Hs 293 and the launching aircraft.[32] As the missile was fired, the wires would connect it to the aircraft and the operator would feed control inputs over these wires. Such a wire-guidance system, very much a feature of many postwar missile systems, would have been immune to the Allies' jamming systems. The basic version of the advanced Hs 294, designed to strike underwater, was also wire-guided, although the backup Hs 294 A variant used the Kehl-Strassburg system. In the end, as with the Fritz-X, the wire-guided variant was never deployed.

The second challenge—that the performance of the Hs 293 could be enhanced by more-precise timing of its detonation—was addressed in the Hs 293 H, a variant in which a command signal to detonate the weapon would be issued not by the launching aircraft, but by another aircraft in a better position to track the weapon and target. However, as the second aircraft would now also be vulnerable, it is unclear what advantage this system would have provided operationally; there are indications that it was not designed as an antiship weapon but instead put forward as a weapon to use against enemy bomber aircraft, then in the process of reducing large parts of urban Germany to burned-out rubble.[33]

The third challenge, of ensuring better aiming, was addressed by inserting a radical new technology of the time—television-based guidance—into the nose of the missile in a variant designated the Hs 293 D. A TV camera would send back to the operator a picture of what lay in front of the missile. By adjusting the flight of the missile to keep the target in the middle of the TV picture, the bomb operator would be assured of a direct hit. This provided a much more precise method of aiming at the target, and the technology would allow the operator to continue to aim his missile even as the launching aircraft maneuvered to avoid enemy defenses. A small television camera was developed by the firm Fernseh GmbH. At least 70 and perhaps up to 255 of these advanced missiles were developed and tested against targets early in 1944.[34] A variant of the larger Hs 295, the Hs 295 D, also used the TV guidance system. However, the technology proved too immature and, according to most sources, the system was never deployed operationally.[35]

The failure to deploy these advanced variants was a function not only of their technical readiness but also of the lack of any perceived need. German technicians had concluded that the level of disturbance of the command radio signal could reach 70 percent before the risks justified a move to a more-advanced guidance system.[36] Moreover, to the extent that strange signals within the relevant frequency range had been detected by the Luftwaffe, it was dismissed as interference from the British Gee navigation system.[37] The Luftwaffe evidently concluded that, to the extent any jamming was taking place, it was sufficiently remote a threat that the newer designs could wait.

Final Missions Before Normandy

As the battle of Anzio faded in February 1944, the glide-bomb groups of the Luftwaffe embarked on different paths. Squadrons 4./KG 100 and 5./KG 100 of II./KG 100 remained at Aalborg, transitioning from the Do 217 E-5 to the new He 177 in preparation for the anticipated invasion of Europe. Only the hard-worked 6./KG 100 was available for antishipping operations in the Mediterranean with the Hs 293.

✦ ✦ ✦

Meanwhile, 7./KG 100 and 9./KG 100 of III./KG 100 remained at Toulouse-Francazal, awaiting opportunities to deploy their Fritz-X against suitable targets in the Mediterranean, should they ever emerge. They did not. Since the Allies did not oblige by bringing heavy cruisers or battleships within range, the Luftwaffe prepared its own plans to take the weapons to the enemy in England. Meanwhile, 8./KG 100 remained at Fassberg, continuing its sluggish transition to the He 177.

The He 177 bombers of II./KG 40 were stationed off the Atlantic at Bordeaux-Mérignac, upgrading from the He 177 A-3 to the more capable He 177 A-5 while preparing for the inevitable invasion of continental Europe. The Fw 200 Condors of III./KG 100, some of which were equipped to launch Hs 293 glide bombs, were still stationed at Cognac. Because Allied air cover over the convoys had improved markedly, the good old days when Condors could stalk their prey for hours on end had long vanished and their use to screen or attack convoys became problematic.

In March and most of April 1944 the glide-bomb war against Allied shipping was essentially the sole responsibility of the overtasked crews of 6./KG 100. Six convoy attacks were launched between 8 March 1943 and 20 April 1943.[38] In all cases these missions were part of orchestrated attacks against vital Allied convoys operating off North Africa, bringing materiel and troops to reinforce operations in Italy. Usually 6./KG 100 operated alongside the torpedo bombers of KG 26. Unfortunately for the Luftwaffe, despite claims to the contrary, the loss of not a single ship can be attributed to the glide bombs during this period. Unlike the days in autumn 1943 when often-uncontested glide bombers took a withering toll on ships and crews, by 1944 the Allies operated air bases across many parts of the Mediterranean and could provide almost constant air cover over the convoys.

Action began on 8 March when convoy KMS-43, code-named "Hannah," was attacked by multiple units of the Luftwaffe.[39] KMS-43 (from the United Kindom ["K"] via the Mediterranean ["M"] at slow ["S"] speed) departed Liverpool on 23 February for Gibraltar. On 8 March the thirty-five merchant ships of KMS-43, many loaded with fresh troops for the Italian campaign, found themselves along the coast of Oran in north-western Algeria. The Luftwaffe sighted this convoy and dispatched roughly a dozen aircraft of 6./KG 100 to intercept for a dusk bombing mission. Unfortunately for the Germans, Allied intelligence knew of the attack in advance, most likely from Ultra intercepts, and long-range RAF Beaufighters were ordered from airfields in Sardinia to intercept. The preemptive fighter attack broke up the raid and the soldiers on board the transports of KMS-43 proceeded unmolested, with one Do 217 lost in the effort.[40]

The next attempt was against KMF-44, code-named "Illicit." This convoy had departed Liverpool on 3 March 1944 and separated from OS-70 on 15 March. KMS-44 arrived in Gibraltar on 17 March and the roughly three dozen ships readied themselves for the likely onslaught of attacks by the Luftwaffe. In this they were not disappointed: 6./KG 100 and KG 26 mounted attacks at dusk on 19 March. Once again, the attacks proved unsuccessful and 6./KG 100 limped home with one of its aircraft lost on its return flight.[41]

KMS-45 ("Thumbs Up") was the next target, having departed Liverpool on 14 March and separated from its twin OS-71 on 25 March. Passing Gibraltar on 27 March, the three dozen ships continued east into the Mediterranean. Once again 6./KG 100 and KG 26 rose to confront, and once again Allied air cover proved too capable. No ships were hit and 6./KG 100 lost another three of the precious Do 217 E-5 aircraft with their critically valuable aircrews.[42]

Having lost five aircraft with nothing to show in return, 6./KG 100 next turned its attention to convoys operating on the United States–to–Gibraltar route. Across the first three weeks of April, this *staffel* launched three attacks on troop-filled and supply-laden convoys in the Atlantic. UGS-36 (code-named "Tennant") was the first, attacked by 6./KG 100, KG 26, and KG 77 on 1 April 1944. No glide bombs scored, and the Luftwaffe lost two more Do 217 aircraft.[43] The next convoy, UGS-37, having departed Hampton Roads on 24 March, was attacked by 6./KG 100 on 11 April, again without any ships being hit. Yet another of the dwindling fleet of Hs 293–equipped Dorniers was lost on this raid.[44]

An even more concentrated attack was made against UGS-38 (code-named "Whoopee"), which departed Hampton Roads on 3 April 1944 en route via Gibraltar to points in the Mediterranean. The surviving aircraft of 6./KG 100, along with torpedo-carrying aircraft of KG 27 and KG 77, were assigned to attack. Accompanying the American convoy were twenty-one escorting warships including *Lansdale*, a destroyer outfitted with the second-generation jamming gear designed to defeat the glide bombs. Overall command of the escort force was by Captain William H. Duvall on board U.S. Coast Guard cutter *Taney*, a survivor of the attack on Pearl Harbor on 7 December 1941. Perhaps because of sheer numbers, the attack in aggregate was a success from the Luftwaffe standpoint. Approaching at low altitude from the east (out of the darkness) some twenty-five minutes after sunset, and without the harbinger of flares, the Ju 88 torpedo bombers found their targets illuminated against the darkening sky.

Lansdale was sunk by a torpedo, its advanced missile-jamming gear of no use against this conventional threat. Liberty ship *Paul Hamilton* also was torpedoed; unfortunately for the 504 troops, 47-member crew, and 29-member Armed Guard, *Paul Hamilton* was filled with high explosives, and the torpedo lit these, instantly obliterating the ship without trace. All 580 on board perished. Other ships were struck, including *Royal Star* (sunk) and *Stephen F. Austin* (abandoned but later saved). *Samite*, met earlier in these pages, also was torpedoed but survived.

A few of these victims may have been claimed by the pilots of 6./KG 100, as reported by their unit biographer, Ulf Balke. The claims included *Samite* and *Royal Star*.[45] However the evidence from the Survivors' Reports from those two ships confirms that conventional torpedoes were to blame for their losses. For example, the master of *Samite*, Captain L. Eccles, reported,

> The explosion was dull, but violent, and judging by the large column of water thrown up, which swamped the forward part of the vessel as far as the bridge, I think that most of the force of the explosion was outside the ship. I did not see a flash. Two pieces of the torpedo were found on the boat deck abaft the funnel. These were examined by the Naval Intelligence Officer in Algiers, who defined one piece as the part of the engine casing, and a heavier piece as part of the warhead.[46]

Likewise, the evidence seems clear that *Royal Star* was the victim of a torpedo in the same attack. As its master, Captain T. F. McDonald reported, an aircraft approached from our starboard beam at less than mast-head height, and when at right angles launched a torpedo, banked steeply and vanished astern, barely missing our balloon wire. . . . No-one saw the track of the torpedo, which struck between the engine room and stoke-hold on the starboard side, but several of my crew reported seeing the wake afterwards. There was a violent and what appeared to me to be a double explosion, with a bright flash; a huge column of water and fuel oil was thrown up, which cascaded over the ship.[47]

The Do 217s did not emerge unscathed from the raid on UGS-38: two of them were shot down, including the aircraft of the squadron commander, *Hauptmann* Willi Scholl.[48]

Thus ended II./KG 100's campaigns against the Mediterranean convoys, and, essentially, the role of II./KG 100 as an operational unit. In May 1944 an organizational switch led the remnants of 6./KG 100, the one unit of II./KG 100 still operating Do 217s, to be transferred to III./KG 100 and reassigned squadron code 8./KG 100. In return, 8./KG 100, the one unit of III./KG 100 that had begun transitional training on the He 177, was redes-ignated 6./KG 100 and reassigned to II./KG 100. Therefore, III./KG 100 remained the sole operator of Do 217 aircraft employed in the glide-bomb role, possessing at its Toulouse bases a mix of Hs 293–bearing Do 217 E-5 bombers, Fritz-X-laden Do 217 K-2 bombers, and newer Do 217 K-3 aircraft able to deploy either weapon. II./KG 100's three squadrons were united at Aalborg for training on the He 177. In the end, fuel shortages soon grounded training missions with the fuel-guzzling He 177, and II./KG 100's role in the glide-bomb campaigns had come to an end.

Two of III./KG 100's *staffeln*, 7./KG 100 and 9./KG 100, had been inac-tive since September 1943, awaiting further opportunities to use the Fritz-X. The anticipated missions against Scapa Flow had never taken place, nor had the bombing missions against industrial targets in Russia. With few battle-ships or heavy cruisers offering themselves as targets within the range of the Toulouse base, in late April 1944 these units of III./KG 100 were rede-ployed for missions against the English home base at Plymouth. This was part of a major offensive against the buildup of Allied invasion forces along the English coast, all too visible and threatening to German defenders in Europe. Of particular interest to the Germans was evidence that two British battleships were moored in Plymouth at that time, perfect targets for the Fritz-X. No doubt the Luftwaffe anticipated a repeat of its prior success in sinking *Roma* and disabling *Warspite*. Perhaps the invasion could even be delayed, if the massive attack at Plymouth sank or disabled a sufficient num-ber of ships.

Luftwaffe general Ulrich Kessler reviewed airmen of II./KG 40 just before the attack on *Rohna*. Trailing him was Hans Dochtermann, commander of the aircraft that destroyed *Rohna*. On the far left side of the photo was II./KG 40 leader Rudolf Mons, who was killed in the attack. *Dochtermann Family Archives*

He 177 bombers of II./KG 40 at Bordeaux-Mérignac were prepared for a mission with Hs 293 missiles. *The Deutsches Museum—Heinkel Archives, FA001-01773*

These bombers of II./KG 40 departed from Bordeaux-Mérignac for an attack with Hs 293 glide bombs. *The Deutsches Museum—Heinkel Archives, FA001-01773*

The greatest loss of life of American servicemen at sea in all wars took place on 25 November 1943 when one Hs 293 destroyed transport *Rohna. Courtesy of the Rohna Association*

Rockwood was written off after being hit by an Hs 293, even though the missile did not explode. *Imperial War Museum, FL10260*

The unexploded Hs 293 ripped through *Rockwood's* bulkhead, from upper left to bottom right. The missile fragments recovered by the crew provided an intelligence bonanza. *UK National Archives, ADM 234-502*

The Royal Navy's new light cruiser *Spartan* was destroyed by a single Hs 293 while anchored at Anzio, suffering sixty-six officers and crew killed. *Imperial War Museum Archives, FL3094*

Destroyer *Meredith* was destroyed off Normandy after being hit with an Hs 293 and other bombs. *Navsource*

Liberty ship *Charles Morgan* was crippled off Normandy, its stern torn apart by an Hs 293. *Naval Historical Foundation, G 252657*

LST-282 was the last ship destroyed by a glide bomb during the invasion of southern France in August 1944. Forty sailors and soldiers were killed. *Courtesy of John A. Hickman*

German scientist Hans Ferdinand Mayer provided advanced warning of glide-bomb developments to British agents in 1939. He survived a Nazi concentration camp. *Siemens Corporate Archives, Munich*

Vital clues to the impending glide-bomb attacks were obtained following the capture of Luftwaffe pilot Hans-Joachim Zantopp in August 1943.
Courtesy of Rainer Zantopp

Royal Navy Lieutenant Commander Roger Hill witnessed glide-bomb attacks in the Bay of Biscay and at Anzio and Normandy. He provided vital intelligence–and developed techniques to evade Hs 293 missiles. Destroyer Captain *by Roger P. Hill*

This Do 217 K-2, abandoned at a Luftwaffe airbase at Foggia, Italy, in September 1943, provided the Allies with their first look at the Fritz-X guidance system. *UK National Archives, AIR 14-3611*

This smashed Strassburg receiver, recovered by the British in September 1943, offered only slight clues to the glide-bomb guidance system. *UK National Archives, AIR 14-3611*

This largely intact Strassburg receiver was salvaged from an Hs 293 missile recovered when an He 177 was shot down over Corsica in late January 1944. *UK National Archives, AIR 14-3611*

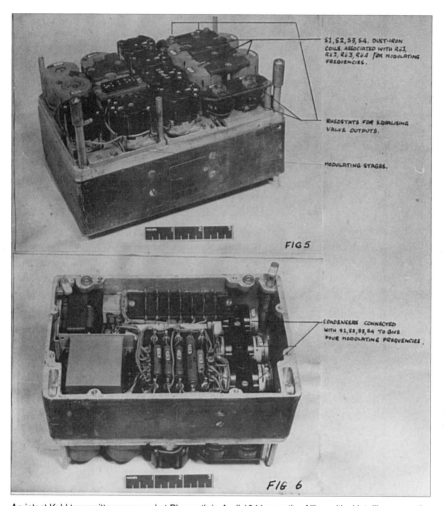

An intact Kehl transmitter recovered at Plymouth in April 1944 gave the Allies critical intelligence and allowed for development of advanced jammers. *UK National Archives, AIR 14-3611*

Frederick C. Davis was one of the first two ships equipped with glide-bomb jamming gear.
U.S. Naval Institute Photo Archive

Herbert C. Jones was the other "guinea pig" used in early (and flawed) glide-bomb jamming efforts.
U.S. Naval Institute Photo Archive

Lieutenant Commander Alfred W. "Skeeta" Gardes commanded *Herbert C. Jones* on vital missions to uncover the glide-bomb control signals. *Courtesy of Chip Gardes*

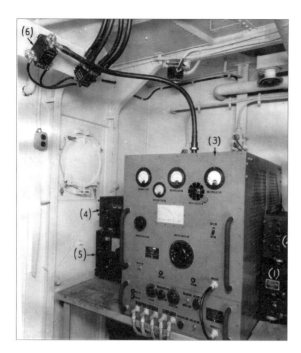

This second-generation XCJ jamming system, installed aboard *Hilary P. Jones*, had been upgraded to jam the correct Kehl-Strassburg frequencies. *U.S. Naval Research Laboratory Report, R-2241*

These receivers (RDC, RBW, RBK), along with the DuMont oscilloscope, provided U.S. ships with the first signs of impending glide-bomb attacks. *U.S. Naval Research Laboratory Report, R-2241*

On 29 April the surviving bombers of 7./KG 100 and 9./KG 100 shifted base from Toulouse-Francazal in the south of France to a forward airport at Orleans. Fifteen crews made the initial journey, though in the end only twelve aircraft, each armed with one Fritz-X, could be provided for this mission out of the nominal twenty-three Do 217 K-3 (and six older Do 217 K-2 aircraft) operating within the group. A critical role in the mission was assigned to I./KG 66 to illuminate the harbor with flares at precisely 0330 hours, just in time for the aircraft of III./KG 100 to launch their optically tracked glide bombs. In the end, I./KG 66 did not release its flares at the proper time, and III./KG 100 arrived over Plymouth to find the darkened harbor enshrouded in smoke. It was simply impossible for the bomb aimers to identify any targets; the weapons were dropped blindly in the faint hope that they might strike something of importance.[49]

Not surprisingly, no targets were hit in the blind attack. The raid was a disaster for the Luftwaffe for other reasons, also. Two aircraft were lost to flak in the raid, including the aircraft commanded by the III./KG 100 commander, *Hauptmann* Herbert Pfeffer.[50] More critically still, one of the two aircraft hit by antiaircraft fire crash-landed outside Blackawton with its Kehl transmitters still relatively intact.[51] As was reported in a British Top Secret assessment at the time, "In spite of the disintegration and burning of this aircraft several units of FuG 203 radio control were recovered. The transmitter and modulator units were in good order, and, with certain valve [vacuum tube] replacements, can be made to work."[52]

In addition to the intact Kehl transmitter, an unexploded Fritz-X bomb was discovered near the wreckage of each of the two downed aircraft and taken to the RAE for complete dissection and evaluation. Now the British scientists had specimens of both German glide bombs for use in fine-tuning the Allied electronic countermeasures. U.S. intelligence reports confirm that well before the war in Europe ended the Allies' description of the Fritz-X was complete and accurate.[53]

After Plymouth, the activity of the glide-bomb squadrons of KG 100 and KG 40 effectively came to a halt for a while. The only suspected operational mission was by one or more Fw 200 Condors, presumably from III./KG 40, against the convoy UGS-40 on 11 May 1944. (As indicated below, an attack by a Ju 290 from FAGr[5] is another scenario.) This was part of a massive orchestration of Luftwaffe raids against this convoy. As with the previous Fw 200 missions, this one ended without any success against Allied targets.[54] The escort fleet leader, Commander Jesse C. Sowell, reported in his action report,

Glide bombs were sighted by Lt.(jg) Paul A. Kinsey, USNR, Armed Guard Commander aboard the SS *Abraham Lincoln*. The first one turned in on ship No. 11 or No. 12 but failed to hit the intended target. The second approached outside of Column 1 and turned to the outside of Column 1 abeam of No. 14 or No. 15. . . . . The attacking planes were identified as JU-88 torpedo bombers, Heinkel HE-111 bombers, Dornier DO-217 bombers, and at least one 4-engine FW-200 (Kondor) bomber guiding radio-controlled glide bombs. (The FW-200 was one of those shot down and crashed in the convoy.)[55]

However, from the German side, the evidence to back up Sowell's report is lacking.[56] The only unit equipped with glide bomb–carrying Fw 200 aircraft was III./KG 40, and at this time that unit had been relocated outside the combat area with its crews on month-long leaves.[57] It is certainly conceivable, instead, that the Ju 290 A-7 aircraft of FAGr(5) were involved. By that date *Staffel* 1./FAGr(5) and its sister unit *Staffel* 2./FAGr(5) each had one Ju 290 A-7 in service; while normally engaged in patrols in the Atlantic, these units were occasionally redeployed from airports near Montpellier, France, against convoys in the western Mediterranean. However, there is no specific evidence that FAGr(5) flew a mission on 11 May 1944 and no evidence that a Ju 290 A-7, or any Ju 290 variant, was lost on that date.[58]

In any case, notable in the case of UGS-40 was the effectiveness of the convoy's preparation for defense against air attack. Captain Thomas H. Taylor, the convoy commodore, and Commander Sowell, based on board Coast Guard cutter *Campbell*, prepared a detailed plan of defense against air attack. The plan was practiced and refined through four rehearsals. Defense against glide bombs was a particular emphasis; American minesweepers *Steady* and *Sustain*, equipped with advanced glide-bomb jamming systems, accompanied the convoy. As a result of these measures, not a single ship was lost despite extensive and repeated air attacks, and the Allies claimed that nineteen of the sixty-two attacking aircraft were shot down.[59]

One last preinvasion attack was scheduled but aborted just one week before troops were to storm ashore at Normandy. On 30 May II./KG 100 was ordered to take its new He 177 bombers on a mission to the south of England. For six hours the crews waited patiently in their aircraft for the launch order, but in the end the mission was scrubbed.[60]

Ongoing Intelligence Operations

While recovery of almost-intact Hs 293 missiles on Corsica gave Allied intelligence units a huge advantage in the wizard war against glide bombs, the intelligence operations did not end at that point. Two other developments took place in the spring of 1944 that, in combination, furthered the Allies' ability to win the electronic war.

✦ ✦ ✦

The first led to very detailed technical German-source information about the Hs 293 coming into British and American possession via the Japanese naval attaché in Berlin, Rear Admiral Kojima Hideo. For several years the Germans had shared technical information on advanced weapons with the Japanese.[61] This collaboration proved to be an intelligence bonanza for the Allies, more significant even than the ability of the Allies to read encrypted Luftwaffe communications. The reason was that the intercepted Luftwaffe communications were messages between informed parties that assumed a basic level of understanding of Hs 293 designs and operation, and thus had many holes that could only be filled via intelligent guessing on the part of Allied analysts. In contrast, the reports made by Admiral Hideo to Tokyo assumed nothing and therefore provided a first-rate primer on the basic of design and operation of these systems, starting from first principles.

Thus in April 1944, when the Hs 293 was described and shown to Hideo, he communicated this detailed technical briefing back to Japan.[62] This he did using a diplomatic code broken the month before by U.S. and British cryptographers. There was a wealth of data in that transmission that largely filled in any gaps in knowledge on the part of the Allies. By this point, combined with the physical evidence already obtained, the Allies could now reverse engineer the entire Hs 293 weapons system. Apparently the Fritz-X was not discussed with the Japanese; because it had largely been withdrawn from operations by that point, though, the Allies were more concerned about the Hs 293.

The second action at that time was a continuation of Project Simmons, the OSS operation to gather intelligence on Hs 293 glide bombs we last visited in Greece and Italy in autumn of 1943. The Allies learned by early 1944 that a major storage facility for the Hs 293 was located in Portes-lès-Valence, a town between Lyons and Marseilles. The OSS hatched a complex mission to obtain vital components of the missiles from that depot—perhaps the Kehl transmitter or Strassburg receiver, or perhaps any upgraded systems prepared in response to Allied jamming. The mission would start with a raid by U.S. Army Air Force bombers on the facility. As the sounds of the explosions faded along with the drone of the passing bombers, they would be replaced by the alarms of the local fire-protection service on their way to help rescue survivors and put out the blazes. However, the local firefighters were going to be disguised French Resistance fighters, intending to rescue for the Allies as many components of the Hs 293 as they could obtain.

The first attempt was planned for the night of 10–11 May 1944. Twelve bombers were assigned to attack the warehouse. Unfortunately, poor weather meant the Allied bombers were unable to find the weapons depot and the mission could not be completed. A second attempt was planned for 10–11 June, but it never came off: the Germans evacuated the warehouse, taking all remaining Hs 293 weapons with them, a couple of days after the Allies had secured the beachhead at Normandy.[63]

One wonders, admittedly in the absence of any clear indications of such, whether the raid on Portes-lès-Valence might have been a diversion, designed to distract German counterintelligence from the vulnerability of the tremendously valuable Berlin–Tokyo communications channel. Should the Allies suddenly demonstrate tactics or countermeasures that indicated a deep understanding of the Hs 293 shortly after such technical information was passed to the Japanese it could only have alerted the Germans to the potential that the Japanese diplomatic code had been broken. It is conceivable that the entire Simmons mission in France was designed to provide a plausible alternative source for the sudden upgrading of Allied data on the Hs 293.

CHAPTER ELEVEN

LAST GASPS:
THE INVASIONS *of* FRANCE

A dolf Hitler had envisioned all along that the Hs 293 and Fritz-X glide bombs would be instrumental in the crushing of any invasion fleet brought by the Allies to the beaches of continental Europe, which is why many glide bombs were stockpiled near expected invasion sites. As the failed preemptive strike against Plymouth telegraphed, the German high command was all too aware of the growing threat of an invasion; large numbers of troops and ships were seen congregating in southern England. According to Hitler's original plan, the inevitable invasion would be met by the full weight of the available Luftwaffe bomber forces and destroyed with these precision weapons.

◆ ◆ ◆

Luftwaffe Order of Battle at Normandy: I./KG 40 Enters the Fight

It was to be an all-hands effort by the Luftwaffe, at least in theory. The units deployed included II./KG 40, now able to launch hordes of Hs 293 glide bombs from upgraded He 177 A-5 heavy bombers, especially given the relatively short distance (about 500 kilometers or 270 nautical miles) from their Bordeaux base to the invasion site. The defense planning also included III./KG 100, which would strike with both types of glide bombs.[1] Given the longer distance from III./KG 100s based in Toulouse, each aircraft would be able to carry only one Hs 293 or Fritz-X. The Nazi defense plans supposed that II./KG 100 would similarly attack with Hs 293 weapons deployed from their new He 177 heavy bombers, then in the process of being introduced into the fleet.

✦ ✦ ✦

A new unit entered the fray just in time for D-day. *Gruppe* I./KG 40 had long played a major role in maritime attack and reconnaissance missions, employing Fw 200 Condor and He 111 aircraft in that role. In early 1943 *Staffel* 2./KG 40 transitioned from its bases in Norway back to Germany to begin conversion training on the new He 177 A-3. Once the basic aircraft familiarization had taken place the unit began to train on the Hs 293 and Fritz-X glide bombs, operating from bases in Fassberg, Schwäbisch-Hall, Giebelstadt, and Garz for this purpose. In early 1944 *Staffel* 1./KG 40 began its transition process to the He 177 and Hs 293 missile. By the start of June 1944, *Staffeln* 1./KG 40 and 2./KG 40 could muster about two dozen He 177 A-5 aircraft and four other A-3 variants (used, apparently, for training).[2]

This meant that four glide-bomber *gruppen* would be deployed as the spearhead against the invasion fleet at Normandy. While it sounded impressive, the reality at the level of individual *gruppen* was quite different. For example, III./KG 100 was but a shadow of its former self by the time the Allied troops poured onto French beaches. *Gruppe* III./KG 100 could muster only thirty aircraft across all three of its *staffeln*.[3] Moreover, reinforcements would be limited. The production line for Do 217 had been shut down in May 1944, so replacement aircraft would be hard to come by after a final tranche of eleven new M-11 variants arrived in June and the same number in July. (Offsetting these two new batches were losses of thirty-two bombers in the same period, more than two-thirds of them to enemy action.)

While *Gruppe* II./KG 40 was in better condition because the production of its He 177 A-5 aircraft was ongoing, at the outset of June 1944 it could assemble only thirty-one of those aircraft for glide-bomb missions, adding to the twenty-three such aircraft available in its sister unit, I./KG 40. *Gruppe* I./KG 40 was new to glide-bomb missions, still transitioning to its new He 177 A-5 heavy bombers. It was far less experienced in these missions than were the survivors of II./KG 40.

Finally, *Gruppe* II./KG 100, the mainstay of antiship operations with glide bombs for the previous ten months, never entered the fight over the beaches at Normandy. That unit was unable to complete the transition from the dwindling fleet of Do 217 aircraft to the trouble-plagued He 177, and thus played no role in efforts to turn back the invasion. Some of its officers and men were redeployed to other units.

Table 11.1—Commanders of Primary Luftwaffe Glide-Bomber Units

Commander	Command	Notes
II./KG 100		
Hauptmann Franz Hollweg	7 May 1943 to 10 September 1943	Reassigned
Hauptmann Heinz Molinnus	10 September 1943 to 4 October 1943	Lost in action
Hauptmann Heinz-Emil Middermann	4 October 1943 to 16 February 1944	Lost in action
Major Bodo Meyerhofer	5 May 1944 to 14 May 1944	Lost in action
Oberstleutnant Bernhard Jope (acting)	14 May 1944 to 11 June 1944	Temporary assignment
Hauptmann Hans Molly	11 June 1944 until group disbanded	
III./KG 100		
Hauptmann Bernhard Jope	28 July 1943 to 10 September 1943	Promoted
Hauptmann Gerhard Döhler	10 September 1943 to December 1943	Reassigned; later KIA
Hauptmann Herbert Pfeffer	December 1943 to 30 April 1944	Lost in action
Hauptmann Wolfgang Vorpahl	12 June 1944 to August 1944	
Hauptmann Heinrich Schmetz	August 1944 until group disbanded	Survived war
II./KG 40		
Major Rudolf Mons	September 1943 to 26 November 1943	Lost in action
Major Walter Rieder	December 1943 to February 1944	Lost in action
Major Hans Dochtermann	February 1944 until group disbanded	Survived war
I./KG 40		
Major Karl Henkelmann	September 1942 (?) until August 1944	
Major Siegfried Freiherr von Cramm	August 1944 until group disbanded	Reassigned

Moreover, the quality of the bomber force could not be assessed only in the context of its aircraft. The condition, training, and morale of the crews were equally vital, and here KG 40 and KG 100 had suffered. The two original *staffeln* of III./KG 100 (7./KG 100 and 9./KG 100) had flown only one combat mission, the 30 April raid on Plymouth, since the battles over Salerno in September 1943. They were out of operational practice, somewhat offset by recurring training missions designed to maintain operational readiness. However, a sizable number of aircraft and crews had been lost in those very training exercises. Meanwhile, 8./KG 100 (until May 1944 operating as *Staffel* 6./KG 100 of *Gruppe* II./KG 100) had been in intense operations since Anzio in January 1944; by D-day it was seriously depleted. Newly promoted Colonel-General Werner Baumbach, reassigned in early 1944 to lead development and training of glide-bomber units, recalls the state of affairs: "[In Italy] the year 1943 had brought no change. The gaps in the [glide-bomber] formations were only made good by young, insufficiently-trained crews. A few sorties—sometimes the very first—saw the end of them. The back of our bomber and fighter crews had been broken and they never recovered."[4]

Turnover in leadership had become a critical issue as well. From the period July 1943 to June 1944, II./KG 40 had lost two of its commanding officers on combat missions, II./KG 100 had lost three commanders in battle, and III./KG 100 had lost one.[5] Increasingly, the ranks of the glide-bomb units had been depleted of their most experienced and highly trained personnel. Complicating that state of affairs was lowered morale, driven by high crew losses, uncertain combat results, and lack of support from senior officers. *Major* Hans Dochtermann, commander of the aircraft that sank *Rohna*, recalls how his unit of II./KG 40 was brought before Werner Baumbach in his capacity as General of Bombers, expecting praise for the successful mission in the Bay of Bourgie in which *Rohna* was sunk. Instead, he and his colleagues received a tirade of insults from Baumbach, who criticized the courage and competence of the bomber crews, suggesting they demonstrated "a complete misunderstanding of the Hs 293 weapon."[6]

If the aircraft and command structure of glide-bomber units had been compromised prior to D-day, the state of affairs with respect to the glide bombs themselves was barely improved. Production of these weapons had never approached the levels once anticipated. As Colonel Baumbach explained in his autobiography,

> The wildest confusion prevailed in the production of the guided missile. In the spring of 1943 the output of the Hs 293s was to be raised from 300 to 950 a month within a few months. [Walter] Hertel, the Engineer General

responsible, reported that from April onwards 750 Hs 293 and 750 FXs would be produced monthly and an increase to 1,200 was possible. At the same time, Staff Engineer [Rudolph] Bree, the technical expert in the manufacture of guided missiles, told us that production, especially in the case of the FX, was in a very bad way, mainly because of a lack of factory space. We had a fully developed weapon but could not produce it in quantity and employ it. When [Karl-Otto] Sauer took over the Fighter Staff, one of his first steps was to order the immediate transfer to fighter construction of the technical personnel engaged in guided missile production. That was the end of the new weapons.[7]

Preparation by the Allies for Normandy

It was with this depleted force that the Luftwaffe sought to hold back the massive Allied invasion of France. Moreover, Normandy was a invasion of the highest priority, supplied with prodigious air support and naval bombardment forces, unlike the invasion at Anzio, in which the Allies tried to scrape by with limited air cover and naval support. The full weight of Allied industrial and technical might was to be evident across the beaches and in the skies over Normandy at dawn on 6 June 1944. Some 5,400 Allied fighters were ready to repel any efforts by the Luftwaffe to disrupt Operation Neptune, the seaborne element of the landing. The air cover over the invasion fleet was continuous: as the sun set, the American P-38s patrolling the skies in daylight were replaced by radar-guided British Mosquitoes working the night shift. The air defense was in depth: as short-range fighters patrolled the littorals, American P-51 and P-47 fighters roamed deep into France and Germany to disrupt any incoming raids. While the fighters provided the tactical defense, long-range bombers of the American and British air forces pummeled the airbases used by the Luftwaffe to assemble strikes against Allied naval forces in the English Channel.

✦ ✦ ✦

The intense Allied air cover over the battlefield, enabled by abundant airfield capacity nearby in southern England, vastly complicated the tactical situation for the Luftwaffe. Daylight attacks using the Fritz-X, in which the Do 217 had to fly a steady slow course, would have been suicidal, and daytime standoff missions with the Hs 293 also would have been problematic. Dusk attacks, the preferred tactical solution for just over half of all glide-bomb missions flown since the initial raids at Salerno almost a year before, would be impractical as well because the bomber force would have to cross fighter-patrolled territory in daylight on the way to the target, which would be difficult at best. Therefore, the only viable option was to conduct attacks just after midnight, in which the aircraft would depart their bases and join up in attack formation at dusk, fly on to Normandy during the night, and launch their weapons at Allied ships either in the black of night or early morning twilight. All this would need to take place while Allied night fighters, supported by shipboard radar vectoring, would seek to peel off bomber after bomber before they could even reach the invasion site.

Even in the absence of concerted defenses, night missions with radio-controlled glide bombs were difficult at best; up to this point only ten had been flown, with disappointing results. Not only were targets difficult to detect in the dark, but also the bomb aimers in the forward part of the aircraft often had difficulty in tracking the weapon and its target at night, a prerequisite for accurate targeting.

If the airborne defenses over Normandy were designed to prevent the Luftwaffe from even approaching the invasion force, the seaborne component of the invasion force would have overwhelmed German pilots accustomed to the thin escort fleets at Anzio. More than two hundred warships were assembled in Operation Neptune, not including the vast numbers of minesweepers, amphibious assault ships, transport ships, and auxiliary vessels. The warships were organized into two fleets, generally corresponding with the American and the British–Canadian sectors. Covering the western (American) invasion sites of Utah and Omaha was Task Force 122, the Western Naval Task Force, commanded by Rear Admiral Alan G. Kirk on board cruiser *Augusta*. To the east was the appropriately named Eastern Task Force under Rear Admiral Philip Van on board cruiser *Scylla*. Two screening forces also covered the invasion force, positioned to anticipate any attempts by U-boats or German surface forces to reach the invasion site. The Western Covering Force encompassed eight light warships; the Eastern Covering force had a similar number.

Should any bombers penetrate the Allied naval and aerial armada, they would confront the new electronic countermeasures emanating from American, British, and Canadian workshops. Moreover, the tactics and training in the use of this equipment had improved considerably since the ad hoc measures of late 1943. Radioman Second-Class Orus Kinney, stationed at Normandy on board Utah Beach command ship *Bayfield* described how he was trained to operate the new jammer, most likely the CXGE system based on his description:

> "We have discovered how the bomb works," the trainer announced, "And your mission is to jam those bombs with this equipment that I have shown

you. We have rigged the oscilloscope so that it will cover three radio bands instantaneously. On the oscilloscope you will be able to spot a Controlled Bomb because it will cause a 'Pip' to show on the screen, a fixed pip, one that will stick straight up. . . . All the other pips on the screen will modulate up and down because they will be voice transmissions or CW (Dots and dashes)." He went on to tell us that when a "Bomb Pip" was spotted, the oscilloscope screen would display the approximate frequency at which time we were yell it out along with the approximate power being used by the Germans; the radioman working the panoramic adapter would tune in the exact frequency. Meanwhile, the sailor at the transmitter would insert the proper coil for the band, set the power, and pull the lever to jam the bomb, that is disrupt the German control of the bomb. After we worked through the procedure a few times, each of us getting a chance to operate at each position, we were ready to set up shop aboard the Bayfield and begin to train for speed; our target was to identify a "Pip," call out the approximate frequency, put exact frequency, get the right coil in the transmitter and JAM within a 10 second span of time. . . . By the first of June, 1944, we were ready to go.[8]

In short, the correlation of forces had come full circle since August 1943, when the novel German wonder weapons had overwhelmed Allied defenses and when Luftwaffe airmen celebrated victory after victory over Allied seamen. Now the weight of technical advance had passed to the Allies. Likewise, the courage of the Allied sailors that led them to continue their dogged advance in the face of superior German weaponry in autumn 1943 would now be equaled by that of their Luftwaffe adversaries, who in summer 1944 embarked on mission after mission at Normandy against virtually insurmountable odds.

Early Action at Normandy

On the morning of 6 June 1944, German soldiers and French civilians at Normandy were roused by the sound of massed naval gunfire, and simultaneously were startled by the sight of the vast invasion force arrayed in front of the beaches. As local Wehrmacht defenders attempted to hold back the assault force, the Luftwaffe High Command marshaled its available resources for an attack on the fleet and beachhead. Glide bombs from I./KG 40, II./KG 40, and III./KG 100 figured prominently in these plans. Göring had called them the "spearhead of the anti-invasion force."[9]

✦ ✦ ✦

As with Anzio, the operations of II./KG 40 and III./KG 100 at Normandy remain mired in uncertainty, and, in a few cases, controversy. No definitive list of missions has surfaced, and any accounting, including this one, is based on integration of available German records (limited), evidence put forward during interrogations of captured Luftwaffe pilots (always suspect), data from Allied fighter pilots who engaged German bombers (subject to exaggeration), and the records of navy and merchant ships placed under attack (at times confusing). By piecing these together, it is possible to create only a plausible picture of what happened in the weeks following D-day.

Missions began the very first night as He 177 bombers of I./KG 40 took off from Orleans-Bricy, joining He 177 aircraft of II./KG 40 departing from Bordeaux-Mérignac. All were headed for Normandy, aiming to reach the fleet offshore just before dawn on 7 June. Radar-equipped ships picked up the incoming raids and vectored British and Australian night fighters to intercept. The ship-based radar controllers provided precise target information, guiding the RAF and RAAF Mosquitoes into attack position behind the often-unsuspecting Luftwaffe bombers, leading author Brian Cull to call this part of the battle the "slaughter of the Heinkels."[10]

For the Luftwaffe the results were indeed disastrous: it was a turkey shoot, though the exact number of bombers lost that day remains uncertain.[11] It is known that Australians of 456 Night Fighter Squadron took credit for four He 177s, most of which were seen to be carrying glide bombs. Shortly after midnight, Flying Officer Ron Pratt and Flight Lieutenant Stew Smith maneuvered their Mosquito night fighter behind an He 177 over the beaches. A short burst of machine-gun and cannon fire caused the unsuspecting aircraft to explode. At about 0100 hours another crew of 456 Squadron picked up an He 177 with glide bombs under each wing. Flying Officer Fred Stevens recalls the incident:

> I turned the gun button to "Fire" as we hurtled in the last half mile. He opened fire first, well over 600 yards off. The coloured balls curled lazily away from the rear of the cabin, then accelerated rapidly past our right wing. The dot of the sight settled between the engine and wing root and I pressed the gun button. The armourers had loaded the cannons with incendiary and high-explosive. One of the first incendiaries must have ruptured a fuel cell, for it seemed the moment I pressed the gun bottom a huge ball of flame engulfed the Heinkel. The crew would have died instantly. The left wing broke off, the rest of the wreckage disintegrating as it fell 10,000 feet into the Channel.[12]

Stevens and Kellet were not finished for the evening: they destroyed a second He 177 off Le Havre. Another Mosquito piloted by Wing Commander Keith Hampshire encountered an additional He 177 carrying two glide bombs off Barfleur and destroyed it with explosive shells from the fighter's four 20-mm cannons.[13] At least six of the four-engine bombers failed to return.[14]

The losses of Luftwaffe aircraft and men this first evening were unmatched by any parallel destruction inflicted on the naval fleets of Normandy. Only one Allied ship reported an attack from this raid by II./KG 40: destroyer-escort *Bates* off Utah Beach, which saw an incoming missile pass safely distant at 0412 hours the morning of 7 June.[15] However, on that same morning on several occasions destroyer *Hambleton* detected and jammed glide-bomb control signals.[16] There were no hits or damage.

Certainly the first raid can be seen as a clear Allied success, combining aggressive air defense to thin the ranks of the enemy with local electronic countermeasures to defeat any weapons that actually could be deployed. However, not all the jamming equipment worked as hoped. The newly developed Canadian Naval Jammer had particular problems with interference. As described by radio operator Kenneth C. Garrett, "[HMCS] *Algonquin* had one installed about two weeks before 'D' day. All you had to do was turn the set on position and it did its own work. Jamming signals. It was very secretive, our instructions were given at various times when to turn it on. On 'D Day' it did destructive work to the *Rodney* a British battleship. We were told to turn the set off as it blocked signals to the guns and wireless office."[17]

The following night, 7–8 June, saw III./KG 100 join the survivors of I./KG 40 and II./KG 40 in missions off Normandy. Once more, fighter aircraft swarmed over the lumbering He 177 bombers of KG 40, with Squadron 456 again serving as primary adversary. Squadron Leader Bas Howard and Flying Officer Jack Ross claimed two missile-laden He 177 bombers; another Mosquito crewed by Pilot Officer "Butch" Hodgen and Flight Sergeant A. McCormick destroyed another He 177.[18] Luftwaffe records for KG 40 confirm at least two aircraft lost that night.[19]

However, the Allies did not escape unscathed this night, or so the evidence suggests. U.S. destroyer *Meredith* was patrolling the Western Task Force area when at 0152 hours on 8 June an explosion ripped apart the port side of the hull, leaving a twenty-meter gap where the hull plates used to be. Seven men were killed in this attack and many others were wounded. *Meredith*, barely surviving, was towed to safety where the next morning a conventional bomb struck the ship and broke the destroyer's back, killing an additional twenty-eight officers and sailors. Exactly what caused the initial damage to *Meredith* remains unclear. Early reports from the scene, including the captain's report, indicate that a bomb of some kind caused the explosion. A subsequent report changed this finding to a mine, perhaps in accordance with the policy (at least in effect prior to Normandy) of disguising the causes of damage in cases of glide-bomb attacks. Certainly the crews of II./KG 40 claimed credit for this attack, which is consistent with the mission profile flown by that unit.[20] Destroyer *Nelson* also reported a miss from a glide bomb that morning in the same vicinity.[21]

Nor was II./KG 40 the only glide-bomb unit to bloody the Allies that night. On the other side of the invasion force, off the mouth of the Seine River, the older Do 217s of III./KG 100 made their initial presence felt at Normandy. In the way was British frigate *Lawford*, built in the United States as a destroyer-escort, transferred to the Royal Navy under Lend Lease, and subsequently converted into a headquarters ship and deployed off Juno Beach. At 0515 hours on 8 June a massive blast ripped apart *Lawford*, killing thirty-seven sailors. For years it had been reported officially that an "aerial torpedo" had been responsible for this hit. Some have interpreted this to mean an air-launched torpedo, though that term also was used for a glide bomb in some early British reports. An investigation of the wreck decades later provided compelling evidence that a penetrating weapon—such as an Hs 293—was responsible, as opposed to a mine or torpedo.[22] Moreover, III./KG 100, which was operating in the area, claimed *Lawford* as a victim, though to be fair they also claimed success against headquarters ship *Bulolo* at that same time when no such hit was made.[23] The Do 217 of III./KG 100 also suffered losses on this mission, with two of nine aircraft never to return.[24]

Two nights later III./KG 100 was back in action, this time targeting the western extremity of the invasion force at Barfleur. Again, it is uncertain exactly what happened that night; the story can only be pieced together from disparate accounts of participants. What is known is that a convoy bringing supplies to Utah Beach came under aerial attack early in the morning of 10 June. At 0200 hours destroyer-escort *Amesbury* was detached from its patrol duties and ordered to come to the aid of this convoy. Sometime later the crew observed a glide bomb hitting the sea about fifteen yards away, covering the ship with water and scattering shrapnel across the decks.[25] At 0400 hours Liberty ship *Charles Morgan* was hit in hold #4, with the resulting explosion blowing out the port hull plates, causing the ship to settle on the bottom while the crew attended to the twelve killed and wounded on board. At 0415 hours crew and passengers on board supply ship *William N. Pendleton* reported a near miss from a glide bomb, the explosion from which buckled bulkheads.[26] *Bayfield*, the headquarters ship for Utah Beach, also reported coming under attack from Luftwaffe bombers the same morning, though no damage was reported. While the evidence remains circumstantial, it appears that all of these ships could be victims of what KG 100 historian Ulf Balke characterized as a "heavy attack" by III./KG 100 that morning in which Hs 293 glide bombers were employed.[27] In return for the damage to two ships, the Luftwaffe lost two of its few remaining Do 217 bombers in that raid.[28] One of them was shot down by Flight Lieutenant Bill Cowper and Flying Officer Bill Watson from 456 Squadron.[29]

KG 100 was not the only glide-bomb unit attacking the beaches on the night of 9–10 June. Aircraft from 2./KG 40 (at least) were also engaged in missions that evening: two of the dwindling number of He 177 bombers were lost, one to Cowper of the 456 RAAF Squadron.[30]

Staffel 1./KG 40 and multiple *staffeln* in II./KG 40 also flew raids on the night of 10–11 June, with five additional aircraft lost.[31] Allied records of 456 Squadron also record two of these losses.[32] Results were minimal: Canadian-owned but British-flagged *Fort McPherson* reported damage from an unexploded glide bomb at about 0330 hours. *Fort McPherson* went back to London for repairs, only to be hit again a few weeks later by a more substantial unguided glide bomb in the form of a V-1 "buzz bomb."

According to German sources, the next attacks were on the night of 12–13 June. One by III./KG 100 was aimed farther north in the channel off the British harbor of Portland.[33] According to these accounts, the Do 217 bombers caught *Boadicea*, leading a supply convoy of from seven to eleven small transports (accounts vary) from Milford Haven in the United Kingdom for Seine Bay near Omaha Beach. At about 0445 hours on 12 June this convoy, named EBC-8, came under air attack. At this point we are again frustrated by inconsistent accounts. Official British records indicate clearly that a German Ju 88 torpedo bomber sneaked into proximity of the convoy by following a formation of RAF Beaufighters returning from a mission. Upon reaching the convoy, and without defensive measures on the part of the convoy, the Ju 88 suddenly broke away and launched two torpedoes in the path of *Boadicea*. According to this account one of the torpedoes hit the destroyer's magazine and destroyed the forward part of the ship. The aft part sank within three minutes; 174 of the 186 on board were killed. However, it has been suggested that an Hs 293 was responsible for *Boadicea*'s loss. While the evidence is underwhelming, one cannot rule it out given the inevitable confusion surrounding nighttime attacks.[34] That same evening 1./KG 40 and 6./KG 40 attempted missions over Normandy only to lose two more aircraft.[35]

If indeed *Boadicea* was a victim of a glide-bomb attack, it was the last to suffer that fate during the Normandy landing. Additional missions were flown but results were elusive. The evidence suggests that II./KG 40 flew a raid on the night of 13–14 June, losing another five aircraft in the process.[36] A raid by III./KG 100 on the following night of 14–15 June over Cherbourg achieved no successes and led to three more losses of Do 217 aircraft.[37]

British command ship *Hilary* reported a glide-bomb attack off Juno Beach on 22 June. Upon detection of the Kehl control signal, operators of the Type 650 jammer on board *Hilary* began transmitting and the missile was seen to deviate. While it was unclear the extent to which the jamming led to this deviation, the success in avoiding a hit while operating the Type 650 jammer led to greater confidence in that system.[38] That same attack on British light cruiser *Scylla* also diverted an incoming glide bomb with its Type 650 jammer.[39] The available records for III./KG 100 do not indicate a mission flown that night, so if the attack was made, it was most likely another mission flown by the dwindling *staffeln* of I./KG 40 or II./KG 40.

Another raid on 25 June by III./KG 100 near the mouth of the Orne River also ended in failure with no targets confirmed hit for the loss of another Luftwaffe aircraft.[40] However, British cruiser *Arethusa* reported damage from a mine exploding astern at 0045 hours on 26 June.[41] This cruiser was operating off Sword Beach, which was the precise target area for the III./KG 100 attack; because the timing is consistent with a nighttime bombing mission, it is at least possible that what *Arethusa* actually witnessed was a glide bomb hitting astern.

One large mission was flown on 4–5 July, combining the remaining aircraft of II./KG 40 and III./KG 100, perhaps in a final effort to break the beachhead with Luftwaffe airpower. Once again there were no successes and the Luftwaffe lost a staggering ten aircraft, including four He 177 bombers.[42] Again, 456 Squadron was the most destructive of the Allied defenses, reporting three kills of He 177 bombers that night.[43] After these missions II./KG 40 had essentially ceased to exist and was withdrawn from the battle line. Following eight months of troubled and frustrating operations, and after losing fifty-three aircraft to enemy action, II./KG 40 had flown its last mission with glide bombs. Likewise, I./KG 40 was taken off the line and dispatched to the rear, never to fly with glide bombs again.

For its part, III./KG 100 likewise scored no hits that night when a combined raid of aircraft carrying Hs 293 missiles and Fritz-X glide bombs took place near the Seine River. Six aircraft with Fritz-X bombs departed from Blagnac, followed by a similar group of aircraft equipped with Hs 293 missiles. No targets were hit or seriously damaged, though the small patrol boat *PC 617* reported two near misses.[44] Meanwhile, another six of the rapidly dwindling number of irreplaceable Do 217 bombers were lost.[45] Squadron 456 claimed one of these as well.[46] A last attempt on 7 July led to claims of a destroyer sunk—no such loss occurred—and the sound of Do 217 glide bombers over Normandy was gone for good.

The massive losses over Normandy inflicted on the Luftwaffe could not be offset with new aircraft or crews. *Gruppe* II./KG 40 started the month of June with thirty-two aircraft and ended with twenty-three: the addition of seventeen new aircraft and four transfers could not offset the loss of twenty-three aircraft to enemy action and another seven to other causes. *Gruppe* I./KG 40 had similar losses. *Gruppe* III./KG 100 started the month with thirty-one aircraft and ended with twenty-five. Even the addition of eleven newly built aircraft and six inbound transfers could not offset the losses of eleven aircraft to enemy action and twelve to other causes. In the case of III./KG 100, the losses in *Staffel* 9./100 were so great that it was effectively disbanded, and the surviving crews and aircraft redistributed to 7./100 and 8./100.[47]

Back to the Bay of Biscay

If the Allied defenses over Normandy's beaches proved virtually impregnable, it was only logical for the Luftwaffe to refocus its efforts to less-prickly targets. This appeared to be the strategy followed in early July 1944 that accounts for some of the last Luftwaffe glide-bomb missions against Allied ships.

✦ ✦ ✦

The last mission against a transport convoy was flown on 4 July by the Fw 200 Condors of III./KG 40, the same day the He 177s of II./KG 40 were preparing to fly their final mission. The day before a Luftwaffe patrol plane had spotted convoys SL-162 (from Freetown) and MKS-53 (from Gibraltar), then sailing together in a convoy of twenty-five ships, bound via the Atlantic for Liverpool. On the morning of 4 July, six of the specially equipped Fw 200 aircraft departed Cognac with Hs 293 missiles under the nacelles of their outboard engines, targeting this convoy. However, the patrol aircraft had related a faulty position report, and the attacking Condors never found the intended target. The last mission with glide bombs against a convoy ended in failure, and all three glide-bomber *gruppen* in KG 40 were now out of the glide-bomb business.[48]

It was then left to III./KG 100 to run down the dwindling supply of glide bombs. As the missions against naval targets had been a major disappointment, production of new glide bombs had come to a halt and the production and research efforts were redirected against air-to-air guided missiles.[49] However, the remaining inventory of Hs 293 missiles was not to go to waste, and the few surviving Do 217 aircraft equipped to carry them operated against naval targets off Brest and in the Bay of Biscay, where the first hits had been made against British and Canadian warships some eleven months previously.

III./KG 100 took ten days away from the battle to regroup before launching its next raids against the ships blockading the port of Brest and other locations along the Bay of Biscay. The entire glide-bomber fleet of the Luftwaffe was now down to a handful of serviceable aircraft, perhaps a dozen new Do 217 M-11 models, and three or so each of the older Do 217 K-3 and Do 217 E-5 variants.

The first mission against the Brest Blockade Group took place on the night of 16–17 July as four Do 217s lumbered into the sky from Toulouse toward the northwest. No targets were encountered and no hits were recorded, though two of the four aircraft never returned from the mission.[50]

The second attack yielded a rare success for the Luftwaffe. On 20 July 1944 Escort Group 9, which included Canadian River-class frigates *Matane*, *Meon*, *Stormont*, and *Swansea* was patrolling off Brest looking for German submarines. The weather was warm with a broken ceiling tending toward heavy overcast. Without warning, the crew of *Meon* was astounded by a large eruption just aft of the ship. It was initially thought that a submarine had managed to launch a new acoustic torpedo (a model G7es, known to the Allies as the Gnat) and that this torpedo had exploded in the wake of the ship. The advocates of the submarine theory were overruled when a Dornier Do 217 appeared briefly through gaps in the cloud layer, confirming that a glider bomb had been responsible for the explosion.[51]

With only one or two 4-inch guns, these four ships, designed primarily for antisubmarine patrol, were relatively lightly equipped for air defense. The primary antiaircraft armament was up to ten 20-mm Oerlikon cannons, which, while devastating when used against aircraft at short ranges, were relatively useless against more-distant targets. The German bombers exploited this vulnerability by keeping well out of range of the ships' guns while launching and guiding their Hs 293 missiles.

The crew of *Matane*, now on alert, was not surprised when another Do 217 appeared out of the clouds and fired an Hs 293 toward the frigate. Seaman Martin Bondy, on board *Matane* at the time, recalled the feeling of helplessness as the Dorniers stood outside the range of the ships' light antiaircraft armament:

> We could not reach the planes, so we had to concentrate on hitting their incoming glider bombs instead. Suddenly we could see a bomb coming directly at us! It struck our ship's upper structure, then deflected downward into the sea, exploding near the waterline. The explosion blew a hole in the port side (left rear), flooding the engine room, and causing

the boiler to burst. The latter caused a rush of hot steam to pour forth, shrouding us briefly in a fog. If the bomb had landed just 20 feet inboard it would have gone down our magazine hatch, and the ship would have been destroyed.[52]

According to Bondy, the Hs 293 exploded in the sea just beside the hull, caving in the steel plates and causing massive flooding in the engine room. Another crewmember remembers it differently. Sonarman Russell Heathman was on the bridge during the attack and remembers watching the missile approach the ship until it impacted "on the foc'sle, and then through three decks where it exploded inside the ship."[53] In any case, *Matane* staggered under the blow but remained intact and was able to survive.

The attack continued without additional success by the Luftwaffe. As reported by the official Royal Canadian Navy damage report, "It is considered . . . that the attacking force consisted of three aircraft, each carrying two bombs. Two were seen to fall astern of *Meon*, one appeared to get out of control and fall a very long way short of *Swansea*, a second one [besides the one that hit] fell close to the port side of *Matane*, and one between *Swansea* and *Stormont*. . . . *Swansea* claims to have hit and deflected one which was heading for her."[54]

Meon took *Matane* in tow and eventually both ships made it back to Plymouth. *Matane* suffered three killed and many others injured in the attack.[55]

Additional missions took place over the following few weeks, including one by eight aircraft on 21 July, in which two or three of the bombers were shot down by fighters.[56] Four aircraft attempted missions on each of the nights of 25–26 July, 27–28 July, and 28–29 July, all to no avail. A larger attack of eight aircraft was made during the night of 31 July–1 August, again without success; after this the Do 217s and their crews stood down for a week. Activity resumed on the night of 7–8 August with a raid on a ship near the town of Avranches, again without success.[57]

The last three missions in the Bay of Biscay were flown just two weeks shy of the annual anniversary of the first successful glide-bomb attack, the one that so startled those on board *Landguard* and *Bideford*. This time no ships were hit, although plenty of crews were startled by attacks and near misses. Canadian destroyer *St. Laurent* was attacked by four Do 217 M-11s of 7./KG 100 on the night of 8–9 August but escaped without damage, with two of the Do 217s lost.[58] An attack on 11 August off the Gironde estuary narrowly missed British destroyer *Onslow;* a similar attack the next evening missed light cruiser *Diadem*.

Bridges Under Attack

KG 40 and KG 100 were unable to stop the Allied tide from washing ashore at Normandy. Given that the beaches were now uncontested, the next best thing the Luftwaffe could do was to stop the Allied forces from moving inland until the Wehrmacht could mount an effective counterattack. It was vital that the Allies remain bottled up in Normandy. This became problematic when on 31 July lead elements of General Patton's Third Army broke through the town of Avranches, which guarded the way to the Atlantic province of Brittany and to the vital port of Brest, a primary Allied objective. The next day, those forces captured the intact bridges at Pontaubault over the Selune River along the road to Brest.

✦ ✦ ✦

Unable to stop Patton's forces on the ground, the German high command attempted to slow them by destroying the vital railroad and road bridges across natural barriers, including the Selune River at Pontaubault, and farther west, over the Couesnon River at Pontorson. The urgency of the situation led the German high command to authorize, for the first time, the use of glide bombs against land targets, something that Hitler himself had forbidden up to this point. The urgency was understood by Patton, who immediately reinforced his presence at the Pontaubault Bridge with hundreds of antiaircraft weapons. An almost continuous umbrella of Allied fighters was imposed above the town.

The day after Patton captured Pontaubault, the Luftwaffe responded. On 2 August a flight of nine Do 217s from III./KG 100 departed Toulouse heading for the town of St. Malo, from there turning east toward the bridges at Pontaubault, arriving around 2100 hours. Heavy cloud cover and intense antiaircraft defenses caused the bombers to abandon their primary target and to proceed instead to the secondary target of Avranches. Some aircraft upon returning to base were reloaded for a second raid that same night. It is not clear if glide bombs were deployed on either of these missions because the aircraft attempted a surprise low-level attack and it is known that at least some of the aircraft carried ordinary bombs. There was no damage to the vital bridges.

Another attempt was made to strike at Pontaubault two days later, on 4 August. Six Do 217 bombers arrived at the scene just minutes before midnight. Some of the aircraft carried conventional ordnance and others took Hs 293 glide bombs into battle. Again, there were no hits with the glide bombs, and this time two of the attacking aircraft were lost.[59] A mission against Pontaubault was made the following night when all eight serviceable aircraft of III./KG 100 attempted to destroy the bridge. Intense defensive fire and night fighter support made the mission impossible, and one more aircraft was lost in the effort.[60]

On the night of 6–7 August a final mission was mounted against the bridges at Pontaubault and Pontorson, farther into the interior of Brittany. Ten aircraft departed Toulouse heading directly for the target, six to Pontaubault and four to Pontorson. Another failure ensued, with no confirmed hits and two aircraft lost, including that of *Leutnant* Rudolf Englemann of 9./KG 100 who had already survived more than four hundred operational missions.[61] A Mosquito night fighter of 604 Squadron had shot him from the sky.

Operation Dragoon

While the invasion force at Normandy continued to push inland, and while the Allied naval escorts blockaded French ports along the Bay of Biscay, additional naval activity was forming in the western Mediterranean, which had been mostly quiet since the battle for Anzio and the convoy attacks of early 1944.

✦ ✦ ✦

This changed on 15 August when almost 100,000 Allied troops—mostly Americans with support from French units—were landed on the southern coast of France between the cities of Toulon and Cannes. This location was designed to split the German forces in France as well as to secure the nearby port of Marseilles, the city from which many of the early glider-bomb missions had been launched in mid- to late 1943. With the strong commitment by the United States, and with grudging acquiescence by the British, a major land and naval force was assembled for this assault. From a naval and air support perspective, Operation Dragoon bore a closer resemblance to Neptune (Normandy) than it did to Shingle (Anzio).

The assault force was organized around four large amphibious task forces: Task Force 86 under Rear Admiral Lyal A. Davidson had the task of landing the First Special Service Force at Île du Levant, an island off the mainland coast. Securing this island was considered critical to protecting the left flank of the invasion zone. The primary assault on the mainland involved three American divisions being put ashore in three zones codenamed, left to right, Alpha, Delta, and Camel.[62]

Many of the veterans from Salerno or Anzio also were part of the overall escort force, including the two original destroyer-escorts equipped for glide-bomb jamming: *Herbert C. Jones* and *Frederick C. Davis*. Minesweeper *Prevail*, another early jamming ship, was also present, as were the surviving countermeasures-equipped destroyers of Destroyer Division 14, including *Madison* and *Hilary P. Jones*. (*Lansdale* had been sunk early in April.) Another early glide-bomb jamming ship, *Woolsey* of Destroyer Squadron 25, also was available, as was destroyer *Livermore*, recently equipped with a jamming system. Taking up the position on the far right flank, closest to St. Raphael, was Destroyer Division 14 destroyer *Charles F. Hughes*. No doubt many of the other Allied ships had also been updated with either British Type 650/651 jamming systems or the upgraded "Type MAS" jammers from AIL.

It was logical that the aircraft of III./KG 100 would redirect their efforts from the distant Bay of Biscay to the attack in their operational backyard in southern France. Over a period of four days, missions were launched in the daytime designed to arrive over the battlefield toward dusk, a protocol achievable because long-range Allied fighter patrols did not roam behind the lines at the French Riviera as they did at Normandy. These were scratch missions often involving composite crews and whatever aircraft and weapons were available. Sometimes aircraft carrying Fritz-X missiles flew missions alongside other aircraft carrying the Hs 293.

The first mission was flown the evening the Allies landed, part of a coordinated strike at dusk on 15 August. Nine Do 217 aircraft departed Toulouse-Blagnac with a mixture of Fritz-X and Hs 293 weapons on board, hoping to sink the thin-skinned transports as well as the heavily armored battleships. Three aircraft never made it: one turned back with mechanical problems and two others were lost en route.[63] The six remaining aircraft arrived over the battlefield at 1838 hours; for the next hour and ten minutes they attempted to destroy the invasion fleet with their Fritz-X and Hs 293 weapons. The attack was cleverly planned, with the aircraft arriving from overland, putting their intended targets between themselves and the escorting warships, which were farther out to sea.[64] This complicated the task of the two dozen or so escorts in the area equipped with missile-jamming systems. From the surface, it appeared that only four aircraft approached the Camel landing zone and released their glider bombs: most likely the two aircraft carrying Fritz-X bombs were far overhead. *Frederick C. Davis* did report a glide-bomb signal and endeavored to jam it, claiming success in the process.

Reports made by the bomber crews suggested a great victory: *LST-282* sunk, a large freighter (seven thousand gross register tons) sunk, *LST-312* damaged, *LST-384* damaged, and an American destroyer called *Le Long* damaged.[65] The claims were considerably exaggerated, especially the account regarding the destroyer *Le Long*, which does not correspond to any identifiable ship. One missile landed close to *Bayfield* (probably the seven-thousand-ton freighter claimed in Luftwaffe reports) but did no damage. However, an Hs 293 did plow directly amidships into *LST-282*, as described in the official loss report:

> The object began to move ahead of the plane and downward on the same course as the plane until its elevation was approximately 25 degrees. At this point it turned approximately 90 degrees to starboard and apparently headed for the *LST 282*. Bright red flame and white smoke were seen coming from the tail of the object which resembled a miniature plane. The speed of the object was exceedingly fast. The Captain told the Gunnery Officer it was a radio controlled bomb and to open fire. The number one forty millimeter located on the bow opened fire. The bomb came in across the starboard side at an elevation of approximately fifty feet. It appeared to be about to cross the ship when suddenly it turned about 45 degrees to port and dove into the ship. An explosion followed immediately. . . . The bomb apparently hit a few feet forward of the superstructure, to the left of the centerline, penetrating the main deck and exploding below.[66]

The crew on board *LST-282* was plunged into a chaos of flame and ripped metal. Forty died, either instantly and mercifully from the explosion, or more agonizingly over time from burns and wounds. The shattered hull of *LST-282*, a burned-out wreck, drifted ashore where it remained as an ongoing reminder of the cost of war. *LST-282* has the distinction of being the last ship before 1967 destroyed in combat by a remotely guided weapon.[67]

Why did the electronic defenses not deflect the incoming Hs 293 in this case? One answer is provided by Radioman Orus Kinny, operator of a glide-bomb jamming system on board the *Bayfield* at the time. As he reports,

> It [was] late in the afternoon of the first day of the operation. As the *LST 282* was cruising into Green Beach to unload troops and equipment, we spotted a "Radio Controlled Bomb" PIP on our screen. We were ordered not to jam, Yes, ordered not to jam. The reason? Apparently there was some suspicion that the ships with the jamming equipment, jammed each other at Normandy. A Navy Officer, a full Lieutenant, was sent to specifically to [sic] observe our procedure and to give us the order when to jam. When we saw the "PIP," we yelled out the frequency and the power and a coil was placed in the transmitter, ready to jam. No order to jam was given. We heard the explosion![68]

The next day brought another attack from III./KG 100. Six Do 217 bombers departed with Hs 293 glide bombs. One aircraft aborted, one was shot down before it could reach launch position, and one was lost after the attack.[69] Again, the bombers approached over land at dusk, frustrating the seaward-deployed jamming ships. Among the four aircraft able to make attack runs, only one hit was claimed, that of an Hs 293 against a destroyer. It turns out, however, that the *Charles F. Hughes* escaped harm as the weapon targeted against her went wide, perhaps due to jamming efforts from *Herbert C. Jones* and *Frederick C. Davis*.[70] Several of the aircraft reported technical failures of missiles on this mission, perhaps also due to jamming by Allied ships.

Like clockwork, the Luftwaffe mounted yet another attack the following day at dusk, with five Do 217s—some carrying Hs 293 missiles and others carrying Fritz-X glide bombs—arriving over the invasion site at 2045 hours. Again they targeted the *Charles F. Hughes,* deployed on the eastern flank of the invasion site, and Luftwaffe intelligence reports intercepted by the Allies reported two near misses by Hs 293s off a six-thousand-ton transport, though no damage was caused. Poor cloud cover forced the aircraft with Fritz-X to jettison their weapons, and one aircraft was lost in the attack.[71] In this case *Ulster Queen* picked up the glide-bomb signals and attempted to jam them with its new Type 651 transmitter.[72]

The following day brings to a close the record of Luftwaffe glide-bomb attacks against Allied ships. It is appropriate punctuation for the entire period of July 1943 to August 1944 and how the once proud Luftwaffe glide-bomb fleet had dwindled to a state of insignificance. On 18 August 1944 the remaining Do 217s were armed and readied for another attack over St. Raphaël. Just after the first few aircraft had departed the runway in Toulouse, an order arrived from headquarters of 2. Flieger-Division (2nd Air Division) for III./KG 100 to abandon the airfield, and return its surviving aircraft from France to Germany.

The Threat Ends

The attacks on Allied forces engaged in Operation Dragoon were the last made by the Luftwaffe using radio-controlled glide bombs against Allied naval targets. Hitler had predicted that massive destruction would result from these attacks and he was right, at least obliquely: the missions flown in June through August had destroyed I./KG 40, II./KG 40, and III./KG 100 as fighting units. The first two had largely ceased to exist after twelve disastrous missions over Normandy and the last had lost thirty-six crews and most of its aircraft in the nine weeks after 6 June 1944.[73] With their bases directly threatened by advancing Allied forces and with the skies over France largely owned by Allied fighters, any further such missions would have been futile, a fact eventually recognized by the Luftwaffe.

◆ ◆ ◆

Moreover, advancing Allied armies had overrun missile depots in France, recovering intact samples of the Hs 293 and Fritz-X glide bombs. By this stage there were no secrets left to these formerly mysterious weapons; the Allied scientists were preparing very sophisticated jammers using this detailed information.

Another factor loomed large: the increasing desperation of German fuel supplies, coupled with the need to mount major airborne defenses against Allied bombers now destroying German city blocks by the gross each day and night. It came down to a choice of powering large numbers of single-engine fighters to protect German cities or small numbers of gas-guzzling bombers to continue a failed antiship campaign. In the end, the heavy bombers were grounded to conserve precious aviation gasoline.

By the end of July 1944, what little remained of II./KG 40 had already been relocated to Gardermoen Airport in Oslo, Norway. The once proud unit was down to only two dozen aircraft equipped for glide bombs. In October 1944 the unit would return to the large base at Schwäbisch Hall where the aircraft would be grounded forever, scattered around the airfield awaiting capture and eventual scrapping. By December there were no aircraft on the roster of II./KG 40, which by then was a paper unit only; it was formally disbanded on 2 February 1945. Two days later, Allied leaders were meeting in Yalta, already planning for the postwar structure of Europe.

The newcomer I./KG 40 (at least Staffeln 1./KG 40 and 2./KG 40) also disappeared shortly after the Normandy campaign. Its surviving aircraft, including only thirteen He 177 bombers, transitioned to Celle, Germany (northeast of Hanover), on 10 July. These two staffeln do not appear to have flown other missions and effectively were disbanded in November 1944.

III./KG 40's fate was similar. Its Fw 200 Condors were withdrawn from the line in July 1944 and relocated to Norway, in this case to Vaernes Airport in Trondheim. Two months later the remnants of the gruppe were brought back to Germany to Blankensee field near Lübeck where the crews were reassigned to other roles, including ground combat. As with II./KG 40, III./KG 40 was disbanded officially on 2 February 1945.

II./KG 100 had been taken off the front line in early March 1944 and reassigned for conversion training to He 177s, a training program that was never completed. For the rest of the war it remained at Aalborg-West airport in Denmark, with its aircraft grounded and its crews largely dispersed. Gruppe II./KG 100 was disbanded on 2 February 1945.

III./KG 100, the unit that had launched the first glide bombs in combat back in July 1943, found itself under emergency evacuation in mid-August 1944, ordered to relocate from Toulouse to Giebelstadt airfield near Würzburg in northern Bavaria. The flight crews made the relatively easy journey by air and parked their aircraft for the last time. It was in Giebelstadt that *Gruppe* III./KG 100 was officially disbanded on 7 September 1944.

While it was easy enough to get the few flyable aircraft to their new home in Giebelstadt, the ground crews and remaining flight crews had additional challenges. They were forced to make their way overland from Toulouse. Led personally by III./KG 100 commander *Hauptmann* Heinrich Schmetz, a hero of the mission against *Roma* in September 1943, these ill-equipped personnel, few of whom had ever been trained in ground combat, found themselves confronted by highly experienced and well-equipped Allied units. Large battles took place at Albi, about fifty kilometers northeast of Toulouse; again at Saint Hippolyte du Fort, about fifty kilometers north of Montpellier; and finally near Lyons. More than three hundred of III./KG 100's personnel were killed or captured during these confrontations, with the few tired survivors eventually reaching Germany in mid-September.

Allied Efforts at Countermeasures Wind Down

The winding down of Luftwaffe glide-bomber formations in Europe after August 1944 was matched by a gradual erosion of Allied efforts at electronic countermeasures. Delays had plagued the advanced XCL transmitter program at NRL and the effort was terminated. The TEA countermeasures system, which was to have used the XCL jammer, instead was programmed around a combined XCJ (the XCJ-4 variant) and XCK transmitters, but delays plagued that system as well and eventually the effort was abandoned. Further development of the CXGE was terminated.[74] Finally, as the threat from glide bombs evaporated in Europe by October 1944, the countermeasures systems on ships in theater were stripped off and redeployed to the Pacific.[75] This battle of warriors and wizards was over.

CHAPTER TWELVE

HOW EFFECTIVE WERE *the* GLIDE BOMBS *and* ELECTRONIC COUNTERMEASURES?

How important and effective were the radio-controlled Fritz-X and Hs 293 glide bombs? Were the original expectations of designers Dr. Max Kramer and Dr. Herbert Wagner validated in practice? Or did the Allies manage to brush off these new weapons or otherwise mitigate their impact? In particular, did the introduction of electronic countermeasures—so ardently pursued by Howard Lorenzen, David Silvester, Norman Davis, Hector Skifter, and J. C. G. Field, among others—affect the outcome of the battles? Unfortunately, these questions are difficult to answer using the available literature; much of the debate has been informed by inaccurate depictions of actual missions and their results. Moreover, the effectiveness of the Allied jamming technology cannot be answered simply: there were about a dozen different types of jammers deployed, sometimes alone and sometimes in combination.[1] It is time to assemble all the data to address these questions, in all their complexity

✦ ✦ ✦

Reconciling German and Allied Claims

Our task is not so simple: while both the Allied and German forces attempted to track the results of the aerial-naval battles, not surprisingly aberrations arise. For example, when placed in the context of information from all sources, wartime Luftwaffe claims of ships sunk with the glide bombs are highly exaggerated. This should not be surprising: it is always difficult to measure mission effectiveness during the confusion and heat of battle and it is a general rule of thumb across all services in all nations that battle claims typically are overstated. To be precise, a Luftwaffe analysis of glide-bomb effectiveness at KG 100, covering the period from their first use through 30 April 1944 (effectively everything prior to Normandy) concludes that 66 weapons achieved direct hits and another 40 were near misses of a nature to cause severe damage, or 106 successes in total.[2] 30 ships were claimed sunk and another 51 were claimed seriously damaged.

✦ ✦ ✦

Table 12.1—Luftwaffe Claims for KG 100 Glide-Bomb Hits and Near Misses Through 30 April 1944

	II./KG 100	III./KG 100	Total
Direct Hits	52	14	66
Near Misses	33	7	40
Total	**85**	**21**	**106**

Table 12.2—Luftwaffe Claims for Ships Sunk or Severely Damaged by KG 100 Glide Bombs Through 30 April 1944

	II./KG 100		III./KG 100		Total for KG 100	
Number of Ships Claimed Sunk or Damaged	Sunk	Severely Damaged	Sunk	Severely Damaged	Sunk	Severely Damaged
Battleships			1	4	1	4
Cruisers		2	2	4	2	6
Destroyers & Escorts	11	13			11	13
Amphibious Transports	3		3		6	
Merchant Ships	9	27	1	1	10	28
Total	**23**	**42**	**7**	**9**	**30**	**51**

Even the most generous interpretation of actual strike results—including all victims whether confirmed, probable, or possible—indicates that prior to 30 April 1944 at best twenty-nine glide bombs achieved direct hits (versus sixty-six claimed) and only fourteen were near misses of a kind likely to cause major damage (versus forty claimed). The numbers are in particular conflict for II./KG 100 and its Hs 293 missiles—some twenty-nine actual hits and near misses versus eighty-five claimed. A similarly generous interpretation of ships sunk or damaged in any meaningful way (not just "severely") by glide bombs in this period produces a number closer to thirty-five or forty than to the eighty-one claimed.

The contemporary Germans were not the only ones to make unsupported claims. Even decades after the war, authors still make statements about glide-bomb performance greatly at odds with available data. For example, author Harold Skaarup, a former Canadian army intelligence officer, reports in a 2005 book that the Fritz-X was next to useless as a weapon after September 1943 due to Allied jamming: "The FRITZ-X was vulnerable too, once its control frequencies were discovered using EWSM [Electronic Warfare Surveillance Measures] techniques. At first, Allied ships used improvised jammers as an ECM reaction; later, they quickly developed a specialized jammer to counter the threats. After September 1943, the FRITZ-X achieved virtually no hits against allied vessels."[3]

Technically this is true, and the "virtually" is superfluous. However, it also should be pointed out that only a handful of missions were flown using the Fritz-X after September 1943, and none of these involved the use of the weapons against ships known to possess electronic countermeasures. For the next seven months after Salerno there were no Fritz-X combat missions flown at all. The next attempted attack after Salerno in September 1943 was the disastrous midnight mission at Plymouth on 30 April 1944 in which the bombers could not even see their targets because of the late arrival of the Luftwaffe aircraft with their illuminating flares. The other missions were desperate gambles against escort ships at Normandy and in the Bay of Biscay in July and August 1944. These raids, involving a handful of aircraft each, were quickly scattered by Allied air defenses, and were hardly a test of electronic countermeasures versus glide bombs.

Published sources do not err only on the side of dismissing the effectiveness of these radio-controlled weapons: at times the error flows in the opposite direction, with commentators overstating the effectiveness of German glide bombs. For example, while, as indicated above, historian Harold Skaarup concludes the Fritz-X had trivial success after the strike on *Roma*, other authors writing just a couple of years before concluded something quite different: "The Fritz-X, a free-fall bomb steered by radio control, sank the Italian battleship *Roma*, on September 8, 1943. It sank or damaged eighty other vessels, including the veteran battleship HMS *Warspite*, in the course of the war."[4] This is greatly in error: only one ship was sunk with the Fritz-X and six others damaged.

A Mission-by-Mission Analysis of Performance

The only way to address the question empirically is to build a database at a mission level for the 118 antiship missions flown by KG 40 and KG 100 using glide bombs across the entire period of July 1943 to August 1944. (This analysis excludes the missions against the Pontaubault and Pontorson bridges because they were not antiship in nature.) For each mission one can document or, when needed, estimate the number of aircraft involved, the number that actually reached the target and launched weapons, and the number aborting or shot down en route to or from the target. Likewise, the number of missiles brought to bear—and their success or failure—can be estimated and in many cases confirmed by shipboard observation and Luftwaffe accounts. Importantly, for the period July 1943 through April 1944 the results can be validated against and corroborated by relatively precise Luftwaffe records on KG 100 and KG 40, thus accounting for 630 of the estimated 903 sorties flown using glide bombs. The remaining missions of KG 100, and for KG 40, need to be compiled from tidbits of data from multiple sources including surviving Luftwaffe records, POW interrogation reports, shipboard observations, and so on.

✦ ✦ ✦

A second set of required data pertains to losses of and damage on board ships as a result of these raids. Fortunately, the data on ship losses and damage are more readily available, though a judgment call must be made as to the level of confidence that an Hs 293 or a Fritz-X was responsible. A thorough analysis of naval, intelligence, and aerial records suggests that for the full period July 1943 through August 1944 eighteen ships were sunk by glide bombs: thirteen of them confirmed glide-bomb victims, three probable glide-bomb victims, and two possible glide-bomb victims. Six other ships were so badly damaged that they were written off or scuttled: four confirmed glide-bomb victims, one probable victim, and one possible victim. Nine others were so heavily damaged that they were put out of action for an extended period: eight confirmed glide-bomb victims, one probable victim, and one possible victim. Finally, twelve others were damaged to such an extent they had to be temporarily taken off front line duties: seven confirmed glide-bomb victims, four probable victims, and one possible victim. Thus the number of ships sunk or otherwise lost ranges from seventeen if only confirmed glide-bomb victims are counted to twenty-four if probable and possible glide-bomb victims also are included. The number of ships damaged ranges from fourteen (including only confirmed glide-bomb victims) to twenty-one (including confirmed, probable, and possible victims).

Table 12.3—Ships Sunk or Damaged with Hs 293 or Fritz-X Glide Bombs

	Confirmed (31)	Probable (9)	Possible (5)
Sunk (18)	HMS *Egret* RM *Roma* HMS *LST-79* MV *Marsa* HMT *Rohna* HMHS *St. David* SS *Samuel Huntington* MV *Birchbank* HMS *Spartan* SS *Elihu Yale* USS *LCT-35* HMS *Inglefield* USS *LST-282*	SS *Bushrod Washington* HMS *Janus* HMS *Lawford*	MV *Indian Prince* HMS *Boadicea*
Written off or scuttled (6)	HMHS *Newfoundland* HMS *Rockwood* HMS *Dulverton* SS *John Banvard*	SS *James W. Marshall*	SS *Charles Morgan*
Heavily damaged (9)	HMCS *Athabaskan* USS *Savannah* HMS *Uganda* HMS *Warspite* HMS *BYMS-2072* HMS *Jervis* HMCS *Matane*	USS *Meredith* (sunk after additional attacks)	USS *Mayo*
Damaged (12)	HMS *Landguard* HMS *Bideford* RM *Italia* HMS *Loyal* SS *Samite* SS *Delius* SS *Hilary A. Herbert*	HMNLS *Flores* SS *Hiram S. Maxim* SS *Selvik* SS *Fort McPherson*	USS *Prevail*

Based on the mission database compiled in conjunction with this manuscript, this damage was caused by 903 aircraft sorties across 118 missions from July 1943 through August 1944. These aircraft carried a total of about 1,200 glide bombs (most of the KG 40 aircraft and a handful of II./KG 100 sorties involved two Hs 293 missiles per aircraft) of which about 500 were never launched at a target, either because the aircraft aborted the mission or because it was shot down before it could use its weapons. Of the 700 or so missiles that reached the target area and were launched, about 230—about one in three—did not function properly or otherwise exhibited behavior that suggested the guidance system was inoperative. Of the roughly 470 missiles that were apparently guided, perhaps 51 achieved a direct hit or a near miss sufficient to cause damage to the ship. Of those 51 results (39 direct hits and 12 near misses) only 35 are confirmed, with 8 probable successes and another 8 possible hits or near misses.

In short, at most only one weapon in twenty-four dispatched from a German airfield scored a hit or damage-causing near miss. Only about one in fourteen of the missiles launched achieved similar success, and at most one in nine of those known to respond to operator guidance was able to hit the target or cause significant damage via a near miss. This is very different from the 50 percent hit rate experienced during operational testing in early 1943.

On the Allied side, including losses on board Italian ships on their way to being handed over to the Allies, perhaps 3,657 sailors and passengers perished in glide-bomb attacks—2,181 from destruction caused by Hs 293 missiles and another 1,476 from the Fritz-X bomb. Of these losses, fully two-thirds resulted just from the destruction of *Roma* and *Rohna*. Excluding these two exceptional cases, the average loss of life from a successful Hs 293 or Fritz-X attack was 25. In the final months of the glide-bomb campaign, when Allied air defenses shot down III./KG 100 and II./KG 40 aircraft by the dozen, missions with these glide bombs were likely to result in the loss of a greater number of Luftwaffe pilots than Allied sailors.

What Explains Mission Effectiveness?

Why did the Fritz-X and Hs 293 glide bombs not live up to the expectations of their inventors, or for that matter, to the claims made by the Luftwaffe? It is difficult to know with precision, but the following observations apply.

✦ ✦ ✦

First, there was a striking difference in the effectiveness of individual bomber groups on glide-bomb missions. Both *gruppen* of KG 100 achieved substantially higher success rates for their missions than did the *gruppen* of KG 40. To the defense of the brave crews of KG 40, it should be noted that many of the most successful missions of KG 100 took place well before KG 40 was even operational and in advance of the point at which Allied defenses had risen to the challenge. Eight of the successful missions of KG 100 took place in situations where Allied air cover was nonexistent (in the Aegean, in the Bay of Biscay in August 1943, and over convoy UGS-18). Moreover, problems with the He 177 aircraft plagued II./KG 40 and caused a high abort rate, whereas KG 100 used the older but more dependable Do 217.

Graph 12.1—Success Rates for Glide-Bomb Attacks by Individual Luftwaffe Group

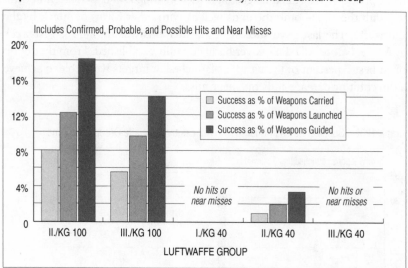

Another factor helps explain the relatively dismal performance of KG 40. More of KG 40's missions took place at night, which was a time of disappointing results for all the groups. About 17 to 18 percent of launches during the day resulted in a direct hit or effective near miss, and 11 to 17 percent of launches at dusk achieved the same. (The lower end of the range reflects confirmed hits and near misses while the upper end includes probable and possible results.) By contrast, only 1 to 5 percent of launches at night caused damage to targets.

Graph 12.2—Distribution of Glide-Bomb Launches by Time of Day

Graph 12.3—Glide-Bomb Success Rates: Day vs. Dusk vs. Night Attacks

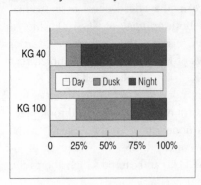

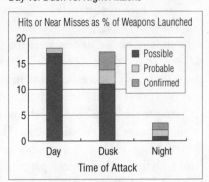

All three groups saw results drop off toward the end of the deployment period when Allied defenses grew more able and experienced in dealing with the glide-bomb threat as well as with other forms of attack by the Luftwaffe. The last great success of the weapons was during the first week at Anzio, before Allied air cover had been fully established. From that point on at best 7 percent of the weapons launched at targets were able to achieve a direct hit or damage-inflicting near miss.

Graph 12.4—Success Rates in Glide-Bomb Attacks by Luftwaffe Group Over Time

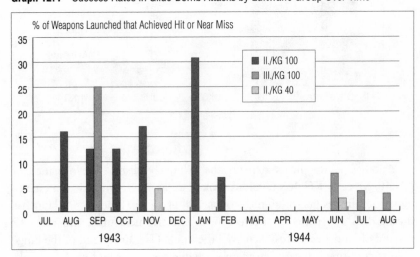

Moreover, in one of those rare cases where the exceptions help to prove the rule, the fact remains that under any circumstances it was rare for the Luftwaffe to score successes against Allied ships except when those ships were stationary or otherwise unable to maneuver, or when they were unable or unwilling to directly engage the aircraft making their bombing runs. Of the ships sunk or damaged with the Hs 293 or Fritz-X, most were either stationary or were restricted in maneuvering either by slow maximum speeds or by operation in congested waters. Likewise, only eight of the forty-five ships hit (confirmed, probable, and possible) were actively deploying weapons that enabled them to strike back at the distant bombers. The other ships were either ill equipped for such defensive measures or were taken by surprise and unable to strike back before impact. Notable is the fact that all of the capital ships sunk or crippled were relatively easy targets: Cruisers *Uganda* and *Spartan* were at anchor. *Savannah* was unable to engage because of friendly aircraft in the vicinity and was still accelerating through twenty knots when it was hit by a Fritz-X. Battleships *Roma* and *Italia* were attacked before they were aware that hostilities with Germany had commenced. Finally, *Warspite*'s defenses were diverted by low-flying aircraft and the defenders saw only the descending Fritz-X bombs when it was too late to do anything about it. Bottom line: ships prepared and equipped to disrupt attacking bombers and able to maneuver at high speed made very difficult targets indeed for the Luftwaffe glide-bomber units.

Cost to the Luftwaffe

The declining success rate of glide-bomb missions after January 1944 corresponded to a continuing and crippling loss of the uniquely configured aircraft and specially trained aircrews involved in these attacks. For example, II./KG 100 suffered total attrition rates of 20 percent in September and October 1943, and another 14 percent in November, leading it to be withdrawn from front-line duties until its deployment at Anzio in January. During each of the first five months of 1944, II./KG 100 lost 12 percent or more of its aircraft, including a stunning 30 percent in February alone. It is no wonder that the remaining Do 217 aircraft and crews of II./KG 100 were consolidated into III./KG 100 after the disastrous spring of 1944.

✦ ✦ ✦

Table 12.4—Defensibility of Ships Sunk or Damaged by Hs 293 or Fritz-X Glide Bombs

	At Anchor, Moored, or Otherwise Stationary	Steady Movement or Moderate-Speed Maneuvering (< 22 knots)	High-Speed and Aggressive Maneuvering (> 22 knots)
No or Minimal Self-Defense Capability Against Launching Aircraft	SS *Bushrod Washington* SS *Elihu Yale* USS *LCT-35* SS *Samuel Huntington* SS *James W. Marshall* SS *John Banvard* HMS *LST-79* SS *Hilary A. Herbert* HMHS *St. David* USS *LST-282*	HMS *Egret* HMT *Rohna* HMHS *Newfoundland* MV *Marsa* SS *Hiram S. Maxim* SS *Selvik* SS *Samite* SS *Delius* MV *Birchbank* MV *Indian Prince* HMS *BYMS-2072* SS *Charles Morgan* SS *Fort McPherson* USS *Prevail*	
Surprised or Otherwise Unable to Engage	HMS *Uganda*	RM *Roma* RM *Italia* HMS *Boadicea* HMS *Warspite* HMCS *Matane* USS *Meredith* USS *Mayo* USS *Savannah* HMS *Dulverton* HMS *Rockwood* HMS *Inglefield* HMNLS *Flores*	
Able to Attack Launching Aircraft	HMS *Spartan*	HMS *Janus* HMS *Jervis* HMS *Lawford* HMS *Loyal* HMS *Bideford* HMS *Landguard*	HMCS *Athabaskan*

Graph 12.5— Monthly Attrition of II./KG 100 Glide-Bombing Aircraft

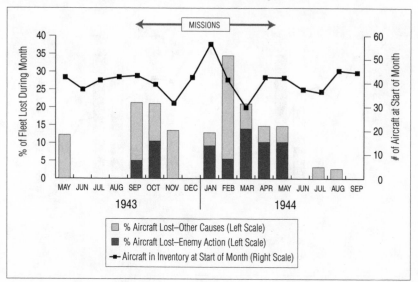

Losses within III./KG 100 are more stunning still and demonstrate the futility of daytime Fritz-X missions, in which the aircraft had to fly slow and straight in conditions of perfect visibility while the glide bomb fell toward its target. Unless surprise was achieved, often in conjunction with low-level diversionary attacks, the crews of the Do 217 K-2 (or K-3 or M-11) bombers were sitting ducks. In September 1943 alone III./KG 100 lost 60 percent of its starting inventory to enemy action at Salerno, resulting in only a dozen aircraft left on hand by the end of the month. The group was rebuilt and only deployed again six months later, in late April 1944, against Plymouth. After that, very few missions with the Fritz-X were flown; many of the III./KG 100 missions after the invasion of Normandy involved a former II./KG 100 *staffel* transferred to III./KG 100 that deployed the Hs 293. Losses during Normandy again rose to staggering proportions with between 50 and 60 percent of aircraft lost each month, only partially made up with replacements. It is no wonder that III./KG 100 ceased to exist after its last missions over St. Raphael in mid-August 1944.

Graph 12.6—Monthly Attrition of III./KG 100 Glide-Bombing Aircraft

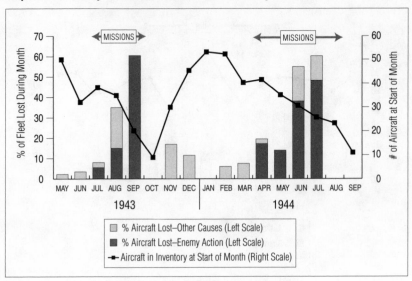

Graph 12.7—Monthly Attrition of II./KG 40 Glide-Bombing Aircraft

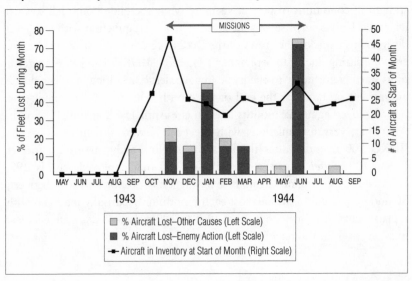

The impact of Allied defenses and the problematic nature of the He 177 are clearly demonstrated in the casualties inflicted on II./KG 40. Losses ranged from 15 to 20 percent per month for most of the period from November 1943 to March 1944, except for a disastrous January over Anzio in which fully 50 percent of the fleet was lost. Constant new shipments of aircraft allowed the inventory to be replenished, though it was much harder to replace the experienced flight crews. In hindsight, these were the good days for KG 40 compared to what happened over Normandy. In the month of June, almost 80 percent of the starting inventory of aircraft was lost, most of it within the first week of the invasion. It is not surprising, then, that II./KG 40 effectively ceased to exist as a functioning unit after June 1944.

While the losses above include multiple causes—accidents in training, aircraft bombed on the ground by Allied aircraft, losses in combat—it would be improper to assume the last was insignificant. Of the 903 aircraft sorties flown for glide-bomb missions, about 112 were lost prior to launching weapons and about another 21 on the way back, for an overall loss rate per sortie of 15 percent. Each time a pilot departed on a glide-bomb mission he had almost a one-in-seven chance of never returning in that aircraft safely. Put another way, the probability that a pilot would return safely after each of the first ten missions was only 20 percent.

Did the Jamming Work: Theoretical Considerations

Now we come to the core question of the role that jamming played in this conflict.[5] How easy should it have been to jam the Kehl-Strassburg system used in the Fritz-X and Hs 293 glide bombs?

✦ ✦ ✦

Over time, the specifications of that Kehl-Strassburg system became known to Allied scientists; after the war, a detailed analysis was prepared that provides insight into the design and operation of that system. From these specifications it is possible to prepare a first-principles analysis of the system, something not available to the Allied engineers working in Washington, Farnborough, Harvard, Mineola, and Sainte-Hyacinthe at the time.

First let us consider the power required to establish a proper command link between the Kehl transmitter in the Do 217 or He 177 and the Strassburg receiver on the Fritz-X or Hs 293. This is the signal that would have to be overcome by jamming. The required power level can be computed from the underlying specifications of the system, the ambient thermal noise at the relevant frequency, the level of signal-to-noise ratio required for effective reception of the Kehl signal, and other assumptions regarding signal attenuation. The design of the German glide bombs, especially the Hs 293, also involved compromises that would reduce the effectiveness of the system. In particular, the antenna on the Hs 293, designed to pick up the Kehl control signal, consisted of a wire of 2.3 meters length, or about three-eighths of the signal's wavelength.[6] This was less than the ideal antenna length at one-half of the signal wavelength. In itself this design compromise would lead to a loss of about 30 percent in the power level of the control signal as it was captured by the antenna.

With the available specifications, one can calculate that about thirty watts of transmitter power would be needed to achieve a link at the maximum (eighteen kilometers) stated range of the system in the absence of any interference.[7] The stated power of the Kehl transmitter has been reported to be about forty-five to fifty watts, though inefficiencies in the Hs 293 antenna design meant that the signal fell to thirty or thirty-five watts when detected by the Strassburg receiver.[8] This means the Kehl transmitter had barely enough power to send a quality signal to the Hs 293 or the Fritz-X Strassburg receiver at the maximum operational distance of 18 kilometers (just under 10 nautical miles). For the Fritz-X this would not be a major issue since that bomb would rarely be more than ten kilometers from the aircraft, given the vertical attack profile. However, with the Hs 293 at maximum range of eighteen kilometers, the transmitter signal was barely enough to overcome background noise to begin with at the far end of the missile's journey. All things being equal—and they were not, as shall be shown below—a jammer operating on the same power level of the transmitter would be able to overcome the Strassburg receiver once the Hs 293 was a third of the way from the launching aircraft to the source of the jamming.

At this stage the issue arises regarding the directional antenna on the Hs 293. While the antenna was exposed to the Kehl transmitter presumably operating astern of it, some of that antenna was hidden from an Allied jammer ahead of the missile, blocked by the rocket motor and missile fuselage. Allied wizards were well aware of this phenomenon and believed that a jammer needed to transmit at least two hundred watts of power to overcome the Kehl signal with any reliability. Indeed, most Allied jammers operated with a maximum power well over two hundred watts, and in some cases produced power levels of one thousand watts. This means that if the proper frequency had been selected, it should have been possible for the Allied jammers to overcome the Kehl signal well before the missile was in its terminal attack phase. Moreover, Allied warriors understood that the jamming ships—often called "jig" ships by their crews—should be placed between the incoming Hs 293 missiles and the convoy or anchorage being protected. Once the missile passed overhead, these jamming ships would have a clear shot of the Hs 293 antenna.

Issues with Multipath Interference

However, there was another factor at play, one not fully appreciated at the time. Years after World War II and long after the last Hs 293 had been launched, engineers and scientists began to understand better the phenomenon of multipath interference on radio-guided weapons, especially in a marine environment.[9] Such interference—the distortion of a signal due to its receipt via direct and reflected sources—could very well have explained the failure of one-third of launched Hs 293 missiles to respond to operator controls, particularly as the weapons approached their targets and moved farther from the launching aircraft.

✦ ✦ ✦

Multipath interference, for our purposes, would occur under a set of special circumstances. The first condition is that a Strassburg receiver unit would see not one but two (or more) separate Kehl control signals. One such signal is the direct line-of-sight transmission from the control aircraft itself. The other is a reflected signal (e.g., off the water) that has traveled a slightly longer path. The second condition is that the longer path followed by the second, reflected, signal has to be of such a distance that when the signal arrives at the receiver it is out of phase with the original control signal. If it is exactly out of phase it will cancel the original signal and the receiver will "hear" nothing. This is the technology principle behind noise-canceling headsets. If the signal is only partially out of phase, it will distort the original command signal and create noise. This is why listeners to FM radio in urban areas sometimes get interference and why they often can achieve clearer signals by moving their radio (and its antenna) to a different location. They are either eliminating a reflected signal path or changing the relative distance so the direct and reflected signals are no longer out of phase.

Unfortunately for designers of radio-guided antiship missiles, the surface of a salty body of water presents an ideal reflective path for radio signals. This would not be much of an issue with a Fritz-X dropped vertically since the reflected signal would not be picked up by the highly directional antenna in the rear of the bomb. For an Hs 293 on a shallow flight path from a distant aircraft, however, it is entirely possible that a reflected Kehl signal would be captured by the Strassburg receiver and added to the line-of-sight control signal, thus causing multipath interference. In short, the transmitter would jam itself. Given the angles involved, this would be true especially as the missile approached its target. Such a phenomenon would appear to the operator on board the aircraft to be either, in the case of exact phase offset, a complete loss of control or, in the case of partial offset, sluggish, sloppy, or squirrelly control responses. Interestingly, such issues would be difficult to detect during developmental testing over land because it typically would not offer the same degree of multipath interference.

A highly trained operator might adjust for this interference by ensuring that the final control inputs were minimal, accomplishing this by careful anticipation of target and missile motion. Thus, we might see a greater incidence of failure due to multipath interference over time as more experienced crews were lost on missions and replaced by less-well-trained air crews. Contrarily, the phenomenon would be more pronounced in cases where targets undertook rapid evasive maneuvers and the bomb operator tried to follow with last-minute major adjustments. Multipath interference, especially in cases where full phase offset occurred, also would make jamming more effective. By silencing the original control signal, multipath interference would allow even a relatively weak jamming signal to get through and overwhelm the receiver.

How real was the potential for multipath interference? The effects can be approximated—assuming calm seas—simply from the height of the aircraft controlling the Hs 293 and the distance of the weapon from that launching aircraft. Two conditions are required. First, the multipath signal must be a sufficiently small number of wavelengths, say 250, away from the original signal as to be detected by the receiver and thus to cause interference. Second, the reflected signal must have a phase-Doppler shift of 100 Hz or less, at which point it erodes or even cancels out the original Kehl control signal. Detailed calculations demonstrate that the second condition would be met as soon as the missile passed one-kilometer distance in the case of a low-altitude launch at 1,500 meters or 3.5-kilometers distance at a high-altitude launch at 4,500 meters. The controlling factor then becomes the point at which the reflected signal approaches the minimum threshold of 250 wavelengths difference (Graph 12.8). In this case, multipath interference would be likely for a low-altitude launch as soon as the missile was five kilometers away from the launching aircraft for a low-altitude attack. It would become an issue for a high-altitude launch after nine kilometers, just as the Hs 293 might be closing in on its target.

Graph 12.8—Doppler Shift of Reflected Kehl Control Signal vs. Aircraft Height and Distance

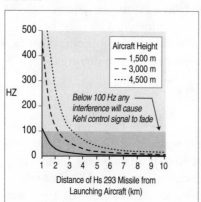

Graph 12.9—Reflected-Path Kehl Signal Difference vs. Aircraft Height and Distance

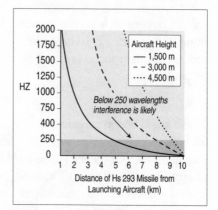

Overall, then, the Luftwaffe's Kehl-Strassburg system as implemented on the Hs 293 had real limitations that facilitated the job of the Allied countermeasure wizards. The compromises in antenna length on the Hs 293 meant that only about 70 percent of the radiated power of the Kehl signal would reach the receiver. The limited power output of the Kehl transmitter provided almost no margin: under ideal conditions the signal was barely enough to control the weapon at maximum range. Finally, multipath interference provided additional self-generated noise in the control signal once the Hs 293 moved beyond a short distance from the aircraft. A well-designed jammer operating on the correct frequencies, at a reasonable power level and at a position where the Hs 293 antenna was not fully shielded from view, should have been highly effective.

This set of limitations also may explain the high percentage of Hs 293s launched—consistently about one in three—that appeared unresponsive to command signals, even before Allied jamming entered the scene.[10] Such losses of control in the terminal phase of the attack also may have been attributed to Allied jamming or operator error, when the Kehl-Strassburg guidance system, in effect, was jamming itself under the right set of conditions. For example, the initial attack on *Egret*, well before any jamming was attempted, saw five of the seven Hs 293 glide bombs targeted against that ship crash into the sea just short of their target. Similarly, the first phase of the attack on convoy KMS-31 failed when all of the Hs 293 missiles crashed into the sea short of their targets—and countermeasures were not a factor in this battle. Such phenomena would be consistent with multipath interference.

Jamming Effectiveness: Empirical Evidence

If the jamming was effective one would expect to see the results in terms of a negative correlation between the availability of jamming systems with the success rates of glide bombs launched by the Luftwaffe. One must be careful in preparing such a correlation because it is always easy to ignore other factors that explain success rates. It therefore is necessary to prepare the analysis from scratch.

✦ ✦ ✦

To start, one must construct a measure of glide-bomb effectiveness for each of the 118 missions on which these weapons were deployed on anti-ship missions. (Of these 118, only about 50 resulted in attacks witnessed by observers on board ship.) The most relevant measure would be the rate of success—direct hits or near misses causing serious damage—as a percentage of those launched weapons that appeared (to the operator in the attacking aircraft) to be responding to guidance signals. A secondary measure would be the success rate as a percentage of all missiles launched, to account for the possibility that what operators interpreted as technical failure was instead evidence of jamming by Allied ships. A third measure, for perspective, would be the number of successes as a percentage of weapons taken on board aircraft embarking on the mission. This last measure tracks the overall effectiveness of Allied defenses including interception by fighters, as well as the rate of aircraft aborts due to failures in the aircraft or Kehl-Strassburg system.

As a reminder, there were about a dozen custom-developed jamming systems against which the various measures of success can be assessed. Some were manually tuned and some were automatically tuned to specific radio frequencies. Still others eliminated the need for tuning at all by jamming all such frequencies simultaneously. Some worked against the direct radio frequency, others attempted to jam the intermediate receiver (used to step down the radio frequency into something that can be converted to move electrical devices), and some may have even operated against the baseband frequency (the frequency of the electrical devices themselves). Most sought to overwhelm the receivers with noise, while one attempted to replace the control signal with one of its own design. Table 12.5 summarizes the approaches taken.

Table 12.5—Summary of Allied Jamming Technologies Deployed Against Kehl-Strassburg System

Radio Frequency Targeted by Countermeasures	Jamming Approach	Type of Jamming	
		Overwhelm Control Signal (Noise Jamming)	Insert False Control Signal (Spoofing)
Kehl Radio Signal (48–50 MHz)	Single Frequency (Spot) Jamming with Manual Tuning	XCJ XCJ-1 JCG Field system XCJ-2 (TX) ARQ-8	
	Single-Frequency (Spot) Jamming with Automatic Tuning	XCJ-3 (CXGE)	Type MAS
	Multiple Frequency (Barrage) Jamming	Jostle CNJ	
Intermediate Frequency (3 MHz)	Interaction of signal from fixed units at 48 MHz and 50 MHz	Type 650 Type 651	
Baseband Frequency (100 Hz)	Fixed at 50 Hz	Electrical razors	

Up through early November 1943, specifically through the attack on convoy KMF-25A on 6 November, the only jamming technology deployed by Allied ships involved such measures as the continuous broadcast of "bollocks" over the radio or the use of electric razors to create electromagnetic interference. Neither solution appeared to have much effect.[11] So, importantly for our purposes of analysis, the intense battles over Salerno took place in the absence of any jamming known to have been effective.

In November and December 1943 the initial deployment of the NRL-developed first-generation XCJ jammers took place on board *Herbert C. Jones* and *Frederick C. Davis*. They could not be everywhere at once, so only a few of the subsequent attacks took place in an environment with jamming as a factor, and these can be isolated from the other attacks according to the presence of one or both of these specially equipped ships. However, because the initial XCJ systems operated on an incorrect frequency, it is reasonable to assume they were ineffective; certainly this seemed to be the case empirically.

Things changed at Anzio in which at least three ships equipped with the NRL's XCJ-1 systems were constantly on patrol. The design of these systems reflected the critical discovery of almost-intact Kehl transmitters at

Foggia in September 1943 and the detailed Kehl signal data obtained during the attack on KMF-25A on 6 November. Unlike the first-generation XCJ system, the follow-on XCJ-1 jammer (and its later upgrade, the XCJ-2) covered the correct frequencies. However, as with Lieutenant Field's interim system, the XCJ jammers were challenged by operational difficulties that allowed the users to become overwhelmed in mass attacks. Hence, we might hypothesize that we would see only limited success of jamming in cases of such large-scale raids, as was the case with Anzio in January, and more-substantial results from countermeasures in other applications where the operators did not have to contend with multiple weapons in the air, such as the attacks at Anzio in February and subsequent attacks on convoys.

This operational problem was addressed with fundamentally different techniques by the British Type 650 system as well as the third-generation jammers from NRL. The former involved a jamming of the Strassburg receiver's 3 MHz intermediate frequency, which eliminated the need to identify specific frequencies in use but which was available for deployment only after the invasion at Anzio. Given this pattern of deployment, we would expect to see an increasing success rate of jamming efforts after the Anzio invasion. The upgraded NRL systems involved a much more capable tuning system coupled with high-power ARQ-8 or CXGE transmitters but these were not deployed until April 1944. One would hypothesize a sharp decline in glide-bomb success rates at that point, especially since the deployment was widespread, with many dozens of ships so equipped.

The final and most-capable U.S. jamming system was the advanced Type MAS prepared by AIL after unexploded Hs 293 missiles were recovered at Anzio and from aircraft F8+AM, the He 177 that crash-landed on Corsica. The Type MAS system allowed the operator to send false control signals that were precisely defined to be interpreted by the Strassburg system as valid. One would expect to see a sharp decline in glide-bomb success following the deployment of these updated systems after April 1944. Two other advanced systems entered the conflict after April 1944: the British Type 651 and Canadian Naval Jammers.

As a practical matter, the XCJ-2, ARQ-8, CXGE (XCJ-3), Type 650, Type MAS, Type 651 system, and the Canadian Naval Jammer were deployed together at Normandy, and this forces us to consider their effectiveness as a group.

The empirical data on effectiveness of glide bombs versus countermeasures, based on an analysis of all 118 missions, is largely consistent with the hypotheses above: the increasing level of jamming effectiveness after April 1944 had a major detrimental impact on glide-bomb missions. Clearly, other factors also help explain the variation in mission effectiveness, especially the number of sorties, the apparent experience level of the crews, and the time of day or night chosen for the attack.

The success rate of glide-bomb missions grew with the level of experience for the first few months, peaking at Salerno when 28 percent of the weapons launched and seen to respond to guidance either hit their target or achieved a near miss sufficient to cause major damage. In October the success rates fell back to the lower levels of August, probably reflecting greater sortie rates against harder-to-hit moving targets compared with the easier missions against stationary targets at Salerno.

Graph 12.10—Glide-Bomb Attack Effectiveness by Campaign and Jamming Technology

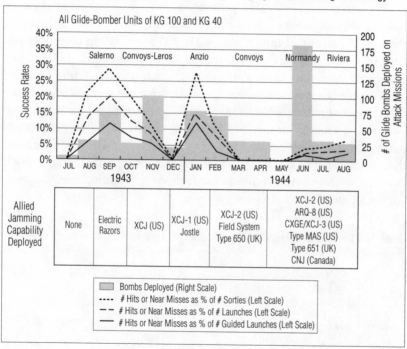

Starting in November 1943 the effectiveness rate fell precipitously. However, the explanation lies not in the use of jamming (a factor in only two missions that month out of twelve flown) but rather in the introduction into battle of large formations of inexperienced crews from II./KG 40. The low success rate of II./KG 40—the loss of *Rohna* notwithstanding—dragged down the total for the Luftwaffe. The success rates in December were zero for similar reasons. Each mission that month was flown by the relatively inexperienced crews of II./KG 40, many missions were undertaken in miserable weather conditions, and in most cases the attacking crews struggled to even find their targets.

The battles over Anzio in late January mark the first time that concentrated jamming was a consistent factor, primarily from the six XCJ-1 systems on board a handful of U.S. ships. The results suggest no change in glide-bomb success rates for the first half of the Anzio battle, a time of large-scale attacks that could overwhelm the jamming ships. There then occurs a major decline in glide-bomb effectiveness starting in February, when smaller-scale attacks were the norm. Once again, the total is dragged down by II./KG 40, which took an estimated fifty-six weapons into battle but achieved no successes.

The effects of KG 40's poor performance on overall success rates can be isolated by considering only those missions flown by KG 100. Furthermore, the variable success of Fritz-X versus Hs 293 missions can be further isolated by considering only KG 100 missions employing the Hs 293 weapon. Finally, the data also can be sorted to distinguish confirmed from probable and possible hits and near misses. These data indicate that glide-bomb success rates were relatively consistent at 20 to 30 percent until the second half of Anzio, at which point they decline to only 10 percent, falling even further during the attacks off Normandy and St. Raphael in mid-1944. Therefore, there is little empirical evidence to suggest that the second-generation NRL jamming systems were effective in the early days at Anzio, at least against large-scale attacks by II./KG 100.

Graph 12.11—Glide-Bomb Hits and Near Misses Over Time by KG 100 Using Hs 293

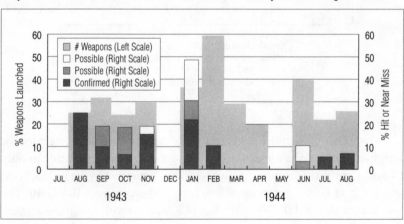

However, there is a noticeable drop in glide-bomb effectiveness in February. The continuing saga of II./KG 40, which was largely ineffective in harassing Allied convoys in the month of February, cannot explain this decline. The effectiveness of II./KG 100 dropped in half from January to February: a weapon seen to be responding to guidance commands had a one-in-five chance of causing damage in January, and only a one-in-ten chance of doing the same in February. Part of this can be explained by the increase in the number of night missions—typically less successful—flown in February as opposed to January. But the possibility certainly remains that the second-generation jamming systems developed by NRL finally proved their value at Anzio in diverting a greater number of missiles than in the first weeks over that invasion site. This is understandable, in that by that time the experience level of the Allied operators using their manually tuned equipment had increased.

The Luftwaffe success rate dropped to zero in March, April, and May 1944 when the targets shifted from ships at anchor off Anzio to convoys moving under air cover and naval escort. These missions were all conducted at night, often in poor weather, so it should not be surprising that the hit rate was low. In all probability the convoys attacked in March did not have the protection of NRL jamming systems. However, certainly by 11 April the convoys were protected by escorts equipped with advanced jamming systems, as can be ascertained by the presence of escorts known to have been so equipped at the time.

The final major contest of Luftwaffe glide-bomb technology versus Allied jamming technology was of course at Normandy in June and July, and in the French Riviera in August 1944. In contrast to Anzio and Salerno, where glide bombs destroyed a number of ships, at Normandy their effect was significantly reduced. There was only a handful of potential cases of glide-bomb damage or sinking over two months, though many of these remain unconfirmed. Once again, the general failure of I./KG 40 and II./KG 40—two ships probably struck (*Meredith* and *Fort McPherson*) in 130 sorties—brings down the success rate. Even III./KG 100, which at that time included remnants of II./KG 100, achieved only minimal success, with only 11 percent of guided weapons hitting targets in June (two possible hits and one probable), falling to 6 percent in July (one confirmed hit) and August (also one confirmed hit). Certainly, the evidence appears that in cases where Allied outer defenses failed and attacking aircraft were able to launch guided weapons at targets the probability that the missile would hit the target in the presence of large-scale application of advanced jamming systems was significantly reduced. Moreover, as the exceptions that prove the rule, the two cases of confirmed hits by III./KG 100 were unusual either in that the ships were outside jamming coverage (*Matane*) or in that the attack strategy intentionally or otherwise was designed to minimize the potential success of jamming by approaching over land with the target between the bombers and the jamming ships (*LST-282*).

In summary, it is hard to construct a case that the early NRL jamming systems (especially the manual XCJ and XCJ-1) had much effect, in keeping with the low expectations by their developers. The second-generation NRL systems appeared to have had a modest effect, especially once the crews became experienced and the ability of the Luftwaffe to overwhelm them with sheer numbers went away. In contrast there is ample evidence that the advanced jammers deployed at Normandy and St. Raphael—especially the CXGE, Type MAS, Type 650, and Type 651—contributed to an otherwise unexplainable and marked decline in the effectiveness of those missiles fired at targets and responding (initially) to operator commands.

Graph 12.12—Summary of Glide-Bomb Effectiveness vs. Jamming Technology

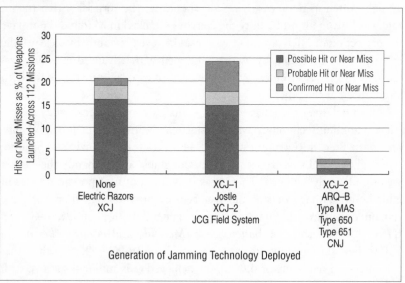

Why Did the Luftwaffe Not React?

The question remains as to why the Germans did not anticipate or detect the presence of jamming operations and why they apparently took no measures to counteract these devices. Certainly the opportunity existed. Throughout

1943 and 1944 the Germans were developing advanced wire-guided and TV-homing versions of the Hs 293, but neither was ever deployed. More conventionally the Luftwaffe had developed transmitters and receivers operating on different frequencies, both below and above 48–50 MHz. The FuG 203-1 and E 230-1 utilized a 60 MHz carrier frequency with nine channels spaced 200 kHz apart. The FuG 203-2 and E 230-2 employed a 27 MHz carrier with nine channels at 200 kHz spacing. Both were produced in large quantities but never deployed.[12]

❖ ❖ ❖

It is not true that the Luftwaffe was unaware of the possibility of electronic spoofing of their Kehl-Strassburg radio links. Two Do 217 aircraft were especially equipped to monitor the airways and look for evidence of radio transmissions in the region of 50 MHz, which would have been a potential indicator of jamming activity.[13] Unfortunately, one of these special aircraft was shot down during the Ajaccio raid in September 1943, before jamming was ever deployed.[14] It remains unclear if additional electronics surveillance missions were ever flown.

There are hints that Luftwaffe pilots were aware of specially equipped naval escorts—reference was made to one of these ships being nicknamed "Old Gossip." However this seems to suggest these pilots believed that these ships were listening in on airborne radio communications. It does not necessarily indicate the pilots believed the ships were jamming the Kehl-Strassburg control link.

The German response was also muted because in April 1944 the Luftwaffe had reported a rate of success far in excess of that achieved, so, for all the Germans knew, the Hs 293 and Fritz-X were performing exactly as intended. Moreover, to the extent that weapons were seen to behave strangely, this was attributed, at least in KG 40, to cases of sabotage of the Kehl transmitter by French workers and to accidental interference by miscellaneous radar and navigation systems, including Gee.[15] (Now we know that multipath interference was also likely a factor.) Provisions had been made to evolve the system toward a wire-guided variant, or to shift the frequencies of the transmitter-receiver, but only in the case that a substantial number of the weapons failed because of known active interference. Evidently, the Luftwaffe believed such a threshold was never met, and they might not have been in error in that conclusion, at least until the invasion of Normandy.

In the end, the best sense of where the Germans stood on the issue of electronic interference is indicated by the views of the inventor of the Hs 293. Herbert Wagner always insisted the Kehl-Strassburg radio-control

links were never effectively jammed and that the eventual failure of the
weapon in operational use was because of Allied attacks on the home bases
of the Hs 293-equipped aircraft. He made this clear in a letter to the edi-
tor of *Scientific American* on 15 September 1981, a short while before his
death: "The sufficiently sophisticated radio link was never jammed but the
allied bomber aircraft finally destroyed the German airfields.[16]

Operational Issues

Questions also can be asked about the operational deployment of the
weapon. What if the Luftwaffe had kept the weapons in reserve for the invasion of Europe as opposed to letting the secret out in August 1943 during
raids against small British patrol ships in the Bay of Biscay? Some observers
have concluded that the Luftwaffe should have used the Fritz-X and Hs 293
in more-concentrated fashion in order to achieve surprise.[17] *Grossadmiral*
Dönitz, by then head of the Kriegsmarine, had proposed a massive blitz
attack on the British naval fortress at Gibraltar, but was vetoed by Hitler
who insisted that the primary objective should be the defeat at long range of
Atlantic convoys, supplanting the U-boats that had taken a heavy beating in
attempting to perform that same mission.

◆ ◆ ◆

As a practical matter, the existence of these weapons likely would have
been compromised even if not used in August 1943. Ultra decrypts had
already begun to point to these new weapons even before the original attacks
in the Bay of Biscay. In the end, the intelligence war, decisively won by the
Allies, trumped the substantial contributions of the technical wizards and
likewise the courageous efforts of Allied and Luftwaffe warriors.

EPILOGUE

B y late August 1944, after only twelve months of combat operations, the era of German radio-controlled antiship glide bombs had come to an end. Only one more mission was flown with the Hs 293, and it was not even against ships but instead against bridges over the Oder River in (then) eastern Germany, in a final effort to slow the final offensive of the Soviet Red Army against the German homeland. KG 100 had long ceased to exist as a functioning group and the remaining Do 217s were operated by a special—and at the time secret—Luftwaffe unit, *Versuchskommando/ Kampfgeschwader* 200. This is the same unit that used to fly captured American B-17 bombers and other Allied aircraft on secret missions. It was commanded after November 1944 by the operational father of the Luftwaffe glide-bomb concept, Werner Baumbach.

◆ ◆ ◆

On 12 April 1945—just hours before U.S. President Franklin Roosevelt died in Warm Springs, Georgia—pilots in KG 200 took twelve surviving Do 217s with Hs 293 weapons on a dusk mission against the Oder bridges. While hits were claimed, the bridge survived, the disruption was minimal, and the massive Soviet advance continued apace.[1] World War II in Europe had but a month to run.

However, the full impact of the German radio-controlled glide bombs, and the Allied efforts to defeat them with electronic countermeasures, extended well beyond World War II. The technologies developed on both sides would see continued use up to the modern day. Although warriors such as Hans Dochtermann, Bernhard Jope, Heinrich Schmetz, "Skeeta" Gardes, and Roger Hill set down their arms, whole industries would be created to expand on the research of electronic wizards such as J. C. G. Field, Max Kramer, Howard Lorenzen, Denys Silvester, Hector Skifter, and Herbert Wagner.

Fate of the Wizards

On 18 May 1945, while smoke still spiraled over the wreckage of Hitler's bunker and the war raged in the Pacific, an aircraft carrying three German passengers landed in Frederick, Maryland. First off the airplane was Dr. Herbert A. Wagner, closely followed by two of his aides. The United States had just begun Operation Paperclip, a massive effort to secure the best scientific minds from Nazi Germany and bring them to the United States. It was hoped these scientists might advance U.S. capabilities in critical areas, both to defeat the immediate enemy in Japan and to prepare for the upcoming struggle foreseen with the Soviet Union. The very first scientist ferreted out of Germany under Operation Paperclip was none other than Dr. Wagner, the inventor of the Hs 293.

◆ ◆ ◆

In May 1945, just after the war ended in Europe, the Allied Naval Technical Mission had located Wagner, along with other German scientists and officials who had sought escape from Allied bombing, in the village of Oberammergau in Bavaria. The Allied scientists and intelligence officials knew who Wagner was, were aware of his importance to the German war effort, and "paid him slavish respect."[2] The U.S. Navy was keen to get Wagner's assistance on its own guided-missile projects, then considered instrumental to the defeat of Japan. Wagner cooperated fully, presenting the Allies with "seven enormous cases of blueprints" and escorting the Allied visitors to the underground manufacturing sites for his secret weapons.

Upon arriving in Washington, Dr. Wagner worked twelve-hour days helping the Navy improve its missile designs. Shortly afterwards he was flown to New York where he was put up at Castle Gould and Hempstead House, the impressive estate of Daniel and Florence Guggenheim at Sands Point, Long Island.[3] Comfortable amongst the manicured lawns, genteel airs, and ocean vistas of Sands Point, Wagner and his colleagues set to work transferring their knowledge of guided weapons to U.S. authorities, then developing their own variants of glide bombs for use against Japan.

Wagner stayed at Sands Point for two years and then relocated to the newly developed Naval Air Missile Test Center in Point Mugu, California, the centerpiece of the U.S. Navy's research into guided missiles.[4] There he earned $27.30 per day working for the Americans. For the next three years he helped develop the guidance systems for many of America's most advanced antiship, land-attack, and antiaircraft missiles, some of which remain in military inventories to this day. While in service of the U.S. government, he was investigated by a counterintelligence team from the Federal Bureau of Investigation (FBI), part of a standard review performed on German scientists working in sensitive U.S. industries. That investigation report characterized Wagner as "an excellent German scientist of good character and who is not interested in politics. . . . He has given no evidence of being either pro-Nazi or pro-Communist and is disinterested politically. . . . Once belonged to the German SS for a four week's instruction course but dropped out of same on his own volition. . . . Is an opportunist who is interested only in science and does not subscribe to any political ideology. . . . Since the death of his wife, Wagner has been drinking considerably but is not a drunkard."[5]

After leaving government service Wagner founded his own Van Nuys–based consulting business, HA Wagner Company. He served as president and chief engineer of that company until 1957, when he sold it to Curtiss Wright after the cancellation of a major missile program that was critical for the company's survival. In 1957 Wagner returned to Germany to become a professor of technical mechanics and space technology at the Technische Hochschule (Institute of Technology) Aachen. Three years later he was awarded an honorary doctorate from the Technischen Universität (Technical University) Berlin. All the while, Wagner continued to consult extensively with the U.S. government and with major corporations, including Raytheon (a major guided-missile producer) and Collins Radio (now part of Rockwell Collins). Missiles he helped develop included the Bullpup, Oriole, and Sidewinder, the last of which is still in use today in vastly upgraded form.

Wagner passed away on 28 May 1982, about a year after he wrote to the journal *Scientific American* insisting his glide bomb had never been defeated by Allied countermeasures. He died in Vienna, Austria, the country where he had been born more than eighty-two years before.

As Wagner journeyed by air to Long Island, Dr. Max Otto Kramer was creating his own postwar legacy, having been squirreled out of Germany to England and then taken by sea to the United States. Kramer, like Wagner, sold his skills to the U.S. government, working from 1947 to 1952 for the Pilotless Aircraft Laboratory at the Naval Air Development Station in

Johnsville, Pennsylvania. He also was subjected to an FBI investigation, which concluded "KRAMER is very conscious of his background and seems to be very cautious in his speech since he appears to realize that he could be very easily criticized for expressing any opinions that were not viewed favorably by his fellow-employees. Hence KRAMER avoids any discussions of a political nature. . . . Attends strictly to duty, rarely absent from work, and applies himself industriously. Produces considerably greater quantity of work than American engineers of the same pay level."[6]

Kramer left government employment in 1952 to take a position as technical director with Coleman Engineering Company, a leading defense and aerospace technology founded by Theodore C. Coleman in Los Angeles. There he continued his exceptional work in fluid mechanics, inventing the completely new field of compliant coatings that he claimed could revolutionize movement of structures through the water. A story has emerged that on his journey by ship to the United States Kramer observed the movement of dolphins and reached conclusions about advanced way to create shapes and material that promote laminar flow, the smooth movement of water (or air) across a surface without the turbulence that slows it down and creates stresses. In 1956, in order to monetize Kramer's research on "Boundary Layer Stabilization by Distributed Damping," Coleman and Kramer founded a jointly owned company, Coleman-Kramer, Inc. The result of this combined effort was a new material designed to reduce drag in underwater vehicles emulating the compliant skin of porpoises. In 1957 the technology was licensed to U.S. Rubber Company for manufacturing, under the trademark Lamiflo. There were great expectations for the technology though it was later suggested the potential of Lamiflo had been significantly overstated. Kramer's entire body of research on compliant coatings had become the subject of intense criticism. Author Mohamed Gad-el-Hak explains what followed in what has been called the Kramer Controversy: "The entire field of compliant coatings became the Rodney Dangerfield of fluid mechanics research, getting no respect from a skeptical community largely because Kramer's original experiments lost credibility. However, . . . the most recent evidence resurrects the good name of this ingenious German-American and with a renewed confidence in this waning and waxing field."[7]

Over time, researchers in Kramer's field—isotropic flows—have taken a deeper look at his research, and especially at his patents for drag-reducing coatings. Some believe the link to porpoises is a convenient cover for research that had actually been sponsored by the Nazis in World War II, a cover designed to make this research more palatable and acceptable to Americans. It also turns out that Kramer's patent filings are incomplete:

there is a critical bit of missing information needed to make sense of them; Kramer evidently kept this information for the use of paying customers only. Only someone who was already highly educated in this obscure field would even know that the information is missing. Perhaps frustrated by his experiences with Lamiflo, Kramer turned away from U.S. customers and looked overseas for parties interested in his research. One of these turned out to be the Soviet Union.

While Kramer's postwar research involving underwater subjects has gained increasing acceptance, he is still best remembered as the inventor of the Fritz-X aerial bomb that in the space of a few weeks sank *Roma* and crippled *Warspite, Uganda,* and *Savannah.* At least one person who worked with his research company after the war describes his reputation using the words "brilliant, very arrogant and truly a Nazi."[8] Kramer became ill in his later years, and passed away in June 1986.[9]

The story of the German glide bombs is not just a battle between pilots and sailors—it is also the story of competing scientific establishments. One of the American players most involved in this battle was Howard Lorenzen, a pioneer in NRL's efforts to build electronic surveillance systems and countermeasures. Lorenzen continued these activities after the war, becoming the pioneer of the art of electronic intelligence (ELINT) and redirecting his activities against the Soviet Union as the Cold War emerged. Virtually every airborne and naval U.S. electronic surveillance system of the 1950s carried his fingerprints, and Lorenzen easily made the transition to the space age. In 1960 he led the successful program to launch an ELINT satellite over the Soviet Union, with the result that U.S. intelligence analysts were overwhelmed with the new data available for their consumption. Lorenzen's early activities in space became a foundation for what would later become the U.S. National Reconnaissance Office. Some of his work remains classified to this day.

Lorenzen continued his work in electronics countermeasures and intelligence throughout the 1960s, retiring in June 1973 as the disabling effects of Ménière's disease (which causes vertigo) became more pronounced. For the next seventeen years he resisted entreaties that he write a book on his experiences and instead maintained contact with friends and former colleagues via "the amateur radio station of his dreams" until his death from pneumonia on 23 February 2000.[10] In October 2008 the U.S. Navy Department announced that its newest missile-range instrumentation ship would be designated USNS *Howard O. Lorenzen.*

Lorenzen's colleagues at the NRL continued their research after the war. Ernest Krause, who led the installation of the early countermeasures systems on *Herbert C. Jones* and *Frederick C. Davis* and who contributed greatly to the development of U.S. atomic weapons after World War II, retired in 1978 from a leadership role in Ford Aerospace, a company he was instrumental in creating. He passed away in 1989.[11] Bill Howe, the NRL engineer who developed the threat receivers used widely to detect glide-bomb attacks, became a highly respected "graybeard" in the field of electronic intelligence. He lives today in Washington, D.C.

Britain's Lieutenant J. C. G. Field, who so ably organized the intelligence efforts on the Hs 293 at Anzio, continued his efforts in electronic counter-measures for the remaining days of World War II, eventually transferring to the regular Royal Navy and reaching the rank of captain in 1955. He supported ongoing efforts in electronics research at the Ministry of Defense and was an avid contributor to academic journals on various topics in physics and electronics, including the best way to teach these subjects to students. Field retired from the Royal Navy in July 1972 and passed away in Cornwall, England, on 15 September 2002.

After the war, Hector Skifter's AIL faced the same extinction that confronted most of the special laboratories created to address radio-related technology issues in the early 1940s. Skifter's group was saved by the intervention of American Airlines, which sought to retain the technical capability assembled by Skifter in hopes of adapting new radar technologies to commercial aviation. An airline subsidiary, Aviation Radio Corporation, acquired AIL from the U.S. Navy. Over time the interests of the airlines and AIL diverged, the parties separated, and the capital needed for further growth was obtained from investor Laurance Rockefeller. In the early 1950s AIL continued its pioneering work in both defense and commercial aviation applications of radar and radio technology for such applications as precision landing systems, electronic surveillance, and ballistic missile defense.

In the late 1950s Rockefeller and the other investors sold their interests to the industrial firm Cutler-Hammer. Skifter continued to bring together innovative scientists and engineers to solve complex problems, and in his spare time managed a small farm in Glen Cove, New York (perhaps five miles from where Herbert Wagner had been based after the war). Skifter maintained his own automobiles, worked in his garden, and provided consulting services to the U.S. military. It was while working in the yard of his Manhasset property that Skifter died of an apparent heart attack in July 1964. His company continues to this day to develop sophisticated jammers as a unit of ITT Corporation.[12]

Fate of the Warriors

Many of the warriors encountered in the story of the German glide bombs never survived the six-year-long conflict. This includes the roughly 3,500 sailors killed on board the ships hit by these innovative weapons. Likewise, casualties amongst the crews of KG 100 and KG 40 were numerous, and relatively few pilots from the year of the glide bombs lived to relay their experiences. It is estimated that fewer than 10 percent of the Luftwaffe bomber pilots who began combat in September 1939 survived through May 1945.[13]

✦ ✦ ✦

One of these survivors was Hans Dochtermann, the pilot of the aircraft that scored the hit on HMT *Rohna* which led to the deaths of more than one thousand U.S. servicemen. Dochtermann had begun his combat duties even before World War II, joining the Kondor Legion in Spain in 1936 and flying combat missions in support of the Nationalists. Following the outbreak of World War II, he flew missions over France and England and later piloted cargo flights to the Russian front. He ended his military career attempting to stem the tide of invading Americans, British, and Canadians at Normandy. On balance, it is estimated he flew perhaps two thousand combat missions during his career, possibly a record for a Luftwaffe pilot flying medium or heavy bombers.[14] The mere fact that he survived the war is amazing in itself.

Dochtermann was taken into captivity after the surrender of Germany and was confined in England until 10 May 1946, the first anniversary of VE day. After release, he worked as a technical interpreter at a U.S. airbase at Oberpfaffenhofen, about twenty kilometers west of Munich. He continued his technical consulting career until his retirement in 1982.

In 1960 Dochtermann was contacted by a former flight sergeant on behalf of a U.S. colonel, John A. Virden, who was conducting research on the 26 November 1943 attack.[15] Hesitant at first, fearing "a hot-blooded relative of a soldier lost on the ship who wanted to extract his revenge upon me," he was eventually persuaded to cooperate.[16] Corresponding with Virden, and eventually meeting with a correspondent from the U.S. Army newspaper *Stars and Stripes*, Dochtermann learned for the first time the identity of the ship sunk by his order and the consequences of his attack. Writing years later to author Carlton Jackson, Dochtermann expressed his feelings on the subject: "I was a front-line soldier, had sworn the oath of allegiance and must obey the commands given me. I condemn every war. The remembrance of all soldiers—from every nation—makes me deeply sad."[17]

The survivors of *Rohna* also remembered and honored their lost colleagues, holding reunions periodically. Many years after the ship was destroyed, and after Hans Dochtermann's death in 1999 at the age of eighty-seven, his son and two grandsons attended some of the *Rohna* reunions and confronted the survivors of that November 1943 attack. The potential for anger melted away, and the Dochtermann descendents were warmly embraced by the elderly *Rohna* survivors and their families. Recalls his grandson, KC Dochtermann,

> My father, brother and I have all attended *Rohna* reunions, and we were all welcomed, almost as family. It was great to meet the survivors and their families, as it brought so much closure to them. It is hard to demonize someone, when their offspring is standing in front of them, 60 years later, with a warm smile and firm handshake. We wish only that my grandfather could have met all the survivors face-to-face. I hope there is a special place in heaven for all of them to share together, as they were all men that were just doing their job for their country.[18]

Heinrich Schmetz, who had scored hits on both *Roma* and *Warspite*, also survived the war. Schmetz had been present throughout the years of aerial conflict in Europe, from September 1939 to May 1945, seeing combat in Poland, France, the Netherlands, Norway, the Mediterranean, and during the battle of Britain. He flew as an observer or pilot on all four of the most common German bombers—He 111, Ju 88, Do 217, and He 177—and was the officer who led the support units of III./KG 100 on their perilous overland trek across France in September 1944. Awarded the Knight's Cross of the Iron Cross (Germany's highest award in World War II for battlefield bravery and combat leadership), the German Cross in Gold, the Iron Cross (First Class), and the Iron Cross (Second Class), he was one of Germany's most illustrious surviving Luftwaffe pilots. Taken into captivity by American troops, he was released in June 1945 and spent the years 1946 and 1947 as a test pilot with both the French navy and and the French armaments ministry. Aviation always remained part of his life. He reentered the new German air force in 1956 and was stationed in Dayton, Ohio, with the U.S. Air Force, even obtaining a U.S. private pilot license in 1967. Schmetz was active in support of collaboration between the air forces of France, Germany, and the United States until his retirement in 1974. Many of the programs on which he worked are still around: the Panavia Tornado fighter-bomber, the Milan antitank missile, and the Roland antiaircraft missile are examples. Four years later he ceased flying as pilot-in-command, renewing his pilot's license no further. Schmetz died at the age of eighty-nine on 22 July 2004.

Bernhard Jope also survived the war. He had commanded III./KG 100 during the early days of glide-bomb missions in 1943, later commanded all of KG 100, and even for a while was acting commander of II./KG 100. Born in Leipzig in 1914, by 31 December 1941 he had already achieved fame for destroying the troop transport *Empress of Britain*, for which he was awarded the Knight's Cross (subsequently upgraded to Knight's Cross with Oak Leaves), complementing his other awards of the German Cross in Gold, Iron Cross (First Class), and Iron Cross (Second Class). Following the dissolution of KG 100, Jope was reassigned on 17 October 1944 as the commander of KG 30, a conventional bomber force employing Ju 88 aircraft operating from bases in Germany and Czechoslovakia. On 23 November 1944 this unit was redesignated KG(J) 30; Jope was to lead it until the end of the war.

KG(J) 30 was a special *Mistel* guided-bomb unit, except in this case the guided weapons were obsolete and worn-out Ju 88 bombers. The unmanned bomber was loaded with explosives and directed into battle by an Fw 190 fighter mounted atop the bomber's fuselage. The pilot of the Fw 190 would fly the composite aircraft toward the target, release the bomber upon approach, then direct it via remote control into targets. The intent was to use this technology to destroy high-value targets such as hydroelectric plants and bridges. In the end, the *Mistel* program achieved indifferent results at best.

Jope survived these final months of the war and ended up a captive of Allied forces, freed to return to private life in 1946. With the rebirth of Lufthansa airlines, his employer before the war, Jope returned to a life of civilian flying and served as a senior pilot with Lufthansa for many years. He died at the age of eighty-one on 31 July 1995, in the spa town of Königstein im Taunus, just outside Frankfurt.

Pilot Hans-Joachim Zantopp, whose capture by the British on 10 August 1943 provided the first tangible evidence of glide-bomb operations, also survived the war. Taken prisoner by the British a few weeks after his twenty-first birthday, he was interrogated in the infamous Tower of London, and was forced to remain in his confinement aboveground during Luftwaffe bombing raids while his interrogators sought safety in the underground bunkers. Zantopp was later transferred to an American POW camp in Tennessee. Treated there with respect and dignity, Zantopp developed a life-long affection for America. Following his release in late 1945, he was reunited with his family who had escaped the Russian invasion of East Prussia during the massive evacuation in spring 1945. Zantopp returned to his lifelong passion of flying, becoming a pilot with Lufthansa and ultimately rising to a very senior position: Boeing 747 captain on the transatlantic routes. He enjoyed these

frequent opportunities to visit the United States. Zantopp trained a generation of Lufthansa pilots—and even once looped a Boeing 707 on a training
flight with a Boeing flight instructor. Ultimately, this survivor of the war and a
career in aviation succumbed to cancer, passing away on 22 August 1977.[19]

A warrior of a different kind during the war was Dr. Hans Ferdinand
Mayer, the courageous author of the Oslo Report that provided British
authorities with their first intelligence clues regarding German research on
radio-controlled glide bombs. Reginald V. Jones, who coordinated scientific
intelligence gathering for Churchill during the war, called the Oslo Report
"probably the best single report received from any source during the war"
on the topic of German scientific research.[20] The Nazi regime never found
out about the Oslo Report during World War II and Mayer's role in the episode was hidden until years afterwards. However, Mayer's anti-Nazi views
did catch up to him and he was sent by Hitler's regime into Dachau concentration camp in August 1943—the same month as glide bombs scored their
first success—after having been exposed by the maid of a neighbor.[21] While
in Dachau, forced into service to the Third Reich, he formed a research institute with other imprisoned physicists, which possibly explains why he survived the war. Certainly, had his role in the Oslo Report been known, the
likely result would have been torture and execution.

In 1946, Mayer, as was the case with so many German scientists, relocated to the United States, working for the U.S. Air Force out of Dayton,
Ohio, while teaching at Cornell University in Ithaca, New York. At the time
his role as the author of the Oslo Report remained hidden. Even R. V. Jones,
the ultimate recipient of the letter in British intelligence, did not know who
the author was. The existence of the Oslo Report itself was not made public
until 1947 (by Jones, during a lecture); even then he withheld many details.

In 1950 Mayer returned to his native Germany and spent the next
twelve years back at his old employer, Siemens & Halske AG, ultimately
rising to a position as the director of research and then serving on the company's board of directors. In 1953 Jones began to receive indications that
Mayer had written the Oslo Report. The two scientists finally met in 1955
at which point Mayer acknowledged being the author and was able to con-
vince Jones of his claim by accurately depicting the letter in ways that had
not to that point been made public. Jones again kept this information to
himself. It was not until nine years after Mayer died in 1980, just shy of his
eighty-fifth birthday, that the information was finally made public by Jones
in his 1989 book *Reflections on Intelligence*.[22]

If pilots Dochtermann, Schmetz, and Jope had first-row balcony seats
in the yearlong theater of glide-bomb threats and countermeasures, and

if Mayer worked behind the scenes, naval officer Roger P. Hill witnessed the same struggle from the orchestra seats. He was present when the first ship was sunk by these Wellsian weapons in August 1943, barely escaping destruction himself. He witnessed the battles between bombers and ships at Anzio in January and February 1944, even taking command of *Jervis* after she had her bow blown off by an Hs 293. Hill also was present during the last wave of glide-bomb attacks at Normandy, when the colleagues of Jope, Dochtermann, and Schmetz were shot down en masse.

Hill survived five years of combat ranging from the Kola Run (including PQ-17), to Operation Pedestal in Malta (for which he was awarded a DSO), to operations in the Bay of Biscay (for which he was awarded a DSC), and in Greece, Anzio, and Normandy, only to be invalidated from the Royal Navy after suffering head injuries during an automobile accident on a seemingly rare occasion on land in Britain. His first marriage failed after he returned to civilian life and he seems to have struggled to adjust to his postmilitary status. Hill himself describes the difficulty of securing civilian employment in Britain after the war:

> The English post-war world had no use for damaged destroyer captains, which was fair enough—no-one owed us a living; but some took it a bit far. One oil company personnel manger said to me when I sought any kind of work, "You boys have got to find out the facts of life. You have had all of the glamour of the war, whilst we were being bombed in London . . . " and so on. I knocked him right out of his beautiful leather chair: (I did not get the job).[23]

By his own admission, Hill's "health cracked up" in 1965. He had remarried and the family decided to immigrate to New Zealand, settling in the quiet town of Nelson on the north end of New Zealand's South Island. There Hill wrote his autobiography *Destroyer Captain* in the evenings and earned wages as a casual laborer during the day, working the docks of Nelson. In his later years he taught at Nelson Technical College and built a house, which he named "Jervis," outside town. Roger Hill died at the age of ninety-one on 5 May 2001. The following year relatives and friends took his ashes to Malta and scattered them over the Grand Harbour at Valetta.

"Skeeta" Gardes remains notable as the first ship captain (along with O. William Goepner) to deploy countermeasures against guided missiles. He was reassigned in December 1943 from his beloved *Herbert C. Jones* to duty in the Pacific in command of another new destroyer-escort, *Richard S. Bull*. There he and his ship would see extensive combat and receive several decorations, including five battle stars. During service off the Philippines,

Gardes was an active participant in the Battle off Samar and saw action in Lingayen Gulf. Later he and his ship supported the invasions of Iwo Jima and Okinawa.

After the war Gardes was assigned as an instructor at the Naval War College. In 1946, perhaps because of his prior experience in Asia, he was sent to Siam (now Thailand) as naval attaché. There he earned the "Order of the White Elephant" from the King of Siam, allegedly, according to family lore, for teaching the King to play a mean game of poker.[24] By special act of Congress, he was permitted to retain the award and wear it on his uniform.[25]

After returning from Siam, Gardes spent another two decades in the Navy, retiring with the rank of captain in 1967. He maintained his interest in boating by operating a marina and running a yacht brokerage on Coronado Island in San Diego. San Diego grew and Coronado's real estate values rose, and after two years running the marina Gardes sold the waterfront property for a tidy profit. (Today the site is occupied by the popular Chart House restaurant.) His last years were spent sailing his yacht and traveling around the world. "Skeeta" Gardes passed away in July 2000, two days short of his eighty-seventh birthday.

Plus Ça Change . . .

By the time of this writing, just about all of the witnesses of the year of warriors and wizards have left us. Their legacy persists in the form of guided weaponry and sophisticated electronic countermeasures, which are now taken for granted, but which in 1943 represented major technical marvels.

✦ ✦ ✦

Our connections with that era remain strong. On 19 March 2003 the U.S. military and its coalition allies invaded Iraq. For the first few months, as the Iraqi army collapsed, the power of U.S. forces was seen as supreme. However, in July 2003, some sixty years to the month after the Do 217 K-2s of III./KG 100 first tested their Fritz-X bombs in combat in the Mediterranean, forces in opposition to the United States deployed a weapon for which U.S. forces were ill prepared. Known as improvised explosive devices (IEDs), these roadside bombs—often triggered using radio links—wreaked havoc on U.S. and coalition forces, causing more than 40 percent of all casualties inflicted on those forces. Once again, as they did in September 1943, the United States scrambled to provide an effective defense.

One avenue exploited was the vulnerability of the tenuous radio links between bomb and detonator. A business unit of EDO Corporation in Simi

Valley, California had been working on a product called Shortstop that involved the jamming of radio-frequency fuses.[26] After the IEDs made their presence felt, the Shortstop technology was adapted into a product named Warlock, designed to jam the vital radio controls between roadside bombs and their controllers, presumably hiding some distance away. EDO's legacy in electronic warfare was broader than its Simi Valley operation. In 2000 EDO had purchased AIL Technologies, the descendent of Hector Skifter's World War II team at Columbia University, which had developed the Type MAS jammer in 1944.[27] Sixty years after the group of technical wizards had been tasked to develop a jamming technique to defeat a new and asymmetric weapon, their metaphorical grandsons (and now granddaughters) had been charged with the same urgent task.

As this is written the threat of guided weapons looms large at sea as well. In 2008 the U.S. Navy concluded that China was developing an advanced weapon derived from one of the latter's ballistic missiles. The warhead of this advanced missile would be able to maneuver in its terminal phase and target specific warships as it hurtled from space to the ocean's surface. This Dong Feng 21 (or CSS-5) missile turned a formerly imprecise weapon into one that could be steered directly into the hull of high-value ships, such as aircraft carriers, much in the way that the Fritz-X targeted battleships some sixty-five years before. Max Kramer would be proud. No doubt the Americans are considering jamming as one of the defensive options, though understandably such things are confined to the world of secrets. The legacy of the wizards continues.

The legacy of the warriors is less evident, for a naval battlefield offers no permanent monuments to those who struggled there, at least none on the surface. One finds no abandoned fortifications, no green pastures with retired artillery pieces, and no crumbling stone walls marking the site of past desperate and heroic last stands. The warriors are leaving us as time moves on, and few of their ships or aircraft are left behind. For example, not a single intact example of an He 177 or Do 217 bomber remains. Only one of the ships on the receiving end of glide-bomb attacks remains afloat—the former USCG cutter *Taney* now in service as a museum ship in Baltimore.

A few other artifacts do survive, including many examples of the Hs 293 and Fritz-X weapons in aviation and military museums. The occasional tourist to Anzio may wander across a plaque emplaced in a wall there honoring those who perished on board *Spartan*. Visitors to the Fort Mitchell National Cemetery in Seale, Alabama, will find a memorial to the victims of *Rohna*. The wrecks of *Boadicea* off England and *Meredith* off Normandy are destinations for highly experienced technical scuba divers. Some of the crosses at the Sicily–Rome American Cemetery and Memorial in Nettuno, Italy, mark the burial sites of those who perished on board *Savannah*.

Not surprisingly, almost all the lasting relics of the war between airmen and sailors can be found not in the ephemeral air or on the ocean but instead on solid land. Many of the most important sites from this year of warriors and wizards remain in use today. The white buildings of Washington's Naval Research Laboratory, where Bill Howe, Howard Lorenzen, and Carl Miller did their work, still line the Potomac River and provide a vista for those seated on the right side of aircraft landing to the north at Ronald Reagan National Airport. Many of the airports used by the Luftwaffe to launch attacks on Allied fleets are in active use today, albeit as air terminals rather than attack bases. Istres airfield outside Marseilles remains active and, as the longest runway in all of Europe, serves as an emergency landing site for the U.S. space shuttle. Toulouse-Blagnac is a major international airport and the assembly site for Airbus S.A.S., with signs of its role as the primary base for II./KG 100 long erased. Nearby Toulouse-Francazal airfield, from which III./KG 100 operated, remains in use by the French air force. Visitors flying to Bordeaux arrive at Bordeaux-Mérignac airfield, from which II./KG 40 launched its attacks in the Mediterranean and Atlantic. As those who participated in these struggles inevitably leave the stage, these few relics—and the written word—suffice to carry forward their memory.

Appendix

Ships Sunk *or* Damaged *with* Glide Bombs

Results of Ship Attacks with Hs 293

Month/Year	Ship	Hits or Near Misses	Result	Killed	Status
08/43	HMS *Landguard*	1 Near miss	Damaged	0	Confirmed
	HMS *Bideford*	1 Hit (did not explode)	Damaged	1	Confirmed
	HMCS *Athabaskan*	1 Hit	Heavily damaged	5	Confirmed
	HMS *Egret*	1 Hit	Sunk	198	Confirmed
09/43	HMHS *Newfoundland*	1 Hit	Scuttled	21	Confirmed
	HMS *LST-79*	1 Hit	Sunk	4	Confirmed
	SS *Bushrod Washington*	1 Hit	Sunk	7	Probable
	SS *James W. Marshall*	1 Hit	Scuttled	63	Probable
10/43	SS *Samite*	1 Hit	Damaged	5	Confirmed
	SS *Hiram S. Maxim*	1 Hit	Damaged	0	Probable
	SS *Selvik*	1 Hit	Damaged	5	Probable
11/43	MV *Birchbank*	1 Hit	Sunk	0	Confirmed
	MV *Indian Prince*	1 Hit	Sunk	0	Possible
	HMS *Rockwood*	1 Hit (did not explode)	Written off	0	Confirmed
	HMS *BYMS-2072*	1 Hit	Heavily damaged	3	Confirmed
	HMS *Dulverton*	1 Hit	Scuttled	77	Confirmed
	MV *Marsa*	1 Hit	Sunk	5	Confirmed
	SS *Delius*	1 Hit	Damaged	0	Confirmed
	HMT *Rohna*	1 Hit	Sunk	1,179	Confirmed

continued on next page

continued from page 207

Month/Year	Ship	Hits or Near Misses	Result	Killed	Status
	HMS *Jervis*	1 Hit	Heavily damaged	0	Confirmed
	HMHS *St. David*	1 Hit	Sunk	60	Confirmed
	SS *John Banvard*	1 Near miss	Written off	0	Confirmed
	SS *Hilary A. Herbert*	1 Near miss	Damaged	0	Confirmed
01/44	SS *Samuel Huntington*	1 Hit	Sunk	4	Confirmed
	HMS *Spartan*	1 Hit	Sunk	66	Confirmed
	HMS *Janus*	1 Hit	Sunk	158	Probable
	USS *Prevail*	1 Near miss	Damaged	0	Possible
	USS *Mayo*	1 Hit	Heavily damaged	7	Possible
02/44	SS *Elihu Yale / LCT-35*	1 Hit	Sunk	12	Confirmed
	HMS *Inglefield*	1 Hit	Sunk	35	Confirmed
	HMS *Lawford*	1 Hit	Sunk	37	Probable
	USS *Meredith*	1 Hit	Heavily damaged	7	Probable
06/44	SS *Fort McPherson*	1 Hit (did not explode)	Damaged	8	Probable
	SS *Charles Morgan*	1 Hit	Written off	170	Possible
	HMS *Boadicea*	1 Hit	Sunk	0	Possible
07/44	HMCS *Matane*	1 Hit	Damaged	4	Confirmed
08/44	USS *LST-282*	1 Hit	Sunk	40	Confirmed

Result of Attacks on Ships with Fritz-X

Month	Ship	Hits or Near Misses	Result	Killed	Status
	RM *Roma*	2 Hits	Sunk	1,352	Confirmed
	RM *Italia*	1 Hit	Damaged	?	Confirmed
	HMNLS *Flores*	2 Near misses	Damaged	0	Probable
09/43	USS *Savannah*	1 Hit	Heavily damaged	197	Confirmed
	HMS *Uganda*	1 Hit	Heavily damaged	16	Confirmed
	HMS *Loyal*	1 Near miss	Damaged	0	Confirmed
	HMS *Warspite*	1 Hit and 2 Near misses	Heavily damaged	9	Confirmed

Notes

Introduction: "Wellsian Weapons from Mars"

1. For the price of almost four thousand aircraft and pilots, Japanese kamikaze missions sank three small escort carriers, fourteen destroyers, three APDs (destroyers converted to high-speed transports), twelve landing ships, and seventeen merchant ships or auxiliaries. No large warships (carriers, cruisers, or battleships) were sunk, though several were heavily damaged.

2. "Nazi Rocket Glider Bomb Is Seen for First Time, Diving at Convoy," *New York Times*, 20 December 1943. The article describes the raid on a convoy, most likely SL 193 / MKS 30, on 21 November 1943.

3. Some 1,045 U.S. service members were killed on board transport ship *Rohna* in November 1943, more than the approximately 880 who perished on board the heavy cruiser *Indianapolis* when it was sunk on 30 July 1945. The number killed on board battleship *Arizona*, which was not at sea during the attack at Pearl Harbor, was higher, with about 1,170 killed.

4. It is particularly difficult to obtain information on Luftwaffe operational losses; this work therefore is based on an integration of reports from various sources. The first and ideal source would be the Luftwaffe "loss reports" compiled by Generalquartiermeister 6. Abteilung (QM6). Unfortunately, the detailed QM6 records for most of 1944 have been lost, though monthly totals are available for the units relevant here. As a substitute, researchers rely on Namentliche Verlustmeldung (NVM) reports, which describe the injury or loss of individual Luftwaffe personnel and are of course highly correlated with aircraft losses. However, if an aircraft was shot down but all personnel parachuted to safety behind Axis lines, or if an aircraft crash-landed upon its return to base but without injury to crew, there would be no NVM report of the incident. A final and indirect source includes the records of Luftwaffe POW interrogations by the Assistant Director of Intelligence (ADI[K]) of the Air Ministry in the United Kingdom. These ADI(K) files provide, within the bounds of accuracy of any interrogation report, useful data on aircraft lost on specific missions. Of course, ADI(K) reports do not help in cases where an aircraft was lost without survivors.

5. For example, Seaman Colin MacKenzie witnessed glide-bomb attacks against a U.S. light cruiser and a merchant ship at Salerno. His book, published before

the war's end, makes no mention of these special weapons despite providing considerable detail about other aspects of these attacks. See Colin MacKenzie, *Sailors of Fortune* (New York: E. P. Dutton & Co., 1944), 172, 178.

6. Don Whitehead, *Beachhead Don: Reporting the War from the European Theater* (New York: Fordham University Press, 2005), 108.

7. "Tätigkeitsbericht über Einsatzperiode das K.G. 100 mit F.K. in der Zeit von 12.7.43–30.4.44 [Activity Report of Missions of KG 100 with Guided Weapons in the Period from 12.07.43 to 30.04.44]," Bundesarchiv-Militärarchiv in Freiberg, Germany, file RL 10/493. This report contains data on the number and type of missions flown by II./KG 100 and III./KG 100 through April 30, 1944. It therefore provides a check against any mission-level data compiled from other varied sources.

8. Williamson Murray, *Strategy for Defeat: The Luftwaffe 1933–1945* (Maxwell Air Force Base, Montgomery, AL: Air University Press, 1983), 303. Murray indicates that the attrition for German fighter pilots "was probably well into the 90th percentile" and that the equivalent figures for bomber pilots "could not have been much better."

Chapter 1

1. Using Royal Navy nomenclature of the time, corvettes, frigates, and sloops were designed for convoy escort duties with primary missions of air defense and antisubmarine warfare. Lightly armed, with a top speed of only sixteen to twenty knots, they made up for combat limitations with long-range endurance. Corvettes weighed in at about 900 to 1,050 tonnes displacement and mounted one 4-inch gun. Frigates were slightly larger; like corvettes, they used relatively inexpensive reciprocating engines to maximize endurance. (The U.S. Navy employed destroyer-escorts in that same role.) Sloops, about the same size as larger frigates (up to 1,350 tonnes) mounted six 4-inch guns and were powered by higher-performance steam turbines for slightly higher speed. Destroyers, by contrast, were designed for antiship roles as well as submarine and air defense; driven by large steam turbines, they were twice as fast as corvettes, frigates, or sloops. More powerfully armed with torpedoes and guns, they displaced up to 1,700 tonnes. Light cruisers were significantly larger ships at about 8,000 tonnes, were heavily armed with twelve 6-inch guns, and could almost match the speed of destroyers.

2. "German Radio Controlled Bombs," Report No. 3007, Air Ministry: Bomber Command: Registered Files, HS and FX bombs: Technical Information, 1943 September–1945 June," UK National Archives, file AIR 14-3611.

3. In this way, Boardman became the first person in history killed by a remotely guided weapon, an unfortunate distinction at best.

4. Roger P. Hill, *Destroyer Captain* (London: William Kimber, 1975). Hill received the Distinguished Service Order for his actions during Operation Pedestal while in command of Royal Navy destroyer *Ledbury*.

5. Admiralty and Ministry of Defense, Department of the Director of Naval Construction, "*Athabaskan*: Damaged by a Bomb, 14 Aug. 27," UK National Archives, file ADM 267/8.

6. Ibid.
7. Hill attributed this to the aerodynamic design of the missile. Another plausible explanation for this behavior is multipath signal error, which is discussed in some detail later in this book.
8. Paulus's identity and that of Vorpahl earlier is provided by Luftwaffe researcher Ulf Balke in *Kampfgeschwader KG 100 "Wiking"* (Stuttgart, Germany: Motorbuch Verlag, 1981).
9. The figure usually quoted is 194 killed from a crew of 229. However, the official Royal Navy casualty list identifies only members of the Royal Navy who perished on the ship. Three RAF personnel are excluded from that number, which brings the total loss of life on *Egret* to 197. This assumes that telegraphist Shields, identified as one of the Y-Service personnel killed in the attack, was Ordinary Telegraphist Robert N. Shields, whose name does appear on the Royal Navy's casualty list. If in fact this is a different individual, than the casualty list grows to 198.
10. Alfred Price, *Dornier Do 217 Variants* (Windsor, Ontario, Canada: Profile Publications, 1974), 59.
11. "Message from Admiralty to Commander-in-Chief U.S. Fleet (COMINCH)," O.I.C. Serial 630 of 27 August 1943, #272059 NCR 3483.
12. Sönke Neitzel, *Der Einsatz der deutschen Luftwaffe über dem Atlantik und der Nordsee 1939–1945* [The Missions of the German Luftwaffe over the Atlantic and North Sea 1939–1945] (Bonn, Germany: Bernard & Graefe Verlag, 1995), 172.
13. Waldemar B. Kaempffert, "The New Weapon: Radio-Controlled Bomb Is Unlikely to Help Germans," *New York Times*, 26 September 1943.
14. Francis H. Hinsley, *British Intelligence in the Second World War*, Vol. III, Part 2 (London: Her Majesty's Stationery Office, 1988), 339.
15. Hill, *Destroyer Captain*, 115.
16. Peter C. Smith, *Ship Strike: The History of Air-to-Sea Weapon Systems* (Shrewsbury, UK: Airlife, 1998), 100–102.
17. Records of the Admiralty; Admiralty, and Ministry of Defence, Navy Department: Correspondence and Papers, UK National Archives, file ADM 1-14507. There also might have been another individual lost, a leading telegraphist signals officer whose surname remains unidentified.

Chapter 2

1. Albert C. Piccirillo, "The Origins of the Anti-Ship Guided Missile," American Institute of Aeronautics and Astronautics, November 1997. Technical paper presented at the 1997 World Aviation Congress, Anaheim, CA, 13–16 October 1997.
2. Max Otto Kramer, "The Wave Drag of Ships," *Naval Engineers Journal*, August 1951, 575.
3. Balke, *Kampfgeschwader KG 100 "Wiking,"* 246.
4. Manfred Griehl, *Do 217-317-417: An Operational Record* (Washington, DC: Smithsonian Institution Press, 1971), 104.
5. Balke, *Kampfgeschwader KG 100 "Wiking,"* 245.

6. Konrad Zuse, *The Computer—My Life* (Berlin: Springer-Verlag, 1993, trans. P. McKenna and J. A. Ross), 60.
7. George Emil Knausenberger and Monica Wagner-Fielder, *Herbert Wagner* (Monterey, CA: Martin Hollmann, 2003).
8. Griehl writes that aircraft KC+NX conducted the first carry tests and DC+CD was used for the first drop tests. See Griehl, *Do 217-317-417*, 102. The four-letter codes here are Stammkennzeichen (Skz), a permanent four-letter factory code assigned to each unique aircraft upon completion (or, if already built, when the system was put in place in 1939). This is different from the operational code represented by a Verbandskennzeichen (Vbkz), which could evolve over time as an aircraft was transferred from one unit to another. Also, if an aircraft with one Vbkz code was lost, another aircraft might be assigned that same code. Hence, Vbkz codes might be shared by more than one aircraft. In this book, Vbkz codes are provided when available. If the Vbkz code is unavailable, an Skz code is provided where available. If the code has a number, typically starting with 6N (for KG 100) or F8 (for KG 40), it is a Vbkz. If all four characters are letters, it is an Skz.
9. Griehl, *Do 217-317-417*, 103.
10. This frequency range was not chosen at random. German engineers were concerned that frequencies outside that narrow range would encounter interference from the British hyperbolic navigation system Gee, which was set up to transmit across four bands between 20 MHz and 85 MHz. Likewise, frequencies below 48 MHz were seen to conflict potentially with the British "Chain Home" coastal radar stations, which were set up to operate between 20 MHz to 50 MHz. This precluded use of frequencies in the 27 MHz range in the Atlantic, though these frequencies might have been viable in the Mediterranean. See Fritz Trenkle, *Die Deutschen Funklenkverfahren bis 1945* (Heidelberg, Germany: Huthig, 1986), 36.
11. The FuG 203a variant (Kehl II) was developed specifically for the Do 217 K-2 aircraft guiding a single Fritz-X. The FuG 203b (Kehl III) was similarly designed for a Do 217 E-5 aircraft equipped for a single Hs 293 missile. A modified version, the FuG 203c (Kehl IV), would allow a launching aircraft to steer either an Hs 293 or a Fritz-X, depending on mission requirements. Later variants were equipped to accommodate up to four weapons on a single larger launching aircraft: the FuG 203d (Kehl IIIm) for multiple Hs 293 launches, the FuG 203e (Kehl IVm) to handle either multiple Hs 293 or Fritz-X weapons, and the FuG 203h (Kehl IVh) to allow for either multiple Hs 293 or Fritz-X launches with an additional ignition command. See Trenkle, *Die Deutschen Funklenkverfahern*, 36, for a complete description (in German). Other sources provide a different definition for the various Kehl units. See, for example, Manfred Griehl and Joachim Dressel, *Heinkel: He 177, 277, 274* (Shrewbury, UK: Airlife, 1998), 116. This text, which focuses on the aircraft rather than the electronic systems, has different designations: FuG 203a (Kehl I), FuG 203b (Kehl II), FuG 203c (Kehl III), and FuG 203d (Kehl IV).
12. For the Fritz-X, this unit was the FuG 230a (Strassburg a); the equivalent system for the Hs 293 was the FuG 230b (Strassburg b). A final variant, the FuG 230h (Strassburg h) had an additional ignition command and was paired with the FuG 203h transmitter. See Trenkle, *Die Deutschen Funklenkverfahern*, 36.

13. Thomas L. Boardman, "German Bombs & Fuzes, Land Mines & Igniters." Report prepared jointly by the U.S. Navy Bomb Disposal School (which Boardman supervised) and the U.S. Army Bomb Disposal School, 14 March 1944, U.S. Air Force Museum archives, File F5-A, Box 819.

14. Gordon Davis, "Rocket and Radio Bombs," an intelligence report prepared by Headquarters RAF, Middle East, on 14 November 1943, archives of the U.S. Air Force Museum, File "F5/1942-1943/German Radio Controlled Weapons," Box 814.

15. A total of 32 He 111 H-12 variants were produced for the Hs 293 test program, the aircraft entering production in August 1942. Many of these special bombers were lost while conducting transport or conventional bombing missions against the Soviets. See Werner Baumbach, *The Life and Death of the Luftwaffe* (New York: Ballantine Books, 1967), 105.

16. The E-5 variant of the Do 217 was powered by BMW 801 C engines and had additional armor and fuel capacity compared to earlier models. For reasons of weight, and in keeping with needs of the mission, the dive-bombing capability was scrapped on the Do 217 E-5. This variant was equipped with a 13-mm MG 131 machine gun mounted in a dorsal turret, a similar gun mounted in a ventral compartment, three 7.92-mm MG 15s in the forward fuselage, and a 15-mm MG 151 cannon mounted in the nose.

17. Price, *Dornier Do 217 Variants*, 69.

18. The QM6 monthly records for II./KG 100, the unit that deployed the Do 217 E-5, indicate that seventy-four newly built aircraft were delivered to this group between April 1943 and February 1944.

19. "Tätigkeitsbericht über Einsatzperiode das K.G. 100."

20. Griehl, *Do 217-317-417*, 111.

21. Ibid.

22. Balke, *Kampfgeschwader KG 100 "Wiking,"* 249.

23. "Tätigkeitsbericht über Einsatzperiode das K.G. 100."

24. Ibid.

25. The Fw 200 C-3/U1 and Fw 200 C-3/U3 variants were equipped to carry the glide bomb, many of which were modified later to an Fw 200 C-6 standard. The Fw 200 C-8 variant was produced new as the definitive production version of the C-6 modified aircraft, though only small numbers ever left the Focke-Wolf factories.

26. Baumbach, *The Life and Death of the Luftwaffe*, 105.

27. Ibid., 104–106.

28. Charles H. Bogart, "German Remotely Piloted Bombs," U.S. Naval Institute *Proceedings* 102 (November 1976), 65.

29. Luftwaffe units were structured into formations of aircraft organized by mission. Thus, bomber organizations were designated as Kampfgeschwader (KG) units. KG 100 was therefore bomber wing number 100. Within KG 100 would be several *gruppen*, or groups, enumerated with Roman numerals (I, II, III, IV, and V) as well as a headquarters unit (*stab*). The second group of KG 100 was specified as II./KG 100, the third group was III./KG 100, and so on. The headquarters unit is designated *Stab* KG 100. Within each *gruppe* were a series of *staffeln*, or squadrons, typically three, in addition to a squadron headquarters

unit (another *stab*). Each squadron, which consisted of perhaps nine to fifteen aircraft, was numbered sequentially with Arabic numerals. *Gruppe* II./KG 100, operating the Hs 293, consisted of a headquarters unit (*Stab* II./KG 100) and three squadrons: 4./KG 100, 5./KG 100, and 6./KG 100. (The three squadrons of I./KG 100, none of which operated glide bombs, were 1./KG 100, 2./KG 100, and 3./KG 100.) Likewise, *Gruppe* III./KG 100 consisted of a *stab* unit and three squadrons of Fritz-X–carrying aircraft: 7./KG 100, 8./KG 100, and 9./KG 100. Within each squadron the aircraft often were organized within units of three, called a *kette* (chain).

30. Order-of-battle information is from a very detailed database compiled from Luftwaffe QM6 records and assembled by Michael Holm. It is available on his Internet site, "The Luftwaffe, 1933–45: Flugzeugbestand und Bewegungsmeldungen, 3.42–12.44." Retrieved June 2008 from http://www.ww2.dk/oob/bestand/kampf/bkampf.htm

31. S. D. Felkin, "Radio Controlled Bombs," ADI(K) Report No. 465A/1943, 14 November 1943, UK National Archives, Air Ministry Directorate of Intelligence: Intelligence Reports and Papers, Assistant Director of Intelligence, AIR 40/2876.

32. The first use of the Hs 293 was the 25 August mission in the Bay of Biscay. One source suggests the glide bomb was used on 13 August during an attack by the Luftwaffe on convoy MKS-21 off the Alboran Islands in the Mediterranean. (See Paul Deichmann, "Luftwaffe Methods in the Selection of Offensive Weapons," *Air Force History Project*. Study Prepared at Karlsruhe, Germany, 1956.) However, the attack on MKS-21 was carried out by Luftwaffe He 111 aircraft using conventional ordnance. See Robert Cressman, *The Official Chronology of the U.S. Navy in World War II* (Annapolis, MD: Naval Institute Press, 2000), 175.

33. Chris Goss, *Sea Eagles: Luftwaffe Anti-Shipping Units 1942–45*, Vol. II (Hersham, UK: Ian Allen Publishing, 2006), 147.

Chapter 3

1. Kopp mistakenly attributes the destruction of *Egret* to II./KG 40. See Carlo Kopp, "The Dawn of the Smart Bomb," *Air Power Australia*, July 2006.

2. This is a bit earlier than the date suggested in most accounts, which typically place the first combat mission in August. Christopher Staerk and Paul Sinnott mistakenly report this attack as taking place on 21 August. See *Luftwaffe: The Allied Intelligence Files* (Dulles, VA: Brassey's, 2002), 92.

3. Samuel Eliot Morison, *History of United States Naval Operations in World War II*, Vol. IX, *Sicily–Salerno–Anzio, January 1943–June 1944* (Boston: Little, Brown & Company, 1954), 191–192.

4. Barbara Tomblin, *With Utmost Spirit: Allied Naval Operations in the Mediterranean, 1942–1945* (Lexington: University of Kentucky Press, 2004), 219.

5. Military Intelligence Division of the U.S. War Department, *World War II: A Chronology August 1943* (Washington, DC: War Department, 1943). This report identifies the merchant ship in question as *Uskide* of 2,708 tons; this information has been repeated by others. See, for example, Brian Cull, *Spitfires*

Over Sicily: The Crucial Role of the Malta Spitfires in the Battle of Sicily, January–August 1943 (London: Grub Street, 2000), 178. This is most likely a misspelling of the *Uskside*, a ship of 2,706 tons (sometimes specified as 2,708 tons), built in 1937, which was operating in the theater at the time. If sunk in Palermo, it was later raised and salvaged because it reappears in service in 1947 as *Teseo*.

6. The first of the two lost aircraft wore the Vbkz 6N+IT and had the manufacturer Werke Nummer (Wk.Nr.; a type of serial number) 4563. The second wore the Vbkz 6N+KT (Wk.Nr. 4554). Individual Luftwaffe aircraft markings, or Vbkz, for bomber units consisted of a Geschwader (wing) designation, which in the case of KG 100 was 6N and in the case of KG 40 was F8. This was followed by the German cross (symbolized here with a plus sign [+]) and a letter, which indicated the aircraft's specific sequence within its *staffeln*, or squadron. The final letter indicated the squadron and, by inference, *gruppe*. For our purposes the relevant *staffel* letters for II./KG 100 are "C" (*stab* or headquarters unit for II./KG 100), "M" (4./KG 100), "N" (5./KG 100), and "P" (6./KG 100). The relevant Vbkz for III./KG 100 are "D" (*stab* of III./KG 100), "R" (7./KG 100), "S" (8./KG 100), and "T" (9./KG 100). Thus, Bürckle's and Schenk's aircraft, 6N+IT and 6N+KT, were aircraft from squadron 9./KG 100 within III./KG 100. Throughout this book, the author attempts to specify exactly which aircraft are lost in specific circumstances. This information is based on the integration of multiple sources, of which the most important are Ulf Balke, *Kampfgeschwader KG 100 "Wiking,"* and Griehl and Dressel, *Heinkel: He 177, 277, 274.*

7. Do 217 K-2 with Vbkz 6N+BD (Wk.Nr. 4574) of the *stab* (headquarters) unit of KG 100, commanded by *Leutnant* Hans-Joachim Zantopp.

8. The reference to Calabria is from Enigma intercepts as reported by Hinsley, *British Intelligence in the Second World War*, Vol. III, Part 1, 111. The raid in the Strait of Messina is described by Balke, *Kampfgeschwader KG 100 "Wiking,"* 255.

9. This was 6N+CD (Wk.Nr. 4573) of the *stab* (headquarters) unit of III./KG 100.

10. The name *Littorio* has Fascist connotations. Upon the overthrow of Mussolini, it was deemed appropriate to rename *Littorio* to *Italia*.

11. Balke, *Kampfgeschwader KG 100 "Wiking,"* 259.

12. For the Italian perspective, see Erminio Bagnasco, *Regia Marina: Italian Battleships of World War II* (Missoula, MT: Pictorial Histories Publishing, 1986). For the German perspective, see Balke, *Kampfgeschwader KG 100 "Wiking,"* 259.

13. Erminio Bagnasco and August De Toro, *Le Navi da Battaglia Classe Littorio 1937–1948* (Parma, Italy: Albertelli, 2008), 293.

14. Baumbach, *The Life and Death of the Luftwaffe*, 107–108.

15. KG 3's previous leader, *Oberstleutnant* Walter Lehwess-Litzmann, was captured in an audacious attack by Soviet partisans in September 1943.

16. Molinnus often is spelled as Molinus. Hollweg is sometimes written as Hollweck.

17. Balke, *Kampfgeschwader KG 100 "Wiking,"* 265.

18. "Tätigkeitsbericht über Einsatzperiode das K.G. 100."

19. After the war, Bax published in his native Dutch an account of his naval experience. See Johannes S. Bax, *Batterij gereed . . . vuur!: Hr. Ms. "Flores" Vecht in de Middellandse Zee* (Rotterdam, The Netherlands: Uitgevers Wyt, 1948).

20. It is sometimes erroneously written that *Flores* was sunk in this attack. See, for example, William Wolf, *German Guided Missiles: Henschel Hs 293 and Ruhrstahl SD 1400X "Fritz-X"* (Bennington, VT: Merriam Press, 2006), 59.

21. There is confusion as to whether *Philadelphia* was actually hit by a missile. A hit was reported by Bogart ("German Remotely Piloted Bombs," 66). Wolf also writes that a glide bomb "hit" *Philadelphia*, even though in the previous paragraph he says the weapon achieved only a near miss. See Wolf, *German Guided Missiles*, 59. Tomblin (*With Utmost Spirit*, 273) makes it clear that the ship was not hit, citing original combat action reports.

22. It has been erroneously reported that an Hs 293 struck *Savannah*. See Walter Karig, *Battle Report: The Atlantic War from the Neutrality Patrol to the Crossing of the Rhine* (New York: Farrar & Rinehart, 1946), Plate 68.

23. James P. Melanephy and John G. Robinson, "Savannah at Salerno," *Surface Warfare* 6, no. 3 (March 1981): 5–7.

24. The aircraft were 6N+DM (Wk.Nr. 5555) from 4./KG 100 and 6N+NP (Wk. Nr. 5654) from 6./KG 100.

25. "Sinking of the Hospital Ship SS Newfoundland," *Newfoundland Times*, September 1994, 9–15. The *Newfoundland Times* is a publication of the HMS *Newfoundland* Association, formed by veterans of the Royal Navy cruiser (not hospital ship) *Newfoundland*. The article quotes the report of Captain Wilson, as obtained from the British Public Records Office.

26. Others have written that the bomb that struck HMHS *Newfoundland* was a Fritz-X. This is unlikely, given Wilson's depiction of events. Moreover, the armor-piercing Fritz-X would have most likely gone completely through the bottom of the hull before exploding. The bomb in this case went through the side of the ship and exploded within, which was more typical of the Hs 293.

27. "Sinking of the Hospital Ship SS Newfoundland," *Newfoundland Times*.

28. It has been reported that the attack on *Newfoundland* was made by a Luftwaffe pilot who decided to engage the hospital ship rather than jettison his weapon after having found no other targets. This account is based on a Y-Service intelligence intercept reporting that a Luftwaffe pilot had radioed during the attack the following message: "I've hit a hospital ship. She's on fire and will certainly sink" (Tomblin, *With Utmost Spirit*, 522).

29. It is sometimes reported erroneously that *Uganda* was sunk in this attack. See Bradley Lightbody, *The Second World War: Ambitions to Nemesis* (London: Routledge, 2004), 185.

30. The aircraft were Skz ZY+MA (Wk.Nr. 4577) and Vbkz 6N+WN (Wk.Nr. 4561), both of them from 9./KG 100.

31. Wolf (*German Guided Missiles*) suggests III./KG 100 was involved in this raid. It seems improbable, given the nature of the target, an unarmored merchant ship. Moreover, Luftwaffe records confirm that III./KG 100 flew six missions at Salerno between 11 and 17 September and these are all accounted for with the two missions on 11 September (at 0630 and 0930), two on 13 September (morning and afternoon), one on 15 September, and one on 17 September.

32. See, for example, Alfred Price, "Guided Missile Genesis," *Flying Review International* 19, no. 10 (July 1974).
33. "Tätigkeitsbericht über Einsatzperiode das K.G. 100." This report states that II./KG 100 executed nine attacks over Salerno, three of which took place during the day and six of which took place at night.
34. Account of Joseph Anthony Yannacci, as reported in his diary. Retrieved June 2008 from http://www.armed-guard.com/ag85.html.
35. Wainwright was the son of U.S. Army Lieutenant General (later General) Jonathan M. Wainwright IV, who earned fame as commander of forces defending Bataan.
36. Robert M. Browning Jr., *U.S. Merchant Vessel War Casualties of World War II* (Annapolis, MD: Naval Institute Press, 1996), 361.
37. See, for example Wolf, *German Guided Missiles*, 60.
38. Tomblin, *With Utmost Spirit*, 285. Also, see Browning, *U.S. Merchant Vessel War Casualties of World War II*, 360.
39. The aircraft was 6N+HP (Wk.Nr. 5552) of 6./KG 100.
40. Yannacci, his diary.
41. Browning, *U.S. Merchant Vessel War Casualties of World War II*, 360.
42. Tomblin (*With Utmost Spirit*) writes, apparently in error, that the ship was declared a total loss and sunk by gunfire from *Hambleton* that same morning at 0910 hours.
43. From Captain Packer's formal report, as quoted by his wife of thirty-seven years, Joy Packer, in *Deep as the Sea* (London: Corgi Books, 1975), 277.
44. Quoted by B. R. Coward in *Battleship at War* (London: Ian Allen, 1987), 92.
45. As quoted by Joy Packer, *Deep as the Sea*, 278.
46. Carlton Jackson reports testimony from a survivor of the raid that another British battleship, *Winchelsea*, had been hit off Salerno by a Fritz-X. See his excellent book, *Allied Secret: The Sinking of HMT Rohna* (Norman: University of Oklahoma Press, 2002), 44. Jackson's source was a taped account from a crewmember of a ship in convoy KMF-26. Jackson does not actually give credence to this account, but to be clear *Winchelsea* was a World War I–era destroyer, not a battleship, and there are no indications it was hit by a Fritz-X. It was, however, targeted by an He 177 carrying two Hs 293 glide bombs during an attack on convoy SL 139 / MKS 10 on 21 November. Neither Hs 293 missile hit during that attack. See *Air Ministry Weekly Intelligence Summary*, no. 235, 4 March 1944, 22.
47. The aircraft was 6N+KN (Wk.Nr. 5630) from 5./KG 100.
48. III./KG 100 lost an aircraft to an Allied fighter with unknown Skz and Vbkz (Wk.Nr. 4575). II./KG 100 lost 6N+FP (Wk.Nr. 5609), 6N+EN (Wk.Nr. 5616), and 6N+IN (Wk.Nr. 5626).

Chapter 4

1. Mayer's claims about *Franken* were not wild speculation but rather a case of badly mistaken identity. There was a ship named *Franken*—a very large fleet oiler under construction for the Germany navy—and right next to it on the Deutsche Werke Kiel AG slipway in 1938 was the actual German carrier under

construction, *Graf Zeppelin*. He probably thought *Franken* was to be another carrier along the lines of already-revealed *Graf Zeppelin*.

2. Hinsley, *British Intelligence in the Second World War*, Vol. I, 508–511. An exact transcript of the German text can be found at Frithjof A. S. Sterrenburg, "The Oslo Report: Nazi Secret Weapons Forfeited." Retrieved June 2008 from http://www.wlhoward.com/id1089.html. The Bv 143 was ultimately abandoned in favor of continued development of the Hs 293.

3. R. V. Jones, *The Wizard War: British Scientific Intelligence 1939–45* (New York: Coward, McCann & Geoghegan, 1979), 69–70. Jones was one of the few who took seriously the information in the Oslo Report.

4. Hinsley, *British Intelligence in the Second World War*, Vol. III, Part 1, 338.

5. Ibid.

6. The Allies would later realize that they had photographic evidence of an Hs 293 being carried by a Do 217 bomber in June 1943, while II./KG 100 was still in training mode operating out of Garz Heringsdorf Airfield. Photoreconnaissance missions over that airfield revealed unusual shadows under the wings of a parked Do 217 aircraft. Later, in December 1943, similar aircraft were encountered in the air over The Netherlands by a patrol of Typhoon fighters of the RAF 198 and 609 squadrons, at which point the Allies had substantial evidence of the Hs 293. Pilots of the Typhoons identified the Do 217 over The Netherlands as carrying Hs 293 missiles; the gun camera photographs from those Typhoons led photoreconnaissance analysts to review the original photos from June of that same year. Technical analysis confirmed that the image not previously identified in the June photographs was an Hs 293. See Staerk and Sinnott, *Luftwaffe*, 92.

7. Hinsley, *British Intelligence in the Second World War*, Vol. III, Part 1, 337.

8. Hinsley mistakenly reports *Savannah* was hit by an Hs 293.

9. Hinsley, *British Intelligence in the Second World War*, Vol. III, Part 1, 499–500.

10. Cull, *Spitfires Over Sicily*, 178.

11. Balke, *Kampfgeschwader KG 100 "Wiking,"* 256. Bürckle's aircraft was 6N+IT (Wk.Nr. 4563) and Schenk's was 6N+KT (Wk.Nr. 4554).

12. Balke, *Kampfgeschwader KG 100 "Wiking,"* 256. Zantopp's aircraft was 6N+BD (Wk.Nr. 4574). This account is confirmed via the author's (Bollinger's) communication with Rainer Zantopp, son of Hans-Joachim Zantopp, 25 July 2009.

13. Felkin, "Radio Controlled Bombs." The report makes clear that the detailed (and highly accurate) information in this interrogation report was obtained from the pilot and observer of aircraft 6N+BD (Zantopp and Arnold), though the report does not provide the actual names.

14. Ibid., 3–4.

15. Hinsley, *British Intelligence in the Second World War*, Vol. III, Part 1, 339.

16. Correspondence between Winston Churchill and Roundell Cecil Palmer, 16 October 1943, Records of the Special Operations Executive, UK National Archives, file HS 8/897.

17. Max Corvo, *The O.S.S. in Italy 1942–1945: A Personal Memoir* (New York: Praeger, 1990), 112.

18. Patrick K. O'Donnell, *Operatives, Spies and Saboteurs: The Unknown Story of the Men and Women of WWII's OSS* (New York: Free Press, 2004), 106–108.

19. Wolf is an example of an author who lists these ships as victims of the Hs 293. See Wolf, *German Guided Missiles*, 23.

20. Adrian Seligman, *War in the Islands: Undercover Operations in the Aegean 1942–4* (Phoenix Mill, UK: Alex Sutton Publishing, 1996), 59.

21. Roger P. Hill, *Destroyer Captain* (London: William Kimbler, 1975), 127.

22. Hinsley, *British Intelligence in the Second World War*, Vol. III, Part 1, 388.

23. Not included here is an action (falsely) rumored to have been taken in September 1943. As indicated by Lieutenant (jg) Malcolm Stearns Jr., a U.S. naval officer working in the Office of the Naval Attaché in London, "[T]he story is also whispered that the inventor of this device has been shot by a British spy." See memo to Captain A. W. Ashbrook, 2 October 1943, from Lt (jg) Malcolm Stearns, Jr., Office of the Naval Attaché, American Embassy (author's collection.) The rumor was of course incorrect.

24. Information on these raids is from Kit C. Carter and Robert Mueller, *The Army Air Forces in World War II: Combat Chronology, 1941–1945* (Washington, DC: Office of Air Force History, 1973).

25. Balke, *Kampfgeschwader KG 100 "Wiking,"* 257.

Chapter 5

1. Terrence Robertson, *Walker, R.N.: The Story of Captain Frederic John Walker, C.B., D.S.O. and Three Bars, R.N.* (London: Evans Brothers, 1956), 142. Walker, then commanding the sloop *Starling* off the coast of France, is legendary for his success in sinking U-boats, being credited with more "kills" than was any other Allied ship captain. He died at age forty-eight in 1944 while serving in the Royal Navy. (His son was killed in action in the war as well.) Walker earned the Distinguished Service Order with three bars for his exploits, meaning he was awarded one of the highest military honors in the Royal Navy for four separate exploits.

2. Biographical information for Lorenzen is from Naval Research Laboratory (NRL), "A Tribute to the Father of Electronic Warfare," Press Release 32-00r, 22 May 2000. Retrieved 13 March 2010 from http://www.nrl.navy.mil/pao/pressRelease.php?Y=2000&R=32-00r.

3. Howard O. Lorenzen, "A History of Electronic Warfare (Countermeasures) at the Naval Research Laboratory," 4 February 1983. This is an unpublished and formerly classified manuscript by Lorenzen describing early development of electronic warfare systems at NRL. It was declassified at the request of this author.

4. These missile fragments are described in a report from the RAE, Farnborough, "Enemy Aircraft Hs 293: Interim Note on the Examination of Fragments of Three Hs 293 Aircraft," 10 September 1943, E. A. Note No. 52/1, UK Archives AIR 14-3611.

5. Interview by the author with William Howe, 4 August 2008.

6. Ibid.

7. Alfred Price, *The History of U.S. Electronic Warfare*, Vol. I (Washington, DC: Association of Old Crows, 1984), 93.

8. Ivan Amato, *Pushing the Horizon: Seventy-Five Years of High Stakes Science and Technology at the Naval Research Laboratory* (Washington, DC: Naval Research Laboratory, 1997), 121.

9. Price, *The History of U.S. Electronic Warfare*, 93.

10. Ibid., 93–94. The XCK and XCL jammers were not completed prior to the end of the glide-bomb threat and thus were never deployed operationally.

11. Norman Friedman, *Naval Radar* (Annapolis, MD: Naval Institute Press, 1981), 128.

12. "Search for Frequency of and Countermeasures to Remote Controlled Bombs: Memo from the Director of Signal Department, 30 July 1943," UK National Archives, Records of the Admiralty, Admiralty, and Ministry of Defence, Navy Department: Correspondence and Papers, file ADM 1-12940. As has been reported earlier, this information came in part from interrogation of the crew of aircraft 6N+BD.

13. Communication on 15 July 2008 between the author and Alfred W. ("Chip") Gardes III. Chip Gardes is the son of the first captain of *Herbert C. Jones*.

14. As such, Goepner is the only major figure in this book to have served as a character in a major Hollywood movie. His role in this incident at Pearl Harbor is documented in the 1970 film *Tora! Tora! Tora*!

15. "Radio-Transfer of Material to the Navy Yard, Washington, for the DE-136: Memo from the Chief of the Bureau of Ships, Radio Division, to the Director of the Naval Research Library, 30 September 1943," U.S. National Archives and Records Administration, Record Group 19 (Bureau of Ships, Radio Division), Entry 1270 (Genera Correspondence, 1943, Counter, Box 140.

16. Placzek is quoted by Lewis M. Andrews Jr. in *Tempest Fire & Foe: Destroyer Escorts in World War II and the Men to Manned Them* (Victoria, Canada: Trafford Publishing, 2004), 59.

17. A. Hoyt Taylor, *The First 25 Years of the Naval Research Laboratory* (Washington, DC: The Navy Department, 1948), 69.

Chapter 6

1. Balke, *Kampfgeschwader KG 100 "Wiking,"* 257.

2. Wolf mistakenly says 24 September. See Wolf, *German Guided Missiles*, 22.

3. The aircraft were 6N+MP (Wk.Nr. 5667), 6N+AN (Wk.Nr. 5605), and 6N+KA (Wk.Nr. 1169). Aircraft 6N+KA was special, a Do 217 E-4 (and thus not a glide bomber) equipped with radio receivers able to detect the presence of Allied jamming. Its loss on this mission, before the Allies had deployed any jamming, would have significant consequences later.

4. Interview with Pierre Perruquet. *Simulation France Magazine*, 9 May 2007. Retrieved 13 March 2010 from http://www.france-simulation.com/sections.php?op=viewarticle&artid=86. Perruquet puts the date of the attack as 29 September.

5. Also lost was a smaller landing craft, *LCT No. 2231*, which was on board *LST-79* at the time and which shared its fate.

6. S. Peter Karlow, *Targeted by the CIA: An Intelligence Professional Speaks Out on the Scandal that Turned the CIA Upside Down* (Paducah, KY: Turner Publishing, 2001), 61.

7. Memo from Lieutenant G. H. Sturge, Bomb Safety Officer, to Commander-in-Chief Mediterranean, 16 November 1943, UK National Archives, Admiralty and Ministry of Defense, Navy Department: Correspondence and Papers. Search for enemy radio-controlled bombs at Salerno and Ajaccio (ADM 1-12938). Some have mistakenly claimed that two intact missiles were found at Ajaccio. Indeed, in early 1944 two nearly intact Hs 293 glide bombs were recovered from another location in Corsica and this might explain the confusion.

8. Trenkle, *Die Deutschen Funklenkverfahern*, 51.

9. Balke, *Kampfgeschwader KG 100 "Wiking,"* 269, names *Fort Fitzgerald* as the ship sunk by an Hs 293.

10. John Slader, *The Fourth Service: Merchantmen at War 1939–45* (Wimborne Minster, Dorset, UK: New Era Writer's Guild, 1995), 244–245.

11. Ian M. Malcolm, a radio operator on board *Samite*, witnessed the attack and glide-bomb impact on *Samite*. Personal communication with the author, 9 February 2008. See also Malcolm's recorded oral history, *Merchant Navy Book 1: Voyage 1 of the* Samite *(World War II)*, self-published, Dundee, UK, 2008.

12. Browning indicates the damage was from a bomb that exploded fifteen feet off the port side. See Browning, *U.S. Merchant Vessel War Casualties of World War II*, 368. Since the only aircraft involved in the raid carried either torpedoes or Hs 293 missiles, it appears the latter was most likely responsible.

13. The aircraft was 6N+GM (Wk.Nr. 5637).

14. The aircraft was 6N+CC (Wk.Nr. 5660).

15. Balke, *Kampfgeschwader KG 100 "Wiking,"* 270.

16. "Report of an Interview with the Master—Captain William Wilson: s.s. SALTWICK—3,775 g.t.," Shipping Casualties Section—Trade Division, 16 November 1943, UK National Archives, Records of the Admiralty; Admiralty, and Ministry of Defence, Navy Department: Trade Division, Admiralty: War History Cases and Papers, Second World War, file ADM 199-2166.

17. Andrews, *Tempest Fire & Foe*, 59.

18. Herbert C. Jones *Radio Press News*, 7 November 1943. This was an internal newsletter typed up and mimeographed for the crew.

19. Andrews, *Tempest Fire & Foe*, 59.

20. Friedman, *Naval Radar*, 129.

21. "Guided Missiles Countermeasures—Report of Performance of DE Equipment, Comment on Memo from the Director of the Naval Research Laboratory to the Chief of the Bureau of Ships, 14 January 1944," U.S. National Archives and Records Administration, Record Group 19 (Bureau of Ships), Entry 1271 (Radio Division General Correspondence, 1944, Countermeasures), Box 10. Gardes was relieved of command of *Herbert C. Jones* on 7 December 1943, two weeks after he wrote this letter. It is not known if these events are connected.

22. Balke, *Kampfgeschwader KG 100 "Wiking,"* 271.

23. See, for example, Roger W. Jordan's highly respected book, *The World's Merchant Fleets 1939: The Particulars and Wartime Fates of 6,000 Ships* (Annapolis, MD: Naval Institute Press, 1999), 488.

24. "Report of an Interview with the Master—Captain A. Ellis: m.v. BIRCHBANK—5,151 g.t.," Shipping Casualties Section—Trade Division, 21 December 1943, UK National Archives, Records of the Admiralty; Admiralty, and Ministry of Defence, Navy Department: Trade Division, Admiralty: War History Cases and Papers, Second World War, file ADM 199-2166.

25. "Report of an Interview with the Master—Captain R. C. Proctor: m.v. INDIAN PRINCE—8,587 g.t.," Shipping Casualties Section—Trade Division, 14 December 1943, UK National Archives, Records of the Admiralty; Admiralty, and Ministry of Defence, Navy Department: Trade Division, Admiralty: War History Cases and Papers, Second World War, file ADM 199-2166.

26. Thierry Bressol, "Après l'épouvantable escale du belge Carlier à Dakar [After the Terrible Port Call of the Belgian *Carlier* in Dakar]," *Souvenirs de Mer*, 9 April 2006. Retrieved March 2009 from http://souvenirs-de-mer.blogdns.net/spip.php?article158.

27. "Tätigkeitsbericht über Einsatzperiode das K.G. 100."

28. Balke, *Kampfgeschwader KG 100 "Wiking,"* 271.

29. Sam Lombard-Hobson, *A Sailor's War* (New York: St. Martin's Press, 1983), 168–169.

30. Ibid., 170.

31. Lombard-Hobson had served as the commanding officer of *Guillemot;* serving under him at the time was Nicholas Monsarrat. Monsarrat is the author of *The Cruel Sea.* He based some elements of this famous novel on his experiences while serving with Lombard-Hobson on *Guillemot.*

32. David D. Bruhn, *Wooden Ships and Iron Men: The U.S. Navy's Coastal & Motor Minesweepers, 1941–1953*, manuscript pending publication. Retrieved January 2009 from http://www.naval-history.net/WW2Ships-BYMS72.htm.

33. Seligman, *War in the Islands*, 69.

34. The aircraft was 6N+EP (Wk.Nr. 8011).

35. Balke, *Kampfgeschwader KG 100 "Wiking."* The information is gleaned from the appendix of aircraft losses, 436–458. The aircraft from 5./KG 100 destroyed in the attack were Wk.Nr. 5613 and 1148. Aircraft damaged from 5./KG 100 were Wk.Nr. 5618, 5658 (6N+KP), 4572, 5639 (6N+KN), and 5411. A Do-217 K-3 from III./KG 100 (Wk.Nr. 4710) was slightly damaged.

36. See Carter and Mueller, *The Army Air Forces in World War II.*

Chapter 7

1. Luftwaffe QM6 records as compiled by Michael Holm on *The Luftwaffe, 1933–45: Flugzeugbestand und Bewegungsmeldungen, 3.42–12.44.* Retrieved January 2009 from http://www.ww2.dk/oob/bestand/kampf/bkampf.htm.

2. Alfred Price, *Aircraft Profile: Heinkel He 177* (Windsor, UK: Profile Publications, 1972), 267.

3. J. Richard Smith and Eddie J. Creek, *Heinkel He 177 Greif: Hitler's Strategic Bomber* (Hersham, UK: Ian Allan Publishing, 2008), 48–50.

4. Griehl wrote that the first use of the He 177 on a glide-bomb mission was on 23 August 1943 against the same British escorts attacked on 25 August and 27 August by II./KG 100. See Griehl, *Do 217-317-417*, 114. This seems highly

improbable, however, because the first He 177s did not even arrive in II./ KG 40's inventory until August 1943 and it would have taken some time to effect the transition.

5. KG 40 was not the only unit to receive the He 177 for maritime attack missions. The first He 177 aircraft were delivered to II./KG 100 in October 1943 and another major tranche would arrive in March 1944. II./KG 100 never actually deployed the He 177 in operational use, however. See Griehl and Dressel, *Heinkel: He 177, 277, 274.*

6. C. R. Shelley, "HMCS *Prince Robert*: The Career of an Armed Merchant Cruiser," *Canadian Military History 4* (1995): 56.

7. Wolf, *German Guided Missiles*, 25.

8. Smith and Creek, *Heinkel He 177 Greif*, 112.

9. Air Ministry Weekly Intelligence Summary no. 235, 4 March 1944, 20.

10. Ibid., 21–22.

11. Griehl and Dressel, *Heinkel: He 177, 277, 274*, 130.

12. The aircraft lost include F8+BN (Wk.Nr. 535443) and an aircraft with Wk.Nr. 535683 and unknown Vbkz and Skz. Two aircraft were lost in accidents: the first was F8+DP (Wk.Nr. 535445) lost to engine fire; this aircraft often is referred to via its Skz, GJ+RG. The second aircraft with Skz NN+QR (Wk.Nr. 535551) was lost in a landing accident.

13. Price, *Aircraft Profile: Heinkel He 177*, 274.

14. Price, *The History of Electronic Warfare*, 94–95.

15. This density of loading is equivalent to that of the notorious Soviet KGB prison ships that carried Gulag convicts to their fate. See Martin J. Bollinger, *Stalin's Slave Ships: Kolyma, the Gulag Fleet and the Role of the West* (Annapolis, MD: Naval Institute Press, 2008).

16. The aircraft that crashed appears to be NN+QW (Wk.Nr. 535556).

17. Herbert C. Jones *Action News*, 27 November 1943. This was the internal newspaper of *Herbert C. Jones*.

18. Price, *Aircraft Profile: Heinkel He 177*, 275.

19. Nuss's aircraft was F8+BP (Wk.Nr. 535684) and Mons was lost on board F8+KM (Wk.Nr. 535367). Other aircraft lost in combat include F8+MM (Wk. Nr. 535369), F8+EP (Wk.Nr. 535444), F8+IM (Wk.Nr. 535566), and F8+DM (Wk.Nr. 535677).

20. Anthony W. Pieper, "An Informal History of the 414th Night Fighter Squadron," unpublished manuscript, date unknown. The pilot in this case most likely is Lieutenant Burton Clark.

21. Survivors' Report by *Rohna's* 2nd Officer, J. E. Wills, made to the Admiralty on 17 December 1943. Retrieved May 2009 from http://www.merchantnavyofficers. com/rohna2.html.

22. Hans Dochtermann, "Attack on U.S. Convoy KMF-26 off the Bay of Bourgie," 14 July 1992. This is a personal memoir prepared by Hans Dochtermann for Professor Carlton Jackson in preparation of Jackson's book *Allied Secret*. The song, from World War I, translates loosely as "And so we sail, and so we sail, and so we sail against England."

23. See accounts in Jackson, *Allied Secret*.

24. James E. Wise Jr. and Scott Baron, *Soldiers Lost at Sea: A Chronicle of Troopship Disasters* (Annapolis, MD: Naval Institute Press, 2004), 147.

25. Numerous anecdotes to this effect are reported in Jackson, *Allied Secret*.

26. "1,000 Saved of 2,000 on Ship in Biggest Transport Loss: War Department Gives European Waters as Disaster Scene—'Enemy Attack' Is Attributed to Submarine," *New York Times*, 18 February 1944, p. 1.

27. "3,604 Troops Were Lost on Ships Taking 4,453,061 Men to Europe," *New York Times*, 14 June 1945, p. 5.

28. See Andrews, *Tempest Fire & Foe*, 59. Andrews is somewhat dismissive of the losses from this attack, which total more than one thousand dead, writing simply that "only one ship was hit."

29. Ibid.

30. William Leonard, *In the Storm of the Eye: A Lifetime at CBS* (New York: Penguin Group, 1987), 40–41.

31. In addition to F8+BP (Wk.Nr. 535684) and F8+BP (Wk.Nr. 535684) reported above, four others were lost during the operation: F8+EP (Wk.Nr. 535444), F8+IM (Wk.Nr. 535566), F8+KM (Wk.Nr. 535367), and F8+MM (Wk.Nr. 535369). Two aircraft are reported to have crashed when landing after the raid: GP+WV (Wk.Nr. 535371) and NN+QT (Wk.Nr. 535553).

32. F8+LM (Wk.Nr. 535562) on 24 December. See Griehl, *Do 217-317-417*, 238.

33. Vbkz and Skz unknown (Wk.Nr. 535672). See Griehl, *Do 217-317-417*, 238.

34. Neitzel, *Der Einsatz der Deutschen Luftwaffe*, 184.

35. Sydney David Waters, *The Royal New Zealand Navy* (Wellington, New Zealand: Historical Publications Branch, 1956), 355. Other writers put the first attack at 1425 hours and the second at 1427 hours. See, for example, Joseph Schull, *Far Distant Ships: An Official Account of Canadian Naval Operations in World War II* (Toronto, Ontario, Canada: Stoddard Publishing, 1987.) Wolf mistakenly puts this attack on 20 December. See Wolf, *German Guided Missiles*, 27–28.

36. Neitzel, *Der Einsatz der Deutschen Luftwaffe*, 181.

37. Goss, *Sea Eagles*, 154.

38. According to some accounts, *Duchess of York* and *California*, both luxury liners converted into large troop transports, were each hit by Hs 293 missiles on 11 July 1943 while off the coast of Portugal in an attack by Fw 200 Condors from III./KG 40. However, the most detailed assessments of the attack, including direct reports from participants on both sides of the battle, indicate the damage to these two ships was the result of conventional 250-kilogram bombs dropped from high altitude. See Goss, *Sea Eagles*, 141–142. Moreover, the roster of aircraft of the unit involved, III./KG 40, did not begin to include Hs 293–enabled variants of the Fw 200 Condor (the C-3/U1, C-3/U3, C-6, or C-8 models) until December 1943.

39. F8+IN (Wk.Nr. 535557) was missing in action and NN+QY (Wk.Nr. 535559) crash-landed upon return. It is not certain that the loss of NN+QY is related to this mission. See Griehl, *Do 217-317-417*, 237.

40. See Michael D. Roberts, *Dictionary of American Naval Aviation Squadrons*, Vol. II (Washington, DC: Naval Historical Center, 2000), 716. Reedy was the commanding officer of VB-110, a patrol unit operating from Northern Ireland.

Years later, as a read admiral, he rose to fame for his aviation exploits over Antarctica. One of the pilots serving in Reedy's unit at the time was Joseph P. Kennedy Jr., the elder brother of President John F. Kennedy.

41. See Carter and Mueller, *The Army Air Forces in World War II.*

Chapter 8

1. G. E. F. Proctor, "German Radio-Controlled Glider Bombs," Air Ministry Memo A.I.2(g) 3009, 1 September 1943, UK National Archives, catalog reference AIR 14-3611.
2. RAE, Farnborough, "German Jet Propelled Glider with Radio Control Hs 293: General Reconstruction," Technical Note No. ARM 231 (S.I.) E.A. No 52/4, December 1943, UK National Archives, catalog reference AVIA 6/12166.
3. Ibid., 2. A *kopfring* was a metal ring welded to the front of Luftwaffe bomb cases to ensure they exploded on contact with the water, as opposed to ricocheting off or penetrating the water too deeply. Trialen 105 was a standard German bomb filling made from a formulation of TNT (70 percent), RDX (15 percent), and aluminum powder (15 percent).
4. Ibid., 5.
5. Ibid., 4.
6. RAE, Radio Department, "An Appreciation of a Radio Unit and Other Pieces Recovered from Hs 293 Glider Bombs," Technical Note No. Rad. 183 (EA 52/5), December 9, 1943, 2, UK National Archives, catalog reference AVIA 6/12355.
7. Trenkle, *Die Deutschen Funklenkverfahern*, 49.
8. See for example, Kopp, "The Dawn of the Smart Bomb." See also Trenkle, *Die Deutschen Funklenkverfahern*, 49. Trenkle also reports that crated weapons were left behind.
9. Moreover, the weapons were not stored intact in crates. Individual components of the Hs 293, for example, were shipped and stored in five separate boxes. The Strassburg receiver and other control devices constituted one of those five boxes. See "Hs 293 Aufgaben u. Organisation des Betr. Zuges 15," RL 10/605: Records of II./KG 100 from 1943, Bundesarchiv-Militärarchiv, Freeburg. This is a field manual for the maintenance and installation of the Hs 293 prepared for ground crews of II./KG 100 in 1943.
10. RAE, "An Appreciation of a Radio Unit and Other Pieces."
11. G. W. Calvert, "Preliminary Report of Examination of Radio Equipment Associated with German Radio Controlled Bombs," Report No. 3021, 2 November 1943, Air Force Museum Box 814, FS/1942-43/German Radio Controlled Weapons.
12. According to contemporary British intelligence reports, seven Do 217 K-2 aircraft of III./KG 100 were left behind. Four contained relatively intact FuG 203e transmitters: 6N+BW (Wk.Nr. 4550), 6N+KR (Wk.Nr. 4560), 6N+HT (Wk. Nr. 4517), and an aircraft with uncertain markings (Wk.Nr. 4564). Three of the Do 217 K-2 bombers had only traces of the FuG 230e transmitters: 6N+BT (Wk.Nr. 4535), 6N+RT (Wk.Nr. 4571), and 6N+CT (Wk.Nr. 4557). In addition, two Do 217 E-5 aircraft were abandoned, both with relatively intact

FuG 230d transmitters: 6N+KP (Wk.Nr. unknown) and 6N+GP (Wk.Nr. 5615). None of these aircraft is mentioned in Balke's book on KG 100 aircraft losses (Balke, *Kampfgeschwader KG 100 "Wiking"*). Their absence helps explain the exceptionally high loss rates for aircraft of KG 100 reported by the Luftwaffe QM6 reports for September 1943, a loss rate in excess of what can be explained by enemy action on individual missions.

13. Aileen Clayton, *The Enemy Is Listening* (London: Hutchinson, 1980), 283–284.

14. C. M. Palmer, "Part of Receiver E.230 from an FX Bomb," Tech. Note No. Rad. 184 (EA56/1) from the Radio Department, Radio Aircraft Establishment, UK National Archives, catalog reference AIR 14-3611. Specifically, the Allies discovered a preselector stage from a partially dismantled Fritx-X receiver that indicated the frequency range was between 47.5 MHz and 50 MHz. It was connected to a 3-MHz transducer, which suggested the intermediate-receiver frequency was 3 MHz. This conclusion was supported by the discovery of an Hs 293 intermediate-frequency amplifier also tuned to 3 MHz. See U.S. Naval Research Laboratory, "General Instructions for Guided Missile Countermeasure Systems," NRL Report No. R-2241 (Washington, DC: Navy Department, 3 March 1944), 2.

15. G. E. F. Proctor, "FX Radio-controlled High-level Armour Piercing Bomb," Report No. 3024, UK National Archives, catalog reference AIR 14-3611. The estimated power output was deduced from aircraft wreckage. In one of the damaged aircraft was found a dummy antenna circuit connected to two fifteen-watt resistors, which led the Allies to believe that the radiated power of the Kehl transmitter was no more than thirty watts. See NRL, "General Instructions for Guided Missile Countermeasure Systems," 3.

16. Naval Cipher communication of 7 November 1943. UK National Archives, Records of the Admiralty; Admiralty, and Ministry of Defence, Navy Department: Correspondence and Papers, UK National Archives, catalog reference ADM 1-12940.

17. See Davis, "Rocket and Radio Bombs."

18. Ibid., 12.

19. "Countermeasures Equipment—Procurement: Memo from Chief of Naval Operations to Chief of Bureau of Ships, 3 December 1943," U.S. National Archives and Records Administration, Record Group 19 (Bureau of Ships), Entry 1240 (Radio Division General Correspondence, 1943, Countermeasures), Box 12. Eight sets were ordered, the first two of which had been installed in *Herbert C. Jones* and *Frederick C. Davis*.

20. Stanley E. Smith (Ed.), *The United States Navy in World War II* (New York: William Morrow & Company, 1966), 573. Involvement by *Woolsey* in jamming glide bombs is confirmed by that ship's cruise book. See Navy Department, *War Cruise: Woolsey*, Ships Data Section, Public Information Division of the Office of Public Relations, Navy Department, 37.

21. Ships with the designations matching *Madison* and *Hilary P. Jones* are reported to have been outfitted with the second-generation equipment in the United States, according to Louis A. Gebhard, in *Evolution of Naval Radio-Electronics and Contributions of the Naval Research Laboratory* (Washington, DC: Naval

Research Laboratory, 1979). *Lansdale* also is known to have been equipped with a jamming system about that time; it is likely that *Lansdale*, *Madison*, and *Hilary P. Jones* formed the second wave of escorts designed to relieve the first wave in mid-February 1944.

22. Gebhard, *Evolution of Naval Radio-Electronics*, 305.

23. This is quite a sophisticated approach to electronic surveillance. When the description of this system was presented to contemporary experts in electronic warfare known to the author, these experts were quite surprised that the engineers of that era would have appreciated such a threat and taken measures to address it. The contemporary experts came away with a renewed appreciation for the capability of those earlier engineers, who preceded them by more than six decades.

24. "Enemy Radio Controlled Missiles," enclosure to ASE memo 34464/43, 2. The precise date of this attachment is unclear. The copy in the UK archives is hand-annotated 27 January 1944, but the content of the memo suggests it was written in December 1943. ADM 1-12940.

25. "Search for Frequency of and Countermeasures to Remote Controlled Bombs: Memo from the Director of Signal Department," 30 July 1943, 3, UK National Archives, catalog reference ADM 1-12940.

26. Ibid., 4.

27. Frederick A. Kingsley, "History of Naval Radar 1935–1945: Radar Countermeasures in World War II, Part 2," *Journal of Naval Science* 17 no. 2 (1991): 96.

28. "Enemy Radio Controlled Missiles," 17 January 1944, 2–3. See ADM 1-12940.

29. Ibid., 2. The date of November is from "Provision of Radio Transmitters for Countering Enemy Radio Controlled Missiles," Director of Admiralty Signal Department, 13 November 1943, UK National Archives, catalog reference ADM 1-12940.

30. The equipment could not save *Woodpecker* from being torpedoed by U-256 on 20 February 1944 and foundering a week later in heavy weather while under tow.

31. The specific reference to Lieutenant Field is from Derek Howse, *Radar at Sea: The Royal Navy in World War 2* (London: MacMillan Press, 1994), 219.

32. Llewellyn N. Morgan, Director of Admiralty Signal Department, "Minutes from 2 December 1943," UK National Archives, catalog reference ADM 1-12940. The plan was to procure two hundred units fitted in pairs, thereby accommodating the needs of one hundred ships.

33. "Message 0318850A dated 3 January 1944 from Admiralty to C. in C. Mediterranean," UK National Archives, catalog reference ADM 1-12940.

34. "General message 202122A/January from Admiralty dated 20 January 1944," UK National Archives, catalog reference ADM 1-12940.

35. A 13 January 1944 memo from Llewellyn N. Morgan, Director of the Admiralty Signal Department, indicates that units for six ships "would be available shortly" and that, unlike the Type 650, they were to be fitted singly rather than in pairs. See ADM 1-12940.

36. Frederick A. Kingsley, "History of Naval Radar 1935–1945: Radar Countermeasures in World War II, Part 2," *Journal of Naval Science* 17 no. 2 (1991): 97.

Chapter 9

1. Henry Maitland Wilson, *Report by the Supreme Allied Commander Mediterranean to the Combined Chiefs of Staff on the Italian Campaign: 8th January 1944 to 10th May 1944* (London: His Majesty's Stationery Office, 1946), 15.
2. The transition training was more complicated than originally planned, with shortages of aircraft and fuel hampering instruction. *Staffel* 4./KG 100 never did deploy its He 177 aircraft in antiship roles.
3. I./KG 1 and III./KG 1 were equipped with the Ju 88 bomber, and I./KG 26 and III./KG 26 flew He 111 and Ju 88 bombers.
4. Balke (*Kampfgeschwader KG 100 "Wiking"*) supplies the information on II./KG 100. The information on II./KG 40 reflects the conclusions of this author (Bollinger), based on the available information, including POW interrogation reports, Ultra communications intercepts, and other Allied reports.
5. 6N+CC (Wk.Nr. 5406).
6. Piccirillo reports, clearly in error, that *Janus* was sunk at Salerno. See Albert C. Piccirillo. "The Origins of the Anti-Ship Guided Missile," American Institute of Aeronautics and Astronautics, November 1997. Technical paper presented at the 1997 World Aviation Congress, Anaheim, CA, 13–16 October 1997, 16.
7. Tomblin, *With Utmost Spirit*, 329.
8. Wilson, *Report by the Supreme Allied Commander Mediterranean*, 22.
9. G. G. Connell, *Mediterranean Maelstrom: HMS Jervis and the 14th Flotilla* (London: William Kimber, 1987), 227.
10. As quoted by Rob Jerrard in his Internet site "Ships That Deserve to Be Remembered: HMS *Janus*." Retrieved August 2009 from http://www.rjerrard.co.uk/royalnavy/janus/janus.htm
11. Tomblin, *With Utmost Spirit*, 329.
12. The aircraft lost was 6N+CC (Wk.Nr. 5406).
13. Goss, *Sea Eagles*, 162.
14. It is difficult to state with absolute confidence how many and which aircraft from II./KG 40 were lost in this and other raids at Anzio. The QM6 "loss reports" are not available for this period. Available Namentliche Verlustmeldung (NVM) records only report cases where crewmembers were killed or missing. If an aircraft was shot down and all crewmembers parachuted to safety behind Axis lines, or if a badly damaged aircraft was written off after landing without loss to crew, then that aircraft loss would not be recorded in the NVM records. What we do know is that on this raid an aircraft commanded by a *Hauptmann* Kobrink from 4./KG 40 did not return, and that all on board were declared missing in action. Likewise, an aircraft commanded by *Oberleutnant* Paul Dietrich from 4./KG 40 with marking F8+AM (possibly Wk.Nr. 535753) did not return, with five crewmembers taken as POWs and one missing in action. (We will hear more of this aircraft later in this chapter.) In contrast to the two aircraft with lost crewmembers reported by the Luftwaffe, British fighters that night claimed four aircraft shot down. It is well known, however, that such claims often were exaggerated.
15. Hill, *Destroyer Captain*, 191–192.

16. Morison, *History of United States Naval Operations in World War II*, 345.
17. Tomblin, *With Utmost Spirit*, 332.
18. Navy Department, "War Cruise: USS *Mayo*," Ships Data Section, Public Information Division of the Office of Public Relations, Navy Department. This is the "cruise book" of the *Mayo*, a contemporary account of events by the ship's own crew.
19. According to Balke's (*Kampfgeschwader KG 100 "Wiking"*) appendix on aircraft losses, these were 6N+KP (Wk.Nr. 5658) from 4./KG 100, 6N+HN (Wk. Nr. 5631) from 5./KG 100, and 6N+FP (Wk.Nr. 5509) originally assigned to 6./KG 100 but flying with another squadron that day. Balke reports that 6N+KP was commanded by *Oberfeldwebel* Herbert Wellny and was attacked by fighters on the way to the target, crash landing with no survivors. Curiously, Balke also indicates an aircraft commanded by *Unteroffizier* Stolzenberg was damaged in that same fighter attack, crash-landing on the beach with all crewmembers surviving. He lists only three aircraft lost in the raid that night from II./KG 100, however, and these are all accounted for in the aircraft above.
20. Most likely these were two aircraft from 5./KG 40. One was commanded by *Hauptmann* Ebersberger and may have been shot down while laying down flares at the onset of the raid. The other was commanded by *Oberleutnant* Fritz Hoppe. His aircraft, F8+NN, was shot down by a Beaufighter night fighter.
21. See Cressman, *The Official Chronology of the U.S. Navy in World War II*, 208. Cressman writes that the ship was hit by a German fighter-bomber first and then suffered a near miss of a glide bomb. Conversely, historian William Askew writes that the ship was actually struck by the Luftwaffe dive-bomber and that the two bombs from that dive-bomber both barely missed the ship. He does not mention a glide bomb at all. See William C. Askew, *History of the Naval Armed Guard Afloat—World War II* (Washington, DC: Office of Naval History, 1946), 171.
22. Browning, *U.S. Merchant Vessel War Casualties of World War II*, 394. Browning says the ship was hit by two bombs, but did not specifically mention glide bombs.
23. Two near misses are reported by Askew, *History of the Naval Armed Guard Afloat*, 171. Browning, *U.S. Merchant Vessel War Casualties of World War II*, 393, describes only one.
24. These include the aircraft commanded by *Leutnant* Siegfried Bonacker of 6./KG 40, which suffered an engine failure and crashed with no survivors. It also includes another aircraft from 5./KG 40 with three missing and three returned to German lines, and an aircraft commanded by *Hauptmann* Paul Hofmann of 6./KG 40. This last aircraft was set afire by an Allied fighter and crashed ten kilometers northeast of Anzio with no known survivors. Given the absence of definitive QM6 data and other vagaries of loss reports from II./KG 40 at this time, it is certainly possible other aircraft were lost.
25. "The Battle of Anzio: World War II," an unpublished firsthand account written by an unidentified radio communications specialist on board Liberty ship *Lawton B. Evans*, anchored at Anzio during the time of the attack. The written account was given by the anonymous author to Nimrod G. Anderson, a U.S. Navy gunner on board the same ship. It has been made available by Anderson's

family on the Internet. Retrieved March 2009 from http://www.richfieldveterans memorial.org/Battle%20of%20Anzio.pdf.

26. Wolf reports, in error, that this attack was made with a Fritz-X. See Wolf, *German Guided Missiles*, 63. This is extraordinarily unlikely. First, the only aircraft able to carry the Fritz-X were based out of theater at the time and none participated in this raid. Second, the missile that struck *Samuel Huntington* entered the port side of the ship and exploded in the engine room, which is characteristic of the Hs 293 flight profile and very unlike the vertical attack profile of the Fritz-X.

27. That aircraft was 6N+GM (Wk.Nr. 5659).

28. Board of Enquiry, "Loss of HMS *Spartan*: Report by the Admiralty," Department of Naval Construction, 9 February 1944. Results of the inquiry into the loss of *Spartan*, transcribed by David Hughes. Retrieved March 2010 from http://artsweb.aut.ac.nz/hmsspartan/sinking_1.html.

29. Nick Beale, *The Bombers of the Luftwaffe Summer 1943–May 1945*, Vol. IV (Hersham, UK: Ian Allen Publishing, 2005), 324.

30. 6N+DN (Wk.Nr. 5601) from 5./KG 100 was shot down by a night fighter and 6N+CU (Wk.Nr. 4363) from *Stab* 100 was shot down by another fighter near Lake Constance.

31. Balke, *Kampfgeschwader KG 100 "Wiking,"* 283.

32. Ibid. The German claims are documented by Balke, *Kampfgeschwader KG 100 "Wiking,"* 283. It is possible Balke has misstated the date of these claims as 16 February when they should apply to an attack on 15 February in which a transport ship and landing craft were indeed hit and sunk.

33. Ibid.

34. "Tätigkeitsbericht über Einsatzperiode das K.G. 100."

35. The lost aircraft was 6N+AC (Wk.Nr. 5646) from *Stab* II./100.

36. Balke, *Kampfgeschwader KG 100 "Wiking,"* 283.

37. Smith, *The United States Navy in World War II*, 572–573. Smith incorrectly writes that the first use of glide bombs against "Allied" forces was at Salerno when that was the first use against *American* forces. Prior to Salerno, British and Canadian forces had been attacked and suffered losses in the Bay of Biscay.

38. Ibid., 574.

39. Ibid., 573–574.

40. The aircraft seriously damaged was 6N+BP (Wk.Nr. 5607).

41. Balke, *Kampfgeschwader KG 100 "Wiking,"* 286–287. The lost aircraft was 6N+BC (Wk.Nr. 5511) from *Stab* II./100.

42. Askew, *History of the Naval Armed Guard Afloat*, 173–174.

43. The aircraft lost was 6N+BP (Wk.Nr. 5607).

44. Once again, Wolf states that a Fritz-X was responsible, a point of view shared by authors Steven J. Zaloga and Peter Dennis in *Anzio 1944: The Beleaguered Beachhead* (Oxford, UK: Osprey Publishing: 2005), 41. This is contradicted by Luftwaffe records that confirm that III./KG 100, the only unit equipped operationally with the Fritz-X, flew no missions over Anzio.

45. Eric Alley, "The Landings at Anzio—A View from the Sea," as reported in "WW2 People's War, An Archive of World War Two Memories," prepared by

the BBC and available at http://www.bbc.co.uk/ww2peopleswar/stories/43/a4015243.shtml.

46. Goss (*Sea Eagles*) presents a thorough account of this attack using firsthand reports and identifies the lost aircraft of II./KG 40 as one commanded by *Oberfeldwebel* Oskar Adam of 4./KG 40. Balke (Balke, *Kampfgeschwader KG 100 "Wiking"*) provides a detailed firsthand account of this battle and attributes it to II./KG 100.

47. Neitzel, *Der Einsatz der Deutschen Luftwaffe*, 184.

48. F8+PN (Wk.Nr. 535679) according to Griehl and Dressel, *Heinkel: He 177*, 277, 274, 238. See Goss, *Sea Eagles*, 168, for relevant names.

49. Kenneth Poolman, *Allied Escort Carriers of World War Two in Action* (Annapolis, MD: Naval Institute Press, 1988), 96–97.

50. Order of battle information is from QM6 monthly records compiled by Michael Holm and made available through his Internet site The Luftwaffe, 1933–45: Flugzeugbestand und Bewegungsmeldungen, 3.42–12.44. Retrieved June 2008 from http://www.ww2.dk/oob/bestand/kampf/bkampf.htm.

51. See Poolman, *Allied Escort Carriers of World War Two in Action*, 97. For a contemporary account, see "Convoy Saved from Air Attack," *London Times*, 18 February 1944, p. 4.

52. The number is uncertain. Ten A-7 variants were completed and delivered to FAGr(5): Wk.Nrs. 186 (9V+FH), 187 (9V+LK), 188 (9V+FK), 189 (9V+KK), 190 (9V+MK), 191 (9V+AB), 192 (9V+HH), 193 (9V+FK), 195 (9V+LK), and 196 (9V+IH). See Karl Kössler and Günther Ott, *Die großen Dessauer: Junkers Ju 89, Ju 90, Ju 290, Ju 390—Die Geschichte einer Flugzeugfamilie* (Berlin, 1993).

53. Ibid., 240. In addition, it would have been unusual to immediately deploy such an aircraft on combat missions. In the case of the He 177 and Do 217 there were several months between the delivery of initial aircraft to the operational unit and their first use in combat.

54. Those aircraft were 9V+DK, Wk.Nr. 0177 of 2./FAG 5 and 9V+FH Wk.Nr. 0175 of 1./FAG 5. Neither aircraft could deploy the Hs 293.

55. Kössler and Ott, *Die großen Dessauer*, 186.

56. Kingsley, "History of Naval Radar 1935–1945," 96.

57. Howse, *Radar at Sea*, 192. The reference to *Inglefield* is from Eric Alley's witness account above. Incidentally, Piccirillo writes that the Hs 293 was captured at a German airfield in Italy in February 1944, and is therefore probably confusing this intelligence find with that from Foggia in September 1943. See Piccirillo, "The Origins of the Anti-Ship Guided Missile," 24.

58. Joe Gray Taylor, *Development of Night Air Operations, 1941–1952*, Historical study #92 prepared for the Historical Division, Air University, U.S. Air Force (Maxwell Air Force Base, Montgomery, AL: U.S. Air Force, 1953), 26.

59. Parts of the aircraft can be seen today, used as structural elements in an old mill at Chjarasjinca, Corsica.

60. C. M. Palmer, "Radio Control Mechanism from the German Glider Bomb Hs 293," RAE, Radio Department, March 1944, 1, UK National Archives, AVIA 6/14424 (Records of the RAE, German Glider Bomb Hs 293: Radio Control Mechanism). It is possible this recovery of missiles from aircraft

F8+AM, clearly documented in contemporary intelligence files, has spawned two other reported cases of recovery of Hs 293 missiles that are less well substantiated. First is the incorrect account of two reasonably intact Hs 293 missiles being recovered at Ajaccio, a different location in Corsica, in September 1943. Second is the report described by Howse that an intact Hs 293 was found on the beach at Anzio on February 22, an account this author has been unable to substantiate from primary source material. It could well be that Howse's report is accurate. It might also be a garbled account of the recovery on February 23 of the missiles from F8+AM, an aircraft that was on its way to bomb Anzio.

61. Boardman, "German Bombs & Fuzes, Land Mines & Igniters." The detailed description of the Hs 293 is dated June 1944.

Chapter 10

1. NRL, "General Instructions for Guided Missile Countermeasure Systems," 2.
2. Ibid., 16.
3. Lorenzen, "A History of Electronic Warfare," 2. This was an unpublished classified manuscript by Lorenzen describing early development of electronic warfare systems at NRL. It was declassified at this author's request in 2008.
4. NRL, "General Instructions for Guided Missile Countermeasure Systems," 9.
5. This often is incorrectly written as DINA-MITE. DINA is an acronym for Direct Noise Amplification, a jamming technique in which band-limited Gaussian noise from a low-power source is passed to a high-power amplifier and then radiated. In this context, MATE referred to the attached receiver unit on the ARQ-8.
6. C. G. Suits, George R. Harrison, and Louis Jordan (Eds.), *Applied Physics: Electronics, Optics, Metallurgy* (Boston: Little, Brown & Company, 1948), 44. This book is one in a series describing the activities of the Office of Scientific Research and Development in World War II.
7. "Guided Missile Countermeasures—Model MAS Jammer—Interim Report on Problem S705R-S: Memo from Director of Naval Research Laboratory to Chief of the Bureau of Ships, 13 Jun 1944," U.S. National Archives and Records Administration, Record Group 19 (Bureau of Ships), Entry 1271 (Radio Division General Correspondence, 1944, Countermeasures), Box 10. Subsequently identified as NARA RG 19 / Entry 1271 / Box 10.
8. "Guided Missiles Countermeasures—Transmitters For: Memo from NRL Section 920 to the Chief of Naval Operations, 24 March 1944," U.S. National Archives and Records Association, Record Group 19 (Bureau of Ships), Entry 1271 (Radio Division, General Correspondence, 1944, Transmitters), Box 239.
9. "Guided Missile Countermeasures—Model MAS Jammer—Interim Report on Problem S705R-S: Memo from Director of Naval Research Laboratory to Chief of the Bureau of Ships, 13 Jun 1944," NARA RG 19 / Entry 1271 / Box 10.
10. Suits et al., *Applied Physics*, 44.
11. C. Steward Gillmor, *Fred Terman at Stanford: Building a Discipline, a University and Silicon Valley* (Stanford, CA: Stanford University Press, 2004), 207.

12. "Radio—Countermeasures—Type CXGE Transmitter, Development of: Memo from Director of Naval Research Laboratory to Chief of the Bureau of Ships, 7 July 1944," U.S. National Archives and Records Administration, Record Group 19 (Bureau of Ships), Entry 1271 (Radio Division General Correspondence, 1944, Transmitters), Box 240.

13. The specific ships that received the CXGE systems that were sent to Exeter remain uncertain. It is known that battleship *Texas* and command ship *Bayfield* had the system on board. Other logical candidates include two other battleships (*Arkansas* and *Nevada*) and three heavy cruisers (*Augusta*, *Tuscaloosa*, and *Quincy*) that provided fire support both at Normandy and then on the French Riviera. Other likely candidates include the other command ship at Normandy (*Ancon*) and the three command ships in southern France (*Catoctin*, *Biscayne*, and *Betelgeuse*). The smaller ships, including light cruisers and destroyers, seem to have been equipped instead with the Type MAS system or ARQ-8 interim jammer.

14. "Radio Countermeasures and Enemy Equipment," RAE Radio Department, Appendix III (J.T.D. No. 6), 1 July 1944, U.S. National Archives and Records Administration, Record Group 38 (Records of the Chief of Naval Operations 1875–1989), Top Secret Reports of Naval Attaches 02/1944—08/1947. ARC ID 595101.

15. The company became AIL. It was acquired by Cutler-Hammer, then sold to the Eaton Corporation, and then sold to EDO Corporation. It is now owned by ITT Corporation.

16. The account in this and the following paragraphs of the role of Skifter and AIL is taken from Gregory S. Hunter, *Hector R. Skifter: Radio Pioneer, Industrial Leader and Defense Advisor, 1901–1964* (Northfield, MN: St. Olaf College Press, 1997), 99–102.

17. Hunter, *Hector R. Skifter*, 101.

18. "Guided Missiles Countermeasures—Model MAS Equipment—Interim Report on Problem S705R-S: Memo from NRL Director to the Chief of the Bureau of Ships, 21 June 1944," NARA RG 19 / Entry 1271 / Box 10.

19. "Guided Missiles Countermeasures—Model MAS Equipment—Reduction of Receiver Local Oscillator Frequency Pulling and Reradiation: Memo from NRL Director to the Chief of the Bureau of Ships, 27 June 1944," NARA RG 19 / Entry 1271 / Box 10.

20. Eight new systems were dispatched to the Pacific, with one retained as a spare at the Norfolk Navy Yard. On 29 July one unit was shipped for installation on board a cruiser, probably *Cincinnati* (CL-6). Between 1 August and 12 August 1944 seven more systems were dispatched for installation on board destroyer-escorts: *Price* (DE-332), *Coolbaugh* (DE-217), *Rudderow* (DE-224), *Robert Brazier* (DE-3435), *Gentry* (DE-349), *Carter* (DE-112), and *Riley* (DE-579). None of these ships supported the invasion of Normandy. In October two units were shipped to New York Navy Yard for installation on board destroyer-escorts, identified only as in Escort Division (CORTDIV) 76 and 79. See various memos from Chief of Naval Operations to the Chief of Bureau of Ships on "Countermeasures Equipment—Distribution of, for 14 July, 26 July, 29 July, 1 August, 12 August, and 31 October 1944," NARA RG 19 / Entry 1271 / Box 10.

21. Kingsley, "History of Naval Radar 1935–1945," 96.

22. As described by Alan Raven and John Arthur Roberts in *British Battleships of World War Two: The Development and Technical History of the Royal Navy's Battleships and Battlecruisers from 1911 to 1946* (Annapolis, MD: Naval Institute Press, 1976).

23. William Edgar Knowles Middleton, *Radar Development in Canada: The Radio Branch of the National Research Council of Canada 1939–1945* (Waterloo, Ontario, Canada: Wilfrid Laurier University Press, 1981), 63.

24. Gebhard puts the number of U.S. ships armed with jammers deployed in the invasion of southern France in mid-August 1944 at sixty-five. See Gebhard, in *Evolution of Naval Radio-Electronics*, 303–304.

25. The landing ships were *Prince Henry* and *Prince David*. Their escorts were modern V-class destroyers *Algonquin* and *Sioux*. Other possible candidates include the Tribal-class destroyers *Haida* and *Huron*. The only ship known to the author for certain to be so equipped is *Algonquin*. This is based on personal correspondence on 23 August 2008 between the author and Kenneth C. Garret, a leading seaman and radar operator on board *Algonquin*.

26. The number of ships equipped for Overlord with these systems is from Kingsley, "History of Naval Radar 1935–1945," 97. Specific ships equipped with the Type 650 included the three Eastern Task Force headquarters ships (*Largs*, *Hilary*, and *Bulolo*), three landing force command ships (*Albrighton*, *Goathland*, and *Nith*), three fighter direction tenders converted from U.S.-built LSTs (*FDTs -13*, *-216*, and *-217*), and an assortment of bombardment ships. For this list of ships see "RCM Equipment for Operation Overlord," UK National Archives, Records of the Admiralty; Admiralty, and Ministry of Defence, Navy Department: Correspondence and Papers, UK National Archives, file ADM 1-16254.

27. Piccirillo, "The Origins of the Anti-Ship Guided Missile," 25.

28. Deichmann, "Luftwaffe Methods in the Selection of Offensive Weapons," 49.

29. Piccirillo, "The Origins of the Anti-Ship Guided Missile," 25.

30. Rowland Pocock, *German Guided Missiles of the Second World War* (New York: Arco Publishing, 1967), 74–75.

31. Ibid., 105.

32. Ibid., 76.

33. Piccirillo, "The Origins of the Anti-Ship Guided Missile," 25.

34. Piccirillo writes that 70 weapons were expended in tests. See Piccirillo, "The Origins of the Anti-Ship Guided Missile," 25. Kopp reports that (unnamed) German sources indicate 255 were built. See Kopp, "The Dawn of the Smart Bomb."

35. Kopp, "The Dawn of the Smart Bomb," quotes unnamed sources as suggesting one British ship was sunk by an Hs 293D.

36. Wolf, *German Guided Missiles*, 14.

37. Trenkle, *Die Deutschen Funklenkverfahern*, 52.

38. See "Tätigkeitsbericht über Einsatzperiode das K.G. 100." This report indicates seven missions were launched between 1 February and 20 April. The mission of 1 February, against UGS-30, has already been described in Chapter 9.

39. Goss, *Sea Eagles*, 168. Goss supplies the code names for this and the other convoys of March and April 1944.

40. The lost aircraft was 6N+MN (Wk.Nr. 5643).

41. The aircraft 6N+UP (Wk.Nr. 5513) was lost during an emergency landing at Istres.

42. The aircraft include 6N+KP (Wk.Nr. 5622), 6N+NP (Wk.Nr. 5638), and 6N+SP (Wk.Nr. 5619). The crew of the first aircraft managed to return from internment in Spain to German lines within a few days. The crew of the other two aircraft perished, except for a gunner rescued from the water by minesweeper *Sustain*, one of the ships especially equipped for jamming glide bombs.

43. The lost aircraft were 6N+BP (Wk.Nr. 5403) and 6N+OP (Wk.Nr. 5405).

44. The lost aircraft was 6N+GP (Wk.Nr. 5657), originally assigned to 5./KG 100.

45. Balke, *Kampfgeschwader KG 100 "Wiking,"* 293. It is not clear from Balke's account that the losses are attributable specifically to KG 100, because he also mentions KG 77 and KG 27 as having played a role in the combined attack.

46. "Report of an Interview with the Master—Captain L. Ecclis: s.s. SAMITE, Shipping Casualties Section—Trade Division, 19 October 1944," UK National Archives, Records of the Admiralty; Admiralty, and Ministry of Defence, Navy Department: Trade Division, Admiralty: War History Cases and Papers, Second World War, file ADM 199-2167.

47. "Report of an Interview with the Master—Captain T. F. McDonald: s.s. ROYAL STAR, Shipping Casualties Section—Trade Division, 16 May 1944," UK National Archives, Records of the Admiralty; Admiralty, and Ministry of Defence, Navy Department: Trade Division, Admiralty: War History Cases and Papers, Second World War, file ADM 199-2167.

48. The aircraft 6N+EP (Wk.Nr. 5558) was shot down by a night fighter after the attack. The aircraft 6N+PP (Wk.Nr. 5641), the aircraft of *staffel* captain Willi Scholl, also was lost.

49. Balke, *Kampfgeschwader KG 100 "Wiking,"* 294.

50. His aircraft was 6N+AD (Wk.Nr. 4701). *Hauptmann* Pfeffer was killed and only his radioman, *Unteroffizier* Wilhelm Friedrich, survived into captivity. 6N+IT (Wk.Nr. 4716) also was lost with only the observer, *Unteroffizier* Erich Katzenberger, surviving as a prisoner.

51. This was aircraft 6N+IT, a relatively new model Do 217 K-3.

52. G. W. Calvert, "Preliminary Report on FUG.203 Recovered from Do 217 K3 6N+IT Crashed 30.4.44 at 0430 Hours, FX and HS Technical Information, Report No. 3026, 3 May 1944," UK National Archives, AIR14-3611.

53. Boardman, "German Bombs & Fuzes, Land Mines & Igniters." The document appears to have been updated over time. The specific page describing the Hs 293 is dated October 1944.

54. See also Morison, *History of United States Naval Operations in World War II*, 271.

55. As cited in Roy W. Brown, *Jig How: A Story of the U.S. Navy Armed Guard During World War II* (Baltimore: PublishAmerica, 2003), 74. Brown's book tells of his firsthand experiences as a signalman in the Armed Guard. He served on board the SS *John Dickinson* and observed the attacks on UGS-40.

56. No such reference is made by Goss (*Sea Eagles*) in his comprehensive study of Luftwaffe maritime attacks. Balke (*Kampfgeschwader KG 100 "Wiking,"* 294) in his detailed history of KG 100, makes no mention of this raid, suggesting that II./KG 100 and III./KG 100 were not involved.

57. Henry L. (Larry) de Zeng in personal communication with the author, March 2009. De Zeng is coauthor with Douglas G. Stankey of *Bomber Units of the Luftwaffe: A Reference Source*, Vol. I (Hinckley, UK: Midland Publishing, 2007).

58. One Ju 290 A-7 aircraft from FAGr(5) was lost in May 1944. On 26 May this Ju 290 A-7 (9V+FK) is reported to have gone missing after it failed to return from a reconnaissance mission off the west coast of Portugal. If this information is correct, then the loss is not connected with UGS-40. See Ott, *Die großen Dessauer*.

59. Morison, *History of United States Naval Operations in World War II*, 269, 272.

60. Balke, *Kampfgeschwader KG 100 "Wiking,"* 296 and 301.

61. Late in the war German submarine U-234 was dispatched to Japan carrying samples, drawings, and technical experts on a variety of advanced systems, including the Hs 293. See Joseph Mark Scalia, *Germany's Last Mission to Japan: The Failed Voyage of U-234* (Annapolis, MD: Naval Institute Press, 2000), 108–109.

62. Hinsley, *British Intelligence in the Second World War*, Vol. III, Part 1, 391.

63. Anthony Cave Brown, *The Secret War of the OSS* (New York: Berkley Publishing Corporation, 1976), 117. Brown writes the name of the town as "Portes des Valence."

Chapter 11

1. Do 217 E-5 bombers of 8./KG 100 (formerly 6./KG 100) would use Hs 293 missiles while the surviving Do 217 K-2 bombers would use Fritz-X bombs. The new Do 217 K-3 and Do 217 M-11 variants could use either weapon.

2. The third *staffel* in I./KG 40, 3./KG 40, continued to fly the Fw 200 on support missions and did not transition to glide bombs. See de Zeng and Stankey, *Bomber Units of the Luftwaffe*, 130–131.

3. According to QM6 records this included six Do 217 K-2 able to carry the Fritz-X, and three Do 217 E-5 able to carry the Hs 293. It also included sixteen Do 217 K-3 and five Do 217 M-11 able to carry either weapon.

4. Baumbach, *The Life and Death of the Luftwaffe*, 162.

5. De Zeng and Stankey, *Bomber Units of the Luftwaffe*, 274.

6. Hans Dochtermann, "Attack on U.S. Convoy KMF-26 off the Bay of Bourgie," 14 July 1992. This is a personal memoir prepared by Hans Dochtermann, found at Manuscripts & Folklife Archives, Kentucky Library & Museum, Western Kentucky University, Bowling Green.

7. Baumbach, *The Life and Death of the Luftwaffe*, 106.

8. Orus Kinny, "Nazi Smart Bombs." Retrieved January 2010 from http://www.kilroywashere.org/003-Pages/03-OrusKinney.html. Collected as part of the Veterans History Project of the Library of Congress.

9. The "spearhead" reference is from Dr. Alfred Price, *The Last Year of the Luftwaffe: May 1944 to May 1945* (Mechanicsburg, PA: Stackpole Books, 1991), 58.

10. Brian Cull, *Diver! Diver! Diver!* (London: Grub Street, 2008), 16.

11. It is commonly reported that for II./KG 40 alone half of the twenty-six aircraft deployed that day were lost. See, for example, de Zeng and Stankey, *Bomber Units of the Luftwaffe*, 133. See also Griehl and Dressel, *Heinkel: He 177, 277, 274*, 134. However, this appears to be a mistaken interpretation of Luftwaffe records that II./KG 40 in only one month—the month of June 1944—lost thirteen of twenty-six deployed aircraft on operations over Normandy. See Smith and Creek, *Heinkel He 177 Greif*, 135–137. This is consistent with the tally from NVM records that account for twelve individual aircraft of II./KG 40 lost in June, the difference being easily explained if one aircraft was lost or written off without any crew members being killed, injured, or declared missing.

12. John Bennett, *Fighter Nights: 456 Squadron RAAF* (Belconnen: Banner Books, 1995), 131–132.

13. Ibid., 133.

14. Based on NVM records these include two aircraft from 5./KG 40: F8+HN (Wk. Nr. 550117) commanded by *Unteroffizier* Hauke and an unknown aircraft (possibly Wk.Nr. 550112) commanded by an *Oberfeldwebel* Müller. *Staffel* 1./KG 40 lost aircraft F8+MH (Wk.Nr. 550206) commanded by *Oberleutnant* Müller. *Staffel* 2./KG 40 lost three aircraft: F8+KK (Wk.Nr. 550197) commanded by *Oberfeldwebel* Timm, F8+LK (Wk.Nr. 535731) commanded by *Oberfähnrich* Bernrieder, and F8+FK (Wk.Nr. 550204) commanded by *Oberfähnrich* Hein. The NVM report for the last one incorrectly lists the date as the following night.

15. Andrews, *Tempest Fire & Foe*, 109.

16. David G. Chandler and James Lawton Collins Jr. (Eds.), *The D-Day Encyclopedia* (New York: Simon & Schuster, 1994), 538.

17. Personal correspondence with the author, 23 August 2008.

18. Bennett, *Fighter Nights*, 133.

19. Those aircraft were F8+MK (Wk.Nr. 550211) commanded by Wadle of 2./KG 40 and an aircraft of 6./KG 100 (Wk.Nr. 550083) commanded by Büsch. There are indicators that the third aircraft claimed that night was from II./KG 40 and if the crew survived and made it back to German lines, it would not be described in an NVM report. That would explain the difference between the twelve losses recorded in NVM records and the total of thirteen losses reported in monthly QM6 totals.

20. Morison concludes without reservation that a glide bomb launched from an He 177 was the cause of *Meredith*'s destruction. See Morison, *History of United States Naval Operations in World War II*, 170.

21. *Dictionary of American Naval Fighting Ships.* Retrieved August 2009 from the U.S. Naval History and Heritage Command site, http://www.history.navy.mil/danfs/n3/nelson.htm

22. The investigation of the sinking of *Lawford* was described on the television series *Wreck Detectives*. See Jeremy Seal, *Wreck Detectives*, "Episode 4" (Croydon, UK: EMAP Maclaren, 2003).

23. Balke, *Kampfgeschwader KG 100 "Wiking,"* 302.
24. One was a Do 217 K-3 (6N+OR, Wk.Nr. 4742) and one was a Do 217 E-5 (6N+MP, Wk.Nr. 5514). The former was from *Stab* III./KG 100.
25. Andrews, *Tempest Fire & Foe*, 103–104.
26. Bob Welch, *American Nightingale: The Story of Frances Slanger, Forgotten Heroine of Normandy* (New York: Simon and Schuster, 2004), 19.
27. Balke, *Kampfgeschwader KG 100 "Wiking,"* 302. The reference to Hs 293 is an inference based on the fact that the targets were suitable for this type of weapon and that all of the aircraft lost in the raid were new models of the Do 217 equipped to carry Hs 293 missiles.
28. One aircraft lost was a new Do 217 M-11 (6N+JP, Wk.Nr. 336473) with 8./KG 100 captained by Siegfried Koezle. In addition one Do 217 M-11 (Wk.Nr. 723052) was accidentally shot by German antiaircraft defenses on the way back. The crew bailed out and was captured by French resistance forces and executed on the spot. Talk about having a bad day.
29. Bennett, *Fighter Nights*, 134.
30. From 2./KG 40 were lost F8+SK (Wk.Nr. 535670) commanded by *Oberfeldwebel* Henze and F8+BK (Wk.Nr. 550198) commanded by Winarski (rank and first name not known).
31. Aircraft F8+BN (Wk.Nr. 550067) from 4./KG 40 and commanded by *Unteroffizier* Hille was shot down by an Allied fighter. Aircraft F8+LN (Wk.Nr. 550074) from 5./KG 40 and commanded by *Oberfeldwebel* Matschke was lost to Allied antiaircraft fire. An aircraft of 4./KG 100 commanded by *Stabsfeldwebel* Rainer also was lost. From 1./KG 100 were lost two aircraft: F8+JH (Wk.Nr. 550175) commanded by *Oberfeldwebel* Konopek and F8+DH (Wk.Nr. 550199) commanded by *Unteroffizier* DeVries.
32. Bennett, *Fighter Nights*, 134–135. One was claimed by Pilot Officer Ivor Sanderson and Flight Sergeant Charles Nicholas and the other by Squadron Leader Geoff Howitt and Flight Lieutenant "Red" Irving.
33. Balke, *Kampfgeschwader KG 100 "Wiking,"* 302–304.
34. See, for example, David Woodward, *Ramsay at War: The Fighting of Admiral Sir Bertram Ramsay* (London: W. Kimber, 1957), 160.
35. These were F8+FH (Wk.Nr. 550215) commanded by *Unteroffizier* Brühan of 1./KG 40, and an aircraft (Wk.Nr. 550221) from 6./KG 40, commanded by *Oberfeldwebel* Neuenfeldt.
36. On the morning of 14 June the following aircraft were lost: Wk.Nr. 550080 from 4./KG 40 and commanded by *Leutnant* Reichmüller, F8+IM (Wk.Nr. 550146) from 4./KG 40, F8+IM (Wk.Nr. 550146) commanded by *Oberleutnant* Meissner, Wk.Nr. 550087 from 6./KG 40, and Wk.Nr. 550078 commanded by *Unteroffizier* Klavehin of 6./KG 40. Aircraft F8+FH, possibly from KG 40 (Wk.Nr. 550216), also was reported missing in action that day but it is not clear if it was operating on this mission.
37. A Do 217 K-3 with marketing 6N+KT (Wk.Nr. 4748) of 7./KG 100 commanded by *Leutnant* Dietrich Leydhscher was shot down, a Do 217 K with marking 6N+HR (Wk.Nr. 4749) of 9./KG 100 commanded by *Feldwebel* Rudolf Stoll was lost, and a Do 217 K-2 with marking 6N+LT (Wk.Nr. 4555) commanded by *Oberfeldwebel* Kurt Faust never returned. This last aircraft is

of some interest because it was equipped to carry only the Fritz-X, suggesting these might have been deployed on this mission.

38. Kingsley, "History of Naval Radar 1935–1945," 97.

39. Chandler and Collins Jr., *The D-Day Encyclopedia*, 494.

40. A Do 217 K-3 with marking 6N+AR (Wk.Nr. 4706) commanded by *Leutnant* Roland Faude of 7./KG 100.

41. Notes taken from *Arethusa*'s "Log Book," June 1944. UK National Archives, Records of the Admiralty; Admiralty, and Ministry of Defence, Navy Department: Ships' Logs: file ADM 53-118866.

42. From 4./KG 40 was lost an aircraft commanded by *Oberleutnant* Hunold (Wk. Nr. 550210). From 5./KG 40 was lost an aircraft commanded by *Oberleutnant* Hauke (Wk.Nr. 550213). *Staffel* 6./KG 40 lost two aircraft, TM+IG commanded by *Feldwebel* Dotsch (Wk.Nr. 550203) and one commanded by *Oberleutnant* Schulte-Vogelheim (Wk.Nr. 550195.)

43. Victories were credited to the teams of Cowper–Watson, Radford–Atkinson, and Sanderson–Nicholas. See Bennett, *Fighter Nights*, 137.

44. Douglas L. Roberts, *Rustbucket 7: Chronicle of the USS PC 617 During the Great War* (Newcastle, ME: Mill Pond Press, 1995), 112–113.

45. Three Do 217 K-3 were lost: Wk.Nr. 3061 from 7./KG 100, Wk.Nr. 4710 of 9./KG lost off the mouth of the Gironde River, and 6N+DT (Wk.Nr. 5718) of *Stab* III./KG 100 under the command of *Leutnant* Erich Keller. Three Do 217 M-11 aircraft also were lost: Wk.Nr. 3037 from 7./KG 100 commanded by *Feldwebel* Simon Obermeier (with all crew taken prisoner), Wk.Nr. 3060 from 7./KG 100 under the command of *Feldwebel* Karl Hipp (who was killed, with the rest of the crew surviving), and Wk.Nr. 6547 commanded by *Leutnant* Siegfried Kynast of 8./KG 100 (shot down by night fighters).

46. The team of Williams and Havord appear to have shot down *Leutnant* Kynast's aircraft. See Bennett, *Fighter Nights*, 137.

47. Beale, *The Bombers of the Luftwaffe Summer*, 342.

48. Neitzel, *Der Einsatz der Deutschen Luftwaffe*, 224.

49. Ibid., 221.

50. Aircraft Wk.Nr. 4579 under *Unteroffizier* Alfred Borowitzka was lost and aircraft Wk.Nr. 4739 returned in such damaged condition that it had to be written off.

51. See Record Group 24 (Royal Canadian Navy), Headquarters (D1), Damage Reports (8340), Document 381-30: Damage report for HMCS *Matane*, 23 August 1944, 3–4. Another excellent account, entirely consistent with (and quite possibly derived from) the official damage report is Fraser M. McKee, *HMCS Swansea: The Life and Times of a Frigate* (St. Catherines, Canada: Vanwell Publishing, 1994), 109–111.

52. Martin Bondy, personal account as featured in the Windsor Historical Society Veteran's Memories Project. Retrieved March 2009 from http://www.windsor historicalsociety.com/Veterans%20Stories/Protecting_the_Sea_Lanes_for_the_ Invasion.php.

53. Interview by the author with Russell Heathman, 22 August 2008. Heathman was a leading seaman and ASDIC operator whose action station was on the bridge, which provided him a clear view of the attack.

54. Damage report for HMCS *Matane*, Record Group 24 (Royal Canadian Navy), Headquarters (D1), Damage Reports (8340).

55. Schull, *Far Distant Ships*, 345–346. The ship itself survived the missile strike and ended up in 1948 as a breakwater at Oyster Bay, south of Campbell River, Vancouver, Canada. Twelve years later, the rusting hull was deemed a hazard to navigation and was removed.

56. These were two Do 217 M-11 aircraft. The first was 6N+GS (Wk.Nr. 3038) commanded by *Oberleutnant* Karl Lamp and the second was 6N+CS commanded by *Leutnant* Wolfgang Schirmer. Many of the Luftwaffe crewmembers survived to be taken as POWs.

57. Neitzel, *Der Einsatz der Deutschen Luftwaffe*, 223.

58. The Do 217 commanded by *Leutnant* Armin Garbe of 8. *Staffel* did not return. The aircraft commanded by *Unteroffizier* Erich Scheler of 7. *Staffel* was shot down.

59. Both were aircraft from 8./KG 100. One was a Do 217 M-11 6N+DR (Wk.Nr. 2926) under *Unteroffizier* August Stolzenberg. The other was an aircraft commanded by *Oberfeldwebel* Konrad Doser, shot down on the returning flight.

60. The lost aircraft was a Do 217 M-11 6N+MS (Wk.Nr. 3057), commanded by *Feldwebel* Helmut John.

61. The other aircraft was a Do 217 6N+GR commanded by *Leutnant* Hans Kieffer of 7./KG 100.

62. Task Force 84 (Rear Admiral Frank J. Lowry on board *Duane*) landed the 3rd Division along two beaches in the Bay of Cavalière (Alpha) west of St. Tropez. Task Force 85, under Rear Admiral Bertram J. Rodgers on board *Biscayne*, landed the 45th Division at Sainte-Maxime (Delta). Task Force 87 under Rear Admiral Spencer Lewis (on board *Bayfield*) landed forces at four beaches off St. Raphael (Camel). In overall command of the Western Naval Task Force was Vice Admiral H. Kent Hewitt on board his flagship *Catoctin*. Air support was provided by Task Force 88 (Rear Admiral T. H. Troubridge) organized around British and American escort carriers.

63. The aircraft lost that evening were a Do 217 M-11 6N+AS commanded by *Oberfeldwebel* Rudolf Blab which went missing, and another aircraft commanded by *Oberfeldwebel* Rudolf Freiberg. The latter ditched after having been shot up by antiaircraft fire from the assembled fleet. The crew survived, was rescued by Spanish fishermen, then was interned in Madrid.

64. See Nick Beale's Internet site Ghostbombers: Operation Dragoon, http://www.ghostbombers.com/dragoon/odnav.html. Beale is a highly respected and published author on Luftwaffe operations in World War II who has compiled material on Operation Dragoon from Allied intercepts of German communications as well as from primary source material from participants.

65. Balke, *Kampfgeschwader KG 100 "Wiking,"* 314. There was no such destroyer by that name. The nearest one can find is destroyer-escort *DeLong* (DE-684), which never left U.S. coastal waters during World War II and which was sunk as a target in 1970. Nor is there a French, Canadian, or British destroyer by that name.

66. Loss Report on *LST-282* written by the commanding officer, 2 September 1944. Retrieved August 2009 from http://www.landingship.com/282/sunk.htm.

67. On 21 October 1967 the Israeli destroyer *Eliat* (formerly HMS *Zealous*) was attacked and sunk by three or four Russian-built P-15 Termit (Nato designation SS-N-2 Styx) missiles fired from Egyptian Kumar-class missile boats stationed within the harbor of Alexandria, Egypt. Of the 190 officers and sailors on board *Eliat*, forty-seven were killed and a similar number injured.

68. Kinny, "Nazi Smart Bombs."

69. Most likely the aircraft that aborted was 6N+DR (Wk.Nr. 6230). One of the aircraft lost was a Do 217 K-3, most likely 6N+GT (Wk.Nr. 4733), and the other was a Do 217 M-11 (Wk.Nr. 6429).

70. Andrews, *Tempest Fire & Foe*, 60.

71. It was a Do 217 M-11 Wk.Nr. 6461.

72. Beale, "Ghostbombers."

73. Balke, *Kampfgeschwader KG 100 "Wiking,"* 315.

74. "Model CXGE—GMCM Transmitter—Shipment of and Modifications of: Memo from Chief of Naval Operations to Chief of the Bureau of Ships, 6 November 1944," U.S. National Archives and Records Association, Record Group 19 (Bureau of Ships), Entry 1271 (Radio Division—General Correspondence, 1944, Transmitters), Box 239.

75. "Countermeasures Equipment—Shipping Instructions: Memo from Chief of Naval Operations to Chief of Bureau of Ships (1950B), 5 Oct 44," U.S. National Archives and Records Administration, Record Group 19 (Bureau of Ships), Entry 1271 (Radio Division General Correspondence, 1944, Countermeasures), Box 9. The memo reports that all electronic countermeasures for guided missiles were to be removed and shipped to CincPac. This included, as specifically named, the following systems: XCJ, ARQ-8, MAS, and CXGE.

Chapter 12

1. In rough order of introduction, these are XCJ, XCJ-1 (TX), Jostle, Lieutenant Field's interim system, Type 650, XCJ-2 (TX), ARQ-8 (DINA-MATE), XCJ-3 (CXGE), Type MAS, Type 651, and Canadian Naval Jammer. Development of several others, including the XCJ-4, XCK (TY), and XCL jammer were terminated before they were deployed operationally.

2. "Tätigkeitsbericht über Einsatzperiode das K.G. 100."

3. Harold Aage Skaarup, *Out of Darkness—Light: A History of Canadian Military Intelligence*, Vol. II, *1983–1987* (New York: iUniverse, 2005), 50.

4. Walter J. Boyne and Ronald R. Fogleman, *Operation Iraqi Freedom: What Went Right, What Went Wrong, and Why* (New York: Macmillan, 2003), 100. Boyne and Fogleman do not provide a source for this declaration, which overstates the actual post-*Roma* success of the Fritz-X by a factor of at least 1,500 percent. A similar case of overstatement can be attributed to *Destroyer: An Anthology of First-Hand Accounts of the War at Sea: 1939–45* (London: Conway Maritime Press, 2003), edited by Ian Hawkins. This book contains an appendix (Appendix VII) that identifies more than sixty ships sunk or damaged by German glide bombs. There are many mistakes in this account, starting with the statement that the Hs 293 and Fritz-X weapons were launched by Dornier 217's and Heinkel 111s. In fact the He 111 did not deploy the missile in

combat, whereas the Heinkel 177 was a major launch platform for the Hs 293. In addition, that appendix identifies the American destroyer *Le Long* as a victim (no such ship ever existed) as well as a dozen or more ships known to have been lost to torpedoes. The appendix also includes, as victims of the Hs 293 or Fritz-X, two ships (*LST-312* and *LST-384*) damaged while in a British port by a V-1 "buzz bomb."

5. This technical analysis is well beyond the abilities of the author. It has been prepared by Dr. Allan Steinhardt, an expert in military applications of radio-frequency technologies and a former chief scientist with the U.S. Defense Advanced Research Projects Agency (DARPA). The author is very thankful to Dr. Steinhardt for his expertise, graciousness, humor, and patience.

6. Length of the antenna is from Wolfgang-D. Schröer, *Fernlenk- und Zielweisungsgeräte der deutschen Luftwaffe* [Remotely Guided and Precision Strike Systems of the German Luftwaffe] (Berlin: Wolfgang-D. Schröer, 2008), 69. The optimum antenna configuration for a system transmitting from 48 MHz to 50 MHz would be 2.85 meters to 2.98 meters, given the wavelength of 5.95 meters to 5.70 meters.

7. It is possible to approximate roughly the effective range of the control signal from the information available regarding the Kehl transmitter and the Strassburg receiver. The baseband signal for each of the control channels on the receiver is about 100 Hz, and the transmission bandwidth is 5 MHz. The noise level at the controller is then computed as kTB, where "k" is Boltzman's constant, "T" is the temperature of the air in Kelvin, and "B" is the bandwidth. (This formula would have been known in the 1940s.) A modern signal-processing system would squeeze all energy in the 5 MHz band into 100 Hz with no loss, a technique known as "pulse compression" or "matched filtering." It is hard to tell how much compression one would have had in the 1940s, so we will take the bandwidth to be the 5 MHz transmit band, which is conservative. The Kehl system needs to generate a signal above that noise level to be effective, so now we consider other factors. There is not much antenna gain in the wire design so we can safely ignore that factor both on the transmit end and the receive end (the large wavelength roughly cancelling the low gain, given a net loss, or gain, of one in linear units). Since the wave spreads after leaving the aircraft (like ripples from a rock dropped in a lake) the energy drops as the square of the distance from the airplane. It turns out we must add a factor of 4π as well since the energy drops as the surface area of the ripple. Hence, at twenty kilometers the energy will have dropped by about 5 billion in watts/meter² from spreading loss. An antenna mismatch in the Hs 293 design would lead to more losses, as would background environmental noise (by boosting power required to travel through it), and various losses in the electronics on both transmit and receive. We can estimate these effective losses as another factor of one thousand above the primitive compression mentioned above. We would want the signal at the receiver after effective losses to be about one thousand times larger than the thermal noise, so we have transmit power ÷ effective losses ÷ spreading loss = 1000 x kTB. The value of kTB for 5 MHz can be found from textbooks to be about one 160-trillionths of one watt. We see that transmit power = 5,000 trillion x 160 trillionth ~ 30 watts.

8. Pocock, *German Guided Missiles*, 38. Some Allied intelligence reports during the war estimated the power at forty-five watts.
9. The pioneering work in this field was by Peter Swerling of the RAND corporation in the early 1950s. Swerling first modeled the effects of multipath interference on radar signals and radio guidance.
10. Data regarding the 33 percent rate of failure in launched missiles are from "Tätigkeitsbericht über Einsatzperiode das K.G. 100."
11. It is not inconceivable that the use of electric razors, as has been claimed in the Royal Navy, could affect the guidance system. They would operate on 50 Hz given standard shipboard power in the Royal Navy; this could affect, conceivably, the 100 Hz baseband signal (a simple multiple of 50 Hz) used in the Hs 293 guidance system. The length of the power cord—the antenna—was about right. However, the power output of a typical electric razor, perhaps eight to ten watts, would be far below that required to offset the Kehl signal even at very close range. A very large number of razors operating in harmony may have been able to pull off this task.
12. Pocock, *German Guided Missiles*, 40.
13. Ibid., 46.
14. Trenkle, *Die Deutschen Funklenkverfahern*, 51.
15. Ibid.
16. As reported by George Emil Knausenberger and Monica Wagner-Fielder in *Herbert Wagner* (Monterey, CA: Martin Hollmann, 2003), 63.
17. Michael L. Handel, *War Strategy and Intelligence* (London: Frank Cass & Co., 1989), 167.

Epilogue

1. Price, *Dornier Do 217 Variants*, 67.
2. Clarence G. Lasby, *Project Paperclip: German Scientists and the Cold War* (New York: Atheneum, 1971), 3.
3. Daniel Guggenheim's son, Harry, had served as a pilot in the U.S. Navy in World War I and was a staunch supporter of aviation. Daniel and Harry later established the prestigious Daniel Guggenheim Medal for achievement in aeronautics. The 162-acre manor had been given to the Institute of Aeronautical Sciences in 1942 and subsequently leased to the U.S. Navy, who established their secret Special Devices Center there. Later the Navy would buy the estate and operate it until 1967 when it was declared surplus. It is now a public park.
4. It remains active today as the U.S. Navy's Pacific Missile Test Center.
5. His abridged FBI file, source of much of this information, is available through the U.S. National Archives and Records Administration, College Park, Maryland, Record Group 65 (Records of the Federal Bureau of Investigation), FBI HQ: Investigative Reports; Classified Subject Files. Released under the Nazi and Japanese War Crimes Disclosure Acts. Classification 105: Foreign Counterintelligence. File 105-10525 for Herbert Alois Wagner.
6. His abridged FBI file is available through NARA Record Group 65. File 105-10717 for Max Otto Kramer.

7. Mohammed Gad-el-Hak, *Flow Control: Passive, Active and Reactive Fluid Management* (Cambridge, UK: Cambridge University Press, 2000), 129.
8. Interview by the author with Kenneth J. Moore. K. J. Moore is the founder of Cortana Corporation, a company specializing in the development and assessment of technologies suitable for submarine warfare. He interacted with Max Kramer in the 1970s and early 1980s.
9. Obituary for Dr. Max Kramer, *Naval Engineers Journal*, January 1987, 19.
10. NRL, "A Tribute to the Father of Electronic Warfare."
11. Obituary, *New York Times*, 29 August 1989, p. B6.
12. Hunter, *Hector R. Skifter*.
13. Williamson Murray, *Strategy for Defeat: The Luftwaffe 1933–1945* (Maxwell Air Force Base, AL: Air University Press, 1983), 303. Murray indicates that the attrition for German fighter pilots "was probably well into the 90th percentile" and that the equivalent figures for bomber pilots "could not have been much better."
14. Dochtermann's logbook did not survive the war. This estimate is from his grandson, K. C. Dochtermann, who reviewed Dochtermann's service record in detail and provided this information in personal communication to the author, 28 March 2008.
15. Dochtermann refers to this individual once as John M. Wirdon and later as John Virden. This is almost certainly U.S. Air Force Colonel John M. Virden (1908–1968), a journalist and military historian who worked during World War II with the *Army Times* and later with the Armed Forces Radio & Television Service.
16. Hans Dochtermann, "Attack on U.S. Convoy KMF-26 off the Bay of Bourgie," 14 July 1992. Personal memoir prepared by Hans Dochtermann, Manuscripts & Folklife Archives Coordinator Kentucky Library & Museum, Western Kentucky University, Bowling Green.
17. Dochtermann, "Attack on U.S. Convoy KMF-26 off the Bay of Bourgie."
18. K. C. Dochtermann, personal correspondence with the author, 28 March 2008.
19. Personal correspondence with Rainer Zantopp, son of Hans-Joachim Zantopp, July 2009.
20. Reginald V. Jones, *Reflections on Intelligence* (London: Heinemann, 1989), 275.
21. Louis Brown, *A Radar History of World War II: Technical and Military Imperatives* (London: Taylor & Francis, 1999), 314.
22. Jones, *Reflections on Intelligence*.
23. Hill, *Destroyer Captain*, 11.
24. Details provided by Gardes's son, Alfred W. ("Chip") Gardes, in personal communication with the author, 13 August 2008.
25. This was the second time Gardes was the beneficiary of an act of Congress, the first being dispensation allowing him and his wife, also an active naval officer, to continue their careers as naval officers after their marriage. This was contrary to official policy at the time.
26. The original business was known as Whittaker Electronic Systems, a unit of Whittaker Corporation. Whittaker sold this business in 1997 to Condor Systems, Inc. In turn, Condor Systems was acquired by EDO in 2002.

27. In the years since World War II, AIL had become a major force in the new field of electronic warfare. It was acquired by Cutler-Hammer in 1958, became part of Eaton in 1979, and finally was bought out by its management and employees in 1997 to become once again an independent company. Later it was acquired by EDO, after which EDO was acquired by ITT.

Selected Bibliography

Archival Holdings in the Bundesarchiv-Militärarchiv, Freiburg

"Hs 293 Aufgaben u. Organisation des Betr. Zuges 15." Records of II./KG 100 from 1943. This is a field manual for the maintenance and installation of the Hs 293 manual that was prepared in 1943 for ground crews of II./KG 100. RL 10/605.

"Kampfgeschwader 100 'Wiking' 1938–1945." Short unit history of KG 100 drafted by a former *gruppe* member, 18 April 1972. RL 10/561.

"Report 74: X. Fliegerkorps. Die Entwicklung der Fluggeräte: 'Die Fliegenden Körper' (FX und Hs 293)." A history of guided weapons development in the Luftwaffe. RL 8/77.

"Tätigkeitsbericht über Einsatzperiode das K. G. 100 mit F. K. in der Zeit von 12.7.43–30.4.44 [Activity Report of Missions of KG 100 with Guided Weapons in the Period from 12.07.43 to 30.04.44]." RL 10/493.

Archival Holdings of United States Air Force Museum

Air Materiel Command, Headquarters, Freeman Field. "Foreign Equipment Descriptive Brief: The German Fritz-X-1400 Glide Bomb." Serial No. 46-5, 21 March 1945. U.S. Air Force Museum Archives, Box 814: FS/ND/German "Fritz" Glide Bomb Photos and Text Material File.

Boardman, T. L. "German Bombs & Fuzes, Land Mines & Igniters." Report prepared jointly by the U.S. Navy Bomb Disposal School and the U.S. Army Bomb Disposal School, 14 March 1944. Available in U.S. Air Force Museum archives, File F5-A, Box 819.

Calvert, G. W. "Preliminary Report of Examination of Radio Equipment Associated with German Radio Controlled Bombs." Report No. 3021, 2 November 1943. Air Force Museum Box 814: FS/1942–43/German Radio Controlled Weapons.

Davis, Gordon. "Rocket and Radio Bombs." Intelligence report prepared by Headquarters Royal Air Force, Middle East, 14 November 1943. Available in the archives of the U.S. Air Force Museum, File F5/1942–1943/German Radio Controlled Weapons, Box 814.

Archival Holdings of the U.S. National Archives and Records Administration

Record Group 19 (Bureau of Ships), Entry 1270 (Radio Division General Correspondence, 1943). Files DE-136 *Frederick C. Davis* and DE-137 *Herbert C. Jones* (Box 140).

Record Group 19 (Bureau of Ships), Entry 1271 (Radio Division General Correspondence, 1944). Files for Countermeasures (Boxes 9–10) and Transmitters (Boxes 239–240).

Record Group 38 (Records of the Chief of Naval Operations). Intelligence Division: Top Secret Reports of Naval Attaches 1944–1947. Document 640: "German Radio Controlled Glider Bomb Data, U.S. Naval Forces in Europe, London, 12 August 1944."

Record Group 38 (Records of the Chief of Naval Operations). Entry UD 351: "World War II Action and Operations Reports." War diaries for *Frederick C. Davis* (Box 992) and *Herbert C. Jones* (Box 1028).

Record Group 65 (Records of the Federal Bureau of Investigation). FBI HQ: Investigative Reports; Classified Subject Files. Released Under the Nazi and Japanese War Crimes Disclosure Acts. Classification 105: Foreign Counterintelligence. File 105-10525 for Herbert Alois Wagner (Box 7) and 105-10717 for Max Otto Kramer (Box 14).

Archival Holdings of the United Kingdom National Archives

Admiralty and Ministry of Defence, Department of the Director of Naval Construction. "*Athabaskan*: Damaged by a Bomb, 27 August 1943" (ADM 267/8).

Admiralty and Ministry of Defence, Navy Department: Correspondence and Papers. Search for enemy radio-controlled bombs at Salerno and Ajaccio (ADM 1-12938); enemy radio-controlled air missiles (Types FX and HS293): countermeasures (ADM 1-12940). HMS *Egret* sunk by enemy air attack: Awards to personnel, various reports concerning ADM 1-14507; Radio countermeasures: fitting of radio jammers for use against guided missiles to ships taking part in Operation Overlord (ADM 1-16454).

Admiralty and Ministry of Defence, Navy Department: Reference Books. Damage Reports: HMS *Rockwood* 11 November 1943 (ADM 234/502).

Admiralty and Ministry of Defence, Navy Department: Reference Books. Damage Reports: HMS *Spartan* 29 January 1944. Board of Inquiry dated 9 February 1944 (ADM 234/507).

Admiralty and Ministry of Defence, Navy Department: Trade Division, Admiralty: War History Cases and Papers, Second World War: "Survivors' Reports" file ADM 199-2166 and ADM 199-2167.

Air Ministry: Bomber Command: Registered Files. "HS and FX bombs: technical information, 1943 Sept.–1945 June" (AIR 14-3611).

Department of Scientific and Industrial Research: Aeronautical Research Council: Reports and Papers. "German jet propelled glider with radio control Hs 293: general reconstruction, 1944" (DSIR 23-13372).

Ministry of Defence: Royal Aircraft Establishment. "German jet-propelled glider with radio control Hs 293: general reconstruction, 1943" (AVIA 6-12166); "Appreciation of a radio unit and other pieces recovered from Hs 293 glider bombs, 1943" (AVIA 6-12355); "German glider bomb Hs 293: Radio control mechanism, 1944" (AVIA 6-25651); Hs 293 and FX radio-controlled enemy bombs, 1943–45 (AVIA 6-14424).

Ministry of Home Security: Intelligence Branch: Registered Files. "Remote-controlled high-explosive glider bomb type Hs 293" (HO 199-365).

Archival Holdings of the National Archives of Canada

Record Group 24 (Royal Canadian Navy), Headquarters (D1), Damage Reports (8340). Document 355-3. "Damage report for HMCS *Athabaskan*, 23 September 1943."

Record Group 24 (Royal Canadian Navy), Headquarters (D1), Damage Reports (8340). Document 381-30. "Damage report for HMCS *Matane*, 23 August 1944."

Published Firsthand Accounts

Baumbach, Werner. *The Life and Death of the Luftwaffe*. Translated by Fredrick Holt. New York: Ballantine Books, 1967.

Bax, Johannes S. *Batterij gereed . . . vuur!: Hr. Ms. "Flores" Vecht in de Middellandse Zee*. Rotterdam, Netherlands: Uitgevers Wyt, 1948.

Connell, G. G. *Mediterranean Maelstrom: HMS* Jervis *and the 14th Flotilla*. London: William Kimber, 1987.

Coward, B. R. *Battleship at War*. London: Ian Allen Ltd., 1987.

Deumling, Klaus. *41 Sekunden bis zum Einschlag: Als Bomberpilot im Kampfgeschwader 100 Wiking mit der geheimen Fernlenkbombe Fritz X* [41 Seconds to Impact: A Bomber Pilot in Kampfgeschwader 100 with the Secret Guided Bomb Fritz X]. Garbsen, Germany: HEK Creativ Verlag, 2008.

Hill, Roger P. *Destroyer Captain*. London: William Kimbler, 1975.

Jackson, Carlton. *Allied Secret: The Sinking of HMT Rohna*. Norman: University of Oklahoma Press, 2002.

Karlow, S. Peter. *Targeted by the CIA: An Intelligence Professional Speaks Out on the Scandal that Turned the CIA Upside Down*. Paducah, KY: Turner Publishing, 2001.

Leonard, William. *In the Storm of the Eye: A Lifetime at CBS*. New York: Penguin Group, 1987.

Lombard-Hobson, Sam. *A Sailor's War*. New York: St. Martin's Press, 1983.

MacKenzie, Colin. *Sailors of Fortune*. New York: E. P. Dutton & Co., 1944.

McKee, Fraser M. *HMCS Swansea: The Life and Times of a Frigate*. St. Catherines, ON, Canada: Vanwell Publishing, 1994.

Melanephy, James P., and John G. Robinson. "Savannah at Salerno." *Surface Warfare*, 6, no. 3 (March, 1981): 2–11.

Packer, Joy. *Deep as the Sea*. London: Corgi Books, 1975.

Plevy, Harry. *Battleship Sailors: The Fighting Career of HMS Warspite Recalled by Her Men*. London: Chatham Publishing, 2001.

Roberts, Douglas L. *Rustbucket 7: Chronicle of the USS PC 617 During the Great War*. Newcastle, ME: Mill Pond Press, 1995.

Robertson, Terrence. *Walker, R.N.: The Story of Captain Frederic John Walker, C.B., D.S.O. and Three Bars, R.N.* London: Evans Brothers, 1956.

Seligman, Adrian. *War in the Islands: Undercover Operations in the Aegean 1942–44*. Phoenix Mill, UK: Sutton Publishing, 1996.

"Sinking of the Hospital Ship SS Newfoundland." *Newfoundland Times*, September 1994. The *Newfoundland Times* is a publication of the HMS Newfoundland Association.

Slader, John. *The Fourth Service: Merchantmen at War 1939–45*. Wimborne Minster, Dorset, UK: New Era Writer's Guild, 1995.

Waters, Sydney David. *The Royal New Zealand Navy*. Wellington, NZ: Historical Publications Branch, 1956.

Whitehead, Don. *Beachhead Don: Reporting the War from the European Theater*. New York: Fordham University Press, 2005.

Unpublished Firsthand and Personal Accounts

Dochtermann, Hans. "Attack on U.S. Convoy KMF-26 off the Bay of Bourgie." 14 July 1992. Available in the Manuscripts & Folklife Archives, Kentucky Library & Museum, Western Kentucky University, Bowling Green.

Dochtermann, K. C. Personal communication with the author, March and August 2008. K. C. Dochtermann is the grandson of Hans Dochtermann and has studied his grandfather's Luftwaffe career.

Erpobungsstelle der Luftwaffe Karlshagen, "Bericht des Stabsing. Thiele über eine Reise zu den FK-Einsatzverbänden vom 11.3.43–3.4.44" Trip report on audit of KG 40 and KG 100 glide-bomb performance. Personal collection of Ulf Balke.

Gardes, Alfred W., III. Personal communication with the author, July and August 2008. Alfred ("Chip") Gardes is the son of Alfred ("Skeeta") W. Gardes Jr., the commanding officer of U.S. destroyer *Herbert C. Jones* during the first deployment of U.S. countermeasures against Luftwaffe glide bombs.

Garrett, Kenneth C. Personal communication with the author, August 2008. Garrett was a radio operator on board Canadian destroyer *Algonquin* during the D-day invasion.

Heathman, Russell. Telephone interview with the author, 22 August 2008. Heathman was a leading seaman on the bridge of Canadian frigate *Matane* during the glide-bomb attack of July 1944.

Howe, William E. W. Telephone interview with the author on 8 July 2008. Howe helped develop the very first electronic countermeasures for glide bombs while employed at the U.S. Naval Research Laboratory in 1943.

Kinney, Orus. "Nazi Smart Bombs." A personal account of a Navy radioman during the invasions of Normandy and southern France. Collected as part of the Veterans History Project of the Library of Congress. Available on http://www. kilroywashere.org/003-Pages/03-OrusKinney.html. Kinney was a glide-bomb countermeasures operator on board *Bayfield*, a U.S. Navy command ship.

Lorenzen, Howard O. "A History of Electronic Warfare (Countermeasures) at the Naval Research Laboratory, 4 February 1983." Unpublished personal memoir, declassified in 2008 at the request of this author.

Navy Department. "War Cruise: USS *Mayo*." Ships Data Section, Public Information Division of the Office of Public Relations, Navy Department, Washington, DC.

Navy Department. "War Cruise: USS *Woolsey*." Ships Data Section, Public Information Division of the Office of Public Relations, Navy Department, Washington, DC.

Pieper, Anthony W. "An Informal History of the 414th Night Fighter Squadron." Unpublished manuscript, date unknown.

Wales, Charles C. Personal communication with the author, April and May 2008. Wales was an officer on board U.S. destroyer *Lansdale*.

Zantopp, Rainer. Personal communication with the author, July and August 2009. Rainer Zantopp is the son of Luftwaffe pilot Hans-Joachim Zantopp.

Firsthand and Personal Accounts Published Online

Bondy, Martin. Personal account of wartime experiences as recorded by the Veteran's Memories Project of the Windsor Historical Society. Bondy was on board *Matane* when it was struck by an Hs 293. Retrieved June 2008 from http://www.windsorhistoricalsociety.com/Veterans%20Stories/Protecting_the_Sea_Lanes_for_the_Invasion.php.

Malcolm, Ian M. Personal communication with the author, February 2008. Supplemented with his oral history, "Merchant Navy Book 1—Voyage 1 of the *Samite* (World War II)." Dundee, UK: Ian M. Malcolm, 2008. Malcolm was a radio operator on board *Samite* during two attacks involving glide bombs in 1943 and 1944.

Perruquet, M. Pierre. "Interview." *Simulation France Magazine*, 9 May 2007. Retrieved June 2008 from http://www.france-simulation.com/sections. php?op=viewarticle&artid=86.

Yannacci, Joseph Anthony. Diary from 3 September to 17 September 1943. Retrieved June 2008 from http://www.armed-guard.com/ag85.html.

Aircraft and Aviation Units

Balke, Ulf. *Kampfgeschwader KG 100 "Wiking."* Stuttgart, Germany: Motorbuch Verlag, 1981.

Beale, Nick. *The Bombers of the Luftwaffe Summer 1943–May 1945*, Vol. 4. Hersham, UK: Ian Allen Publishing, 2005.

Bennett, John. *Fighter Nights: 456 Squadron RAF.* Belconnen, Australian Capital Territory (ACT), Australia: Banner Books, 1995.

Corum, James S. "To Stop Them on the Beaches: Luftwaffe Operations Against the Allied Landings in Italy." *Royal Air Force Air Power Review* 7, no. 2 (Summer, 2004): 47–66.

Cull, Brian. *Spitfires Over Sicily: The Crucial Role of the Malta Spitfires in the Battle of Sicily, January–August 1943.* London: Grub Street, 2000.

de Zeng, Henry L., and Douglas G. Stankey. *Bomber Units of the Luftwaffe 1933–1945,* Vols. 1 and 2. Surrey, UK: Ian Allan Publishing, 2008.

Goss, Chris. *Sea Eagles: Luftwaffe Anti-Shipping Units 1942–45,* Vol. 2. Hersham, UK: Ian Allen Publishing, 2006.

Griehl, Manfred. *Do 217-317-417: An Operational Record.* Washington, DC: Smithsonian Institution Press, 1971.

Griehl, Manfred, and Joachim Dressel. *Heinkel: He 177, 277, 274.* Shrewsbury, UK: Airlife, 1998.

Hitchcock, Thomas H. *Monogram Close-up #3: Junkers Ju 290.* Boylston, MA: Monogram Aviation Publications, 1975.

Holm, Michael. "The Luftwaffe, 1933–45: Flugzeugbestand und Bewegungsmeldungen, 3.42–12.44." This is an online repository of Luftwaffe order of battle data from Generalquartiermeister 6. Abteilung. Retrieved June 2008 from http://www.ww2.dk/oob/bestand/kampf/bkampf.htm.

Neitzel, Sönke. *Der Einsatz der deutschen Luftwaffe über dem Atlantik und der Nordsee 1939–1945* [The Missions of the German Luftwaffe over the Atlantic and North Sea 1939–1945]. Bonn, Germany: Bernard & Graefe Verlag, 1995.

Price, Alfred. *Aircraft Profile: Heinkel He 177.* Windsor, UK: Profile Publications, 1972.

Price, Alfred. *Dornier Do 217 Variants.* Windsor, UK: Profile Publications, 1974.

Smith, Richard J., and Eddie J. Creek. *Heinkel He 177 Greif: Hitler's Strategic Bomber.* Hersham, UK: Ian Allan Publishing, 2008.

Ships and Naval Units

Andrews, Lewis M., Jr. *Tempest Fire & Foe: Destroyer Escorts in World War II and the Men Who Manned Them.* Charleston, NC: Narwhal Press, 1999.

Askew, William C. *History of the Naval Armed Guard Afloat—World War II.* Washington, DC: Office of Naval History, 1946.

Bagnasco, Erminio. *Regia Marina: Italian Battleships of WWII.* Missoula, MT: Pictorial Histories Publishing, 1986.

Browning, Robert M., Jr. *U.S. Merchant Vessel War Casualties of World War II.* Annapolis, MD: Naval Institute Press, 1996.

Cross, Donald E. "USS *Herbert C. Jones* (DE 137)." *DESA News.* November/December 1986. Reproduction of a history of *Herbert C. Jones* prepared 7 November 1946 by the U.S. Navy. *DESA News* is a publication of the Destroyer Escort Sailors Association.

Giorgerini, Giorgio, and Augusto Nani (Eds.). *Le Navi Di Linea Italiane* [Ships of the Line of the Italian Navy]. Rome: Ufficio Storico Marina Militare, 1980.

Karig, Walter. *Battle Report: The Atlantic War from the Neutrality Patrol to the Crossing of the Rhine*. New York: Farrar & Rinehart, 1946.

Morison, Samuel Eliot. *History of United States Naval Operations in World War II*, Vol. II, *Operations in North African Waters, October 1942–June 1943*. Boston: Little, Brown, 1947.

Morison, Samuel Eliot. *History of United States Naval Operations in World War II*, Vol. IX, *Sicily–Salerno–Anzio, January 1943–June 1944*. Boston: Little, Brown, 1954.

Morison, Samuel Eliot. *History of United States Naval Operations in World War II*, Vol. X, *The Atlantic Battle Won, May 1943–May 1945*. Boston: Little, Brown, 1956.

Morison, Samuel Eliot. *History of United States Naval Operations in World War II*, Vol. XI, *The Invasion of France and Germany, 1944–1945*. Edison, NJ: Castle Books, 1957.

Poolman, Kenneth. *Allied Escort Carriers of World War Two in Action*. Annapolis, MD: Naval Institute Press, 1988.

Raven, Alan, and John Arthur Roberts. *British Battleships of World War Two: The Development and Technical History of the Royal Navy's Battleships and Battlecruisers from 1911 to 1946*. Annapolis, MD: Naval Institute Press, 1976.

Rohwer, Jürgen, and Gerhardt Hümmelchen. *Chronology of the War at Sea: 1939–1945*. London: Ian Allan, 1972.

Roscoe, Theodore. *United States Destroyer Operations in World War II*. Annapolis, MD: Naval Institute Press, 1953.

Scalia, Joseph Mark. *Germany's Last Mission to Japan: The Failed Voyage of U-234*. Annapolis, MD: Naval Institute Press, 2000.

Schull, Joseph. *Far Distant Ships: An Official Account of Canadian Naval Operations in World War II*. Toronto: Stoddard Publishing, 1987.

Smith, Stanley E. (Ed). *The United States Navy in World War II*. New York: William Morrow & Company, 1966.

Tomblin, Barbara. *With Utmost Spirit: Allied Naval Operations in the Mediterranean, 1942–1945*. Lexington: University of Kentucky Press, 2004.

Wise, James E., Jr., and Scott Baron. *Soldiers Lost at Sea: A Chronicle of Troopship Disasters*. Annapolis, MD: Naval Institute Press, 2004.

Woodward, David. *Ramsay at War: The Fighting of Admiral Sir Bertram Ramsay*. London: W. Kimber, 1957.

General Military Aspects and Operations

Chandler, David G., and James Lawton Collins Jr. (Eds.). *The D-Day Encyclopedia*. New York: Simon & Schuster, 1994.

U.S. Fleet Headquarters of the Commander In Chief, Navy Department. *Amphibious Operations Invasion of Northern France Western Task Force June 1944: Cominch P-006*. Washington, DC, 21 October 1944.

Wilson, Henry Maitland. *Report by the Supreme Allied Commander Mediterranean to the Combined Chiefs of Staff on the Italian Campaign: 8th January 1944 to 10th May 1944.* London: His Majesty's Stationery Office, 1946.

Zaloga, Steven J., and Peter Dennis. *Anzio 1944: The Beleaguered Beachhead.* Oxford, UK: Osprey Publishing, 2005.

Scientific and Technical Aspects

Amato, Ivan. *Pushing the Horizon: Seventy-Five Years of High Stakes Science and Technology at the Naval Research Laboratory.* Washington, DC: Naval Research Laboratory, 1997.

Brown, Louis. *A Radar History of World War II: Technical and Military Imperatives.* London: Taylor & Francis, 1999.

Friedman, Norman. *Naval Radar.* Annapolis, MD: Naval Institute Press, 1981.

Gebhard, Louis A. *Evolution of Naval Radio-Electronics and Contributions of the Naval Research Laboratory.* Washington, DC: Naval Research Laboratory, 1979.

Gillmor, C. Steward. *Fred Terman at Stanford: Building a Discipline, a University and Silicon Valley.* Stanford, CA: Stanford University Press, 2004.

Howse, Derek. *Radar at Sea: The Royal Navy in World War 2.* London: MacMillan Press, 1994.

Hunter, Gregory S. *Hector R. Skifter: Radio Pioneer, Industrial Leader, and Defense Advisor, 1901–1964.* Northfield, MN: St. Olaf College Press, 1997.

Jones, R. V. *The Wizard War: British Scientific Intelligence 1939–45.* New York: Coward, McCann & Geoghegan, 1979.

Kingsley, Frederick A. "History of Naval Radar 1935–1945: Radar Countermeasures in WWII, Part 2." *Journal of Naval Science* 17, no. 2 (April 1991): 95–107.

Knausenberger, George Emil (Ed.). *Herbert Wagner: Documents of His Work and Life.* Bonn: Deutsche Gesellschaft für Luft- und Raumfahrt e.V., 1990.

Knausenberger, George Emil, and Monica Wagner-Fielder. *Herbert Wagner.* Monterey, CA: Martin Hollmann, 2003.

Knowles Middleton, William Edgar. *Radar Development in Canada: The Radio Branch of the National Research Council of Canada 1939–1945.* Waterloo, ON, Canada: Wilfrid Laurier University Press, 1981.

Lasby, Clarence G. *Project Paperclip: German Scientists and the Cold War.* New York: Atheneum, 1971.

Price, Alfred. *The History of U.S. Electronic Warfare,* Vol. 1. Washington, DC: Association of Old Crows, 1984.

Suits, C. G., George R. Harrison, and Louis Jordan (Eds.). *Applied Physics: Electronics, Optics, Metallurgy.* Office of Scientific Research and Development, NDRC Summary Technical Report of Divisions 15, 16, 17 and 18. Boston: Little, Brown, 1948.

Taylor, A. Hoyt. *The First 25 Years of the Naval Research Laboratory.* Washington, DC: The Navy Department, 1948.

Trenkle, Fritz. *Die Deutschen Funklenkverfahern bis 1945*. Heidelberg, Germany: Huthig, 1986.

U.S. Naval Research Laboratory. "General Instructions for Guided Missile Countermeasure Systems." NRL Report No. R-2241. Washington, DC: Navy Department, 3 March 1944.

Intelligence Aspects

Brown, Anthony Cave. *The Secret War of the OSS*. New York: Berkley Publishing Corporation, 1976.

Clayton, Aileen. *The Enemy Is Listening*. London: Hutchinson, 1980.

Corvo, Max. *The O.S.S. in Italy 1942–1945: A Personal Memoir*. New York: Praeger, 1990.

Handel, Michael L. *War Strategy and Intelligence*. London: Frank Cass & Co., Ltd., 1989.

Hinsley, Francis H. *British Intelligence in the Second World War*, Vols. I–III. London: Her Majesty's Stationery Office, 1988.

O'Donnell, Patrick K. *Operatives, Spies and Saboteurs: The Unknown Story of the Men and Women of WWII's OSS*. New York: Free Press, 2004.

Staerk, Christopher, and Paul Sinnott. *Luftwaffe: The Allied Intelligence Files*. Washington, DC: Brassey's, 2002.

Previous Works on German Glide Bombs

Bogart, Charles H. "German Remotely Piloted Bombs." U.S. Naval Institute *Proceeding* 102 (November 1976): 62–68.

Kopp, Carlo. "The Dawn of the Smart Bomb." *Air Power Australia* (July 2006).

Piccirillo, Albert C. "The Origins of the Anti-Ship Guided Missile." *American Institute of Aeronautics and Astronautics*, November 1997. Technical paper presented at the 1997 World Aviation Congress, Anaheim, CA, 13–16 October 1997.

Pocock, Rowland. *German Guided Missiles of the Second World War*. New York: Arco Publishing, 1967.

Price, Alfred. "Guided Missile Genesis." *Flying Review International* 19, no. 10 (July 1974): 54–55, 59.

Saxton, Timothy. "Kehl: The German Use of Guided Weapons Against Naval Targets, 1943–44." *Defence Studies* 3, no. 1 (Spring 2003): 1–16.

Schröer, Wolfgang-D. *Fernlenk und Zielweisungsgeräte der deutschen Luftwaffe* [Remotely Guided and Precision Strike Systems of the German Luftwaffe]. Berlin: Wolfgang-D. Schröer, 2008.

Smith, Peter C. *Ship Strike: The History of Air-to-Sea Weapon Systems*. Shrewsbury, UK: Airlife, 1998.

Wolf, William. *German Guided Missiles: Henschel Hs 293 and Ruhrstahl SD 1400X "Fritz-X."* Bennington, VT: Merriam Press, 2006.

Index

A

Admiralty Signal Establishment (ASE), 96, 98, 122
aerial torpedoes, xvii, 63, 64, 105, 107
Afghanistan, xviii
Air Force, U.S.: Army Air Corps personnel in KMF-26 and onboard *Rohna*, 80, 83; 8th Air Force, 87; jamming system, development of, 125; Simmons Project, 143–44; 350th Fighter Group, 81–82
Airborne Instrument Laboratory (AIL), 128–30, 198, 205, 233n15, 245n27
aircraft: antiship missions, 2–3; codes for, 212n8, 215n6; markings on, 215n6; production of, 31; sinking of ships by, challenges of, xiii–xv. *See also* launching aircraft
Algonquin (Canada), 153, 234n25
Alsterufer (Germany), 86
Ancon, 33, 233n13
Anson (Great Britain), 133
antiaircraft defenses, xiv, 21, 34, 50
Anzio: aircraft lost over, 110, 112, 113, 114, 116, 118, 120, 179, 228n14, 229nn19–20, 229n24, 230n27, 230n30, 230n43, 231n48, 231n59; air-defense capabilities for landing, 102; conventional ordnance use at,

104, 105, 112; German troops in, 103; glide bomb use at, xvi; historical accounts of battle, 104–5; II./KG 40 attacks on, 88, 104–11, 228n4; II./KG 100 attacks on, 88, 103–16, 230n32; III./KG 100 attacks on, 113–14; invasion force, landing of, 102–3; jamming systems and ships, 94, 95, 98–100, 186, 187–88, 189, 227n35; naval support for landing at, 101–2; plaque to honor *Spartan* crew, 205; POWs from raids on, 120, 228n14; recovery of Hs 293 missile, 120, 122, 186, 231–32n60; strategy of landing at, 101; success rate of glide bomb mission, 187
Arethusa (Great Britain), 156
Army, U.S.: Fifth Army, 28, 31; Seventh Army, 25; Third Army, 160;
Arnold, Walter, 45–46, 218n13
Athabaskan (Canada): attack on and damage to, 4–5, 6, 24, 171, 207; Bay of Biscay antisubmarine force, 3; defensibility of, 176; Hs 293 fragments, recovery of, 49, 54, 89; maneuverability of, 74
Atherstone, 81
Auffhammer, Fritz, 24, 31
Augusta, 150, 233n13

Australian Night Fighter Squadron, 152–53, 155
Avalanche, Operation, 28, 44

B
Baumbach, Werner, 22, 148–49, 193
Bayfield, 150, 154–55, 163, 233n13, 238n27, 240n62
Beatty, 65
Bergamini, Carlo, 28, 29, 30
Bideford (Great Britain), 2, 3, 6, 7, 24, 89, 159, 171, 176, 207
Birchbark (Great Britain), 68–69, 171, 176, 207
Biscay, Bay of: glide bomb attacks, 2–8, 22, 24, 28, 31, 157–59, 214n32, 230n37; intelligence on glide bombs, 6–8, 44, 46, 49, 57; U-boat attacks in, 1–2
Boadicea (Great Britain), 155, 171, 176, 205, 208
Boardman, Charles W., 3, 210n3
Brewer, Godfrey N., 3–4, 5–6
Bulolo (Great Britain), 154, 234n26
Bushrod Washington, 36–37, 38, 74, 171, 176, 207
BYMS-2072 minesweeper (Great Britain), 71–72, 171, 176, 207

C
Canada 5th Support Group, 2, 4
Carlier (Belgium), 68, 69
Carmen, Operation, 73
casualties of war, xvii, xviii, 41, 172, 199, 205–6, 209n3, 210n8, 244n13
Charles F. Hughes, 162, 164
Charles Morgan, 154–55, 171, 176, 208, 238n27
China, 205
Churchill, Winston, xvi, 6, 47, 101, 103
convoys: aircraft lost during attacks, 63–64, 74, 79, 80, 81–82, 85, 118, 138, 139, 140, 221nn13–14, 223n12,

223n16, 223n19, 224n31, 235nn40–44, 235n48; codes for convoy numbering, 62, 64, 138; defensive measures against air attack, 142; EBC-8 convoy, 155; FAGr(5) attacks on, 118, 119, 141–42, 236n58; Fw 200 antishipping missions, 76; German navy threat to, 9; glide bomb use against, 22, 73; II./KG 40 attacks on, 76–85, 117–18, 157; II./KG 100 attacks on, 60, 62–69, 117, 137–40, 221nn11–14; III./KG 40 attacks on, 117, 141–42, 157; III./KG 100 attacks on, 141–42, 155, 236n56; jamming systems and ships, 186, 189; KMF-25A, 64–67, 186; KMF-26, 80–85; KMF-44/OS-70, 138; KMS-31, 67–69, 70–72, 183; KMS-43, 138; KMS-45/OS-71, 138; MKS-21, 214n32; MKS-28, 64; ONS-29, 118, 119; OS-67/KMS-41, 117; SL-136/MKS-10, 217n46; SL-139/MKS-30, 77–79; SL-147, 117; SL-162/MKS-53, 157; SL-193/MKS-80, 85; success rate of glide bomb mission, 187; U-boat threats to, 1, 6, 10, 22, 77; UGS-18, 62–64; UGS-30, 117; UGS-36, 138; UGS-37, 138–39; UGS-38, 139–40; UGS-40, 141–42, 236n58
Corsica: Ajaccio raids, 61–62, 107, 191, 220n3; recovery of Hs 293 missiles, 62, 122, 186, 221n7, 231–32n60

D
Davidson, Lyal A., 26, 161
Davis, Norman E., 96, 167
defensive measures: air cover, 49, 50, 149, 173, 174; airfields, bombing of, 18, 50–51, 72, 87, 113, 192, 222n35; development of, 41; effectiveness of, 73; high-speed maneuvering, 5, 36, 49, 50, 74, 108, 175; smoke screen for ships, 50; success of Luftwaffe and,

175, 176; of UGS-40 convoy, 142.
See also electronic countermeasures
and jamming systems

Delius (Great Britain), 78–79, 81, 171,
176, 207

Destroyer Captain (Hill), 4, 203

destroyer-escorts, 57–59. See also
Frederick C. Davis; *Herbert C. Jones*

dive-bombers, xiv, 37–38

Dochtermann, Hans, 82–83, 118, 147,
148, 199–200

Dodecanese campaign, 70–72

Döhler, Gerhard, 32, 147

Dornier (Do) 217 bombers: air cover
and loss of, 60; airfield bombings,
loss of during, 50–51, 72, 222n35;
airway-monitoring equipment on,
191; Anzio raids, 103–4, 106–16;
Bay of Biscay raids, 2–3, 4–5,
157–59, 239n50, 240n56, 240n58;
convoy raids, 62–69, 138, 139, 140,
235nn40–44, 235n48; dependability
of, 173; E-5 variant, 19, 213n16;
example of, 205; French Riviera and
Dragoon Operation, 162–64, 240n63,
241n69, 241n71; Fritz-X sorties,
20; glide bomb deployment role,
19, 20–21, 140, 236n1, 241–42n4;
guidance system for glide bombs,
212n11; Hs 293 sorties, 19–20,
73; intelligence on, 48, 218n6; K-2
variant, 20; K-3 variant, 20; loss of
during raids and accidents, 175; M-11
variant, 20; modifications for glide
bomb deployment, 19; Normandy
raids, 149–50, 154–57, 238n24,
238nn27–28, 238–39n37, 239n40,
239nn45–46; number built and
operational, 19, 23, 213n18; Oder
River bridges raid, 193; Plymouth
raids, 141, 235nn50–51; Pontaubault
Bridge raids, 160–61, 240nn59–61;
production of, 146; range of, 19–20,

22, 49; recovery of by Allies, 92–93,
225–26n12; replacement for, 19;
Salerno raids, 34, 36, 37, 40, 216n24,
216n30, 217n39, 217n48; Sicily
raids, 27, 45–46, 215nn6–7, 215n9,
218nn11–13; vulnerability of, 60

Dragoon, Operation, 161–64, 187, 189,
190, 240n62

Dulverton (Great Britain), 72, 171, 176,
207

E

Egret (Great Britain): attack on and loss
of, 5–8, 24, 171, 207; Bay of Biscay
antisubmarine force, 3; casualties
aboard, 5, 7–8, 211n9, 211n17;
decoy mission of, 7, 46; defensibility
of, 176; explosion of ship's magazine,
5, 6, 74; Hs 293s, control of, 183

electronic countermeasures and
jamming systems: ARQ-8 system,
125–26, 128, 129, 133, 185, 186,
187, 190, 232n5, 233n13; barrage
jammers, 99, 185; British approach,
123; Canadian Naval Jammer,
132, 133, 153, 185, 186, 187, 190;
criticism of efforts, 66–67; CXGE
system, 126–28, 133, 150–51, 166,
185, 186, 187, 190, 233n13; design
of Kehl-Strassburg system and success
of jamming signals, 66; detection
equipment installation on aircraft, 62,
220n3; development of, xvi, xviii, 53,
54–57, 122, 165, 166, 198, 204–5;
effectiveness of, xvi, 115, 123, 133,
153, 156, 167, 169, 184–90, 243n11;
electric razors, 52, 185, 190, 243n11;
electronic jamming, concept of,
53–54; expectations for success with,
59; failure of, 163; false commands
to guidance systems, 121, 122, 129,
133; Field system, 99–100, 185, 187,
190; frequency range for, 55–57, 66,

89, 93–94, 96–98, 120, 122, 123–24, 130; IED jamming technology, 204–5; information about, analysis of, xvii; installation on destroyer-escorts, 57–59, 185; installation on Royal Navy ships, 98–100, 227n32, 227n35; intelligence on frequencies and development of, 46; Jostle jammers, 99, 125, 185, 187, 190; listen-through/look-through capability, 124, 130–31; Luftwaffe knowledge of jamming operations, 54–55, 114–15, 191; Luftwaffe response to jamming operations, 190–92; magnetic recording system, 55, 59, 84–85; MAS system, 128–31, 133, 162, 185, 186, 187, 190, 205, 233n13, 233n20; mass attacks and jamming systems, 84, 95, 96–98; operation of, 150–51; radio signals, interference with, 51; RAO receivers, 94–95, 105, 123–24; RBK receivers, 55–56, 57, 58, 95, 123, 124, 131; RBW receivers, 124; RCK receivers, 55–56, 58; RCX receivers, 124; RDC receivers, 124; RDG receivers, 123–24; shielding of receivers to prevent detection, 94, 227n23; signal recording missions, 66–67, 84–85, 93; spot-jamming approach, 123, 185; termination of jammer development, 166; threat from, Luftwaffe concern about, 136–37; Type 650 jammer, 96–99, 133, 156, 162, 185, 186, 187, 190, 234n26; Type 651 jammer, 132, 133, 162, 164, 185, 186, 187, 190; types of jamming, 184–85; XCJ system, 56–57, 58, 123, 185, 187, 190; XCJ-1 system, 94–95, 105, 114, 123, 124, 185–86, 187, 188, 190, 226–27nn19–21; XCJ-2 system, 124, 132–33, 185, 186, 187, 190; XCJ-3

system, 124, 126–27, 133, 185, 186, 187; XCJ-4 system, 166; XCK system, 56, 124, 126, 166, 220n10; XCL system, 56, 124, 126, 166, 220n10

Elihu Yale, 114, 171, 176, 208

F
Field, John C. G., 98, 99–100, 119–20, 129, 167, 198
Flores (Netherlands), 32–33, 171, 176, 208, 216n20
Focke-Wolf (Fw) 200 Condor: Bay of Biscay attack, 4; blockade-running operations, 86–87; characteristics of and uses for, 2; convoy raids, 117, 137, 141–42; glide bomb deployment role, 21–22, 213n25; intelligence on, 46; replacement for, 118; troop transport raids, 224n38
Fort Fitzgerald (Great Britain), 63
Fort McPherson (Canada/Great Britain), 155, 171, 176, 189, 208
France: Brest, 157–59, 160; French Riviera and Dragoon Operation, 161–64, 187, 189, 190, 240n62; GC 1/7 Squadron, 81–82; operations along coast of, 22; Percussion Operation, 2; Pontaubault Bridge, 160–61; Pontorson, 161; Simmons Project, 143–44; stockpile of glide bombs in, 22, 165
Franken (Germany), 43, 217–18n1
Frederick C. Davis: Anzio jamming mission, 100, 105, 114–15; characteristics of, 57; destroyer-escort role, 57–58, 64–65, 66–67, 80, 84; Dragoon Operation, 162, 164; effectiveness of jamming operations, 115, 123, 133; electronic countermeasure systems installation, 57–59; expectations for success, 59; jamming system installation, 94, 185,

197–98, 226n19; signal recording missions, 66–67, 84–85, 93

Fritz-X (Ruhrstahl PC 1400FX): accuracy of, 13; Anzio raids, 104, 113–14, 230n26, 230n44; characteristics of, 11–12; combat engagement of, 12–13; control of, 12, 135; control of, loss of, 191; control surfaces, 17; development of, 11–13, 197; Do 217 sorties with, 20, 236n1; effectiveness of, 12, 70, 167–72, 175, 176, 188, 241–42n4; enhanced variations of, 134–35; examples of, 205; explosive charge, 12; first deployment of, 25; French Riviera and Dragoon Operation, 162, 164; guidance system for, 16–18, 212nn10–12 (see also Kehl-Strassburg radio guidance system); He 177, deployment with, 75; intelligence on, 41–49, 141; jamming signal between guidance system and, 179–80, 181; launch aircraft, vulnerability of, 12–13, 177; night missions with, 149–50; Normandy raid, 149–50, 156; number carried by launching aircraft, 16–17, 212nn11–12; operational deployment of, 192; operational status of, 44, 73; pilot training, 23–24; production of, 13, 148–49; recovery of by Allies, 89–90, 91–93, 141, 225nn8–9; ships sunk or damaged with, 168–72, 208, 241–42n4; stockpile of, 145, 165; testing of, 13, 18; threat from, 49; weather and deployment of, 21. See also Luftwaffe Gruppe III of Kampfgeschwader 100 (III./KG 100)

G

Gardes, Alfred W. "Skeeta," Jr., 58, 65, 67, 93, 203–4, 221n21, 244n25

Garrett, Kenneth C., 153

Gee hyperbolic navigation system, 137, 191, 212n10

German navy, 9. See also U-boats

Germany: air defenses against Allied bombers, 165; Black Sea operations, 22; blockade-running operations, 85–87; Enigma code and machines, 31, 43–44, 77; Gustav Line in Italy, 101; information sharing with Japan, 143, 144, 236n61; materials from Japan, 85; Oder River bridges, 193; remotely-controlled weapons, development of, 10

Glasgow (Great Britain), 86, 87, 224n35

glide bombs: abandonment of, xv–xvi; aircraft lost during raids with, 179; anxiety of crew about use of, 40; censorship about use of, xvi–xvii, 209–10n5; convoys as target of, 22; damage from, 74; deaths from, xvii, 41, 172, 209n3; development of, xv; effectiveness of, xv, 41, 74, 167–70, 186–90, 209n3, 241–42n4; first deployment of, 25, 230n37; guidance of, xv; historical records on use of, xvi–xvii, 209–10n5, 210n7; mass attacks with, 21, 84, 95, 96–98; stockpile of, 22, 145, 165; threat from, 166. See also Fritz-X (Ruhrstahl PC 1400FX); Henschel Hs 293 A-1 missile

Goepner, O. William, 58, 93, 220n14

Great Britain: Carmen Operation, 73; Chain Home coastal radar stations, 212n10; Gee navigation system, 137, 191, 212n10; Plymouth raids, 88, 140–41, 145, 169, 235nn50–51; signals intelligence network, 6–8, 211n9

Greece, 48, 70–72

Grenville (Great Britain), 3, 4, 5, 7, 49, 50, 74, 102

Guggenheim, Daniel, 194, 243n3
Guggenheim, Harry, 243n3
guidance system. *See* Kehl-Strassburg
  radio guidance system

H
Heinkel (He) 111 aircraft: Anzio raids,
  106–7; convoy attacks, 214n32;
  Fritz-X testing, 13, 18; glide bomb
  deployment role, 241–42n4; Hs 293
  testing, 15, 18, 212n8, 213n15; I./KG
  40 missions, 146
Heinkel (He) 177 Greif (Griffon)
  bomber: A-3/A-5 variants, 75, 118,
  137; Anzio raids, 107–8, 111, 116,
  118, 229n24, 231n48; blockade-
  running operations, 86–87, 224n39;
  characteristics of, 18, 75; convoy
  raids, 76–85, 117–18, 217n46,
  223n12, 223n16, 223n19, 224n31;
  delays in deployment of, 18–19, 22,
  76; engine configuration, 75; example
  of, 205; Fritz-X deployment, 75;
  Hs 293 deployment, 75, 241–42n4;
  I./KG 40 missions, 146; loss of during
  airfield bombings, 87; loss of during
  missions, 104; Normandy raids, 145,
  146, 152–53, 155, 156, 157, 237n11,
  237n19, 238nn30–32, 238nn35–36,
  239nn42–43; pilot training, 103,
  104, 116, 140, 146, 165, 223n5,
  228n2; problems with, 18, 75–76,
  79, 140, 173; range of, 75, 76, 116;
  relocation of, 165; transition to, 73,
  75, 137, 222–23n4
Henkelmann, Karl, 147
Henschel Hs 293 A-1 missile: antenna
  on, 180, 183, 242nn6–7; Anzio raids,
  103–16, 230n26; blockade-running
  operations, 86–87; characteristics
  of, 15, 90; combat engagement of,
  15–16; control of, 135–36; control
  of, loss of, 181, 183, 191; control

surfaces, 17, 90; convoy raids,
  60, 62–69, 70–72, 76–85, 117,
  118–19, 157, 217n46, 221nn11–14;
  development of, 13–16; Do 217
  sorties with, 19–20, 73, 236n1;
  effectiveness of, 15–16, 73, 167–72,
  175, 176, 188, 241–42n4; enhanced
  variations of, 135–37; examples
  of, 205; explosive charge, 16; first
  deployment of, 25, 214n32; French
  Riviera and Dragoon Operation,
  162–64; fuel for, 15, 49, 54;
  guidance system for, 16–18, 179–83,
  212nn10–12, 242–43nn6–9 (*see
  also* Kehl-Strassburg radio guidance
  system); He 177, deployment with,
  75, 145, 241–42n4; intelligence on,
  41–49, 54, 142–44, 218n6, 236n61;
  jamming signal between guidance
  system and, 179–83; multipath
  interference, 181–83; night missions
  with, 149–50; Normandy raids,
  149–50, 154–55, 156, 238n27;
  number carried by launching aircraft,
  16–17, 118, 212nn11–12; Oder
  River bridges raid, 193; operational
  deployment of, 192; operational
  status of, 44, 73; pilot training, 15,
  23–24; production of, 148–49, 157;
  propulsion for, 15; recovery of by
  Allies, 62, 71, 89–90, 91–92, 120–22,
  186, 221n7, 225n8–9, 225–26n12,
  226n14, 231n57, 231–32n60; ships
  sunk or damaged with, 168–69, 170–
  72, 207–8, 241–42n4; stockpile of,
  145, 165; television-based guidance,
  136; testing of, 15, 18, 212n8,
  213n15; threat from, 49; weather and
  deployment of, 21. *See also* Luftwaffe
  Gruppe II of Kampfgeschwader 100
  (II./KG 100); Luftwaffe Gruppe II of
  Kampfgeschwader 40 (II./KG 40)
Herbert C. Jones: Anzio jamming

mission, 100, 105, 114–15; attack
on, 114–15; characteristics of, 57;
destroyer-escort role, 57–58, 64–65,
66–67, 80, 84; Dragoon Operation,
162, 164; effectiveness of jamming
operations, 115, 123, 133; electronic
countermeasure systems installation,
57–59; expectations for success, 59;
Hs 293 missiles, near-miss strikes
by, 81; jamming system installation,
94, 185, 197–98, 226n19; jamming
system, testing of, 66, 67; signal
recording missions, 66–67, 84–85, 93
Hilary (Great Britain), 156, 234n26
Hilary A. Herbert, 110, 171, 176, 208,
229nn21–22
Hilary P. Jones, 94, 100, 133, 162,
226–27n21
Hill, Roger P.: Anzio landing, 102;
attack on *Grenville*, 5, 211n7;
career and life of, 203; *Grenville*
commander, 4; intelligence on glide
bombs, 5, 7, 49, 74; *Jervis* skipper,
108; Malta operations, 4, 203, 210n4
Hiram S. Maxim, 63, 171, 176, 207,
221n12
Hitler, Adolf, 22, 31, 160, 164, 192
Hollweg, Franz, 23, 32, 147, 215n16
Howard O. Lorenzen, 197
Howe, William E. W. "Bill," 55, 56,
58, 198
Husky, Operation, 25–27

I
improvised explosive devices (IEDs),
xviii, 204–5
Indian Prince (Great Britain), 68, 69,
171, 176, 207
Inglefield (Great Britain), 116, 120,
171, 176, 208
intelligence: analysis of, 41; before Bay
of Biscay raids, 6–8, 44, 46; film crew
and equipment, 4, 7, 49; intelligence

organizations and agents, 47–49,
70; from Japan, 143, 144, 236n61;
Kehl-Strassburg radio guidance
system, 43, 46, 54, 89–91, 93,
226nn14–15; Oslo Report, 42–43,
202, 218n3; from POWs, 45–46, 57,
93, 218nn11–13; recovery of Fritz-X
bombs, 89–90, 91–93, 141, 225nn8–
9; recovery of Hs 293 missiles, 62,
71, 89–90, 91–92, 120–22, 221n7,
225n8–9, 225–26n12, 226n14,
231n57, 231–32n60; sources of,
41–49; success of Allies at, 192; Ultra
intelligence, 43–45, 50–51,
115, 192
Intrepid (Great Britain), 48–49, 219n19
Iraq, xviii, 204–5
Italia/Littorio (Italy), 28, 29–30, 171,
175, 176, 208, 215n10
Italy: armistice and control of navy,
28–29; Calabria, 27, 28; Foggia, 13,
91–93, 94, 225n8–9, 225–26n12;
Gustav Line strategy, 101; intelligence
on glide bombs, 47–48; Naples, 40;
navy (Regia Marina), 28–31; Rome,
101; Sicily-Rome American Cemetery
and Memorial, 206; stockpile of glide
bombs in, 22; supplies and resources
for troops about to invade, 1;
Taranto, 28. *See also* Anzio; Salerno

J
James W. Marshall, 37–38, 171, 176,
207, 217n42
jamming systems. *See* electronic
countermeasures and jamming
systems
Janus (Great Britain), 106–7, 108, 110,
171, 176, 208
Japan, 143, 144, 194, 236n61
Jervis (Great Britain), 106–7, 108, 110,
171, 176, 203, 208

John Banvard, 110–11, 171, 176, 208, 229n23
Jones, Reginald V., 202, 218n3
Jope, Bernard, 26, 29, 30, 31, 116, 147, 201
Junkers (Ju) 88 fighter-bombers, 2, 19, 43, 139, 155
Junkers (Ju) 290 aircraft, 118–19, 141, 142, 231nn52–54, 236n58

K
kamikaze missions, xiv–xv, 209n1
Kehl-Strassburg radio guidance system: aircraft modifications for, 18; design of and success of jamming signals, 66; false commands to, 121, 122, 129, 133; flood of signals from transmitters, 123; frequencies used by, 16, 17, 46, 55–57, 66, 89, 93–94, 120, 191, 212n10; information about, analysis of, xvii; intelligence on, 43, 46, 54, 89–91, 93, 119–22, 141, 226nn14–15; jamming, perceived threat from, 136–37; jamming signal between glide bombs and, 179–83; limitation of, 18; multipath interference, 5, 79, 181–83, 191, 211n7, 243n9; operation of, 16–18, 212nn10–12; power output and requirements, 93, 179–80, 226n15, 242–43nn7–8; recovery of by Allies, 119–21, 141, 225n9, 225–26n12; sabotage, 79, 191. *See also* electronic countermeasures and jamming systems
Kinney, Orus, 150–51, 163
Kramer, Max Otto, 11, 33, 46, 134, 167, 195–97
Krause, Ernest H., 58, 197–98

L
Landguard (Great Britain): attack on and damage to, 3, 6, 24, 159, 171, 207; Bay of Biscay antisubmarine force, 2; defensibility of, 176; Hs 293 fragments, recovery of, 89; intelligence before attack on, 7
Lansdale, 94, 95, 100, 133, 139, 162, 226–27n21
launching aircraft: bombing of airfields used to launch, 18, 50–51, 72, 222n35; codes for, 212n8, 215n6; jamming system, equipment to detect, 62, 220n3; limitation of, 18; markings on, 215n6; modifications for Kehl-Strassburg system, 18; number of bombs carried by, 16–17, 212nn11–12; production of, 31; vulnerability of, 12–13, 60. *See also* Dornier (Do) 217 bombers; Heinkel (He) 111 aircraft; Heinkel (He) 177 Greif (Griffon) bomber
Lawford (Great Britain), 154, 171, 176, 208
LCI-12, 116
LCT-35, 114, 171, 176, 208
LCT-209, 36, 37, 38
Leinster (Great Britain), 34, 108–9
Leonard, Bill, 84–85
Littorio/Italia (Italy), 28, 29–30, 215n10
Lombard-Hobson, Samuel Richard le Hunte, 70–71, 222n31
Lorenzen, Howard Otto, 53, 55, 59, 84, 93, 123, 129, 167, 197
Loyal (Great Britain), 35, 171, 176, 208
LST-79 (Great Britain), 61–62, 171, 176, 207, 220n5
LST-282, 162, 163, 171, 176, 190, 208
LST-312, 162, 241–42n4
LST-373, 26
LST-384, 162, 241–42n4
Lucas, John P., 102–3
Luftwaffe: aircraft lost during airfield bombings, 113; airfields used by, 206; antiship weapon for, 10; confidence

in, 9; crews, condition, training, and morale of, 148; jamming operations, knowledge of, 114–15; organization of, 213–14n29; reports and records of, xvi, xvii, 209n4, 210n7; units to deploy glide bombs, 23–24

Luftwaffe Fernaufklärungs Gruppe 5 (FAGr[5]), 118–19, 142, 231nn52–54, 236n58

Luftwaffe Gruppe I of Kampfgesch-wader 40 (I./KG 40): base for, 146; destruction of, 164; disbanding of, 165; fleet size, 146; He 177 training, 146; Hs 293 training and deployment, 146, 236n2; leadership of, 147; maritime attack and reconnaissance missions, 146; Normandy raids, 146, 151, 153, 155, 156, 157, 237n14, 237n19, 238nn30–32, 238n35; ships sunk or damaged by, 165; success of, 172–75, 189

Luftwaffe Gruppe I of Kampfgesch-wader 66 (I./KG 66), 141

Luftwaffe Gruppe II of Kampfgesch-wader 40 (II./KG 40): aircraft lost during raids, 172, 178–79; airfield bombings, aircraft lost during, 87; Anzio raids, 88, 104–11, 116, 118, 120, 179, 228n4, 228n14, 229n20, 229n24, 231n48, 231n59; base for, 76, 137, 145, 206; blockade-running operations, 86–87, 224n39; convoy raids, 76–85, 117–18, 157, 223n16, 223n19, 224n31; crews, condition, training, and morale of, 148; destruction of, 164; disbanding of, 165; fleet size, 76, 104, 146, 165; Fw 200 antishipping missions, 76; He 177 deployment, 76, 145, 173, 222–23nn4–5; leadership of, 147, 148; Normandy raids, 145, 146, 151–54, 155–57, 179, 237n11, 237n14, 237n19, 238nn31–32,

238nn35–36, 239n42; relocation of, 165; ships sunk or damaged by, 170–72; stand-down of, 88, 118; success of, 172–75, 187–89

Luftwaffe Gruppe II of Kampfgesch-wader 100 (II./KG 100): aircraft for, 23; aircraft lost during raids, 175, 177–78; aircraft markings, 215n6; airfield bombings, aircraft lost during, 72, 222n35; Ajaccio raids, 61–62, 220n3; Anzio raids, 88, 103–16, 229n19, 230n27, 230n30, 230n43; bad weather, aircraft lost during, 115, 230n41; base for, 31, 49, 50–51, 73, 103, 137, 140, 206; Bay of Biscay attack, 2–8, 22, 24, 28, 214n32; consolidation into III./KG 100, 175; convoy raids, 60, 62–69, 70–72, 74, 117, 137–40, 221nn11–14, 235nn40–44, 235n48; crews, condition, training, and morale of, 148; disbanding of, 165; Dodecanese raid, 70–72; fleet size, 23, 74, 103; Greek raid, 72; He 177 training and deployment, 165, 223n5; Hs 293 training and deployment, 23–24; intelligence on operations of, 44, 218n6; leadership of, 147, 148, 201; mission report, 210n7; Normandy raids, 145–46; operational status of, 44; organization of, 23, 140, 213–14n29; range of, 31; relocation of, 31; Salerno raids, 32, 34–35, 36–38, 40, 216n24, 216n26, 217n33, 217n39, 217n46, 217n48; ships sunk or damaged by, 168–72; stand-down of, 88, 116; success of, 172–75, 188–90; training of, 23–24

Luftwaffe Gruppe III of Kampfgesch-wader 40 (III./KG 40), 23, 85–87, 117, 141–42, 157, 165, 172–75, 224n38

Luftwaffe Gruppe III of Kampfgeschwader 100 (III./KG 100): aircraft for,
23; aircraft lost during raids, 172,
177; aircraft lost during training,
104; aircraft markings, 215n6;
airfield bombings, aircraft lost
during, 50–51, 72, 222n35; Ajaccio
raids, 107; Anzio raids, 107, 113–14,
230n44; base for, 26, 31, 49, 50–51,
73, 104, 137, 140, 145, 206; Bay of
Biscay attacks, 157–59; convoy raids,
74, 141–42, 155, 236n56; crews,
condition, training, and morale of,
148; crews, overland journey for,
166; destruction of, 164; disbanding
of, 166, 177; Dragoon Operation,
162, 163, 164, 240n63, 241n69,
241n71; England raid, planned, 142;
fleet size, 23, 74, 104, 146, 236n3;
Foggia, items left at, 91–93, 94,
225–26n12; French Riviera and
Dragoon Operation, 162–64; Fritz-X
training and deployment, 23–24;
intelligence on operations of, 44–45;
Italian navy, attack on, 29–31;
leadership of, 147, 148, 200, 201;
mission report, 210n7; Normandy
raids, 145, 146, 151–52, 153, 154–57,
177, 238n24, 238n28, 238–39n37,
239n40, 239n45; operational status
of, 44; organization of, 23, 140, 213–
14n29; Plymouth raids, 88, 140–41,
145, 169, 235nn50–51; Pontaubault
Bridge raids, 160–61, 240nn59–61;
range of, 31; relocation of, 164, 166;
Salerno raids, 32–34, 35–36, 37,
38–40, 60, 216n26, 216nn30–31,
217n46, 217n48; ships sunk or
damaged by, 168–72; Sicily raids,
26–27, 45–46, 214n2, 215nn6–7,
215n9, 218nn11–13; stand-down
of, 88; success of, 172–75, 188–90;
training of, 23–24

Luftwaffe Kampfgeschwader units:
KG 1, 228n3; KG 26, 63, 64, 65,
68, 137, 138, 228n3; KG 27, 139,
235n45; KG 30/KG(J) 30, 201; KG
77, 138, 139, 235n45; KG 200, 193

M
MacKenzie, Colin, 209–10n5
Madison, 94, 100, 133, 162, 226–
27n21
magnetic-anomaly detector (MAD),
128–29
Marnix van St. Aldegonde (Great
Britain), 65
Marsa (Great Britain), 78, 79, 81, 171,
176, 207
Marshall, Gordon, 78
Matane (Canada), 158–59, 171, 176,
190, 208, 240n55
Mayer, Hans Ferdinand, 42–43, 202,
217–18n1
Mayo, 109, 110, 171, 176, 208,
229n18
McCorkle, Francis D., 65
Meon (Canada), 158, 159
Meredith, 153–54, 171, 176, 189, 205,
208, 237n20
Meyerhofer, Bodo, 147
Middermann, Heinz-Emil, 64, 103,
114, 147
Miller, Carl, 56, 58
Molinnus, Heinz, 32, 63–64, 147,
215n16
Mons, Rudolf, 76, 77–78, 80, 81, 85,
147, 223n19

N
Naval Research Laboratory (NRL):
ARQ-8 jamming system, criticism of,
125; establishment of, 53; jamming
system, development of, 53, 55–57,
94–95, 123–24, 129–30; jamming

systems, effectiveness of, 185–86, 187, 189, 190; relics of war, 206
Nelson, 26, 154
Neptune, Operation, 133, 149, 150–51
Newfoundland (Great Britain), 34–35, 171, 176, 207, 216nn25–26, 216n28
night missions, 149–50, 173–74
noise jamming, 54
Normandy: air defenses, 149; aircraft lost over, 152–53, 154, 155, 156, 157, 177, 179, 237n11, 237n14, 237n19, 238n24, 238n28, 238nn30–32, 238–39nn35–37, 239n40; Allied forces, preparation of, 149–51; breakwater (gooseberry) off Omaha Beach, 38; I./KG 40 attacks on, 146, 151, 153, 155, 156, 157; II./KG 40 attacks on, 118, 145, 146, 151–54, 155–57; II./KG 100 attacks on, 145–46; III./KG 100 attacks on, 145, 146, 151–52, 153, 154–57, 236n1; jamming systems and ships, 131, 132–33, 150–51, 186, 188, 189, 190, 233n20, 234nn24–26; naval support for landing at, 101–2; Neptune Operation, 133, 149, 150–51; success of Allies at, 157, 160; success rate of glide bomb mission, 187; timing of attacks, 149–50
North Africa, 1, 22
Norway, 22

O
Office of Strategic Services (OSS), xvi, 47–48, 143–44
Orion (Great Britain), 57, 108
Orsono (Germany), 86
Oslo Report, 42–43, 202, 218n3
Otter, 131

P
Packer, Herbert Annesley "Bertie," 39–40

Paperclip, Operation, 194
Paul Hamilton, 139
PC 617 patrol boat, 156
Pearl Harbor, xiv, 58, 209n3, 220n14
Penelope (Great Britain), 108
Percussion, Operation, 2
Perruquet, Pierre, 61
Petard (Great Britain), 71
Pfeffer, Herbert, 141, 147, 235n50
Philadelphia, 26, 33, 35–36, 40, 216n21
pilots, German fighter/bomber: attrition rate, xviii, 199, 210n8, 244n13; He 177 training, 103, 104, 116, 140, 146, 165, 223n5, 228n2; loss of during raids and accidents, 74–75; shortage of, 75; training of, 15, 17–18, 23–24
Plunkett, 34, 108, 110
Plymouth, 88, 140–41, 145, 169
Prevail, 110, 162, 171, 176, 208
Prince David (Canada), 234n25
Prince Henry (Canada), 234n25
Prince of Wales (Great Britain), xiv, 31
prisoners of war (POWs): from Anzio raids, 120, 228n14; from Bay of Biscay raids, 240n58; glide bomb pilots, 199, 200, 201; intelligence from, 27, 45–46, 57, 93, 218nn11–13; from Salerno raids, 93; from Sicily raids, 27
Pursuer, 117

R
Reedy, James R., 87, 224–25n40
relics of war, 205–6
Repulse (Great Britain), xiv, 31
Rieder, Walter, 85, 117, 118, 147
Rockwood (Great Britain), 70–71, 90, 91, 171, 176, 207
Rodney (Great Britain), 153
Rohna (Great Britain): attack on and loss of, 82–84, 171, 207; casualties

aboard, 172, 199, 209n3, 224n28;
characteristics of and uses for,
80, 223n15; defensibility of, 176;
memorial to victims of, 205; reunions
of survivors, 200
Roma (Italy): attack on and loss of,
29–30, 44, 169–70, 171, 172, 208;
defensibility of, 175, 176; explosion
of ship's magazine, 30, 74; sinking of,
197; striking power of, 28
Royal Air Force (RAF): aircraft shot
down by, 72; Beaufighters, 72,
81–82, 106, 108, 138; glide bomb
attack, response to, 7; intelligence on
glide bombs, 46, 218n6; Normandy
raid, 152; Y-Service personnel, 6–8,
46, 92, 211n9
Royal Aircraft Establishment (RAE),
89–90, 91–93, 98, 120–21, 141
Royal Canadian Navy, 122
Royal Navy: 1st Support Group, 3–6, 7;
40th Escort Group, 2, 77; glide bomb
attack risk, intelligence on, 6–8, 46;
jammer installation on ships of, 98,
227n32; light ships used by, 1–2,
210n1
Royal Star (Great Britain), 139–40

S
St. Andrew (Great Britain), 34, 108–9
St. David (Great Britain), 108–9, 110,
171, 176, 208
Salerno: aircraft lost over, 34, 36, 37,
40, 60, 216n24, 216n30, 217n39,
217n48;
Allied control of coast off, 40;
Avalanche Operation, 28, 44; Fifth
Army landing at, 28, 31; Fritz-X
attacks, 32–34, 35–36, 37, 38–40,
216n26, 216n31, 217n46; glide
bomb attacks, xvi, 230n37; Hs
293 attacks, 32, 34–35, 36–38,
40, 216n26, 217n33, 217n46;

intelligence on glide bombs, 47–48;
intelligence on raids, 44–45; POWs
from raids on, 93; success rate
of glide bomb mission, 187–88;
unexploded Hs 293 missiles, 62
Saltwick (Great Britain), 64
Samite (Great Britain), 63, 139, 171,
176, 207, 221n11
Samuel Ashe, 115–16
Samuel Huntington, 111–12, 171, 176,
208, 230n26
Santa Elena (Great Britain), 65
Savannah, 26, 33–34, 44, 171, 175,
176, 197, 206, 208, 216n22
Schmetz, Heinrich, 39, 147, 200
Scholl, Willi, 103, 140, 235n48
Scylla (Great Britain), 150, 156
Selvik (Norway), 63, 171, 176, 207
Shingle, Operation, 59, 114
ships: light ships used by Royal Navy,
1–2, 210n1; sinking of by aircraft,
challenges of, xiii–xv
Sicily: aircraft lost over, 27, 45–46,
215nn6–7, 215n9, 218nn11–13;
Augusta, 25–26, 27, 214n2;
harbor use by Allied forces, 25–26;
intelligence on glide bombs, 44, 57;
Palermo, 25–27, 28, 44; supplies and
resources for troops on, 1; Syracuse,
25–26
Silvester, David Denys, 96, 97, 132
Simmons Project, 48, 143–44
Skifter, Hector R., 128–30, 167, 198,
205
Slapstick, Operation, 28
Soviet Union, 22, 85, 113, 193, 194,
197, 213n15
Spain, 2, 22
Spartan (Great Britain), 107, 108,
112–13, 171, 175, 176, 205, 208
Steady, 142
Stephen F. Austin, 139
Stormont (Canada), 158, 159

submarines, 128–29. *See also* U-boats
Sustain, 142, 235n42
Swansea (Canada), 158, 159

T
Taney, 139, 205
Tillman, 65
Tivives, 64
torpedo bombers, xiii–xiv
Trialen filling, 90, 225n3

U
U-boats: Bay of Biscay campaign, 1–2,
  6; convoys, threat to, 1, 6, 10, 22, 77;
  failure of, 9, 22; loss of, 1; sinking of,
  22, 219n1
Uganda (Great Britain), 35, 45, 171,
  175, 176, 197, 208, 216n29
Ulster Queen (Great Britain), 164
Ultra intelligence, 43–45, 50–51, 115,
  192
Uskide/Uskside (Great Britain), 26–27,
  214–15n5

V
Vasillisa Olga (Greece), 48–49, 219n19
Virden, John A., 199, 244n15
Vittorio Vento (Italy), 28, 29
von Cramm, Siegfried Freiherr, 147
Vorpahl, Wolfgang, 4, 103, 147

W
Wagner, Herbert A., 13–14, 135, 167,
  191–92, 194–95
Wainright, Jonathan M., V, 36, 38,
  217n35
Walker, Frederic John, 52, 219n1
Warspite (Great Britain), 38–40, 45,
  171, 175, 176, 197, 208
Waterhouse, John Valentine, 3–4, 5
William Dean Howells, 36, 37
William N. Pendleton, 154–55, 238n27

Wilson, Henry Maitland "Jumbo,"
  102, 107
Wilson, John Eric, 34–35
Winchelsea (Great Britain), 77, 217n46
Woodpecker (Great Britain), 98,
  227n30
Woolsey, 94, 100, 105, 115, 133, 162,
  226n20

Y
Yannacci, Joseph A., 36, 37–38

Z
Zantopp, Hans-Joachim, 45–46, 201–2,
  218nn12–13

About the Author

MARTIN J. BOLLINGER is a professional management consultant and senior partner with Booz & Company. He has served the global aerospace and defense industry for over twenty-five years. In his spare time he researches and writes about naval and maritime history. He serves as a director of the Naval Historical Foundation and has supported the publishing efforts of the U.S. Naval Institute.